Tourism in the Middle East

TOURISM AND CULTURAL CHANGE
Series Editors: Professor Mike Robinson, *Centre for Tourism and Cultural Change, Sheffield Hallam University, UK* and Dr Alison Phipps, *University of Glasgow, Scotland, UK*

Understanding tourism's relationships with culture(s) and vice versa, is of ever-increasing significance in a globalising world. This series will critically examine the dynamic inter-relationships between tourism and culture(s). Theoretical explorations, research-informed analyses, and detailed historical reviews from a variety of disciplinary perspectives are invited to consider such relationships.

Other Books in the Series
Irish Tourism: Image, Culture and Identity
   Michael Cronin and Barbara O'Connor (eds)
Tourism, Globalization and Cultural Change: An Island Community Perspective
   Donald V.L. Macleod
The Global Nomad: Backpacker Travel in Theory and Practice
   Greg Richards and Julie Wilson (eds)
Tourism and Intercultural Exchange: Why Tourism Matters
   Gavin Jack and Alison Phipps
Discourse, Communication and Tourism
   Adam Jaworski and Annette Pritchard (eds)
Histories of Tourism: Representation, Identity and Conflict
   John K. Walton (ed)
Cultural Tourism in a Changing World: Politics, Participation and (Re)presentation
   Melanie Smith and Mike Robinson (eds)
Festivals, Tourism and Social Change: Remaking Worlds
   David Picard and Mike Robinson (eds)

Other Books of Interest
Natural Area Tourism: Ecology, Impacts and Management
   D. Newsome, S.A. Moore and R. Dowling
Progressing Tourism Research
   Bill Faulkner, edited by Liz Fredline, Leo Jago and Chris Cooper
Recreational Tourism: Demand and Impacts
   Chris Ryan
Shopping Tourism: Retailing and Leisure
   Dallen Timothy
Sport Tourism Development
   Thomas Hinch and James Higham
Sport Tourism: Interrelationships, Impact and Issues
   Brent Ritchie and Daryl Adair (eds)
Tourism Collaboration and Partnerships
   Bill Bramwell and Bernard Lane (eds)
Tourism and Development: Concepts and Issues
   Richard Sharpley and David Telfer (eds)

For more details of these or any other of our publications, please contact:
Channel View Publications, Frankfurt Lodge, Clevedon Hall,
Victoria Road, Clevedon, BS21 7HH, England
http://www.channelviewpublications.com

TOURISM AND CULTURAL CHANGE 9
Series Editors: Mike Robinson and Alison Phipps

Tourism in the Middle East
Continuity, Change and Transformation

Edited by
Rami Farouk Daher

CHANNEL VIEW PUBLICATIONS
Clevedon • Buffalo • Toronto

Library of Congress Cataloging in Publication Data
Tourism in the Middle East: Continuity, Change and Transformation
Edited by Rami Farouk Daher.
Tourism and Cultural Change: 9
Includes bibliographical references and index.
1. Tourism–Middle East. I. Daher, Rami. II. Series.
G155.M66T68 2006
338.4' 79156–dc22   2006011056

British Library Cataloguing in Publication Data
A catalogue entry for this book is available from the British Library.

ISBN 1-84541-051-3 / EAN 978-1-84541-051-3 (hbk)
ISBN 1-84541-050-5 / EAN 978-1-84541-050-6 (pbk)

Channel View Publications
An imprint of Multilingual Matters Ltd

UK: Frankfurt Lodge, Clevedon Hall, Victoria Road, Clevedon BS21 7HH.
USA: 2250 Military Road, Tonawanda, NY 14150, USA.
Canada: 5201 Dufferin Street, North York, Ontario, Canada M3H 5T8.

The policy of Multilingual Matters/Channel View Publications is to use papers that
are natural, renewable and recyclable products, made from wood grown in
sustainable forests. In the manufacturing process of our books, and to further support
our policy, preference is given to printers that have FSC and PEFC Chain of Custody
accreditation. The FSC and/or PEFC logos will appear on those books where full
accreditation has been granted to the printer concerned.

Typeset by Florence Production Ltd.
Printed and bound in Great Britain by MPG Books Ltd.

Contents

Preface

For the ancient Greeks, the world was essentially divided into an East and a West. This notion of a world of two halves was largely continued by the Romans, despite their forays into the North of Europe, and remains embedded in 'Western' public consciousness to this moment. The area we commonly refer to as the Middle East (and formerly, within a less expansive world, as the Near East) is thus at the very point of cross-over between these two 'halves' of the world; a wonderfully permeable, fluid, real and imagined expanse of lands, landscapes and peoples. In the European tradition, the Middle East marks the point where Europe stops being Europe and gradually, untidily, and somewhat uneasily, morphs into another place and culture. Here, globalization is not a new phenomenon.

Over the years a great imagining of difference relating to the Middle East has constantly veered from romanticized fascination and engagement, to that of suspicion and fear on both sides of this perceptual divide. Travelers, traders, and pilgrims to, and through, the region have long been an outcome and an expression of the region's strategic position, religious significance, and imagined mystique. Thus, the region is well-versed in providing the essential structures and cultures of hospitality, fed as they are through the religious and cultural values that intrinsically pervade all aspects of everyday life.

But within the modern world it would be wrong to portray the Middle East solely as a focus for the Orientalist explorer or spiritual traveler. Through Thomas Cook's Tours, the region was one of the first in the world to experience organized tourism and over the past 50 years or so substantive parts of the region have been engaged with the essentially modernist project of leisure tourism. A drive along the coastal highway of Lebanon, for instance, reveals a plethora of sites and facilities dedicated to domestic tourism and to an international tourism that flourished during the 1950s and 1960s.

It would be true to say, certainly from a European perspective, that when we think of tourism in the Middle East, we generally conceptualize it as a number of destinations: places where international/Western visitors go. In this process, we have been all too happy to reduce the complexity and richness of histories and cultures to a relatively small number of images and signs. Thus Jordan *is* Petra and the Dead Sea, Syria *is* Palmyra, and Egypt *is* Luxor and the Pyramids at Giza. Of course these are the very centres where international visitors do congregate; such is international tourism. But this view neglects three important dimensions. The first is the diversity of landscapes, sites, and locations, which also attract international tourists and have done for many years, such as the Syrian coastline for instance, and particularly the sea-port of Latakia, which is still a call for Mediterranean cruise ships, stopping for excursions to nearby Qalaat Saladin. The second is the incidence of regionalized or domestic tourism in the Middle East, which remains largely poorly understood. Over recent years, the internal patterns and flows of tourists within the region have increased due to significant levels of Arabs preferring not to venture out to European and American destinations. The third dimension relates to the tremendous changes that are taking place regarding the provision for tourism driven by high levels of external investment, particularly from, and in, the Gulf States. The levels of investment and development in tourism are, of course, tremendously uneven across the Middle East, ranging from the hyper-modern, capital intensive, high-rise hotels of Dubai to the development of small eco-tourism projects in Mount Lebanon.

It is these processes and dynamics of change that have long marked out the Middle East region as one of the most significant and indeed, sensitive regions of the world. But change is always set within the contexts of continuity and tradition to produce dialectics of complex engagement and encounter at a variety of levels. Tourism and travel are acts of transformation at the individual and institutional level. Throughout the Middle East region landscapes and lives are being transformed through the provision of infrastructure to support tourism and leisure, and in the process identities and local/global relations are being challenged and re-defined.

Sadly, in common discourse, discussion of tourism in the Middle East continues to fall between a number of extremes: persistent and pervasive Orientalist conceptions or peoples and places, somewhat disjunctive notions of massive post-modernist spatial transformations, and configurations of the region as a series of 'no-go' areas due to military and political instability. All such narratives are accurate to a degree, but between these all too familiar focal points there is a much more complex, deeper and richer set of understandings about tourism and tourists. While aware of the meta-narratives relating to tourism, this volume is a fine attempt to get between the extremes and into the intricacies of tourism in the region. Through its insightful and varied chapters the book sets out to uncover and unravel the multifaceted nature of tourism in the Middle East from a variety of perspectives. Understanding tourism in the Middle East, as a form of social encounter and exchange, as well as in a context of spatial and historical transformation, is critical in helping to understand the region not as a boundary between two notional world halves, but as the very place that as binds them together.

Professor Mike Robinson
Centre for Tourism and Cultural Change
Leeds Metropolitan University

Acknowledgements

I would like to thank my two dear friends and research companions: Mike Robinson and Xavier Guillot for their support and friendship and for the intriguing discussions we enjoyed during our various travels in Jordan, Syria, and Lebanon. I would also like to thank Seteney Shami for her support and for being an inspiration ever since I ventured outside of architecture. My deep gratitude also goes to Nezar AlSayyad and Nelson Graburn who were supportive during my visit to the University of California, Berkeley in 2001 during which the initial ideas of this book were formulating. I am also grateful to Martina Rieker for her great influence on my work and for being an inspiration always. Gratitude and thanks go to my dear friend and colleague Amer Jokhadar for his support and for all the work he has done in support of this book. Finally, my deepest thanks and appreciations go to my parents, wife, and kids who were patient enough to bear with me while I was working on this project.

The Contributors

Peter Burns is a Professor of International Tourism and Development and Director of the Centre for Tourism Policy Studies (CENTOPS; www.centops.org) at the University of Brighton. He is a consultant anthropologist specializing in strategic policy-making for tourism in the developing world and emerging economies. He has extensive international experience in institutional strengthening and working with communities in helping them achieve better access to and participation in tourism enterprise. He is founding Chair of the Association of Leisure and Tourism Studies (ATLAS) special interest group in social identities and a board member of the United Nations World Tourism Organization (WTO) Education Council. He is one of the first tourism scholars to be elected as an academician of the UK national Academy of Social Sciences.

Rami Farouk Daher taught architecture at Jordan University of Science and Technology (JUST) and is currently teaching at the American University of Beruit (AUB), and practices architecture and heritage management through a private consultancy: TURATH, in Amman, Jordan. Daher is interested in research related to politics and dynamics of place and heritage conservation, tourism, and urban regeneration and has conducted research on these issues in places such as Jordan, Syria, and Lebanon. Daher is also a Visiting Research Fellow at the Centre for Tourism and Cultural Change at Sheffield Hallam University, UK. Daher was awarded several research grants from places such as the Social Science Research Council and Fulbright and has published on issues related to heritage, politics of place, tourism, and urban regeneration. Daher has worked as a consultant for several heritage management and urban regeneration projects all over Jordan and abroad.

Xavier Guillot teaches architecture and urban planning at the School of Architecture in St Etienne in France and is a research associate at the

French Institute of Urbanism (University of Paris VIII). Xavier has worked and taught in different places including France, Jordan, Japan, Singapore, and the US. His research interest focuses on the relationship between globalization and the evolution of urban places including issues related to tourism. In parallel to his academic activity, he practices architecture through a private consutancy in the Pyrénées.

David Homa received his BA from the University of Nebraska at Omaha in Education and his MA from the University of Nebraska at Lincoln in Anthropology. Homa has done tourism research in Egypt and Japan. He taught Cultural Anthropology in Tokyo, Japan at a branch of Lakeland College, Wisconsin. Homa currently teaches Anthropology and Economics at Los Gatos High School in Los Gatos, California.

Saba Al Mahadin holds a BA in English Literature and Linguistics from the University of Jordan, an MSc in Hospitality Management from Edinburgh University in Scotland and has recently completed a PhD in Tourism Studies from Brighton University in the UK. Her work focuses on the tourism sector as a field of legitimating discourses. Her work and research centers on Jordanian tourism and she has researched tourism in Aqaba and in other places in Jordan. Al Mahadin has also worked as a consultant for the Ministry of Tourism and Antiquities in Jordan and for Zara Expo.

Salam Al Mahadin is currently Assistant-Professor of English at Petra University in Jordan. Her research emphasizes critical discourse with a particular focus on Jordan and her previous work includes papers on the semiotics of Jordanian Personal Status law, Jordan in post-colonial theory, in power and polity in tourism, and gender and power in education. She is currently working on a book on the cultural aspects of the production of Jordanian national identity.

Scott MacLeod is a post-graduate student in Ethnology at the University of Edinburgh interested in research related to information technologies, UNESCO World Heritage Sites, and the Internet. He holds a BA in the Social Science of Religion (1985) from Reed College, Portland, Oregon, and studied most recently at University of California, Berkeley (2000–1), and at the University of California, Santa Barbara (2001–3) before matriculating at the University of Edinburgh in 2003.

Birgit Mershen is an archaeologist teaching at Sultan Qaboos University in Oman. Mershen has also taught archaeology at Yarmouk University in Jordan and has extensively researched the northern parts of Jordan while living there. Mershen is also an active consultant on projects related to archaeology, tourism, and community development and is well-published on different topics related to archaeology and community involvements in heritage tourism.

Noha Nasser is Post-Doctoral Visiting Fellow at the Birmingham School of Architecture and Landscape, University of Central England. Nasser is an active researcher on issues relating to the architectural heritage of Egypt and the Islamic World and has published extensively on the architecture of Muslim societies in the UK. Nasser is also affiliated with the Center for Middle Eastern Studies at the University of California, Berkeley where she has conducted research. Currently, she is publishing work on the effect of cultural processes on urban form, and the conservation and regeneration influenced by Islam.

Aylin Orbaşli trained as an architect and has specialized in conservation, tourism, and heritage management and is currently teaching at Oxford Brookes University in the UK. She works as an independent consultant and as an educator and has over ten years international experience of working with and advising on historic buildings and areas. Among numerous other publications, she is the author of the book *Tourists in Historic Towns: Urban Conservation and Heritage Management* (Spon, 2000). She chairs the ICOMOS-UK Education and Training Committee and is a member of ICOMOS International Scientific Committee on Training.

Abbreviations

AIC	Abdali Investment Company
APSAD	Association for the Protection of Sites and Ancient Dwellings
ASEZA	Aqaba Special Economic Zone Authority
ATLAS	Association of Tourism and Leisure Studies
AUB	American University of Beruit
BCD	Beirut Central District
CDR	(Lebanese) Council for Development and Reconstruction
CENTOPS	Centre for Tourism Policy Studies
CHTUD	Cultural Heritage, Tourism, and Urban Development (Project)
CPH	Cham Palaces and Hotels
DGA	Directorate General of Antiquities
EFF	Extended Fund Facility
GAM	Greater Amman Municipality
GCC	Gulf Co-operation Council
GDP	gross domestic product
GSM	Greater Salt Municipality
HTML	hypertext markup language
ICCROM	International Centre for the Study of the Preservation and Restoration of Cultural Property
ICOM	The International Council of Museums
ICOMOS	International Council on Monuments and Sites
ICUN	International Union for the Conservation of Nature
IFPO	French Institute of the Near East
IMF	International Monetary Fund
JUST	Jordan University of Science and Technology
JVA	Jordan Valley Authority
KDC	Kerak Development Cooperation

KM	Kerak Municipality
KSA	Kingdom of Saudi Arabia
MOT	Ministry of Tourism
MOTA	Ministry of Tourism and Antiquities
MPWH	Ministry of Public Works and Housing
NAFTA	North American Free Trade Agreement
NGO	non-governmental organization
PMU	Project Management Unit
QIZ	Qualified Industrial Zone
RSCN	Royal Society for the Conservation of Nature
SAL	Structural Adjustment Lending
SCA	Supreme Council of Antiquities
SCT	Supreme Commission for Tourism
SDC	Salt Development Cooperation
SWR	Südwestrundfunk
TDA	Tourism Development Authority
TDD	Technical Development Department
TOR	Terms of References
UAE	United Arab Emirates
UDP	urban development project
UNDP	United Nations Development Program
UNESCO	United Nations Educational, Scientific and Cultural Organization
USAID	US Aid and International Development
WDI	World Development Indicator
WEF	World Economic Forum
WTO	World Tourism Organization
WTO	World Trade Organization
WWW	World Wide Web
ZIH	Zara Investment (Holding) Co. Ltd

Chapter 1

Reconceptualizing Tourism in the Middle East: Place, Heritage, Mobility and Competitiveness

RAMI FAROUK DAHER

Introduction

Tourism is becoming an increasingly global and complex phenomenon, with political, economic, social, cultural, environmental, and educational dimensions. Robinson (1998: 31) considers tourism to be the 'largest of multi-national activities.' When Lanfant (1995b: 26) explains about the omnipresence of tourism, she added that tourism on a world scale makes itself felt at geographical, ecological, and technological levels – as well as in the less visible and symbolic processes. Sheller and Urry (2004: 3) added that ' "Travel and tourism" is the largest industry in the world, accounting for 11.7 per cent of world GDP, 8 per cent of world export earnings, and 8 per cent of employment.' They emphasized that the mobility produced by tourism affects almost everyone everywhere. 'Internationally there are over 700 million legal passengers' arrivals each year (compared with 25 million in 1950) with a predicted 1 billion by 2010' (Sheller & Urry, 2004: 3). AlSayyad (2001b: 1) considers the twentieth century to have

> been the century of travel and tourism. Indeed, the inhabitants of the world in the last two decades have met more other people than at any time in known history. As travel around the world has risen to unprecedented levels, the number of tourists visiting certain countries and cities in a given year often exceeds the numbers of those places' native populations. Global travel has encouraged the phenomenal growth of the tourism industry.

The Middle East, regardless of how it is defined, has been identified as the geographic arena for this edited volume on tourism. Tourism in the

Middle East, within a global culture and competitive world economy, is faced with many challenges such as the leakage of tourism revenues and benefits into First World multi-national agencies and enterprises. Yet, tourism in the Middle East could also be the driving force for valuable opportunities leading to 'progress' and 'development.' The term 'Middle East,' which is politically charged and is considered a post-colonial construct by many intellectuals, has been chosen on purpose to elicit and evoke discontinuities and transformations within this significant region of the world.

Tourism is a multi-industry sector involving transportation, accommodations, attractions, cultural production, representation, distribution and many other sectors as well. Tourism research engages scholars and researchers from diverse fields such as anthropology, economy, geography, architecture, cultural studies, and tourism, which is evolving into a discourse of its own. Yet tourism-related research had mostly addressed tourism processes at the macro scale creating a vacuum and a need for more research that tackles local processes of transformation and change at the micro scale. Tourism is a vibrant vehicle of change that continues to influence the production and nature of 'cultural capital' manifested in heritage sites, cultural landscapes, folklore, and arts and crafts. Since tourism development takes place in real situations and places and affects real people, issues of place representation, authenticity, interpretation, socio-economic and spatial transformation therefore become significant areas for research and contemplation.

This edited volume on tourism in the Middle East embodies a multi-discursive approach to the study of tourism in the region offering not only different perspectives but also qualifying local knowledge and realities. The book reexamines the discourse of tourism within geopolitical contemporary regional realities. It reexamines tourism as a discourse linked to heritage and identity construction, national and global economies, and development of local communities. Alternatively, a new discursive approach to the understanding of tourism emerges out of invigorating and stimulating latent regional realities and the social histories of various towns, villages, and cultural landscapes within the contested and politically charged region of the Middle East. The book investigates issues of national identity, authenticity, definition of heritage, representation of cultures and regions, and tourism-related investments throughout a new vision for the region that transcends current geopolitics or national and formal historiographies.

Place, Heritage, Tourism, and Geographic Categories

Defining and choosing a geographic area for research and comparative analysis can sometimes be a complex and difficult task due to continuously shifting geographic and geopolitical categories and their associated meanings and perceptions. As critical political geographers have shown, it is important to move beyond the acceptance of geopolitics as a reality of world politics and to examine critically the ways in which geopolitical terms are defined and the significant social meanings they hold (Marston & Rouhani, 2001: 101–2). Nevertheless, the following three geopolitical and geo-cultural categories of '*Bilad al Sham*,'[1] the '*Mashreq*,'[2] or the '*Levant*' (though different in meaning, genealogy, and connotations based on the privileged standpoint and the discursive practices that facilitated the inscription of such categories) refer to generally the same physically geographic region that encompasses the countries of Jordan, Syria, Lebanon, and Palestine. While all of these geopolitical and geo-cultural categories are constructed and can be contested and become subject of scrutiny, some have emerged from within the region (such as *Bilad al Sham* or *Al Mashreq al Arabi*) and others have been part of colonial or neo-imperial *imagineering* of the region such as the Middle East or even the *Levant*. The Middle East as a geographical term, and according to Dalby (2003: 8), suggests the historical legacy of imperial specifications of the region. The term comes from 'earlier British designations of the world, which have been maintained on the maps and in the geopolitical imaginations of policy makers.'

In order to understand the genealogy of such geopolitical and geographic categories, one needs to understand and research the moments of transformation and rarity that the region of the Middle East witnessed over the past couple of centuries such as the destruction and replacement of the dynastic religious realm (represented by the Ottoman Empire) with the various post-mandate nation-states of Syria, Jordan, Lebanon, Palestine, Iraq, Turkey, Egypt, and several other nation-states during the first half of the 20th century, and the consequences of such moments and transformations on the definition and practice of nationhood, heritage, and tourism.

When studying the formative influence of colonial encounters in the shaping of national cultures and nation-states, one ought to observe how the various political systems of the newly constructed Middle East, in an attempt to legitimize their new existence (represented in monarchies and republics) consequently constructed several official representations and narrations of national pasts at the expense of regional realities (Kandiyoti,

2002: 282). Such constructed pasts were grounded in a search for distant and ancient origins linked to a disassociation from and varying levels of rejection of the recent past (mainly Ottoman). Due to such ideological, territorial, and cultural transformations, the process of image building and heritage identification and definition became highly contested and problematic especially when it was limited by the physical and political boundaries of the various nation-states and the restrictive and exclusive dogma of nationalism.

The work of Edward Said in general, and *Orientalism* in particular, helps us understand such processes of construction or inscription of a specific *Orient* in the minds of Europeans, local nationals, and the world (Said, 1979). Inscription mechanisms (surveys, documentation, military surveys, travel literature, and others) work to create the 'Other,' the 'Opposite' to Europe, which legitimized and led to, through direct modes of imperialism, control, exploitation, and hegemony. Europe was made to be rational, scientific, virtuous, mature, and 'normal' while the Orient (the opposite) was imagined and made to be irrational, depraved, childlike, non-scientific but exotic and 'different.'

This had considerable ramifications on how the past and tradition were viewed by the community and by institutions of the state, and also on how heritage was defined or marginalized. Furthermore, this also affected how the image of each of the nations in the region was weaved and constructed to fit a particular desired reality through discursive practices such as heritage definition by institutions of the state or academia, education and schooling, archaeology, museums, and tourism. One is intrigued to ask questions such as: How do these inscription mechanisms work to create a certain image for the region? How are the images of each of the nation-states constructed and how is heritage defined accordingly? How does this geopolitical construction and inscription process affect tourism to the region and the choice of sites to be incorporated for tourism purposes and why?

The company Thomas Cook and Son contributed to the development of mass tourism to the *Levant* in the second half of the 19th century. Hunter (2003: 157) stated that

> starting in 1869, Thomas Cook and Son created the tourist trade of Egypt by developing the Nile transit service while simultaneously opening up Syria/Palestine to travelers. The Cook enterprise quickly expanded to other parts of the region. The establishment of tourist offices in Cairo (1872), Jaffa (1874), and Jerusalem (1881) was followed by the opening of Cook agencies in Constantinople (1883), Algiers (1887), Tunis (1901), and Khartum (1901).

Primarily, ancient ruins (e.g. Egypt's ancient Phaeronic sites) and biblical sites of Palestine or Syria were the highlights of such tourism. A typical journey from Europe covered Egypt's ancient monuments, the Nile, the holy sites in Palestine and prime locations in major cities such as Beirut, Jerusalem, and Damascus. Sites such as Temple of Jupiter in Ba'albeck, Dome of the Rock and the Church of the Holy Sepulchre in Jerusalem, the Umayyad Mosque in Damascus, the ruins of Palmyra, and the rose-cut city of Petra were popular sites amongst tourists.

The definition of the region's heritage and the sites that were incorporated into tourism brochures or posters were confined to the classical, religious, and ancient monuments during mandate and early statehood period in the first half of the 20th century. Meanwhile, and according to Maffi (2002: 210–11), Daher (2002), and Schriwer (2002), the heritage of the recent past (manifested by its rural, urban traditions) was marginalized by official state discourses that attempted to disassociate from the recent Ottoman past and local realities and instead to construct legitimacy for the different, newly emerging state systems (Egypt, Jordan, Palestine, Syria, Lebanon) by constructing inks with distant origins (e.g. Phaeronic in Egypt, Nabatean in Jordan, Phoenician in Lebanon). Philipp (1992: ix) had stated that each of the newly emerging nation-states of the Middle East were 'looking too frequently for a definite past for each of the new states within its own limited territory. For the sake of consistency and the desire to find causal connections we are inclined to search for local patterns in the past which will explain the local state of the present.' In the Middle East, the European 'discovery' of the Orient through tourism to the ancient and Biblical '*Levant*' in the 19th century also contributed to the definition of a specific and imagined '*Levant*' and worked to define heritage in the region in a manner that excluded the recent past and regional realties of this region that we now call the Middle East.

According to Said (1979: 2–3), *Orientalism*

> is a style of thought based upon an ontological and epistemological distinction made between 'the Orient' and (most of the time) 'the Occident.' Thus a very large mass of writers, among whom are poets, novelists, philosophers, political theorists, economists, and imperial administrators, have accepted the basic distinction between East and West as the starting point for elaborate theories, epics, novels, social descriptions, and political accounts concerning the Orient, its people, customs, 'mind,' destiny, and so on.

Orientalism for Said was a 'corporate institution' for dealing with the Orient and making statements about it, describing it, and ruling over it

(Said, 1979: 3). The following quotation by Said illustrates how *Orientalism* is a whole discourse that worked to distribute a whole geographical awareness about the Orient into aesthetic, scholarly, economic, sociological, historical and philosophical texts and into a whole series of interests about the region. It is only by examining *Orientalism* as a discourse that one can understand the complexity of this 'systematic discipline' by which Europe was able to manage and even 'produce' the Orient in the 19th and 20th centuries.

> Therefore, *Orientalism* is not a mere political subject matter or field that is reflected passively by culture, scholarship, or institutions; nor is it a large and diffuse collection of texts about the Orient; nor is it representative and expressive of some nefarious 'Western' imperialist plot to hold down the 'Oriental' world. It is rather a distribution of geographical awareness into aesthetic, scholarly, economic, sociological, historical, and philosophical texts; it is an elaboration not only of a basic geographical distinction (the world is made up of two unequal halves, Orient and Occident) but also of a whole series of 'interests' which, by such means as scholarly discovery, philological reconstruction, psychological analysis, landscape and sociological description, it not only creates but also maintains; it is, rather than expresses, a certain will or intention to understand, in some cases to control, manipulate, even to incorporate, what is a manifestly different (or alternative and novel) world. (Said, 1979: 12)

This exercise of power over the Orient could not have been made possible without the production of knowledge about the Orient. According to Foucault (1980), no power is exercised without the extraction, appropriation, distribution, or retention of knowledge. The network and web of power/knowledge are evident in many of his writings (Foucault, 1980). A classical example that might illustrate the relationships between the production of knowledge and the exercise of power is to consider the production of diverse knowledge by the European travelers, scientists, and geographers of the 18th and 19th centuries to North Africa (the *Maghreb*) and the ancient *Levant* (the *Mashreq*) in the form of maps, narratives, investigative reports, art, demographic studies, archaeology, social narratives and studies, military surveys, photography, postcards, and other forms of productions. That knowledge, which was produced in the light of discovery and subordination of the Orient, was used to manipulate and exploit such regions and to rationalize domination and colonization. Colonization was rationalized on the basis of the European man transforming the citizens of these territories into modern and rationale individuals. One of Thomas Cook's newsletters from the 19th century, the *Traveller's Gazette* of November 1928, features an article entitled 'France in Algeria: The Romance of Algeria' that developed the colonial theme of an ancient Roman land in Algiers rescued from barbarism and transformed into a 'happy country by the French' (Hunter, 2003: 164).

Said (1979), who adopts Foucault's concept of discourse to explicate and understand *Orientalism* also adheres to this notion of power/knowledge in the production of the Orient by the discourse of *Orientalism*. Said had elaborated that

> to believe that the Orient was created – or, as I call it, 'Orientalized' – and to believe that such things happen simply as a necessity of the imagination, is to be disingenuous. . . . The Orient was Oreintalized not only because it was discovered to be 'Oriental' in all those ways considered common place by an average nineteenth-century European, but also because it could be – that is, submitted to being – made Oriental. (Said, 1979: 5)

Tourists coming to the constructed *Levant* in the 19th century imagined themselves coming to a cultural landscape that had not changed since antiquity, or since ancient Biblical and Byzantine times. Tourism posters and advertisement in general emphasized the antiquities of the region, and furthermore, romanticized a non-changed village life in Palestine and Syria. Fuchs (1998) elaborates on what he terms the 'timeless paradigm' of Orientalists who systemized an Orient that had remained unchanged for millennia, thus marginalizing centuries of change and transformation, especially during the recent periods before the 'European discovery' of the Orient. In his studies of the Palestinian Arab House of the 19th and early 20th centuries, Fuchs (1998: 157–6) elaborated that

> one problematic aspect of nineteenth- and early-twentieth-century descriptive literature is its predominantly biblical-archaeological inspiration: many authors regarded the landscapes of Palestine as illustrations of the Scriptures, and their texts are frustratingly burdened with biblical quotations. Behind this attitude, lay the assumption, often taken for granted, that traditional life in Palestine had remained unchanged for millennia.

As a consequence, the urban and rural realities were either marginalized or not even included in this *imagineered* discourse of the *Levant* and the region.

This notion of geopolitical *imagineering* of regions and creation of geographic categories is not restricted to the past or to the imperial colonial legacy. More recently, this region, and precisely the geographic region of the Southern Mediterranean encompassing countries such as Syria, Turkey, Lebanon, Egypt, Jordan, Tunis, and Algiers, has been inscribed and incorporated through a new European discourse as part of the Euro-Mediterranean space. To understand this neo-liberal geopolitical *imagineering*, it is crucial to analyze *Euromed* partnership[3] and collaboration in areas related to the cultural heritage and to heritage tourism[4] and its efforts in construction and production of a new understanding of the region: the new Mediterranean. By *imagineering*, the author intends a new term he coined for the process that combines an engineered imagining of geographical space made possible through a discursive practice that uses heritage, trade, collaborative research projects, information technology (IT), and tourism as its tools to inscribe this new geographic category.

The author argues that most *Euromed* initiatives depend on a digital representation of space, heritage, and tourism with minimal physical effects on the ground but, yet, with such serious socio-political and ideo-logical consequences. One of the major socio-economic and political consequences of this geopolitical *imagineering* is the recruiting of the Muslim part of the Mediterranean (Southern and Eastern Mediterranean represented by Middle East and North Africa) as an extension to Europe within a geopolitical framework of pan regions. *Euromed* collaboration is benefiting from the latest developments in IT[5] and particularly in multi-media systems to authenticate this new engineered/imagined region. This new geopolitical *imagineering* of the Mediterranean has several socio-economic and cultural consequences on this part of the Middle East in terms of how heritage is defined and how it is articulated and incorpo-rated into tourism.

If the discourse on *Orientalism* (researched by Said) was meant to create the *Other*, as a demarcation of East and West, the recently evolving discourse on *Euromed* heritage is one of integration rather than demarca-tion within a power network of pan regions. To elaborate, while both discourses deploy mechanisms of *inscription* for purposes of control and socio-economic and cultural hegemony, the nature of the *inscription* and *imagineering* in each case is different. In the discourse on *Orientalism*, inscription mechanisms (surveys, documentation, military surveys, travel literature, and others) work to create the 'Other,' the 'Opposite' to Europe, which legitimized and led to, through direct modes of imperialism, control, exploitation, and hegemony. In the discourse on *Euromed Heritage*, *inscription* of the new 'Mediterranean' acts to create an integrated *pan region* (an extension to Europe) that is still inferior, but nevertheless, is influenced and dependent on superior European advancement in high technology, IT and multimedia. Ultimately this discourse legitimizes and leads to an indirect form of imperialism. The various inscription processes act as a grid for filtering ideas and practices that ultimately establish the positional superiority of the European countries over Southern Mediterranean ones.

Many years later after colonization was over in the Middle East around the middle of the 20th century, and nation-states emerged in a grand attempt to forge national identities and images for each of these states, it is ironic that the same Orientalists and colonial discourses perpetuate. One only has to look at any tourism brochure or poster, or watch any promotional video that defines and promotes each of the countries within the Middle East to find out that practices of governments in the region through their ministries of tourism work to define the region mainly through its classical traditions marginalizing local regional realities of the recent past in particular. One example comes from Jordan Tourism Board brochures where sites such as Petra and Jerash are still the highlights of any tourism trip coming to Jordan; only recently very little attention is directed to promoting Jordan's more recent heritage realities such as agricultural villages in the north, the vernacular, and urban and social heritage of various Jordanian towns such as Salt or Amman. Publications of the Jordan Tourism Board such as the *Map of Jordan* (Jordan Tourism Board, 1998) or the *Visitors' Guide: Welcome to Jordan* (Jordan Tourism Board, 2000) (see Figure 1.1) highlight primarily Jordan's antiquities sites (such as Petra, Jerash, Byzantine Churches of Madaba, and the Umayyad Desert Castles) and Jordan's significant nature attractions (such as Wadi Rum and Dana nature reserves, the Gulf of Aqaba, and the Dead Sea).

Gregory (2001: 112) explores some of the ways in which the fatal attractions of colonial nostalgia are inscribed within contemporary cultures of travel and heritage definition in Egypt. He believes that what makes the histories of colonialism nostalgic is the 'seductiveness of colonial power.'

> Those seductions continue to exercise an extraordinary power at the start of the twenty-first century, which is why I prefer to speak not of the condition of 'postcolonialism' but instead of 'the colonial present', and why I wish to explore some of the ways in which the fatal attractions of colonial nostalgia are inscribed within contemporary cultures of travel. (Gregory, 2001: 112–13)

To illustrate his point of view, Gregory uses two late 20th-century exhibits: one is based on a 1994 guidebook to Egypt by Gallimard, which

Figure 1.1 The cover of a 'visitors' guide' brochure for Jordan produced
by the Jordan Tourism Board. Jordan is defined primarily
through its ancient and classical heritage such as Petra and
Jerash or through nature sites such as the Dead Sea and the
Desert. Other realities of Jordan's heritage such as the rural and
urban sites from the recent past are not incorporated in the
formal definition of what Jordan is.

Source: Jordan Tourism Board, 2000. www.see-jordan.com

Figure 1.2 Thomas Cook's offices in Heliopolis near Cairo, Egypt.
Source: Photograph taken by Rami Farouk Daher, May 2005.

similar to several 'comparable texts, it exquisitely aestheticizes and commodifies a particular visual economy of travel.' The book opens with a view of 'Boats on the Nile' with 'Tourists returning from Karnak'. The second exhibit 'is a tourist brochure produced for Thomas Cook's 1997–98 season on the Nile. In the gracious days of Edwardian cruising, prospective clients are reminded' of Thomas Cook's palatial and luxuriously finished paddle-steamers, which dominated the Nile in the 19th century and represented the era's best in comfort and technology (Gregory, 2001: 113). Figure 1.2 shows Thomas Cook's offices in Heliopolis near Cairo. AlSayyad elaborates that

> Gregory's project is to ask how these images of colonial nostalgia were constructed and, more importantly, what colonial histories are hidden from the views they presented. Eschewing the term 'post-coloniality', Gregory prefers to explore what he calls the 'colonial-present', and to ask why and how, at the end of the 20th century, people may still be seduced by such stories of colonial power. (AlSayyad, 2001b: 20).

Constructed Heritage Places and Emerging Tourist Sites: Marginalization and Qualification Processes

When studying the formative influence of colonial encounters in the shaping of national cultures and nation-states (Anderson, 1983; Kandiyoti, 2002; Maffi, 2000), one ought to observe how the various political systems of the region of the Middle East, in an attempt to legitimize their new existence (represented in monarchies and republics) consequently constructed several official representations and narrations of national pasts at the expense of regional realities. Such constructed pasts were grounded in a search for distant and ancient origins linked to a disassociation from and varying levels of rejection of the recent past (mainly Ottoman). The multi-layered process through which nations, heritage and images are defined, produced, and constructed takes place and emerges with the circulation of official/dominant, popular (local), academic/elitist, and geopolitical discursive practices. Mechanisms for such a construction included several discursive practices, different institutions of the state such as ministries of education, culture, and tourism, and ranged from school curricula to stamps, museums/heritage definition, and tourism attraction and other areas of representation. This process of construction resulted in manufactured images formulated by how each of these states conceptualized itself.

In general, and throughout several places in the Middle East, such rejections of and disassociations from the recent past had roots in pre- and post-mandate and colonial periods when *modernity* was introduced as ever-changing and progressive, and it was contrasted with *tradition*, which was presented as static, non-changing, anti-progress, non-scientific, and non-individualistic (Horner, 1990). The separation between the recent past and present led eventually to a dilution of people's awareness and knowledge of the past, its various moments of transformation and change and the role it played in their everyday life. Out of this separation, the past and heritage become molded into constructed and esoteric periods of 'then' and 'now.'

This dichotomy between past and present occurred in different parts of the world as well. Graburn (1998) shows how history and heritage (the past) could be molded into constructed periods of 'then' (distant) and 'now' (recent) in museums and collection interpretations, thus denying another interpretation of the past that could have addressed significant moments of discontinuities and transformations in the Inuit's history (Inuits of the Central and Eastern Canadian Arctic). He elaborates on the emergence of a 'generalized' and 'total' Inuit history, which is imagined, reproduced, and constructed in most other museums of the Central and Eastern Canadian Arctic.

The various political systems (nation-states) of the current Middle East, constructed official representations and narrations of national pasts and forged 'constructed' national identities at the expense of regional realities. In the process, the recent past and heritage of the region was led into a state of paralysis. Many historic studies on the Ottoman period in the Arab world uncritically lumped it into one long period and labeled it as four centuries of alien domination, neglect, and deterioration. According to Rogan (1994: 32), several national narratives attempted to incorporate the conviction that the Ottoman period was insignificant to the region and that it amounted to 'four centuries of neglect.'

The official rhetoric of post-mandate nation-states, and in their desperate search for foundation, legitimacy, and origins, attempted consciously to create links with the distant, antiquarian, ancient past. Several newly erected 'national' and foreign archaeological institutions facilitated the search for such distant origins. Archaeological museums flourished in the newly constructed ancient *Levant*, the official discourse highlighted the interconnections with such distant 'constructed' points of origins that were conceived to have operated in the past within an approximate territorial boundary similar to that of the contemporary national-state. Maffi (2000) highlights one example that explicates the Jordanian/Hashemite fascination with ancient Nabbattean civilizations that operated in a geographic territory similar to today's modern Jordan.

Hobsbawm and Ranger (1983: 1–2) believe that 'traditions' that appear or claim to be old are often quite recent in origin and sometimes invented:

> 'Invented tradition' is taken to mean a set of practices, normally governed by overtly or tacitly accepted rules and of a ritual or symbolic nature, which seek to inculcate certain values and norms of behavior by repetition, which automatically implies continuity with the past. In fact, where possible, they normally attempt to establish continuity with a suitable past.

Hobsbawm and Ranger (1983: 14) also believe that

> we should not be misled by a curious, but understandable, paradox: modern nations and all their impedimenta generally claim to be the opposite of novel, namely rooted in the remotest antiquity, and the opposite of constructed, namely human communities to 'natural' as to require no definition other than self-assertion.

They also believe that 'the national phenomenon cannot be adequately investigated without careful attention to the invention of tradition' (Hobsbawm & Ranger, 1983: 14).

Reilly (1999: 62) criticizes those who speak of a decisive break between the past and the present in his study of *Bilad al Sham* during contemporary and Ottoman periods. Instead he believes that his study shows that 'elements of contemporary reality were present in the past.' Reilly feels that we are witnessing a critical paradigm shift in Arab historiography. In general, critical historians are turning away from political history to social and economic history. The history of the Syrian lands does not 'consist of a series of famous personalities, they write but of "the people" who produced nourishment and daily necessities for the inhabitants' (Reilly, 1999: 46). This paradigm shift in Arab historiography emerged through socio-economic and ideological change and is part of a larger transformation shared not only by some historians but also by a group of philosophers, critical thinkers, and social scientists in general. This is gradually affecting how critically heritage is being redefined and how new sites are incorporated into the realm of tourism within the region.

One particular outcome is the qualification and granting voice to certain regional realities that were not incorporated into the 'national definition' of heritage or in the promotion agendas of ministries of tourism such as the vernacular villages that transcend national boundaries in places such as the villages in the Hauran between Syria and Jordan or, for example, tracing the heritage of domestic architecture and its evolution throughout the Eastern Mediterranean region. Or they might include 'sites' that had predominantly stayed outside the realm of popular sites promoted by the state for purposes of tourism such as social history of cities (as oppose to official state history), urban heritage of the recent past such as historic city cores in Salt, Jordan, in Muharraq, Bahrain, or in Tirpoli in Lebanon; or the newly emerging sites of heritage, art, and culture that are patronned by rich families evoking different forms of authority and patronage and tackling the social issues and the history of the everyday such as the Soup Museum in Saida, Lebanon or *Darat al Funun* (houses of the arts) in Amman, Jordan. Furthermore, such sites also include heritage corridors, travel and pilgrimage routes such as the Hijaz Railroad Line, which crosses Syria, Jordan, and Saudi Arabia with its various train stations that date to the turn of the 20th century but also with its Hajj forts dating to the beginning of the Ottoman period in the region.

It is very interesting that even though there have been many studies on culture, heritage, and tourism addressing these interrelated independent political units or nation-states (sometimes termed quasi-states) that once enjoyed the sovereignty of a common region in many places of the world (e.g. East and West Germany, North and South Korea, Vietnam, Yugoslavia, Hong Kong, Taiwan and China, Northern Ireland and the Republic of Ireland, and others) (Butler & Mao, 1995), there has been little scholarly work on the region of the Middle East or the Arab world and its various newly erected nation-states regarding similar issues and concerns. Despite the fact that, currently, each of these nation-states constitutes a separate political entity, there had been always, and continuously, during the 20th century and before considerable travel between them. This creates significant methodological and ideological challenges for research on heritage and on tourism regarding the inherent differences, conflicts, and unresolved issues concerning the definition of *the heritage in between* historically and culturally defined vs. politically and functionally defined regions/nations.

The Heritage Industry and the *Kan Zaman* Genre in Middle East Cultural Tourism

One significant cultural change that affected the definition of heritage and the celebration of different types of sites was the shift from modernity to post-modernism where, according to Urry (1990: 82), boundaries between high and low cultures, and also between different cultural forms such as tourism, art, education, shopping, and architecture were dissolved. While modernity, as a mode of cultural ideology, differentiated between high and low art, post-modernism practiced a 'democratic' de-differentiation and the same way it celebrated high-class architecture by other modes of cultural production, it also celebrated the ordinary, the popular, and the folk of everyday. So the same way that tourists can visit and appreciate the splendor of the Umayyad Mosque in Damascus, they could celebrate the local cultural experience provided by the city's ordinary historic houses. And visitors to Cairo can enjoy the Pyramids but also the house where the late notorious singer Abulhalim Hafiz used to reside.

According to Urry (1990: 85), this process of de-differentiation caused signification to become increasingly more figural or visual during which tourists are gradually dealing more with the iconographic reality of places. Also, this process of de-differentiation is leading to a democratization of heritage sites, where the 'ordinary' is now celebrated and becomes subject of the tourist gaze. A visit to Damascus is not complete today without a visit to the *Naufara*, a traditional coffee shop where one enjoys drinking tea or coffee in historic Old Damascus while listening to the *Hakawati* (narrator of historic biographies or storyteller) in the same way that a tourist visiting Istanbul will make sure to visit Ayub Çami (Mosque) to watch the celebrations after male circumcision. Urry (1990: 101) adds that the gaze is socially constructed and 'that both production and consumption are socially organized, and that the gaze must be directed to certain objects or features which are extraordinary, which distinguish that site/sight of the gaze from others.'

More recently, and within the past 20 years or so, it has been interesting to note the emergence of several global trends within the different countries of the world. One very important trend is the appeal of heritage tourism to many governments in developing countries, where heritage is becoming an industry, in attempts to achieve successful economic restructuring signaling a shift to the service sector in a late capitalist era with consequences on heritage/tourism relationships and privatization dynamics (Chang *et al.*, 1996). Robinson (2001: 40) elaborates how 'for developing economies whose natural resource base is depleted, tourism would appear to provide a rather rapid way of generating hard currency and creating employment. Indeed, utilizing the cultural and ethnic resources of a nation or region for tourism may be the only way out.'

> In the presence of such trends, and amidst of the monotony of global high capitalism, at a time when standardized products and services are increasingly marketed world wide, there is an increasing demand for built environments that promise unique cultural experiences. Many nations, meanwhile, are resorting to heritage preservation, the invention of tradition, and the rewriting of history as forms of self-definition. Indeed, the events of the last decade have created a dramatically altered global order that requires a new understanding of the role of tradition and heritage of social space and the shaping of city form. (AlSayyad, 2001b: 4)

This is not a new phenomenon, it had occurred in developed countries as well. Tourism developments continue to play a major role for developed countries in their attempts to restructure and readjust from a manufacturing to a service-sector base (Robinson, 2001: 40). This is evident in many ex-industrial and manufacturing small- and medium-size cities shifting their economy to tourism industry and the service sector.

Kan Zaman in Jordan from the late 1980s is actually one of the very early examples of the heritage industry in the Middle East that used heritage and tradition coupled with entertainment to promote a new heritage tourism product in the region. It represents the adaptation of a *Khirbet* (estate or farm) from the 1850s in the Yadoudeh area outside of Amman that belonged to one landowning family (the Abu Jabers) into traditional restaurant and coffee shop.[6] The old stables, where the traditional restaurant is located, and landowners estate has become a popular tourist attraction for locals and foreign tourists alike where in addition to eating and drinking, they can enjoy niche shopping at the different local crafts and souvenir shops within the same premises. The project, financed in 1989 by Jordan Tourism Investment, became a model for similar adaptations all over the country and elsewhere in the Middle East to the extent that similar places adopted the same name such as Salt Zaman and Madaba Zaman in Jordan where *Zaman* could be loosely translated into English as 'bygone days' and *Kan* is the past verb for being, so *Kan Zaman* could mean 'happened in bygone days.'

One example of invented tradition comes to us from Southern Egypt's village of New Gourna near the ancient site of Luxor. New Gourna was planned by the famous Egyptian architect Hassan Fathy in the 1950s as the new home for residents of the settlement the Egyptian government wanted to evict from their houses among the archaeological sites of the ancient Theban necropolis in Luxor. 'Fathy designed the village using elaborate mud-brick structures that he imagined represented indigenous tradition' (AlSayyad, 2001b: 21). In his search for the ideal vernacular, Fathy turned to the geometries and proportions of Islamic styles that had flourished in Cairo several centuries earlier and these resulted in the use of unfamiliar forms in the use of domes and vaults for example. Kamel (2000) had added that Fathy used the Nubian indigenous architecture as precedent because he was seeking solutions for the crises in architecture and urban environment of the time. The solution was found by re-rooting one's self in tradition and the vernacular. According to AlSayyad (2001b: 14) and 40 years later, his architecture became an invented tradition by becoming the adopted architecture for tourism development, hotels, and resorts, in different places on the Red Sea in Eastern Egypt such as in Al Gourna, Qusair, and Hurghda.

Kamel (2000: 147) added that the famous American architect Michael Graves was commissioned for the design of hotels in Al Gourna on the Red Sea that were inspired by Fathy's designs resulting in a collage of styles and meanings where a combination of the Fathy's Nubian vernacular and 'Pharaonic Monumentalism' served as precedents for his hotel resorts and other tourism developments. In another location on the Red Sea, similar transformations and tourism developments, which were derived from the architectural aesthetics of Hassan Fathy, are taking place. Kamel (2000: 152) also elaborates that in 1989, Orascom, an Egyptian construction corporation established a sister company, Orascom

Projects and Tourist Developments to develop 500 hectares of purchased land 22 kilometers north of Hurghda, the fast developing tourist town at the Red Sea. The aim was to capitalize on the climate, clear waters, and coral reefs of the Red Sea to create a large-scale resort project. The new village and resorts had to display a uniquely exotic attraction not only in services, but also in their image and experience.

Similar 'inventions of tradition' are taking place in other tourist locations in the Middle East. In Jordan, for example, and on the shores of the Dead Sea, Movenpick, the famous hotel chain operators appropriated the Jordanian vernacular, or even the traditional architecture of villages in the region of Bilad al Sham juxtaposed with a flavor of the local mud sandy architecture of the Dead Sea as precedent to create its notorious luxurious hotel and spa on the Eastern shores of the Dead Sea with a twist of tradition (see Figure 1.3). The new hotel complex is divided into

Figure 1.3 Movenpick Hotel and Resort on the Eastern Dead Sea Shore in Jordan. The historic precedents for the architecture fall between Jordan traditional vernacular architecture in the north with its courtyards and village spaces and the local mud architecture for which the Dead Sea area is famous.

Source: Photograph taken by Rami Farouk Daher, 2002.

courtyards (similar to village spaces) and narrow alleys with water drinking fountains before opening up to the sea view. The color and material give the impression of the local mud architecture that the region is famous for. This 'manufactured heritage' became the object of the gaze for a lot of tourists who simply prefer to remain within the premises of the luxurious hotel and rarely venture outside. It also became a preferred topic for photographs where it is sometimes difficult to distinguish between this appropriation of heritage and the real thing; the real thing could have never existed in this form or juxtaposition.

The different examples presented before exemplify how tradition can be subjected to consumption by governments or individuals to create a certain national identity or a different identity and sense of pride. The examples show also how on several occasions, heritage can be subjected to varying degrees of manufacturing where it becomes a mean for capital accumulation by individuals and investors. AlSayyad believes that

> although the two activities, consuming tradition, and manufacturing heritage, are thus produced by different agents, one cannot separate them from each other. In this global era, the consumption of tradition as a form of cultural demand and the manufacture of heritage as a field of commercial supply are two sides of the same coin. And many countries are now actively inventing or re-creating their own heritage, and using tourist revenues to do so. Their design agenda thus has two components: one politically self-serving; the other economically sustaining. (AlSayyad, 2001b: 15)

Yet, the heritage industry can take different forms and engage various types of initiators and actors that also play a role in broadening the definition of heritage and work to qualify and grant voice to subjugated realities and histories. One particular significant actor in the region are elite and notable families who are turning to heritage, culture, and the intelligentsia for their philanthropist endeavors and projects in different places such as Syria, Lebanon, Jordan, Bahrain, Palestine, and Egypt. One prominent example comes from Saida, Lebanon. Endowed by the Audi family in Saida, the Audi Foundation transformed the old family residence (which also functioned before as a soap factory) into the headquarters of the Foundation and into a thematic museum of handmade soap (Daher, 2004). This thematic museum asserts to relate the history of soap to the region at large stretching between Trablus (Lebanon), Haleb (Syira), Nablus (Palestine), and Salt (Jordan) and to show the various stages of its manufacturing and the diversity of its shapes. Furthermore, the family's involvement in the city included the renovation of the façades of the neighboring historic El Chakrieh street and the rehabilitation of various traditional housing units in the same historic neighborhood.[7] In fact, one of its very interesting features is its emphasis on the events of everyday life and histories of the local ordinary citizens. Places such as the Soap Museum in Saida are gradually becoming significant tourist attractions offering the tourist a different angle on local history and culture. Of course, the Soap Museum marks one of the early examples of such projects; several started to appear in Lebanon such as the Bsous Museum, which narrates and displays the heritage of the silk industry in the country (Dahdah, 2004).

First World–Third World Relationships and the Politics of Tourism Development

A recent World Tourism Organization (WTO) report credited domestic and international tourism in 1995 with the creation of 200 million jobs worldwide and an 11.4% contribution to the world's gross domestic product (GDP) (Cheong & Miller, 2000: 372). Yet, tourism is a First World industry presenting uneven and unequal development between First World and Third World economies. People from the First World make up the significant bulk of international tourists and it is they who have the resources to make relatively expensive journeys for pleasure or in seeking cultural difference. In addition, processes of uneven development are reflected through the growing elite and newly wealthy classes in some Third World countries that are now able to participate in tourism. According to Titley (2000), and based on statistics from the World Travel and Tourism Council, the tourist industry is providing one in nine jobs and 80% of travelers come from just 20 countries. 'In other words, in a changing global economy, tourism is a matter of economic imperative for the Majority World and privileged mobility for the Minority' (Titley, 2000: 79).

With the growth of the service sector within a global economy, many developed countries see in tourism the answer in a shift to a service-sector base. With an increasingly competitive global market, many developing countries also view tourism as the vehicle for economic development and growth. The following quotation by Robinson (2001: 45) sketches the realities of uneven development in tourism between the First and the Third Worlds:

> Various researchers have positioned the phenomenon of international tourism as a manifestation of neocolonialism and imperialism. Similarly, in a neo-Marxist vein it is possible to conceive of

the 'pleasure-periphery' idea of tourism as representing the fundamental structural dependency of the developing nations upon the
developed nations. The ideas of neocolonialism and global imbalance
are borne out not only in terms of the direction of tourist flows from
First to Third World, but also by the fact that the necessary enabling
elements for world tourism – the means of production, the ideology
of consumption, capital, credit, and information – are chiefly located
in, and controlled by, the developed nation. (Robinson, 2001: 45)

Whether or not such a competitive global market is part of a deliberate
policy objective of global capital and First World countries is yet to be
seen. But, nevertheless, it is forcing many developing countries into
lowering socio-economic conditions (e.g. labor wages, environmental
standards) in pursuit of 'competitiveness' and First World corporate
tourism investments. One predominant characteristic of tourism policies
in some Middle Eastern countries is the gap between proposed policies
and strategies on one side, and realities and implementation on the
ground on the other. This poses a challenge and a threat to the success
of the tourism industry in the Middle East. While most governments
adopt a *modernist* developmental paradigm that centers on economic
growth and an apparent bias towards the formal tourism sector, the
informal tourism sector is generally excluded from national policies
regardless of the high initial capital cost and leakage to outside economies
characteristic of the formal sector. For example, several national tourism
policies in different parts of the Middle East support the establishment of
key international hotel chains and attempt to attract large tourism investments while small- and medium-size tourism endeavors such as hotel
businesses in the form of 'bed and breakfast' or local family tourist businesses in both urban and rural areas are not encouraged or supported, or
even included in national visions for tourism development in general.

At the national scale of Jordan, the new millennium triggered the
Ministry of Tourism and Antiquities (MOTA) to start thinking seriously
about its tourism strategies. The rhetoric and objectives of the strategy are
reassuring. The Mission Statement for 1999–2000 is 'Sustainable Tourism
Development towards Economic Prosperity.' Tourism objectives include
developing an advanced tourism industry utilizing its competitive advantages, developing archaeological and tourism sites and resources to
enhance the tourism product, expanding the role of the private sector,
and upgrading the quality of tourism services to the highest international
standards (Ministry of Tourism and Antiquities, 1999). In reality, when
it comes to implementation, very few of these objectives are actually

achieved. In addition, implementation strategies do not even come close to fulfilling such objectives. Tourism developments continue to be driven by multi-national capital and large investments, tourism policies and strategies continue to be manipulated by foreign aid endeavors that are conditioned with privatization and induce high leakages of the tourism revenues to outside the country. National tourism strategies seldom accommodate small- and medium-size tourism developments and investments that can be more likely linked to genuine community development.

In the developing world, and with increasing economic problems and mass unemployment, tourism is gradually becoming an attractive sector to invest in because, first, it does not demand huge investments, second, nor does it demand high technology that is not available for most of such countries. AlSayyad (2001b: 3) stated that in the Third World, and due to economic problems and pressures coupled with mass unemployment, 'tourism is an attractive sector to invest in as it does not demand huge investments nor high technology.' Furthermore, many governments of the world turn to tourism as it is often 'presented as the last chance' (Lanfant, 1995a: 3). Tourism plays a significant role in the budgets of different Middle Eastern countries. Table 1.1 illustrates selected Middle Eastern countries' economic dependence on tourism. Syria is seriously starting to provide an 'appropriate environment for tourism investment.'[8] In several occasions, the Syrian Minister of Tourism had declared recently that Syria is very serious about attracting inward investments. Syria invited tenders for more than 100 tourism sites during the Tourism Investment Market, which was held in Damascus in April, 2005.

In 1996, the tourism sector provided more than 770 million Jordanian Dinars in revenues amounting to more than 12% of the GDP of the country to the extent that it had been defined as Jordan's number one foreign exchange earner (Daher, 2000a: 22). Lebanon's whole economy was always dependent on tourism, especially inward Arab tourism from Saudi Arabia and the Gulf states. In fact, after September 11, the circulation of Saudi and Gulf capital investment, after it was no longer welcomed in the US and Europe, found its way to the Lebanese tourism market in the form of several international chain hotels such as the Movenpick of Beirut, but also the Rotana Group of hotels, which is funded by United Arab Emirates (UAE) emirs and sheikhs.

Robinson (2001: 48) states that enclave tourism resorts 'being separate from the ordinariness of the surrounding environment also allows tourist enclaves to develop, ostensibly removing tourists from contact with the host community.' Furthermore, Oppermann (1993: 540) stated that the 'spatial concentration of international tourism in developing countries,

Table 1.1 Selected Middle Eastern countries' economic dependence on tourism

Country	Tourism Industry Share of Country GDP		Tourism Industry Jobs Share of All Employment		Tourism Visitor Exports Share of All Exports	
	Percentage	*Rank*	*Percentage*	*Rank*	*Percentage*	*Rank*
Bahrain	2.5%	6	4%	5	1.7%	10
Egypt	7.0%	1	3%	6	54.0%	1
Israel	2.9%	5	3%	7	1.2%	12
Jordan	6.9%	2	7%	1	6.5%	7
Kuwait	1.9%	9	2%	9	2.2%	9
Lebanon	3.4%	4	7%	2	33.9%	2
Oman	2.2%	7	3%	8	19.5%	4
Qatar	3.7%	3	4%	4	24.5%	3
Saudi Arabia	1.6%	10	2%	10	17.7%	5
Syria	2.1%	8	5%	3	7.3%	6
UAE	1.1%	12	1%	12	1.4%	11
Yemen	1.1%	11	2%	11	2.9%	8
MENA*	2.5%		3%		6.5%	

Source: Ministry of Tourism and Antiquities (2004: 21)

Note: * MENA stands for Middle East and North Africa.

combined with the typical standardization of the tourism product in mass tourism' usually result in the establishment of 'enclave' resorts. According to Sharpley (2000: 10) tourism investments are regularly influenced by power relations that are concentrated within enclave resorts or 'tourist ghettos', thereby 'contributing to socioeconomic inequalities through a developmental process which is, ironically, often promoted by the central governments of the countries in which the resorts are located.'

In spite of its high initial capital costs and high leakage to the outside, the formal sector, within tourism developments, is usually favored by most tourism agencies that promote tourism developments in the Third World. It is a well-known fact amongst tourism experts that the informal sector, manifested in local small- and medium-size endeavors, is capable of higher integration into the local economic structure; it is 'capable of producing a high multiplier effect on the local economy than the formal tourism sector' (Oppermann, 1993: 544). The informal tourism sector is symbolized by its 'open structure' instead of the 'enclave structure' of the formal tourism sector (Oppermann, 1993: 544). In addition, over-dependence on the formal sector within tourism developments leads to a high foreign participation and dependency, for example, through international hotel chains:

> Within developing countries, participation is restricted to the upper class, which has the required funds and insights into the needs and wants of international mass tourists. The upper circuit operation entails high leakage in the form of profit transfers, repatriation of funds from foreigners in managed positions, large imports of food, and other general items. This does not even include all the imports of furniture and decors when international standards hotels are built. (Oppermann, 1993: 534)

Sharm al Sheikh is a new emerging resort city on the Red Sea in Egypt. Large influxes of tourists from different parts of the world dictated the creation of an international airport that receives tourists who directly fly to Sharm (as it is called) from various destinations from Europe and elsewhere in the world. Each one of the resorts and international chain hotels had created its own enclave; tourists rarely venture outside the domains of the resort, and if they do, they remain within a shared space locally called 'Hotels Promenade,' a promenade street between the hotels and the beach which restaurants, clubs, and cafes of the different chain resorts open onto. Though it is interesting to walk along this street promenade, especially at night, in reality, you are not in the city but within the enclave domain and space of the international chain hotels and resorts.[9] Several similar tourism development endeavors in the Middle East, such as in Aqaba, Jordan for example, are starting to consider Sharm al Sheikh as the ultimate example for tourism development to be adopted in the region with maximum leakage of tourism revenues to the outside.

In Jordan, the Eastern Dead Sea Shore Development Project (between Sweimeh and Zara) is located on the Eastern shore of the Dead Sea starting from the town of Sweimeh, then stretching southward to provide infrastructure to existing and planned tourism developments along side the Dead Sea and urban and infrastructure services for Sweimeh village and its future extension. In different parts of the Third World, many tourism development-planning policies are still embedded within 'modernization' paradigms that, according to Sharpley (2000) center on 'economic growth' that, presumably, enables countries to advance through 'stages from traditional to an age of mass consumption. The benefits of economic growth "trickle down" or diffuse through the spread of "growth impulses" or "poles" of growth' (Sharpley, 2000: 4).

The previous primes of economic growth and modernization developmental theories could be critiqued at different levels and on a number of grounds. The 'trickle down' effect in Third World countries remains a myth due to power relations and the fact that 'development' and the right to investment is in the hand of few national elite. The masses (workforce) are exploited as cheap labor and are seldom initiating their own development initiatives. Particularly, the modernization development paradigm could be criticized for its use of 'traditional and modern as ambiguous ideal-type classifications with Western ethnocentric overtones, the modernization paradigm continues to underpin the rationale for tourism-induced development' (Sharpley, 2000: 4–5). Yet, and as explained earlier, many tourism ministries in the Arab world that still adhere to a *classical* 'modernization' development paradigm, depends highly on multi-national large tourism investments (e.g. international five-star hotel accommodations, enclave resorts) with high initial capital cost and leakages of tourism benefits to the outside. In addition, within the tourism industry and its several areas of transportation, accommodation, distribution, and production, First World corporations and transnational companies dominate the scene.

Guillot (2003) focuses on one aspect of the tourism industry: the luxury hotels through the study of entrepreneurs behind their development. He presents a critical comparison between two chains: one local and one international operating between Jordan (Zara Investment Holdings' Movenpick) (Figure 1.3) and Syria (Othman Aidi's Cham Palaces and Hotels) (Figure 1.4). Zara Investment (Holding) Co. Ltd (ZIH) was founded in 1994 by the late Khalil Talhouni (a businessman and banker) along with a group of independent investors, local bankers and investment companies. Cham Palaces and Hotels (CPH) was founded by Osman Aidi (an expatriate who resides between Paris and Damascus) in 1977 as a semi-private and semi-governmental company. The Ministry of Tourism holds 25% of the shares, while the remaining 75% is held by 20,000 private shareholders. One of their very early examples is the Cham Palace in downtown Damascus. Zara had contracts with an international managing company and signed a management contract with Movenpick to operate the hotel in the Dead Sea (Zara's largest in Jordan) (Guillot, 2003).

One aspect of comparison between the two chains is the percentages of tourism revenue leakages to the outside of the country. In the case of

Figure 1.4 Postcard showing Cham Palace Hotel in Damascus, Syria. This
          local chain has spread all over the country.

Source: Postcard bought at hotel lobby, February 2002.

Cham Palace hotels in Syria, a greater percentage of the revenue remains
in Syria. Almost everything is manufactured locally, and the Aidi
Foundation has to pay no royalties to international chain operators as
management and operations are locally based. In the case of Zara's
Movenpick, not only did Zara have to pay for the initial investment to
build the hotel, but also it had to pay Movenpick for its name, management contract, and operations in addition to importing the furniture and
other hotel details concerning the hotel rooms, restaurants, and lobbies
according to Movenpick standards and design profile.

Today, tourism-related research is in need of a theoretical framework
that emphasizes the links between the political economy of tourism and
its social, cultural, and environmental dimensions. Basic imbalances exist

between developed, developing, and lesser-developed nations not only in terms of spatial distribution of tourist activity, but also in terms of the distribution of economic benefits. While many studies address conflict between tourists and host cultures, it is significant to acknowledge the fact that power relations are intensely present in the tourism industry and conflict is conceptualized as present not only at a global level but also at a local level where tourists, host communities, and most strikingly, tourism brokers are agents of power. In addition, tourism research should acknowledge recent fundamental restructuring of the mode of production under conditions of post-Fordism. There is a qualitative shift from mass production and consumption to more flexible systems of production and organization through changes in the way that goods and services are consumed, with rapidly changing consumer tastes and the emergence of niche and segmented markets (Mowforth & Munt, 1998: 26). Termed 'flexible accumulation' by Harvey (1990), this fundamental restructuring in the mode of production is shifting from a product-base to a service-base economy with significant consequences for tourism.

The present phase of globalization involves a marked increase in the pace of economic and everyday life and a phenomenal acceleration in the movement of capital and information. Time–space compression seeks to encapsulate this intensification to overcome the barriers of distance and stretch economic relationships to all parts of the globe. The consequences of this post-Fordist global economy are now seen in the tourism industry through new products, new tourism types, new types of tourists, and new niche markets and competitive strategies. An increasing number of tourist destinations are drawn into the global tourism industry creating more opportunities but also more competition and potential exploitation. Yet, such consequences are becoming more evident in increasing socio-economic and political conflict over space and how it is appropriated and developed. One can easily position many current enclave resorts and tourism developments in the context of this increasingly competitive global economy and financial imperialism.

The Role of International Tourism in Shaping Space: From Luxor to Mkies: Spatial Displacement and Processes of Inclusion and Exclusion

Even through heritage tourism has various cultural and economic benefits, especially for a struggling economy such as in Egypt, Jordan, or Syria, it still induces remarkable adverse impacts on the historic environments and the lives of people associated with the dismantling vital and significant links between the cultural heritage and its respective host-communities (Daher, 2000a: 22). It is true that tourism can create employment opportunities, generate foreign exchange revenues, and spread peace and cultural understanding but still, 'the processes by which tourists experience culture, and the way culture is utilized by the tourism industry and host communities, are increasingly characterized by conflict' (Robinson, 1999: 1–2).

In several parts of the world, primarily in Third World countries, tourism is known to have caused gentrification, breaking down of social and economic structures, social disintegration of family values, varying degrees of environmental degradation, and deterioration of historic and cultural settings due to exploitation practices and commodification of historic environments. The myth of tourism having the ability to generate conflict-free cultural harmony and understanding is largely 'a residual attitude derived from the romantic (and elitist) traditions of travel in the 18th and 19th centuries,' which were dominated by Euro-centric moralistic tradition and ideology (Robinson, 1999: 2–3). AlSayyad (2001a: vii) had elaborated how

> nations, regions and cities have utilized and exploited vernacular built heritage to attract international investors at a time of evertightening global economic competition, and how the tourist industry has introduced new paradigms of the vernacular and/or traditional, based on the production of entire communities and social spaces that cater almost exclusively to the 'other.'

The present phase of globalization involves a marked increase in the pace of economic and everyday life and a phenomenal acceleration in the movement of capital and information. Time–space compression seeks to encapsulate this intensification to overcome the barriers of distance and stretch economic relationships to all parts of the globe. The consequences of this post-Fordist global economy are now seen in the tourism industry through new products, new tourism types, new types of tourists, and new niche markets and competitive strategies that appropriate the 'cultural capital' of places, sites, and host communities for consumption and introduces such 'cultural capital' into cycles of excessive capital accumulation:

> To counter declining sales in mature and traditional Fordist-organized product markets, to take advantage of new flexible production technologies, and also to chase the considerable spending power of the affluent middle classes, capital has begun to emphasize product differentiation, the aesthetic qualities of material commodities, and

proliferate services which embody the requirements of symbolic capital. (Britton, 1991: 469)

An increasing number of tourist destinations are drawn into the global tourism industry creating more opportunities but also more competition and potential exploitation (Mowforth & Munt, 1998: 30). Yet, such consequences are becoming more evident in increasing socio-economic and political conflict over space and how it is appropriated and developed. Many historic places in the region of the Middle East with their rich traditions, heritage, and cultural traits of their associated living communities are being incorporated into major tourist attractions as will be explained through this section of the chapter. One can easily position many current heritage industry projects or even enclave resorts and tourism developments within ancient and historic settings in the context of this increasingly competitive global economy and financial imperialism.

Heritage and cultural tourism is drawn to historic villages for their lure of authentic rural experiences, tourists seek contact with living communities next to ancient sites all over the Middle East where local communities have lived in between such ancient ruins or next to them for ages such as the cases of Luxor in Egypt, Petra or Mkies in Jordan, or Bosra in Syria. The combination of an ancient site that dates back thousand of years intertwined with a traditional living community is extremely attractive from the heritage industry's point of view. Historic urban areas in the Middle East have also attracted tourists seeking a cultural experience; they seek historic urban neighborhoods for a taste of urban historic life with its exoticness, diversity, and vitality such as historic cores of Cairo, Damascus, Jerusalem, or Istanbul. Gradually, international tourism development and the competition for inward investment in such locations have considerable consequences on the relationship between such tourism spaces and their respective communities leading to socio-economic and political conflict over space and how it is appropriated and developed. One crucial question always rises to the surface: Who gets the right to induce development in such places and how?

Several of these places have been used as a stage for local culture and tradition coupled with entertainment and excessive consumption to sugar-coat oppression and to produce 'historic villages,' 'festive markets,' or 'heritage centers' that are dominated by investors who attempt to package culture and heritage as commodities ready for consumption by an uncritical audience where the line between cultural experiences and pure entertainment becomes very thin and boundaries between the two positions become so blurred. Britton (1991: 453) asserts that 'as far as tourism is concerned, leisure activities have become increasingly commodified as a "culture of consumption" has evolved.' Britton borrows his critique from the Frankfurt School's critical position of late capitalism and the commodification and manipulation of culture and public life by the media and icons of consumption. One manifestation of this trend has been the formation of what the Frankfurt School of critical theorists (especially Adorno, Horkheimer as well as Marcuse) called 'the culture industry.' A set of institutions and practices are designed to facilitate the adjustment of individuals to participate with such cultural experiences without challenging the social realities of inequalities and exploitation that such experiences are based upon. This requires that individuals be tuned to commercial entertainment with activities that require attentive yet passive and uncritical participation. This is what is termed by the Frankfrurt School as the 'one dimensional society' that offers no resistance to late capitalists and global commodification of life, places, and experiences (Kellner, 1997).

With the popularity of new modes of post-modern consumerism and consumption that centers around culture (rapidly changing consumer tastes and the emergence of niche and segmented markets), more research is needed to investigate increasingly blur intersections between culture and entertainment where culture, in its classical sense, is being packaged, consumed, and forced into cycles of capital accumulation. Certain intellectuals claim that such transformations lead to a depravation of culture and to an intellectualization of entertainment and amusement thus obscuring social conflict and camouflaging the objectives of a dominating global economy through the commodification of culture, places, and people. Therefore, it is very important to understand processes of tourism not only from a reductionism lens of First World economy, but also from the perspective of the different regions and their respective local dynamics (Daher, 2000b).

The first group of case studies discussed below comes from rural areas with living communities associated with classical tourist sites such as Luxor, Petra, or Mkies. Mkies, which represents a severe case of rural gentrification, is a Jordanian village built during the Ottoman period (see Figure 1.5). Just two decades ago, Mkies, famous for its unique olive produce and strategic location, was a thriving village built next to the classical (Greco-Roman) town of Gadara in the middle of the 19th century. The village underwent a series of battles and conflicts over the rights of its development. In the late 1970s and through the late 1980s, the local community was evacuated and was put in standardized housing units unfit for village life and for an agricultural community. The acquisition

Figure 1.5 The village of Mkies in northern Jordan after evacuation of its residents and their relocation to a nearby housing project. The image shows one of the courtyard houses with the courtyard space.

Source: Photograph taken by Rami Farouk Daher, 1988.

of the land by the government (justified by the rationale of eminent domain) was initially carried out in order to conduct archaeological excavations of ancient Gadara leaving the vacant village to fall into neglect and despair and dismantling vital links and relationship between the settlement and agricultural land and the villagers, who now depend on low-paying jobs in near by urban centers.

The evacuation dismantled this vital relationship between the village and its local community. Even though some of the courtyard houses in the village were conserved and adapted by a wealthy investor into tourist facilities (e.g. archaeological museum, rest-house, and Italian restaurant), the local community was marginalized and never was engaged in the tourism development. By the end of 1990s, and due to the lure of international investment, the government was contemplating selling the whole village to a large tourism company, which was planning to turn the historic village into a five-star hotel (Daher, 2000b). What is interesting today is the collaboration between the local community, archaeologists, architects, and anthropologists against the wealthy investors and processes of capital accumulation. Continuous contestation by the local community and by local activists succeeded recently in 2005 in convincing MOTA into launching a study that would come up with a solution that would ensure the protection of the historic village and genuine engagement of the local community in tourism development. Details of this project are yet to be seen.

The world-famous site of Luxor has been known, for more than a century and a half now, for its archaeological treasures, which were recognized in 1979 by UNESCO and the international community and inscribed as part of world heritage. A small village at the end of the 19th century, madinat-al-Uqsur has grown and become a strategic urban space. The village and the notion of its proximity to the ancient ruins of Luxor (e.g. temple of Karnak) became a major attraction for international experts in heritage management and tourism planning issues (Sandrine, 2005). Over the last 30 years, Luxor has been the focus of about 10 different plans and projects, engaging the Egyptian government, the local authorities and the main international development agencies, from UNESCO in 1980 to UNDP, more recently.

Sandrine (2005) focuses on two periods in the recent history of Luxor. The first period centers on the genesis of Luxor as a modern space.

> In 1893, Maspero, head of the Antiquity department decided to excavate the temple of Luxor where the 'Arab' village was located. In two decades, Luxor the 'miserable village', as it use to be qualified

by travelers, became a modern and cosmopolitan town, thanks to its treasures and international tourism, intimately connected to the European colonial project in Egypt. (Sandrine, 2005)

The second period centers on international agencies attempts to redevelop, plan, and come up with ideal solutions for the city. From 1996 to 2002, the UNDP and the Egyptian government implemented the 'Comprehensive plan of Luxor City Development Project.' According to the plan, Luxor should become an open-air museum and two new settlements should be constructed in the desert, in order to relocate the population and provide international tourists with adequate infrastructures.[10]

Sandrine (2005) is interested in addressing the issue of cultural tourism development as a tool to shape and produce segregated spaces in Egypt in relations to international norms, national constrains, and local patterns. She believes that the 'raison d'etre of Luxor lies somehow in the hand of the Other (Egyptologist, expert, tourist), or on the perception he-she has on the region and its resources.' The two examples presented so far, Mkies from Jordan and Luxor from Egypt, testify to the role international tourism plays in planning, reshaping, and organizing space with consequences on local communities' relationships with such places: 'hot spot' tourist attractions such as the ancient temples of Luxor or the Greco-Roman antiquities of Mkies. On many occasions, processes of inclusion and exclusion work to grant voice to certain realities of these sites while marginalizing others. One can also refer to examples spread all over the Middle East besides the world-famous sites such as Luxor or Mkies. One particular example comes from a rural village Al Taybet dating to the beginning of the 20th century located next to the World Heritage Site of Petra in Jordan, which had been transformed into a five-star tourist resort renamed Taybet Zaman.

Taybet Zaman Tourist Village (see Figure 1.6), originally a rural settlement, had been rented from its inhabitants by Jordan Tourism Investments on the basis of a long-term contract (about 30 years). 'The village was then transformed into a luxurious tourist attraction, and some of the former villagers where offered low-income jobs in the new development as cleaning and custodial work' (Daher, 1999: 35). The village is being packaged and sold to the tourists in a fashion where the tourist deals with the values and imagery of a 'museumized' reality rather than the dynamics and realities of the present. Similar partial or total relocation occurred in other projects in the region such as Khibet al Nawahleh Tourist Village also near Petra. In fact, Petra itself once enjoyed a thriving Bedouin community, which is now housed in the nearby ghetto

Figure 1.6 The village of Taybet in southern Jordan near Petra. The village had been adapted into a tourism village and is now called Taybet Zaman.

Source: Photograph taken by Rami Farouk Daher, July 1994.

UmSaihoun. Ex-residents of Petra are allowed to come during the day to rent horses for tourists and sell souvenirs and replicas of ancient pottery to the visitors of the famous rose city carved in the mountains.

Daher (1999: 34) argues that the current approach to heritage tourism in Jordan, Egypt, and elsewhere in the Middle East continues to empower certain interests, and privilege certain pasts, above others. In particular, the local community has been marginalized and disempowered. The local community, in certain cases, is denied the right to adopt and implement its own approach to development because of excessive governmentalization of social life (manifested in planning ordinances such as restrictive zoning or imminent domain) leading to extreme socio-economic control. The irony is that the same planning and development ordinances that have prohibited one local community's development initiatives can swiftly be changed when the 'right' investor or global capital proposes their own development scheme. Most such investors and transnational tourism companies claim their projects will aid the community at large through heritage or eco-tourism developments by providing job opportunities for local residents. But such claims could be, in many cases, nothing but a mere camouflage for excessive flexible capital accumulation and monopoly control over this golden investment opportunity. By hiring the local community at 'sweatshop' rates, tourist investment companies are further able to eliminate all potential competition from small businesses or local projects (Daher, 1999).

The conflict over the production of tourism space (such as at Mkies, Luxor, or, Taybat Zaman for example) is no longer an argument about vernacular architecture or conservation or even the privileged classical or ancient history at the expense of the recent past. The argument and conflict are also beyond the issues of authenticity of the conservation projects and the tourist experiences (even though these are also important issues for contemplation and research). The argument is gradually developing into a socio-economic and political conflict over space, and how and for whom it is appropriated for development resulting in severe cases of gentrification and territorial dispositioning. It is extremely interesting to see forces of late capitalism of a post-Fordist era manifested over such small sites on a global scale, producing spaces and geographies of inequalities.

It is very common now, within similar cases, for the government to compensate local communities (through monetary compensations or housing units); investors also purchase or conduct long-term (up to 30 years in some cases) rentals of whole settings or vernacular villages. However, this approach to tourism development, not only denies the local community the opportunity to initiate its own development projects and schemes, but also creates an extremely dangerous shift in the cultural capital and property ownerships that will have catastrophic consequences on such communities and on any country at large in the future.

According to Robinson (2001: 45), the concept of compensation for loss of cultural capital, or loss of control of that capital is 'firmly anchored in the same, "traditional," First World view which rationalized the commodification of culture, and has legitimized its trading.' An apparent consequence of such trade-off already in process, is the production of geographies of inequalities and processes of excessive exploitation in addition to the disappearing and obscuring of past economic functions and socio-economic and community patterns of activities. As explained by Daher (1999), many locations are consequently shifting from vibrant functioning places to 'museumized' 'show cases' exhibited for a passing audience and owned by a wealthy segment of society (investors or trans-national corporations). The following quotation by Robinson (2001: 50–1) proficiently and skillfully frames the issue of ownership in the wider context of territorial belonging, sense of place, and governance:

> In both developing and developed economies the power of the tourism industry has manifested itself in often-dramatic changes of ownership. Yet the dynamics of ownership in world tourism has attracted relatively little attention in the literature for several reasons. Because of the fluidity of international capital, the low barriers to entry in the tourism business, and the momentum of tourism development, patterns of ownership are difficult to monitor. This is often compounded by the distance and opaqueness of decision-making among corporate players, and between developers and governments. In addition, because tourism is largely measured by its economic success rather than its cultural integrity, the issue of ownership has not commonly been recognized as a problem. However, if one frames ownership in the wider context of territorial belonging, sense of place, and participation in the decisions regarding how places look and function, there are many problems. Cultural territories are contested, and have been and remain, appropriated from host communities. Arguably in many cases, appropriation is difficult to distinguish from normative processes that accompany it.

The second group of case studies in this section comes from urban historic environments from different places in the Middle East. The historic urban environment together with its exoticism, vitality, and variety is also being incorporated as part of the tourist gaze. The popularity of

urban living, and the ever growing café society are redirecting the interests and attention to historic places in Damascus, Aleppo, or Amman that
had been for long, forgotten and had even fallen into neglect. Old cafés,
warehouses, historic houses, and the likes are being adapted and rehabilitated to cater for a growing tourist demand both local and foreign.
Urry (1990: 192) notes that in order to satisfy the tourist gaze, 'environments, places, and people are being regularly made and re-made as tourist
objects. The reconstruction process is more than cosmetic, it involves
substantive economic and social change.'

One particular historic neighborhood undergoing extensive structural transformation and demographic change is Hamrawi next to the
Umayyad Mosque in Damascus. The neighborhood is famous for its bril-
liant courtyard houses with magnificent *Iwans* that overlook the central
courtyard space, which is usually endowed with a water feature. These
houses are simple on the outside but once one enters into the main
courtyard, the decorations, water, vegetation and exquisite spatial
arrangement make it a pleasurable and relaxing place to rest, contemplate
and regenerate. Narrow alleys with specialty markets bring together the
neighborhood, which is also close to major tourist monuments such as
the Umayyad Mosque but also other places such as historic *Medrassas*
(historic schools), and *Khans* (e.g. The *Khan* of Asa'ad Paşa).

More recently, during the last 10 years or so, several of the neighborhood courtyard houses have been converted into restaurants and cafés
that are increasingly becoming very popular amongst a local Damascene
domestic audience, expatriates, and foreign tourists alike. What is com-
forting is that, first, the source of most of the investments is local (e.g.
families who owned these houses are transforming them themselves).
Second, these places are not being turned into elitist gated tourist
enclaves, on the contrary, they are relatively affordable by the larger
community, and so far have been very inclusive, which is also a positive
trait of the Damascene society in general. But, defiantly, these investments
are causing discomfort for the residents who are still residing in the
historic neighborhood due to the fact that these places stay open until
very late hours each night and sometimes the noise pollution is unbear-
able. Besides, such structural transformations have definitely increased
property values in the area, luring many residents and families to sell up
and move out, which will eventually have a major effect on the demog-
raphy and nature of the whole historic city core.

Beit Jabri (Jabri House) is one of these places within the historic
Hamrawi neighborhood that is becoming very popular amongst the
café society of Damascus (see Figure 1.7). In Beit Jabri, a local Damascene

Figure 1.7 Biet Jabri in the historic neighborhood of Hamrawi in Damascus, Syria. The house has been adapted into a restaurant. The clientele is a favorable mix of different social groups and tourists.

Source: Photograph taken by Rami Farouk Daher, 2003.

individual had changed his grandfather's house into a coffee house and cultural center after it had been used as storage. The house was originally built in the 17th century for the Jabri family. In 1975, the house was deserted as the family could not afford the upkeep and served as a storage space, similar to many historic courtyard houses in Old Damascus. In 1988 the idea came to one of the grandsons of the Jabri family to change it into a restaurant. Now it is visited by politicians, artists, poets, and tourists alike, and there are also plans to use it as an art gallery and for selling used books.[11]

In certain neighborhoods of historic Amman next to the downtown area such as the area of the First Circle/Rainbow Street, spatial and socio-economic transformation is taking place as the area is becoming popular amongst upper-middle-class residents of Western, affluent Amman. The neighborhood is famous for its rich heritage, history, and culture. The neighborhood's architecture spanning from early Ammani houses of the 1920s to the elegant, yet not pretentious architecture of modernity in Amman, to contemporary creative architecture and adaptation to place. The neighborhood is connected to the downtown with a series of steps, a typical Ammani characteristic. What is also interesting about the place is its social diversity where different social and economic strata of society live side by side: a tourist can enjoy a falafel sandwich for less than half a dollar next to a restaurant serving first-class expensive meals. Current socio-economic and structural transformations are completely changing the nature of the area. The several historic houses are being converted into cafés and restaurants, souvenir and craft shops are also a new popular arrival to the neighborhood, property value is increasing rapidly, and multi-national cooperations in disguise are buying property from residents who sometimes are lured by the high prices or are agreeing to sell because their property (the inheritance) is already divided between many family members and descendants to the extent it would be easier to sell out to an investor who will invest and transform the property to tourist or upper-middle-class function.

The architectural heritage in a certain geographic location has become a means for social differentiation and the production of a new social identity for the upper middle class. This 'cultural capital' as termed by Zukin and cited by Britton (1991: 469) is linked to a specific spatial fixity (e.g. inner-city residential areas, downtown, historic waterfronts). The geographic constitution of such gentrified or conserved areas is crucial to the production of such new identities, which usually center on 'urban living' and consumption of high-class cultural products (e.g. alternative music and arts and crafts). Historic residential neighborhoods in Amman (such as the one around Rainbow Street) have become particularly favorable locations for this type of conservation activity. A perfect example from that neighborhood is Books @ Café, a recently completed adaptation of a historic house into a Westernized internet café. The place, popular amongst tourists and affluent Ammanis, sells books (mainly on architecture, urban living, cinema, and art), arts and crafts, and the restaurant serves a Westernized (mainly American) menu while overlooking historic downtown Amman. Britton (1991: 454) added that

> commodities in this form become a mean to an end: the purchase of a life-style: a statement of taste and demonstration of the possession of 'cultural and symbolic capital'; an invigoration of the body; an uplifting of the spirit; a broadening of the mind; a signifier of status, a confirmation of challenge of attitudes.

> Despite its high-minded intensions, the project constitutes an intrusion into a calm residential neighborhood, producing alienation and discomfort among the local community. And it has created a schizophrenic difference between the environments inside and outside the Café, intensifying the separation between the neighborhood and its architectural heritage. (Daher, 1999: 35)

In Aqaba, and after the peace process with Israel and the establishment of several Qualified Industrial Zones (QIZ) in the country coupled with declaring Aqaba as a 'free economic zone,' the Aqaba Special Economic Zone Authority (ASEZA) was created. ASEZA was granted the responsibility of neo-liberal socio-economic transformations in the city and held a position of urban projects, tourism, and infrastructure developer; thus gradually replacing former regulating public bodies such as the Municipality of Aqaba, Aqaba Regional Authority, and Aqaba Governate, which were either dissolved or regressed to a voyeur's position.

In Aqaba, Jordan, the whole city is going through intense socio-economic and territorial transformations as it is being declared a 'Special Economic Zone.' Talking to taxi drivers and shop owners, many have reiterated that 'the city is no longer theirs.' It is very obvious that the whole city is being taken over by multi-national, big money investments in the form of five-star hotels and large-scale development projects. The 'hot' and most desired places on the shore such as popular old beach coffee houses, public beaches, fish restaurants on the beach, or even significant low-rise hotels from the mid-20th century are all being taken over by such 'first-class tourism investments.' Aqaba's distinctive, yet not so recognized heritage of the 1930s and 1940s represented in the Old Town with its residential houses, coffee shops, and open-air cinema, will be completely disguised and submerged by this sweeping 'grand planning' and 'new vision' for the city. Everybody is aware of 'the change' including the ordinary citizen, yet, people such as the taxi driver and the shop owner do not posses the right tools to contest or even mitigate such visions and investments.

ASEZA, equipped with the tropes and slogans of modernity, efficiency, liberalism, and lack of government bureaucracy, is superimposing 'first-class tourism developments' as termed by one of ASEZA's officials. Such developments take the form of multi-national five-star hotels and various 'big money' investments linked with the tourism/entertainment sector in existing 'hot spots' and public places within the city displacing and replacing traditional coffee houses and restaurants by the beach, low-rise historic hotels from the middle of the 20th century, historic neighbor-hoods, and even existing slums in very strategic locations of the city overlooking the Bay of Aqaba. Such developments are causing severe cases of urban cleansing, spatial and social displacement, and exclusion of a certain part of Aqaba's history, heritage, and urban poor and residents. The examples presented before on urban tourism developments from Damascus, Amman, and Aqaba trigger the importance of integrating critical theory and political economy into the study of tourism and analysis of tourism developments. Britton (1991: 451) develops two themes to facilitate an understanding of this integration: 'the capitalistic nature of most travel and tourism production and consumption; and the contribution of tourism to the analysis of territorial competition and economic restructuring.'

> Geographers have tended to treat elements of tourism and travel in isolation from other spheres of social and economic life. By treating tourism almost solely as a discrete economic subsystem, many reveal-ing links have been missed between tourism and other politically and theoretically important geographic issues, which demonstrate the wider role and position of tourism in capitalist accumulation. This simple point can be demonstrated with two examples of how tourism can be regarded as a central element of territorial competition and geographically uneven accumulation. (Britton, 1991: 466)

Popularity of Domestic Tourism in the Region after 9/11: Festivals and Shopping Malls and the Myth of the Cultural Tourist

The Middle East has been divided, as far as incoming tourism is con-cerned, into two major categories: the first category consist of countries with a rich tourism history due to diverse cultural heritage, history, and archaeology such as the cases of Egypt, Tunis, Jordan, Lebanon, Syria, Iraq, and Turkey for example; the second category is countries with insignificant incoming tourism as in the case of the Gulf countries such as Kuwait, Qatar, Saudi Arabia, and the UAE. Yet, citizens of the countries of the second category produced an abundance of outward tourism to Europe and the United States especially after the 1970s and until recently due to the rich oil revenues of these countries, which had enabled their citizens to afford to take extravagant trips to Europe's different capitals (mainly London and Paris). Especially during the late 1970s and 1980s, a considerable amount of oil revenues were spent on the French Riviera or in the hotels and casinos of the fog capital of the world, London.

The events of September 11 had changed the direction of tourism influx in the region; at least, it had decreased the number of Arab Gulf states' citizens venturing into Europe and to the United States due to strict visa regulations and a general feeling that Saudi or Gulf tourists would no longer be welcomed in the Western world. As a reaction and since the beginning of the 1990s, one can easily witness the flourishing of local domestic tourism attractions in the Gulf in the form of 'festivals,' 'spas,' and recreational centers. Most of these tourism developments and investment claim a cultural experience through the different tourism festivals, which flourished all over the Arabian Peninsula, but in reality, most of the events centered on shopping and consumption coupled with entertainment. A recent article in the famous Lebanese newspaper *AlHayat* had shown that many Saudis are staying in the country after September 11 and are spending their summers in such new tourist attractions: theme festivals in cities such as Jeddah, Abha, and other Saudi cities. Each of these festivals claims a theme linked to its region, for example the one in Medina is linked to history and heritage, the Jeddah festival is linked to sea-related activities and so on.[12] Many of these domestic tourism ventures claim to be providing 'cultural experiences' but in reality they primarily center on consumption and entertainment.

Qatar had established recently its Ajaeb Saif Qatar (Summer Wonders of Qatar) Summer 2004 festival and is expecting to receive 50 million travelers by the year 2015, and is therefore planning to built recreational centers and theme parks to lure more local entertainment tourists.[13] Dubai, in the UAE, had of course diversified its economic investments way before September 11, and is no longer dependent on oil revenues. Dubai is considered today a vibrant business center famous for import and export, IT, logistics, and other service industries not only within the Middle East but also in Asia and in the Indian sub-continent. Dubai had developed its tourism industry depending on becoming the Middle Eastern capital of consumption and entertainment. Theme parks of every type are being built starting from thematic shopping malls such as Ibn Battutah[14] Mall to an indoor ski resort in the middle of the desert. Global Gulf and Saudi money is also finding its way to other capitals of the Middle East, Amman for example is unfortunately witnessing a series of shopping malls and different entertainment centers blessed by the government in the efforts to encourage inward investment. Tourism to places such as Dubai is even advertised as pure shopping excursions. Many of these shopping malls and recreational/cultural centers are simply extraordinary tourist attractions in their own right and represent an exceptional degree where the line between culture and entertainment is very blurred.

Furthermore, inter-Arab tourism to the northern Arab countries such as Lebanon and Syria centers also on excessive consumerism and un-involved tourists who hardly attempt to explore the different cultural and historic attractions even though such counties are blessed with a rich and diverse rural and urban cultural heritage dating from ancient times up to the present. In general, Arab tourists visiting Lebanon or Syria, for exam-ple, are mainly not involved and tend to simply explore major attractions from the luxury of the tourist bus leaving the country with only an icono-graphic memory and experience. The author of this chapter signed up with a travel agent and took a typical tourist trip from Jordan to Lebanon to explore the experiences of hundreds or even thousands of tourists.

In general, tourists spent most of their times in the coach and their exposure to the sites visited was minimal, remaining at the fringes and periphery of each site. Mostly, the concentration was on sites that repre-sented cultural icons of Lebanon such as the Rawshe Rock on the sea shore, the Palaces of Beit al Din in the Lebanese mountains, the Cedar Trees in the north, for which Lebanon is famous, and other nature sites such as the cave of Jeitta with its stalagmites and stalactites. Of course, shopping consumed a huge percentage of the itinerary. It was interesting to notice that the urban heritage of the different Lebanese cities was not offered or included in the program. Our experience of Beirut was confined to 30 minutes in the famous post-war reconstruction project of downtown Beirut: Solidere. The cities of Saida and Sour were not on the program, and the visit to Tripoli, which is famous for its urban heritage from the Mamluk period, was confined to visiting the harbor and eating at a famous Arab sweets place.

Urry (1990: 47) reiterates that the contemporary tourist gaze is increas-ingly signposted and that there are markers that identify the things and places worthy of our gaze, which would be restricted to relatively small number of tourist nodes. 'The result is that most tourists are concentrated within a very limited area.' Inter-Arab tourism to Lebanon, Syria, or Egypt is iconographic and signposted in nature and is restricted by the tourist bubble of the bus. Rarely, are tourists interested in engaging in local cultural experiences or an exploration of place beyond the famous icons. The tourist is like a child driven from one place to another in a comfortable, but at the same time, confining bubble (the bus) where the experience of 'being a tourist' is more relevant to most tourists than the experience of 'being in place.' Inter-Arab tourism organized by hundreds of travel agencies in the Arab world is gradually manipulated by excessive consumerism, and is becoming more iconographic and signposted while tourist experiences are increasingly short, intense, and are no longer emerging in culture but are gradually more figural and visual in nature. Most tourists are uninvolved and remain closer to the confinement of the tourist 'bubble' (the bus) without venturing into cities or rural landscapes.

Resistance from below and alternative voices

In the midst of such large-scale tourism developments and excessive commercialization of tourist experiences emerges a genuine and very authentic partnership between tourism and heritage in the region Bilad al Sham represented in family-owned and run small hotels in Damascus, Aleppo, Amman, and Beirut offering a different alternative to the grand luxurious hotels. Whether it is Al Rabi'e Hotel (Figure 1.8) located in an old, historic Damascene courtyard house, or Le Baron Hotel from early 20th century Aleppo, not only do revenues from tourism stay in the country and leakages to the outside are kept to a minimum, but also such places provide a different experience for the tourist or traveler willing to explore the city with its wonders and social realities of everyday life as appose to a 'swift' and 'iconographic' experience of the place that is restricted to 'certain' chosen buildings and places put on a pre-planned itinerary. The families that run these old hotels and enterprises, which are becoming very popular amongst tourists, are definitely very active actors in the definition and in the shaping of heritage, and provide totally different levels of connections to these cities and their historic and public places.

Le Baron Hotel in Aleppo (Figure 1.9) was founded by an Armenian family in 1909, it advertised itself as a modern hotel and is listed as a two-star hotel and is on the itinerary of several tour operators. It is of course famous for the visitor's book with travelers and visitors' impressions

Figure 1.8 Al Rabi'e Hotel in the historic neighborhood of Saruja in Damascus. This hotel is housed in an old courtyard Damascene house and has been run by a local Damascene family since the late 1940s and is a favorable place by tourists and a local heritage-minded clientele.

Source: Photograph taken by Rami Farouk Daher, 2001.

about the place, Aleppo, and Syria in general. Several famous people stayed there such as King Faisal of Saudi Arabia, Agatha Christie, and Lawrence of Arabia, and the hotel is full of relics from early 20th century that remind the visitor of its glorious past.[15] Al Rabi'e Hotel in the historic neighborhood of Saruja in Damascus is located in an old courtyard Damascene house. It has been run by a Damascene family since the late 1940s. It is also listed as a two-star hotel but is famous amongst long-term travelers and tourists in general who seek an involved stay in Damascus that is closer to the public and to the city. The visitors' book of Al Rabi'e Hotel is also famous as it is full of different impressions from visitors in the various languages of the world.[16]

Places like Le Baron or Al Rabi'e work to uncover informal and un-official histories, which are distant from official discourses of Syria. The

Figure 1.9 Le Baron Hotel in Aleppo, Syria. The hotel dates to the early 20th century and is run by an Armenian family from Aleppo.

Source: Photograph taken by Rami Farouk Daher, 2001.

families that run these old hotels and enterprises, which are becoming very popular amongst tourists, are definitely very active actors in the definition and in the shaping of heritage, and provide totally different levels of connections to these cities and their historic and public places.

Another group of actors who are providing a different alternative when it comes to experiencing the historic realities of cities and of everyday life are the different patroned heritage projects by elite notable families of Bilad al Sham in Jordan, Lebanon, Syria, and Palestine. They provide for the more involved tourist another perspective different from the official narrative of history and the past provided by the state by emphasizing the local regional realities of the region and by offering a chance to rewrite and reread history. Sidon (Saida) in Lebanon represents a perfect example where local families are involved in the local cultural scene. While the Debbaneh family are restoring and adapting their old residence into the new Debbaneh Palace and Saida History Museum (Figure 1.10), other notable families in Saida such as Audi, had also adapted their old residence into the famous Soap Museum and had been involved heavily

Figure 1.10 Debbaneh Palace in Saida, Lebanon. This historic palace is being adapted, with funds from the Debbaneh Foundation, into a historic house museum that narrates the social and local history of the city and the house itself.

Source: Photograph taken by Rami Farouk Daher, 2002.

through the Audi Foundation in urban regeneration activities in the city. The Debbaneh Palace was built in 1721 by the Hammoud family, and was acquired in 1800 by the Debbaneh family. Then it underwent several periods of restoration and especially after the war in 1999 when the descendants of Raphael Youssef Debbaneh set up the Debbaneh Foundation, which established the Debbaneh Palace and Saida History Museum. The objectives of the museum are to represent and shed light on the city's urban, socio-economic, and political history. With the aim of constantly renewing the visitor's interest in the city, the project will not only include artifacts from the past, but it will also focus heavily on the societies that produced them. This will involve explanations and extracts from people's daily lives, family social structures, and political circumstances, not to mention construction, architecture, and town planning.[17]

One particular trend that is emerging in tourism in places such as Jordan, Syria, and Lebanon is special agents and travel operators that are slowly recognizing the importance of promoting particular itineraries to discriminating and independent-minded travelers and clientele who are more involved and are interested in particular experiences and sites. Such operations are being run through small niche suppliers as oppose to mass production/consumption operators. Examples are diverse concentrating on both urban and rural itineraries including special agents and tour operators that are starting to run special tours that concentrate on urban social realities of cities in the region. Famous stops on these 'urban itineraries' include coffee houses like Al Fishawi Coffee House near *Sūq* Khan al Khalili in Cairo, Egypt (Figure 1.11); this place, which is now a tourist Mecca, is famous for its association with notorious Egyptian writers and critical thinkers such as the late Najeeb Mahfouz. Other urban tours sometimes concentrate on specific themes within cities such as exploring the different *Sūq* or *Khans* within Damascus or special tours in the old city visiting distinguished Damascene houses. Figure 1.12 shows a unique Damascene house popular on these special urban tours; it was adapted to serve now as the headquarters of the Danish Research Mission in Damascus. Eco-tourism to Dana and Wadi Faynan nature reserves in Jordan and other nature reserves in the country operated by the Royal Society for the Conservation of Nature (RSCN) in Jordan, special guided tours of Old Damascus where the itinerary follows a certain theme such as houses or *Khans*, or other significant heritage feature or experience, or special tours of urban historic sites of Salt in Jordan or along the Hijaz Railroad Line between Syria, Jordan, and Saudi Arabia are some examples of such alternative tourism that is being offered to such discriminating and involved travelers.

Figure 1.11 Al Fishawi Coffee House near *Sūq* Khan al Khalili in Cairo, Egypt. This coffee shop, which is now a tourist Mecca, is famous for its association with notorious Egyptian writers and critical thinkers like the late Najeeb Mahfouz.

Source: Photograph taken by Rami Farouk Daher, 2005.

Figure 1.12 A special tour in the old city of Damascus visiting a distinguished Damascene house which functions now as the headquarters of the Danish Research Mission in Damascus.

Source: Photograph taken by Rami Farouk Daher, 2003.

One particular example of these travel operations is Idrisi Travel operated by a wife and husband team (McQuitty and Eykemduyn) who organize special tours to Jordan, Syria, Libya and other places in the Middle East. Idrisi Travel was named after the famous Arab geographer born in Morocco in AD 1100. Attached to the Royal Court of King Roger II of Sicily, he wrote one of the greatest works in mediaeval geography: *The Pleasure Excursion of One who is Eager to Traverse the Regions of the World*. Idrisi Travel 'attempts to explore the world with the same eagerness, discovering new routes and destinations off-the-beaten track, traveling in small groups and led by specialist guides' as advertised in their brochure.[18] The small company's selling-points lie in the quality of the guides. McQuitty, for example, is an archaeologist who had lived in Jordan and the region for more than 15 years where she had worked as the Director of the Council for British Research in the *Levant*. Her expert knowledge in the archaeology and also heritage of the region, and cultural and environmental backgrounds enables her to transform her tours into a unique cultural and educational experience. She had often led walking tours between Petra and the nature reserve of Wadi Faynan in Jordan, or along Bedouin off-the-beaten tracks in Libya. Furthermore, such tours offer a wide variety of ways to explore nature and the environment such as walking, cycling, camping, and bird watching. They also attempt to collaborate with local non-governmental organizations (NGOs) and organizations and tourism cooperatives (e.g. Wadi Faynan Tourism Cooperative) to make sure the revenues of tourism reach the local communities wherever and as much as possible. The owners of Idrisi Travel do not like to label themselves as study-tours but rather they like to think of themselves as offering to the intelligent-minded tourist a 'well-informed holiday.'

Circulated Images, Competitiveness, Mobility, and Fantasy Cities: The Solidere Phenomenon and Neo-liberal Urban Restructuring

The Gulf Cooperation Council had declared the availability of $80 billion in liquidity awaiting investment (Sadik, 2005). The UAE alone enjoys $26.3 billion in trade surplus, and Dubai declared a 16% GDP growth. This circulating global capital is searching for venues and places to invest in real-estate development all over the Middle East in places such as Dubai, Doha, Manama, Kuwait, but also in Beirut, Cairo, Damascus, Tunis, and Amman as well with future considerable consequences on the nature of the urban environment in these cities and on the future of tourism at large in the Middle East where each of these cities is not only competing for international business and tourism, but is also competing for more consumer- oriented tourism services in the form of themed shopping malls, recreational centers, and theme parks.

Business tourism is flourishing in Dubai with 1000 businesses starting each month. In 2003, Dubai hosted 4.8 million visitors, and enjoyed the position of number one worldwide when it comes to hotel occupancy rates, 85% year round, furthermore, Dubai is planning to add 100 hotels within the next five to seven years and is expecting 10 million visitors by 2007 and 15 million by 2015 (Sadik, 2005). Junemo (2004: 182) elaborated that in the year 2000, Dubai had 2.4 million guests and that the prognosis is that by 2010, some 15 million tourists will arrive to Dubai. Gradually, cities in the Middle East are depending on a highly increased rate of mobility within the region where cities are, for the first time, putting their different urban amenities on the market as a tourist commodity to be explored, invested in, and used to entertain tourists, business people, visitors, and most important of all: affluent clientele from all over the region. Fainstein and Judd (1999: 261) have added how

> there does seem to be a degree of consensus that the present epoch involves a different, more flexible organization of production, higher mobility of both capital and people, heightened competition among places, and greater social and cultural fragmentation. Within the city the unity previously imposed by a manufacturing-driven economy has disappeared, and urban culture itself has become a commodity.

Hall (1996: 155) examines how cities are being packaged and introduced as products for marketing in an age of 'New Urban Tourism,' he investigates how 'although urban centers have long served to attract tourists, it is only in recent years that cities have consciously sought to develop, image and promote themselves in order to increase the influx of tourists.' As far as the Middle East in concerned, we will gradually observe how, whether it be Beirut or Amman, Dubai or Manama, Cairo or Tunis, it is very obvious that cities in the region are competing for inward business and tourism investments with considerable consequences not only on how these cities are being transformed, or how heritage and tourism development is being conceived, but also on how tourism and tourist products, and experiences are taking a central role in this overall transformation.

It is interesting to understand the effect of the circulation of global capital and huge reserves of money in search of high-yielding and secure investments, excessive privatization, and circulating urban flagship projects in Jordan, Lebanon, Egypt, all over the Arab Gulf states, and through out the Arab region on the nature of urban reality, property values and speculation, and the nature of tourism investments. New emerging urban islands of excessive consumption for the chosen elite together with the internationalization of commercial real-estate companies and construction consultancies capable of providing high-quality services signify this neo-liberal urban restructuring in places such as downtown Beirut, Abdali in Amman (Daher, 2005; Summer, 2005), Dreamland in Cairo (Adham, 2004), the financial district in Manama and even in the heart of the Holy City of Mecca through the Jabal Omar Project.[19] Cities are obliged to create the right milieu, competitive business climate, and first-class tourism attractions in order to lure people to come live, invest, and entertain. Developments in Dubai and the current urban reconstruction for the Beirut downtown (know as the Solidere Project) are becoming the models to follow in such developments. Adham (2004: 157) had noted that circulating images of such neo-liberal urban restructuring mimic developments in the West and represent as such an 'Oriental vision of the Occident.'

Hall (1996: 155–7) elaborated how city centers are shifting to leisure and tourism in many parts of the world. He added that the 'primary justification for the redevelopment of inner city areas for tourism is the perceived economic benefits of tourism.' The entire urban core is presently looked upon as a recreational environment and as a tourism resource, and one of the purposes is to 'attract and retain the interest of professionals and white-collar workers, particularly in "clean" service industries such as tourism and communications.' Tyler (2000: 292–3) talks about the creation of the 'Fantasy City,' where the city turns into a 'playful spectacle' and elaborates on city marketing where he sees city marketing as a reaction to economic change – a method of promoting inward investment by marketing, undertaking physical change and image recreation. Sheller and Urry (2004: 3) state that

> many places are being put into play due to the increasingly global character of these contemporary mobilities. The 1990s have seen remarkable 'time-space compression,' as people across the globe have been brought 'closer' through various technologies. There is an apparent 'death of distance' in what is sometimes described as a fluid and speeded-up 'liquid modernity.'

Furthermore, Sheller and Urry (2004: 4) elaborate on the concepts and lifestyles associated with these 'places to play.' They believe that tourism is not only transforming the materiality of many 'real' places, but is also having a deep impact on the creation of virtual realities and fantasized places: 'These are enormously powerful and ubiquitous global brands or logos that increasingly feature tourist sites/sights as key components of the global culture that their brand speaks to and enhances.' These brand companies include many in 'travel and in leisure: Disney, Hilton, Nike, Gap, Easyjet, Body Shop, Virgin, Club Med, Starbucks, Coca Cola, and so on. These brands produce "concepts" or "life-styles": liberated from the real-world burdens of stores and products manufacturing,' and these lifestyle concepts revolve around generic types of places to play: the hotel pool, the waterside café/restaurant, the cosmopolitan city, the hotel buffet, the theme park, the club, the airport lounge, and the shopping mall.

An important question emerges to the surface: Within these places of play of intense mobility, who gets the opportunity to be mobile? And what is the relationship between the local and global within this mobility? It is only global money and a chosen few who are granted this privilege. The rest of the world cannot join 'the play,' entry to these global places of play is restricted to the majority of people and is only permitted through their involvement in the provision of services and infrastructure (e.g. Indian and Pakistani workers in Dubai hotels and resorts) and their involvement in performance for tourists (e.g. exotic dancers and music performers in the Caribbean). The following quotation by Titley (2000: 84) elaborates on the conditions of entry into such global 'places of play':

> Service demands that locals be allowed entry into this carefully managed construction. In a place displaced from surrounding communities, entry is limited to service and performance. Yet this entails contact – as Michael Cronin has pointed out, any tourist/tourist worker encounter is highly personalized, and the 'personality of the transient in paradise surely have a right to expect friendliness from those blessed enough to inhibit, locals are part of the product, and as such have very definite and circumscribed roles thrust upon them. Discrepancies are opened up by a refusal to perform, or at least to maintain a level of presumably manic happiness.'

Junemo's (2004: 181) work on Dubai is informative as it describes the socio-economic, spatial, and demographic transformation taking place in this extraordinary place of constant 'play.' The city had recently begun the construction of the world's two largest man-made islands to boost and enhance the city's image and reputation: 'They are both shaped like palm trees and are called the Palm *Jumeirah* and the Palm *Jebel Ali* respectively. Even though they are separate islands, the whole project is referred to as "the Palm".' Junemo (2004: 185–6) considers projects such as the 'Palm' or Ibn Battutah Shopping Mall or the Dubai Ski Resort and Recreational Center (Figures 1.13a and b) to represent an aesthetic of kitsch and thematic events: 'And to create a place like the Palm is almost

Figure 1.13a and b Interior of the recently developed indoor ski resort and recreational center in Dubai, UAE.

Source: Photographs by Rami Farouk Daher, 2006

an example of divine play – the possibilities of creating land at will in any shape' (Junemo, 2004: 186). 'This imaginative play continues as each buyer of a signature villa or beach house has the choice of different architectural themes, such as Contemporary, Arabic, Mediterranean, Caribbean, or Scandinavian (there are 22 styles in all).' Junemo (2004: 187) asserts that this fragmentation of the aesthetic expression and the playful relation to symbols that lie behind it is widely recognized within post-modern theory where people are concerned with surface images rather than deep meanings.

Yet these 'playscapes' whether in Dubai, Amman, or Beirut are simply gated communities with practices of inclusion and exclusion. These spaces are usually guarded and are closed off for many to ensure a certain type and nature of individuals allowed to participate in these places of leisure and consumption. The following quotation by Junemo (2004: 190), illustrates how these places maintain and enforce a symbolic distinction between those with access to the networks and those without. This distinction, which centers on the ability to consume such places and participate in these 'places of play,' is crucial for the formation of a distinct social identity for the upper middle class where monetary capital is turned into some accepted form of social capital in order to gain access to such exclusive social networks:

> Surveillance and control are also maintained through symbolic distinction (Bourdieu 1984) between those with access to the networks and those without. Those inhabiting the center of a network distinguish themselves from the excluded 'lower classes' through a certain consumer lifestyle. In Dubai this phenomenon even has a name, 'Jumeirah Jane', describing the affluent Western women with a consumer lifestyle represented by mobile phone, sunglasses, a four-wheel-drive car, and color coordinated outfits. This can be contrasted with the working cloths of an Indian or Pakistani working in construction or perhaps as a caretaker. 'Jumeirah Jane' is a person who belongs in the Palm, while the maintenance workers are uniformed in order to signal that they are allowed inside, but are not part of the social activities. In other words, apart from simply possessing monetary capital, this must be turned into some accepted form of social capital in order to gain access to the social network.

Introducing the Chapters

The chapters in this book all share the fact that they center on exploring tourism in the Middle East, yet, they are very diverse in their individual area of concentration, background of authors, and approach to knowledge. This edited volume could be considered as one of very few comprehensive explorations of tourism in the Middle East addressing general issues such as historiography of tourism in the Middle East; tourism, representation, and the transformation of place, history, and culture; tourism and the quest for community development; and tourism and politics of place and heritage through local and global juxtapositions.

In Noha Nasser's chapter, 'A Historiography of Tourism in Cairo: A Spatial Perspective,' she provides a critical historical perspective of tourism in the city of Cairo starting from a time when tourism and travel presented a vital socio-economic activity engaging different people from various parts of the world during the 12th century (when trade, culture, and education were the main reasons for travel demonstrating an early form of urban/cultural tourism). The chapter skillfully moves to the emergence of travel in the 19th century where tourism was linked to a high level of curiosity but was also associated with different forms of dominance, social hierarchies, and the construction of stereotypical realities of the 'Orient.' Tourism was catering to a European-colonialist leisure and taste. Finally, to a recent time where tourism is linked to a consumer-driven society leading to a commodification of tourism in Cairo and to segregated spaces.

By concentrating on Cairo's urban environment, the reader will be exposed to archaic forms (12th century in Cairo for example) of urban tourism, driven by an appreciation of a rich urban culture. This will definitely clarify several misconceptions about the Middle East and shed light on an aspect of Middle Eastern tourism that has not received enough recognition: urban tourism. Furthermore, one of the strengths of Nasser's chapter is that it breaks the boundaries between disciplines. Nasser was able skillfully to bridge the gap between urban historiography, tourism, and urban regeneration studies. The chapter could also be critically linked to two important issues: First, the nature of the relationship between the Islamic world and Europe through time (e.g. medieval Islamic Cairo, Imperial Khediv Ismail era, contemporary (the opening-up era) through focusing on one aspect of 'world making': tourism. Second, the notion of identity vis-à-vis embracing the modernity project linked to the spatial dimension of tourism: where this critical debate is brought under the light in different periods of Cairo's history as well (e.g. Cairo of the 19th century and the grand urban undertakings *à la manierre Haussmann*, or contemporary designation of Cairo as a World Heritage Site and consequent socio-cultural and spatial transformations).

Xavier Guillot's chapter, 'From One Globalization to Another: In Search of the Seeds of Modern Tourism in the Levant, a Western Perspective,' looks at the beginning of international tourism with a critical eye. The chapter brilliantly shows that the concept of travel and the different forms of travel to the region are not a new reality but are rooted in the 19th century (and maybe before). Guillot shows how as early as the 19th century Bilad al Sham was already a prime cultural tourist destination and states eloquently in the introduction of his chapter: 'Looking at this early phase of modern tourism leads us to put international mass tourism into perspective as a long-term cycle evolving industry, and to evaluate its current development patters more objectively.'

Also, by concentrating on the tourism operators or agents (as Guillot terms them) such as transportation, accommodation, the tourist guide-book, and the organized tour, it becomes very obvious that his research is not the outcome of only a literature review, but on the contrary, it is also grounded in an in-depth fieldwork within the area on know-ledge based on extensive travel in the region, and on thorough discourse analysis. Guillot also sheds light on very important concepts such as the impact of the 'schedulable trip' on the rise of mass tourism and the link between the development of mass tourism and improvements in trans-portation. The chapter also skillfully traces the evolution of the 'organized tour' and the role of Thomas Cook in that regard.

Regarding Scott MacLeod's chapter: 'Digital Spatial Representations: New Communication Processes and "Middle Eastern" UNESCO World Heritage Sites Online,' extensive research had been conducted on the Middle East World Heritage Sites online. The chapter crosses boundaries between IT, media, and Internet on the one hand, and cultural represen-tations and cultural productions on the other. The author incorporates and explicates the various novel communication processes (e.g. integra-tion, interactivity, hypermedia, immersion, narrativity) reflecting an in-depth understanding of the concepts. The chapter attempts to be as objective as possible and to reflect a culturally bias-free critique of the various online representations of the World Heritage Sites.

The author critiques the Orientalist construct of the 'timeless desert' as unchanging in the context of modernity; furthermore, the author is critical of the criteria and selection procedures used to nominate World Heritage Sites from the region and uses Turkey as an example. Sites selected to the World Heritage List in Turkey demonstrate that the selec-tion criteria and process privilege those sites with Western links such as the ones linked to Greek, Roman, and Christian histories. Ottoman Islamic pasts (and regardless of their ultimate significance to the local populations and to the identity of Turkey today) are marginalized and are only represented in context of their articulation with Roman and Christian histories. The chapter also shows how 'heritage sites are often used by state regimes to shape identities based on an imagined past rooted in such sites.'

In Saba Al Mahadin's and Peter Burns' chapter: 'Visitors, Visions and Veils: The Portrayal of the Arab World in Tourism Advertising,' the authors consider the promotion of tourism of the Arab world (visions) through images such as veils, camels, and primitive life. Those images, which symbolize backwardness, oppression, and inferiority, are adopted promoters of tourism in order to affect tourists' traveling decisions about these countries. In other words, the authors are looking at how the enterprise of tourism to the Middle East can shape the knowledge and the discourses about this part of the world. Then, they take a key symbol through the media discourse (the veil), and attempt to uncover such practices in the tourism promotion sector where certain discourses have been used to produce knowledge about the Arab world. These discourses, of which *Orientalism* is but one, and the knowledge produced lead to a practice of power. The chapter could be considered an attempt to resist such practices by the uncovering of such power/knowledge mechanisms.

The chapter critically addresses one contested relationship within the tourism industry and that is the unbalanced and unregulated relationship between the local people and those who promote the industry through visual representation. The authors feel that this notion of representing the Arab world through tourism's visual representations is not value free. And by shedding light on this issue, they contribute to the understanding of tourism's complex relationships, not only between the host community and tourists, but between a complicated web of power relations and stakeholders.

Aylin Orbaşli's chapter: 'The 'Islamic' City and Tourism: Managing Conservation and Tourism in Traditional Neighbourhoods,' brings to the foreground the notion of tourism and urban development when addressing the 'Islamic' city. There has been a lot of work on the 'Islamic' city, most of it has addressed the 'Islamic' city from other perspectives (e.g. architecture), but also socio-economic and cultural perspectives. This is one of very few times that tourism is becoming the focus of research while addressing the Islamic city. Orbaşli is skillful in shedding the light on a very important link between urban tourism and urban conservation. Besides, she brings out concepts and issues from both discourses, thus broadening the concept of stakeholders while incorporating management, socio-economic, and cultural considerations. Also, her discussion reflects great depth regarding several issues such as visitor experience, benefits of tourism to medium and small historic towns, critiquing the separation of normal and tourist activities, issues of authenticity, and other issues.

Birgit Mershen's chapter: 'Development of Community-Based Tourism in Oman: Challenges and Opportunities,' is about community-based tourism development in the midst of governmental tourism policies that encourage 'affluent (quality) tourists' and upper-scale tourism. Such national policies in Oman are not isolated cases; it is a phenomenon that exists in other Middle Eastern countries such as Jordan, Egypt, and others. While large-scale tourism investments ('big money') that are encouraged by 'national policies' end up in 'enclave tourism' with high leakages (in terms of the revenues) to the outside; small- and medium-size 'local' tourism accommodations and other forms of tourism developments have a tendency to generate more revenues that stay within a certain country with minimal leakages to the outside. This is a very sensitive and important topic for contemplation in the Middle Eastern context and maybe else where in the world as well. Mershen has beautifully presented for the reader both the formal (tourism enclaves) and informal (community-based) forms of tourism. This chapter should be read not only by academicians and responsible tourists, but also by governmental officials and policy makers as well.

The case study (Wahabi Sands Rashid's Camp) is skillfully presented with all its details in a very contextualized tableau without a pretentious indulgence in theory but in a manner that reflects genuine and extensive ethnographic fieldwork and knowledge of the local truths and narratives. Mershen's case study is a perfect example of a good-quality microanalysis and investigation that beautifully depicts for the reader power mechanisms at international, national, and local levels. The chapter touches also an important phenomenon that is strongly present in many Middle Eastern countries: the discrepancies between the declared policies and strategies and actual governmental implemented actions within the tourism industry. In other words, there is a gap between the rhetoric and reality. In Oman, for example, while governments promises 'vowed not to sell out Oman's fine beaches,' yet the current government's 'enthusiasm for sea-shore resorts and enclave tourism probably has to be interpreted as an attempt to readjust aspirations to the economic realities.' Mershen declares that today in Oman, tourism plans are to be achieved through the large-scale investments through foreign investors without consideration that these 'quick' economic gains are at the expense of local benefits and the environment.

The chapter also attempts to understanding different levels and meanings of public participation within tourism development. Throughout the chapter and also the case study, Mershen has demonstrated how public participation can reach significant levels where the local community (such as the case in Rashid's Camp) could play a very significant role in the 'development' process and risks its own financial resources to achieve development (the family or local community are the initiators of a certain project and not the receivers of a deterministic mode of development).

Peter Burns' chapter: 'From Hajj to Hedonism? Paradoxes of Developing Tourism in Saudi Arabia,' presents a very well-informed and critical analysis on the development of tourism in Saudi Arabia in particular, and a critical analysis of the official (state) discourse in general. Burns presents critical analysis through the dismantling and the analysis of the official Saudi photomontage of the state. If anything, it only reconfirms how the official Saudi discourse uses such iconographies for the creation of its own legitimacy and rationalization. Also, it shows how 'Islam' is used to reaffirm this legitimacy of the Saudis.

Burns links tourism developments in Saudi Arabia and processes of Saudization to 'encouraging new private sector ventures.' Burns reiterates that 'given that in 1996 only 7% of the private sector workforce was Saudi, it is quite clear that the private sector has to meet this challenge, mainly through Saudization and expansion: hence the drive for, among other things, tourism.' The government is trying to transform its notorious responsibility of creating 'relatively undemanding white-collar jobs in the bureaucracy' to the private sector.

David Homa's chapter: 'Tourist Development in Sinai, Egypt: Bedouin, Visitors, and Government Interaction,' is about tourism development in between 'national strategies' of the Egyptian government, which prioritizes the 'affluent tourist,' 'multi-national investors' who want to invest in 'tourist enclaves,' and the 'local community' in the case of the Bedouins of the Sinai who have been taking part in tourism development since the 1960s in the Sinai and are very much interested in maintaining an active role in the tourism development in the area, the tourists flocking to this 'hot spot' in the thousands, and the travelers and backpackers who are interested in a more 'scaled down' type of accommodation and overall experience. The mechanisms of power, negotiations, and conflicts that take place between stakeholders present an outstanding case though which one can understand a pattern or a 'phenomenon' that is emerging in the Middle East at the moment in other places such as in Aqaba, Sharm al Skeikh, and in other places as well. Homa's discussion of authenticity is interesting where he is grounding it in a contextual ethics that is not only culturally based but also depends on the nature and type of the tourist/traveler, level of involvement of the local community, and 'personal frame of reference.'

Rami Farouk Daher's chapter: 'Tourism, Heritage, and Urban Transformations in Jordan and Lebanon: Emerging Actors and Global-Local Juxtapositions,' ventures into the epistemology of urban conservation/regeneration of historic cores in different cities of Jordan and Lebanon within the cultural region of Bilad al Sham. Through its various discourse analysis, the chapter will investigate the nature, scope, and effect of diverse groups of publics, actors, networks, and agencies (international and local) engaged in the definition, production, consumption, and regeneration of 'urban heritage' and its links to place politics, identity construction, and tourism development. The chapter will attempt to reveal the various connections, networks, and discourses operating between these publics, actors, and agencies.

It is very obvious that tourism and its related development has played a significant role in the transformation and reshaping of cities recently. This chapter sheds light on current socio-economic and cultural/spatial transformations affecting urban centers and historic city cores within the region and identifies several significant emerging phenomena: (1) Several emerging urban regeneration/tourism projects within the region that stem from neo-liberal urban restructuring and circulation of surplus global capital as in the case of prime cities of Beirut's Solidere Project in the downtown area and Amman's Abdali Mega Urban Project, which is represented as the 'new downtown for the City.' (2) The emerging role of aid agencies and international donors in the regeneration/tourism projects targeting historic urban centers of secondary cities within the region and circulating a standardized form of heritage and of place in places such as Salt, Kerak, Jerash and Madaba in Jordan, and Tripoli, Jbeil, and Sour in Lebanon. (3) Emerging new/old actors and agents in the form of 'notable families' who reintroduce themselves in the region as patrons of culture, heritage, and history. They work to fund and patronize urban regeneration projects, adaptations into cultural tourism facilities and into heritage museums and interpretation centers. Thought the impact might be minimal at the moment in comparison to other agents of change, such families and philanthropists are reintroducing another alternative to the 'state's formal vision of history and of the past, furthermore, they facilitate different itineraries for tourists and visitors that rest on an informal narration of the past and an emphasis on the "ordinary," on the social history and matters of everyday life.'

The significance of the chapter rests on the fact that it ventures into very contemporary and recent transformations and changes within the region of the Middle East that had stayed predominantly outside the interest of researchers and scholars such as the inseparable relation between tourism and urban change. Observers of the current transformations of the urban scene in the region are likely to conclude that cities are gradually becoming business and tourism spectacles.

In Salam Al Mahadin's chapter: 'Tourism and Power Relations in Jordan: Contested Discourses and Semiotic Shifts,' she qualifies as a local Jordanian intellectual who attempts to unravel and reveal power through discursive shifts where it is most invisible and subtle. She does that through an in-depth analytics of power in a locale that is Jordan where also she is accounting for this particular location in a remarkable and in-depth manner. Not only that, she is dealing with Foucault's concept of 'governmentality' and the emergence of political economy as central to the 'art of government,' but also his 'archaeology' as well. By unraveling the various shifts in discursive practices and how they affect tourism, Al Mahadin has critically presented an in-depth discursive analysis of the Jordanian formal discourse. She shows how tourism and its related 'sites,' such as museums, billboards, websites, pamphlets, and others, are being used and as institutions to legitimize and to reshape state formal discourses along the three layers she uses for her chapter: the nation-state that is 'Jordan', the monarchy, and the community or sense of Jordanianess. Based on not only Foucault, but also critical thinkers of the Frankfurt School such as Adorno and Kellner, such institutions formed parts of the strategies of 'governing' with the objective of producing a disciplined citizenry or creating a forced link between culture and entertainment, thus camouflaging oppression and power relations.

Linked to the previous point, she is beautifully situating tourism as one of the discursive practices of governmentality (with its forms of social planning and policy making) linked to issues of legitimacy and identity construction vis-à-vis the three layers mentioned earlier (the nation-state, the monarchy, and the community or sense of Jordanianess). She mentions how tourism 'forms a node in a web of power relations that delimit and define the possibilities of action and the "forms of knowledge and identities and agencies by which governing operate".'

Notes

1. Bilad al Sham is a very old and archaic local geographic term denoting the land of the East Mediterranean region, the term had been in use since more than a thousand years. The concept of Bilad al Sham introduced in this chapter

is very different from the politically grounded concept of Greater Syria, which is linked to the ideology of Pan Arabism promoted by individuals such as Antoun Saadeh or Nuri al Sai'd in the middle of the 20th century. This book promotes a historical/cultural and popular/local concept of Bilad al Sham from the bottom up, grounded in the ethnographic, cultural, and regional realities of the area. As a concept/reality present in both popular and scholarly discourses, Bilad al Sham exists beyond the limitations of national boundaries or discourses. Also, regardless of how contested this concept is by official historiographies, Bilad al Sham is still a 'living' and 'functioning' conception.

2. Al Mashreq al Arabi is another local concept that emerged recently during attempts of establishing Arab unity within the Arab world with its different cultural formal regions: (1) Al Mashreq al Arabi (Arab East), which encompasses the current nation states of Jordan, Lebanon, Syria, and Palestine; (2) Wadi al Neel (The Nile Valley), which encompasses the nation states of Egypt and Sudan; (3) Al Maghreb al Arabi (Arab West), which encompasses the nation states of Libya, Algiers, Tunis, and Morrocco; and (4) the Gulf and the Arabian Pennisula, which encompasses the nation-states of Saudi Arabia, Kuwait, Bahrain, Qatar, the United Arab Emirates, Oman, and Yeman.

3. The Euro-Mediterranean Conference of Ministries of Foreign Affairs held in Barcelona on November 27–8, 1995, marked the starting point of the Euro-Mediterranean Partnership (Barcelonna Process). A wide framework of political, economic, and social relations between 15 Member States of the Europaean Union and 12 Partners of the Southern Mediterranean countries was initiated (Euromed Partnership, 2002).

4. Some Euromed Cultural Heriage Projects include: CORPUS: Traditional Mediterranean Architecture; IPAMED: Computerized Cartography of the Historical Heritage; MWNF: Museum with no Frontiers (Exhibition Trail on Islamic Art and Civilization in the Mediterranean); ALAMBO: Professional Qualification for Architectural Heritage Arts; UNIMED HERIT: Post-graduate Course in Cultural Heritage and Heritage Management; EXPO 2000 EURO-MED HERITAGE: Exhibition of Euromed Cultural Heritage in connection with the Expo 2000 in Hanover; MEDRESSA: Multi Media and Cultural Heritage; EURO-MEDITERRANEAN HERITAGE DAYS: The European Heritage Days and their extension to the Mediterranean region, in addition to several other projects as well (Euromed Heritage, 2002).

5. New ITs used include GIS (Geographic Information Systems), Multimedia DBMS (Database Management Systems), and others.

6. *AlHayat* newspaper, Thursday, December 17, 1998, Issue No. 13071.

7. Meeting with George Audi and other soap factory staff, Audi Foundation, Saida, Lebanon (February 18, 2002).

8. Syria Live Net: http://www.syrialive.net/tourism.tourism.htm (accessed on April 13, 2005).

9. These observations were taken by the author during a recent visit to Sharm al Sheikh in June 2005.

10. Lecture by Gabriel Abraham on November 23, 2000 entitled: Preserving the City of the Gods: Luxor, Egypt, at Diwan al Mimar (The Center for the Study of the Built Environment's (CSBE) Architectural Forum) in Amman, Jordan. Diwan al Mimar is a discussion forum on the built environment organized by CSBE in association with Darat al Funun–The Khalid Shouman Foundation.

11. Information is based on several field visits to Beit Jabri in Damascus in the years 2002, 2003, 2004, and 2005 and to an interview with Raed Jabri (owner) in February 2002.
12. *AlHayat* newspaper, 'Saudi Arabia is witnessing a surge in tourism festivals: Saudi tourists staying in country make developing excited.' Issue No. 14322, p. 17.
13. *Al Dustour* newspaper, September 9, 2004. Amman, Jordan.
14. Ibh Battutah is a famous Muslim traveler from Morroco who in the 12th century traveled all over the Islamic world from the shores of the Atlantic to China. This shopping mall mimics the built environment of some locations from different parts of the world to entice shoppers. Similar to Disney's Epcot Center, the shopping mall claims to provide a cultural experience for the shopper.
15. The author visited and stayed in Le Baron Hotel in February 2002. During his stay, several informal discussions with the owners and employees took place.
16. The author visited Al Rabi'e Hotel several times from 2001 and up to 2004. These visits provided the chance for informal discussions with the owners, employees, and some of the tourists who happened to be staying there.
17. Meeting with Ms Monique Aggiouri. Debbbaneh Palace, Mutran Street, Saida, Lebanon (February 18, 2002).
18. Idrisi Travel, 2005. Touristic brochure, Netherlands. www.idrisitravel.co.uk. Accessed on December 18, 2005.
19. www.jabalomar.com. Accessed on April 23, 2005.

References

Adham, Khaled (2004) Cairo's urban déjà vu: Globalization and urban fantasies. In Yasser Elsheshtawy (ed.) *Planning Middle Eastern Cities: An Urban Kaleidoscope in a Globalizing World* (pp. 134–68). New York: Routledge.

Al-Sayyad, Nezar (2001a) Preface. In Nezar Al-Sayyad (ed.) *Consuming Tradition, Manufacturing Heritage: Global Norms and Urban Forms in the Age of Tourism* (pp. vii–viii). New York: Routledge.

Al-Sayyad, Nezar (2001b) Global norms and urban forms in the age of tourism: Manufacturing heritage, consuming tradition. In Nezar Al-Sayyad (ed.) *Consuming Tradition, Manufacturing Heritage: Global Norms and Urban Forms in the Age of Tourism* (pp.1–33). New York: Routledge.

Anderson, B. (1983) *Imagined Communities: Reflections on the Origins and Spread of Nationalism*. New York: Vintage Books.

Britton, S. (1991) Tourism, capital, and place: Towards a critical geography of tourism. *Environment and Planning D: Society and Space* 9 (4), 451–78.

Butler, R. and Mao, B. (1995) Tourism between quasi-states: International, domestic, or what? In R. Butler and D. Pearce (eds) *Change in Tourism: People, Places, Processes* (pp. 92–113). London: Routledge.

Chang, T. *et al.* (1996) Urban heritage tourism: The global-local nexus. *Annals of Tourism Research* 23 (2), 286–99.

Cheong S. and Miller, M. (2000) Power and tourism: A Foucauldian observation. *Annals of Tourism Research* 27 (2), 371–90.

Dalby, Simon (2003) Geopolitics, the Bush doctrine, and war on Iraq. *Arab World Geographer* 6 (1), 7–18.

Dahdah, Linda (2004) Bsous museum offers journey into Lebanon's silk heritage. *The Daily Star*, May 28, 2004.

Daher, Rami (1999) Gentrification and the politics of power, capital, & culture in an emerging heritage industry in Jordan. *Traditional Dwellings and Settlements Review (TDSR): Journal of the International Association for the Study of Traditional Environments* X (II), 33–45.

Daher, Rami (2000a) Heritage conservation in Jordan: The myth of equitable and sustainable development. *Les Document Du CERMOC (CERMOC DOCUMENT),* No. 10: *Patrimony and Heritage Conservation in Jordan (Irene Mafi & Rami Daher)* (pp. 17–42). Beirut, Amman: CERMOC (Center for Studies and Researchers on the Contemporary Middle East).

Daher, Rami (2000b) Dismantling a community's heritage: Heritage tourism: Conflict, inequality, and a search for social justice in the age of globalization. In M. Robinson *et al.* (eds) *Tourism and Heritage Relationships: Global, National, and Local Perspectives* (pp. 105–28). Conference organized by the University of Northumria at Newcastle and Sheffield Hallam University, Sheffield, UK, September 2–7, 2000.

Daher, Rami (2002) The heritage [in] between: The discourses of 'region' and 'nation' in Bilad al Sham. *The Eighth Conference of the International Association for the Study of Traditional Environments (IASTE),* Hong Kong, China, December 12–15.

Daher, Rami (2004) Notable families of Bilad al Sham as patrons of art, heritage, and culture. *The Daily Star of the Herald Tribune*, No. 11430, July 3, 2004.

Daher, Rami (2005) Neo-liberalism, glocalization & urban restructuring in Jordan & Lebanon: Swift urban heritage donor recipes & quartering urban space. A paper presented at the *Social Science Fourteenth Annual Symposium: The Transformation of Middle Eastern Urban Landscapes: From Modernism to Neoliberalism,* The American University of Cairo (AUC), Cairo, Egypt, May 12–15, 2005.

Euromed Heritage (2002) Regional program in support of the development of Euro-Mediterranean cultural heritage. List of the projects of the first phase. On WWW at http://europa.eu.int/comm/external_relations/euromed/euromed heritage-proj-en.pdf. Accessed 12/8/2002.

Euromed Partnership (2002) Euromed information notes on dialogue between cultures and civilizations. On WWW at http://www.deljor.cec.edu.int/en/ whatsnew/dialogue.pdf. Accessed 10/8/2002.

Fainstein, S. and Judd, D. (1999) Cities as places to play. In D. Judd and S. Fainstein (eds) *The Tourist City* (pp. 261–72). New Haven and London: Yale University Press.

Foucault, Michel (1980) *Power/Knowledge: Selected Interviews and Other Writing 1972–1977.* (Colin Gordon, trans. and ed.) Brighton: Harvester Press.

Fuchs, Ron (1998) The Palestinian Arab house and the Islamic 'primitive hut'. *Muqarnas* 15, 157–77.

Graburn, Nelson (1998) Weirs in the river of time: The development of Canadian Inuit historical consciousness. *Museum Anthropology* 22 (2), 54–66.

Gregory, Derek (2001) Colonial nostalgia and cultures of travel: Spaces of constructed visibility in Egypt. In Nezar Al-Sayyad (ed.) *Consuming Tradition,*

Manufacturing Heritage: Global Norms and Urban Forms in the Age of Tourism (pp.111–51). New York: Routledge.

Guillot, Xavier (2003) Tourism, hotel entrepreneurship and 'ready-made heritage' in Jordan and Syria: The cases of Zara Investment Holding and Cham Palaces & Hotels. Paper presented in Workshop No. 8 entitled *Reconceptualizing Public Spheres in the MENA Region: New Publics and Spaces of Contestation* at the 4th Mediterranean Social and Political Research Meeting, held at the Robert Schuman Center for Advanced Studies of the European University Institute of Florence, March 12–23, 2003.

Hall, Colin (1996) *Tourism and Politics: Policy, Power, and Place*. Chichester: John Wiley & Sons.

Harvey, D. (1990) *The Condition of Postmodernity: An Inquiry into the Origins of Cultural Change*. Oxford: Blackwell Publishers.

Hobsbawm, E. and Ranger, T. (eds) (1983) *The Invention of Tradition*. London: Cambridge University Press.

Horner, A. (1990) *The Assumption of Tradition: Creating, Collecting, and Conserving Cultural Artifacts in the Cameroon Grassfields (West Africa)*. Berkeley: University of California.

Hunter, Robert (2003) The Thomas Cook archive for the study of tourism in North Africa and the Middle East. *Middle East Studies Association: Bulletin* 36 (2) (Winter), 157–63.

Jordan Tourism Board (1998) Map of Jordan. On WWW at www.jordan-tourism.com.jo. Accessed on November 19, 2005.

Jordan Tourism Board (2000) Visitors' guide: Welcome to Jordan. On WWW at www.see-jordan.com. Accessed on November 19, 2005.

Junemo, Mattias (2004) 'Let's build a palm island!': Playfulness in complex times. In M. Sheller and J. Urry (eds) *Tourism Mobilities: Places to Play, Places in Play* (pp. 181–91). London: Routledge.

Kamel, Basil (2000) Revitalizing of urban heritage – or the commodification of tradition? In M. Robinson *et al.* (eds) *Tourism and Heritage Relationships: Global, National, and Local Perspectives* (pp. 145–58). Conference organized by the University of Northumria at Newcastle and Sheffield Hallam University, Sheffield, UK, September 2–7, 2000.

Kandiyoti, D. (2002) Post-colonialism compared: Potentials and limitations in the Middle East and Central Asia. *International Journal of Middle Eastern Studies (IJMES)* 34 (2), 279–97.

Kellner, D. (1997) Globalization and the postmodern turn. On WWW at http://www.gseis.ucla.edu/courses/ed253a/dk/globpm.html. Accessed on December 12, 2000.

Lanfant, Marie-Françoise (1995a) Introduction. In M.-F. Lanfant, J.B. Allock, and E.M. Bruner (eds) *Internatinal Tourism, Identity and Change: Sages Studies in International Sociology* (pp. 1–23) (Vol. 47). London: Sage.

Lanfant, Marie-Françoise (1995b) International tourism, internationalisation and the challenge to identity. In M.-F. Lanfant, J.B. Allock, and E.M. Bruner (eds) *Internatinal Tourism, Identity and Change: Sages Studies in International Sociology* (Pp. 24–43) (Vol. 47). London: Sage.

Maffi, Irene (2000). Le statut des objects dans la mise en scene museographique du passe en Jordanie: Le discours historique, la narration mythique et la tradition. *Les Document Du CERMOC (CERMOC DOCUMENT)* No. 10: *Patrimony and Heritage Conservation in Jordan (Irene Mafi & Rami Daher)* (pp. 3–16). Beirut, Amman: CERMOC (Center for Studies and Researchers on the Contemporary Middle East).

Maffi, Irene (2002) New museographic trends in Jordan: The strengthening of the nation. In George Joffe (ed.) *Jordan in Transition 1990–2000* (pp. 208–24). London: Hurst & Company.

Marston, S. and Rouhani, F. (2001) Teaching and learning the lesson of complexity. *The Arab World Geographer* 4 (2), 100–2.

Ministry of Tourism and Antiquities (1999) *Synopsis of Tourism Strategy*. Amman, Jordan: MOTA.

Ministry of Tourism and Antiquities (2004) *Jordan National Tourism Strategy 2004–2010*. Amman, Jordan: MOTA.

Mowforth M. and Munt, L. (1998) *Tourism and Sustainability: New Tourism in the Third World*. London and New York: Routledge.

Oppermann, Martin (1993) Tourism space in developing countries. *Annals of Tourism Research* 20, 535–56.

Philipp, Thomas (ed.) (1992) *The Syrian Land in the 18th and 19th Century*. Stuttgart: Franz Steiner Verlag Stuttgart.

Reilly, James (1999) Past and present in local histories of the Ottoman period from Syria and Lebanon. *International Journal of Middle East Studies* 35 (1), 45–65.

Robinson, Mike (1998) Tourism encounters: Inter- and intra-cultural conflicts and the world's largest industry. *Traditional Dwellings and Settlement Review* X (1), 31.

Robinson, Mike (1999) Cultural conflicts in tourism: Inevitability and inequality. In M. Robinson and P. Boniface (eds) *Tourism and Cultural Conflicts* (pp. 1–32). Oxford: CABI Publishing.

Robinson, Mike (2001) Tourism encounters: Inter- and intra-cultural conflicts and the world's largest industry. In Nezar Al-Sayyad (ed.) *Consuming Tradition, Manufacturing Heritage: Global Norms and Urban Forms in the Age of Tourism* (pp.34–67). New York: Routledge.

Rogan, Eugene (1994) Bringing the state back: The limits of Ottoman rule in Transjordan, 1840–1910. In E. Rogan and T. Tell (eds) *Village Steppe and State: The Social Origins of Modern Jordan* (pp. 32–57). London: British Academic Press.

Sadik, Rula (2005) Dazzling Dubai: The 'invisible' hand of global competitiveness. A paper presented at the *Social Science Fourteenth Annual Symposium: The Transformation of Middle Eastern Urban Landscapes: From Modernism to Neoliberalism*, The American University of Cairo (AUC), Cairo, Egypt, May 12–15, 2005.

Said, E.W. (1979) *Orientalism*. London and Henley: Routledge and Kegan Paul.

Sandrine, G. (2005). Shaping the city for the other: Tourism development, heritage management and the urban fabric in Luxor. A paper presented at the *Social Science Fourteenth Annual Symposium: The Transformation of Middle Eastern Urban Landscapes: From Modernism to Neoliberalism*, The American University of Cairo (AUC), Cairo, Egypt, May 12–15, 2005.

Schriwer, Charlotte (2002) Cultural and ethnic identity in the Ottoman period architecture of Cyprus, Jordan and Lebanon. *LEVANT: The Journal of the Council for British Research in the Levant* 34, 197–218.

Sharpley, R. (2000) Tourism and sustainable development: Exploring the theoretical divide. *Journal of Sustainable Tourism* 8 (1), 1–19.

Sheller, M. and Urry, J. (2004). Places to play, places in play. In M. Sheller and J. Urry (eds) *Tourism Mobilities: Places to Play, Places in Play* (pp. 1–10). London: Routledge.

Summer, Doris (2005) Neo-liberalizing the city: Transitional investment networks and the circulation of urban images in Beirut and Amman. Master's thesis in Urban Planning. Beirut: American University of Beirut (AUB).

Titley, G. (2000) Global theory and touristic encounters. *Irish Communications Review* 8, 79–87.

Tyler, Duncan (2000) A framework for analyzing urban tourism. In M. Robinson *et al.* (eds) *Developments in Urban and Rural Tourism* (pp. 287–99). Sunderland: Centre for Travel and Tourism.

Urry, John (1990) *The Tourist Gaze: Leisure and Travel in Contemporary Societies.* London: SAGE Publications.

Chapter 2

A Historiography of Tourism in Cairo: A Spatial Perspective

NOHA NASSER

Introduction

This chapter explores the relationship between the changing nature of tourism on the spatial transformations in Cairo's urban form. It analyses this relationship from the 12th century to the present, examining morphological transformations at two spatial scales: the micro scale of the building, and the dispersion of tourist activities within the city at the macro scale. These spatial transformations are seen to be dynamic, influenced by changes in the social, cultural, economic and political environments. By adopting a political economic approach, three successive periods in Cairo's development will show that Cairo's urban landscape responded to acute political and economic change as a result of its changing relationship with the external world and the changing nature of tourism in the region (see Table 2.1). The chapter concludes by discussing the historical significance of political economy and the evolving nature of tourism on the spatial development of the historic city. The transformations are then measured against principles of sustainability, projecting recommendations for the conservation, development and management of Cairo's cultural heritage.

By virtue of its very nature, travel – tourism's simplest denominator – is spatial, presupposing movement of people from one place to another. This occurs at a number of spatial scales; globally, regionally and locally. In the case of the Middle East, the extent of global travel dates back to the Achaemenid period, when a nexus of land and sea routes from China through Sassanian Persia to the upper Euphrates, and from India and the Yemen through western Arabia, channelled trade of silk and spices to the Mediterranean. The strategic location of the Middle Eastern heartlands between Europe and Central Asia established a network of trading

Table 2.1 The relationship between three political-economic periods in Cairo's history corresponding to changes in the nature of tourism and its dominant spatial transformations

Time period	Nature of tourism	Main features
The Islamic era (969–1798)	Regional people travelling for combination of holy reasons, education and trade	Cairo had dominant position in world economy, flourished as one of the major cultural centres of the Islamic world
The imperialist period (1798–1952)	Travel mainly by European cultural elite for education	Walled city declined as a result of modernisation and colonisation Cairo 'commodified' as popular destination
Post-revolution (1952–present)	Mass tourism of foreigners for cultural tourism and leisure shopping	Cairo inscribed as World Heritage Site in 1979 Dramatic rise in tourist numbers Khan al-Khalili becomes major tourist bazaar

centres and travel architecture distributed across time and space. Regionally, profound changes to trade routes occurred with the rise of Islam, old routes were expanded and new routes forged joining Mecca, the sacred centre, to Iraq, Persia and Oman to cater for the increasing numbers of Muslim pilgrims travelling for *Hajj* (Pearson, 1994). The extraordinary mobility of Muslim culture established urban features responding to the needs of the travelling citizenry. At the urban scale, this mobility created a powerful transforming force claiming space for specialised activities and functions within the urban setting. In the Middle East, specialised buildings such as *khans, wikalas, qaisarriyas, funduqs* and *hammams* as well as specialised markets, such as the 'money-changers', became prominent urban focal points.

The Spatial Dimension of Tourism

The spatial dimension of tourism has only recently been seen as an essential part of policy development and the planning and management process (Ashworth, 1995; Ashworth & Tunbridge, 1990; Dietvorst, 1995;

Jansen-Verbeke & Wiel, 1995). This is true of all tourist destinations, including tourist-historic cities, where tourist activities and the growing number of tourists induce changes in urban form, in the physical structures, in the functional patterns and in the use of public space. Jansen-Verbeke (1997) has shown that different tourist activities have had a physical impact on the artefacts of the urban environment. Tourists visiting historical cities are attracted by the spatial concentration of historic buildings as a setting for sightseeing and the range of opportunities for related cultural activities. The number of attractions and the actual location of interesting artefacts in the historic city explain, to a large extent, the way that tourist activity develops in time and space causing over-crowdedness, traffic congestion, shortage of parking, changing retail trades, rising prices and intrusion in the private domain (Dietvorst, 1995).

This strongly differentiated spatial behaviour has led to land-use selectivity, creating concentrations of 'tourist complexes': mainly core elements, the primary resources that attract visitors, and complementary secondary elements, those functions that support the tourist activity such as restaurants and souvenir shops (Ashworth & Tunbridge, 1990; Dietvorst, 1995). In extreme cases, 'enclave tourism' occurs where the type and location of facilities are created specifically to serve the needs of recreation and particularly the needs of tourists. This 'export' orientation leads to higher priced rents and the emergence of a tourist district isolated rather than functional for the local community (Newby, 1994).

At a smaller scale, building selectivity is governed by both economic pressures and time bias. The pre-eminence of economic forces generated by tourism means that the reuse of individual buildings frequently results in a leisure or tourist dimension conflicting with the building's original form and use (Newby, 1994). The age and rarity of buildings provide the basis for much of the tourist attraction. However, towns that have evolved through many periods, offering a variety of architectural styles, are faced with the problem of tourism's selectivity when certain periods are favoured above others susceptible to changing tastes over time.

The intrusions of the tourist activity and the tourists into the spatial domain of an urban community have been attributed to the ways in which the tourist activity disrupts the interaction pattern of 'people and place'. According to Jansen-Verbeke (1997: 244): 'The new activities related to tourism are interfering with the existing system and therefore hold the risk of imbalancing the system itself.' Therefore, what is required is an understanding of the historical symbiotic relationship between place, users and activities that can be used as a paradigm in which new tourism activities can be introduced sensitively.

The Islamic Era

The nature of tourism in the Islamic world

This period corresponds to the time when powerful dynasties governed by *Shari'a* or Islamic Law. The geographic area that embraced Islam became known as *Dar al-Islam* (literally, The House of Islam), which included at one point in time the regions from Spain to Central Asia. Islam brought with it a new dimension to travel, one that involved spiritual and temporal movement at the same time as physical movement motivated by a combination of holy reasons and social, economic and political concerns (Eickelman & Piscatori, 1990). While *Hajj* (pilgrimage) is usually seen as travel with a uniquely religious purpose, other forms of travel were just as common: *rihla* or *talab al-ilm* (travel for learning and other purposes), and *ziyara* (visits to shrines and religious festivals), which all helped shape the religious imagination.

These journeys crossed gender and ethnic lines creating a significant rise in traffic between urban centres, especially the unique focus on Mecca, and between sacred places within the city, such as *sufi khanaqahs*, shrines, mosques, tombs and mausoleums of notable Islamic figures. Thus a complex 'sacred geography' was established, spatially superimposed along trans-national trade routes and within each city's urban form. The pre-eminence of religious and intellectual motivations for travel created a new genre of urban centres, giving greater sanctity to those already established trading centres that possessed key institutions of religion and/or learning such as Mecca or Al-Azhar in Cairo, but also the emergence of shifting hierarchies of centres in different periods depending on political and economic conditions. In the case of travel for religious scholarship, the institutionalisation of the *madrasa* (colleges of law) system, which replaced the mainly oral tradition, gave rise to a number of cultural capitals attracting large numbers of Muslim students and scholars; Baghdad set the standard in the 9th and 10th centuries, Cairo in the 10th and 12th centuries, and Nishapur in the 13th and 14th centuries (Gellens, 1990). Other cities in Islam rose to prominence by virtue of their political dominance such as Istanbul, or their commercial wealth such as Jeddah and others, which prospered as major ports of call along the pilgrimage and trade routes.

The economic dimensions of travel and pilgrimage in Muslim society are well documented, particularly that it was religiously acceptable to trade whilst on the *Hajj*. Considering that the length of this religious enterprise could take up to a few years, pilgrims carried goods to trade and convert into cash in order to purchase the different commodities that they needed for the journey. It was the caravan trade that was the major sector of the early modern economy of the Middle East, boosted by merchants who also accompanied the pilgrimage caravans, exploiting the protection afforded under military government by the officer in command of the tour, *Amir al-Hajj*, and his guards (Pearson, 1994).

The commercial predilection of Muslim travellers developed specialised travel architecture with a distinctly commercial dimension serving travellers, both merchants as well as pilgrims (Sims, 1978). Buildings that denoted the combined functions of a rest-house, lodging facilities and trading house carried a number of names; *khan, funduq, wikala* and *qaisariya*. These special building types were also known by their founder or owner, or after the merchandise they specialised in such as the Silk Khan, the Soap Khan or the Oil Khan, or after the people using it such as the Egyptian Khan or the Tailors Khan in Tripoli, Lebanon. As a special building type, these buildings were constructed in a uniform manner. The two- to four-storey structures were erected around a large inner court with a grand portal and had a portico that supported a gallery. The ground floor was made up of vaulted storage rooms, and in some cases included shops fronting the street. The upper storeys consisted of separate rooms or apartments dedicated to travellers, merchants and pilgrims. Some of these buildings also provided stables for animals, a mosque and a *sabil* (drinking fountain). Within the city, these building types formed part of the market complex, located between the major city gates and in prime positions within the urban landscape. According to Sims (1978) a combination of specialised buildings, markets and *hammams* (baths) clustered around the congregational mosque constituted the main elements of the Islamic market place segregated according to the nature and value of the goods and trades. Although this is generally true, the public domain of the city also attracted other functions such as the *madrasas* (colleges), *khanqahs* (monasteries) and mausoleums (Nasser, 2001). In essence, the public domain was a place in which buildings for local and tourist activities were concentrated, whether for educational, commercial or religious use.

These amenities were provided by the ruling class and wealthy who established themselves as patrons of public welfare (Nasser, 2002). By virtue of their wealth and power, and as a means of fulfilling one of the five pillars of Islam – almsgiving – the ruling class constructed social welfare buildings and commercial enterprises through the religious endowment system of *waqf khayry*. The endowment was an inalienable gift of money, property or food to be used for a specific purpose such as for spending on public facilities or private bodies, or by dedicating the property itself to serve public or private interest (Nasser, 2002). Once an endowment was made, the gift and its revenues became the property of the community, whether to help the local community, *sufi* brotherhoods, the poor of Mecca and Medina, or for travellers to stay gratis for a specified number of days and to receive food. The endowment also worked to maintain public buildings, such as *madrasas*, *khanqahs* and *sabils*, from the revenues generated through rents, in effect cross-subsidising the retention of culturally significant buildings (Nasser, 2002). In morphological terms, rigid *waqf* property laws protected the fragmentation of land and the change of land-uses. Lands and buildings held in *waqf* constituted a separate form of land tenure, inhibiting the application of traditional patterns of Islamic inheritance and the subsequent subdivision of land parcels. The underlying influence of *waqf* property was that it preserved plot patterns and land-uses to a great degree (Nasser, forthcoming). The extent of patronage was regional. This is particularly evident with the sacred cities of Islam (al-Haramayn) upon which a substantial amount of charity converged from endowments across the Islamic world (Hoexter, 1998). Within each city, the management of real estate was in the hands of the religious notables who ensured maximum returns and appropriate distribution amongst beneficiaries according to the *waqf's* religious sanction. This also involved a thorough knowledge of the property market through speculation and exchange to sustain revenue (Nasser, 2002).

Thus under *Dar al-Islam*, the great cities of Islam flourished as nuclei of wealth, religion, education and power that prompted the mobility of a vast number of people from the eastern extremities to the west for religious, educational and commercial reasons. Travel, or *rihla*, in its broadest definition was for purposes of pilgrimage, trade, scholarship and adventure. Attesting to the culture and civilisation of these urban centres, literary sources of the great Muslim travellers are numerous consisting of geographical writings, local historical accounts, references in belles-lettres, route-books and lists of roads, settlements and cities (Sims, 1978). In addition, and increasingly from the 13th century, European visitors travelling for religious, commercial, diplomatic or military purposes to these cities describe their experiences in their writings (Sims, 1978). Cairo was no exception, as described by Ibn Khaldun in the 14th century (1951: 256–7):

> He who has not seen Cairo does not know of the grandeur of Islam. It is the metropolis of the universe, the garden of the world, the anthill

of the human species, the throne of royalty, a city embellished with castles and palaces, its horizons decorated with monasteries and with schools, and lighted by the moon and stars of erudition. ... I went through the streets of this city which were choked with throngs of pedestrians and through its markets, which overflowed with all the delights of this life. One could talk forever of this city and of the extensive dimensions of its civilisation.

Cairo – city of culture

This section examines the morphological development of the walled city of Cairo during the Islamic era, influenced by its trade links and cultural dispensation. Within the global context of the Middle Ages, Cairo enjoyed a dominant position in the world economy, being strategically located along the land and sea routes of the east–west spice trade, and controlling much of the transit trade in the Red Sea. Over a period of 900 years, Egypt and its commercial centres of Fustat, Cairo and Bulaq, fostered trade of spices and goods between Europe and India. At the same time, Cairo lay on the pilgrimage caravan route serving north and west Africa, becoming a vital regional collection centre for pilgrims and the caravan trade from Muslim Spain and the Yemen. The spice trade was always an important aspect of Cairo's economy shipped from the Indian Ocean via two routes: first, the southerly route beginning at Aden, through the Red Sea to the Sudanese port of 'Aidhab, to be transported by caravan to Quds, then up the Nile to the port city of Fustat (Staffa, 1977). The northerly route stopped at the Red Sea ports of the Hijaz and Qulzum, transporting goods by caravan through the Eastern desert to Cairo.

The Cairo pilgrimage caravan was rigorously timed to arrive in Mecca for the annual *Hajj*, which took approximately 40 days, travelling overland across the Eastern desert via the port towns of Aqaba and Yanbo to Mecca. On the return journey to Cairo, the caravan passed through Medina for a few days (Pearson, 1994). These caravans began and terminated their journeys north of Cairo at the *Birkat al-Hujjaj* (the Pilgrims Lake) where the pilgrims rallied and camels were laden with equipment and provisions. The size of these caravans distinguished them from other trade caravans in the region, reported to have been composed of 30,000 or 40,000 people (Pearson, 1994). The Cairo caravan, one of the largest and richest, was renowned for its delivery of the *kiswa*, or covering for the *Ka'aba* in Mecca. The *mahmal*, as it was called, was carried on a richly adorned litter that accompanied the caravan giving it great prestige.

Cairo was founded in 969 by the Fatimids as an imperial capital constructed for the sole use of the Caliph, his court, slaves and officials, and troops. Cairo's layout reflected the centre of political and religious power. The city was surrounded by high walls and gates, containing two large centrally located palaces, and a mixture of administrative, recreational, as well as residential functions. The original town plan resembled Roman antecedents; orthogonal in plan and characterised by a regular grid, wide streets and *rahbas* (open spaces). Politically, the Fatimids were *shi'ites* whose ideological differences from *Sunni* Islam isolated them from the intellectual currents of Baghdad and Damascus during this time (Staffa, 1977). Nevertheless, the influence of *Shi'ite* free-thinking contributed to progress in science and medicine, as well as philosophy, raising Cairo's image as an intellectual centre on par with *Sunni* Islam. In particular, centres of high learning such as the *al-Azhar* mosque and the two *Dar Al-Ilms* (Houses of Science) in which collections of 20,000 books were made available to everyone, as well as the revered shrine of al-Hussein (the Prophet's grandson), had far-reaching adherents (Staffa, 1977). Economically, the majority of trading took place in Fustat, however, Nasir-i-Khusraw (1993) visiting in the 11th century confirms that within the walled city there are convents, baths and a number of markets occupying a total of 20,000 shops. Al-Maqrizi (1853) the 15th-century topographer also identifies a number of luxury markets catering for the needs of the Caliph and his entourage, including the gold market closely linked to the royal mints, and a *Dar al-Wikala* built for those traders arriving from Iraq and al-Sham (Syria/Lebanon). At this stage, however, the evidence suggests that all commercial real-estate in Cairo was owned by the Caliph, trading in goods associated with government, and concentrated around the great palaces along the major north–south thoroughfare, al-Qasaba, and along the intersection with the main east–west street leading to al-Azhar (Nasser, 2000). Two factors are relevant from the Fatimid era: first, Cairo's initial layout offered a morphological frame for future transformations based on an inertia inherent in the street pattern, plot distribution and political value associated with the palaces that influenced development; second, Cairo's cultural status had found its roots during this time, particularly al-Azhar, and which was to proliferate throughout its development.

Cairo's political, economic and social history from the 12th to the 19th century helped shape the spatial geography of tourism in Cairo, which became linked to the *ziyara* of the shrines, international trade and its corresponding markets, the pilgrimage and the centres of learning. The first major impetus to Cairo's transformation came under the Ayyubids.

Politically, Salah al-Din reunited Egypt with the *Sunni* Abbasids, whose empire had begun to dissolve into semi-autonomous regions administered by means of fiefs allocated to the ruling elite. In this tradition, Salah al-Din distributed agricultural and urban land amongst his family and *amirs* (knights) resulting in prime urban locations coming under an elitist tenure. This is particularly evident with the reallocation of the great palaces to the ruling class that accompanied the shift of political power to the Citadel on the Muqattam hills. Simultaneously, Salah al-Din opened Cairo to the masses, prompted by the burning of Fustat in the 12th century, diversifying Cairo's social and commercial life as quarters were settled and markets created. Under the Ayyubids, Cairo experienced a renewal of government interest in public welfare, with many religious foundations prospering through *waqf* (endowments) particularly the Ayyubid-sponsored establishment of the *madhahib* (schools of law) and the associated *madrasas*. Economically, Salah al-Din's successful campaigns against the Crusaders and the expansion of the Ayyubid Empire secured trade with Europe and the Far East, encouraging commerce with the merchants of Pisa, Genoa and Venice who flocked to Alexandria, and the exclusive use of the Red Sea to Muslim traders exploiting trade with the Indian Ocean (Staffa, 1977).

Cairo continued to prosper under the Mamluks (1252–1517) reaching its apogee during the early 14th century under the reign of al-Nasir Mohammed Ibn-Qalawun with an estimated population of half a million (Abu Lughod, 1971). Cairo's prominence as one of the largest cities in the Muslim world was bolstered by the transfer of the Caliphate from Baghdad to Cairo by Baybars in 1260 as a result of his victory over the Mongols. Cairo's development witnessed cycles of growth and decline closely linked to the Mongol uprisings and Crusader campaigns that disrupted overland trade routes, as well as the numerous appearances of the Bubonic plague from the mid-14th century and famine that severely depleted populations (Abu Lughod, 1971). During times of internal stability and external security, Cairo expanded beyond its city walls, suburbs developed to the north, west and south, with the expansive City of the Dead developing to the east, that included the masterpiece mausoleums of Mamluk rulers and notables. The markets flourished with the growing trade between east and west, monopolised by the Mamluk elite who used their wealth and power to patronise public works and sponsor urban development and regeneration, investing in urban real-estate and land speculation through the *waqf* system (Nasser, 2002).

However, by the time of the Ottomans in the early 16th century, Cairo had begun to decline with the disruption of the spice trade by the

Portuguese. Vasco da Gama's successful circumnavigation of Africa and his arrival in India in 1498, established a virtual monopoly on the spice trade that had been channelled by the Venetians through Cairo for so long (Pearson, 1994). Disruption of trade continued under the Dutch and English in the 17th century controlled by the Dutch East India Company. Nevertheless, the continued use of caravans as the main method of transportation ensured the Middle East remained part of the trade network (Pearson, 1994). The movement of the Caliphate to Istanbul, the Ottoman capital, gave provincial Cairo a new role as the centre for storage of the transit trade before distribution to various regions of the empire. This is reflected in the extraordinary multiplication in the number of warehouses and *waqf* property.

In response to acute political, social and economic changes, the walled city of Cairo experienced greater specialisation of land-uses and buildings, as well as changes in plot patterns and street layouts. This cycle of transformation began under the Ayyubids, initially in the form of markets and structures catering for the local economy to support the increase in Cairo's population as well as luxury goods for the elite, but most evidently in the proliferation of *madrasas* placed in strategic locations as a form of *shi'ite* counter-propaganda (Nasser, 2000). The hiatus in the establishment of Cairo's international markets is due to Fustat's continued importance during this time. Nevertheless, what is significant from this era is the rehabilitation and reconstruction of Fatimid foundations by the Ayyubid ruling class. This had three major influences. First, that redevelopment was superimposed spatially on the major Fatimid mansions and palaces, which were concentrated in the vicinity of Bein al-Qasrein (the square between the two major palaces) and along the east–west thoroughfare linking al-Azhar with the western city gates. Second, that the inertia inherent in these large plots provided the foundation for large structures to be constructed over them, many of which were later placed in *waqf* further preserving their boundaries. Third, these areas were prime locations augmenting land values, underpinning future commercial and cultural proliferation (Nasser, 2001).

Cairo developed first as a cultural centre, augmented by Salah al-din's policy to re-establish *Sunni* orthodoxy. Beside the seventeen Ayyubid *madrasas*, Salah al-Din invited Persian *sufis* (dervishes) to Cairo accommodating them in a former Fatimid House, Dar Said al-Suada, converting it into a *khanqah*. He endowed upon it properties and land to fund travel allowances and daily provisions, he also built a bath nearby (al-Maqrizi, 1853). The Ayyubid introduction of *waqf* in Cairo began a process of defining the public domain, placing areas of highest land values under this rubric. This custom proliferated under the increasing specialisation and densification of Mamluk Cairo. More Fatimid villas and palaces along the major thoroughfares were being dismantled, and in many cases subdivided, and placed in *waqf*. A good example is the four-acre site of Dar al-Wizara in the north-eastern part of the city, which under the Mamluks was developed into two cultural buildings, Madrasa Qaransqur and Khanqah Bibars al-Gashankir, as well as four commercial buildings. Spatially, the impetus for these developments was stimulated by the re-direction of the Sultan's ceremonial route, which encouraged the ruling class to exhibit their benevolence. Also, during Mamluk rule, Bein al-Qasrein, had become well-built up, with four schools adding to the two Ayyubid colleges, Dar al-Hadith and al-Sailihiyya. A great many smaller colleges were also constructed within the neighbourhoods off the main thoroughfares such as Ribat al-Baghdadiya built as a convent for women. An annexed tomb became a common feature. Ibn Khaldun, writing in the 14th century, describes Cairo's cultural vitality (1951: 435):

> We, at this time, notice that science and scientific instruction exist in Cairo in Egypt, because the civilisation [of Egypt] is greatly developed and its sedentary culture has been well established for thousands of years. Therefore, the crafts are firmly established there and exist in many varieties. One of them is scientific instruction. This [state of affairs] has been strengthened and preserved in Egypt by the events of the last two hundred years under the Turkish dynasty, from the days of Salah al-Din b. Ayyub ... they built a great many colleges, hermitages, and monasteries, and endowed them with mortmain endowments that yielded income. ... As a consequence mortmain endowments became numerous, and the profit from them increased. Students and teachers increased in numbers because a large number of stipends became available from the endowments. People travelled to Egypt from the Iraq and the Maghrib in quest of knowledge. Thus the sciences were very much in demand and greatly cultivated there.

During the Ottoman regime, space was very scarce, therefore new religious buildings were built over ruins, mainly small buildings such as *sabil-kuttabs* (fountain and orphan schools) and *zawiyas* (oratories), with no large-scale colleges being constructed.

Similar processes of rehabilitation and redevelopment applied to commercial uses, *hammams*, *wikalas* and *rab'* (apartment blocks for the merchant class). Spatially, the tendency was to locate commercially endowed property in the vicinity of its bequeathed cultural building. This reinforced the relationship between these two functional types within the public domain, but also capitalised on the high land values of this part of the city. The flowering of international trade under the Mamluks, and the subsequent increase in storage facilities under the Ottomans, influenced these prime locations in a number of ways. First, residential land along the major thoroughfares was the most vulnerable, tending to be displaced by commercial buildings. The robustness of the courtyard plan gave great flexibility for rehabilitation, which tended to occur frequently through the re-appropriation of space (Nasser, forthcoming). A second cycle of development was in the building up of former stables. The final cycle was a gradual building up within the plot, and in rare cases a subdivision of the property that was constrained by *waqf* stipulations (Nasser, 2000). Second, the greater specialisation of goods was reflected in the ecological distribution of trade from different parts of the world. An example is trade from Syria and Palestine (*Nablus*) tended to be located near the northern Bab al-Futuh. These were further differentiated by goods arriving by land being housed in Wikalat Qusun, and those arriving by sea in Wikalat Bab al-Juwaniyya (al-Maqrizi, 1853). Of particular interest is al-Maqrizi's mention of Khan al-Sabil, located just outside the northern gate of Bab al-Futuh, which was founded 'for people of the road and travellers free of charge, in it are a well with water scoops and a trough' (Mackensie, 1992: 166). At the centre of the city, in Bein al-Qasrein and the Khan al-Khalili the highest land value (most probably because of this area's association with the great Fatimid palaces) governed the sale of precious goods. Spices, slaves, jewellery and fine cloths were traded in the Khan al-Khalili (the building that later gave its name to the entire district), Khan Masrur al-Kabir and Wikalat al-Gallaba specialising in goods from the Sudan, are among the most famous. South of the east–west thoroughfare up to the southern city gate, Bab Zuweila, were located the merchants of imported fine cloth, the majority of the merchants were Syrian Christians from Aleppo of which Khan al-Hamzawi is most renowned (al-Maqrizi, 1853). With the rise in importance of coffee and tobacco in the 17th century, these goods were accommodated in Khan al-Khalili, and in purpose built *wikalas* north of Bein al-Qasrein housing traders from Turkey, Syria, Morocco and Tunisia. Raymond (1993) attests to the extensiveness of Cairo's markets under the Ottomans with 116 commercial houses and 40 markets in an area of 18 hectares. Ali Pasha Mubarak (cited by Raymond & Wiet, 1979) describes Cairo's ecological distribution at the end of the 19th century: the northern part of Cairo dealt with imports from Syria, Hijaz and Yemen, the central section was mainly Turkish imports, and the southern section remained specialised in fine cloths from Europe and India.

Support services for the entire area were concentrated in Bein al-Qasrein, in particular in the *Sagha* (gold market) which had been constructed over the former Fatimid kitchens. In this area, money-changing transactions proliferated in small stalls within the market and along Bein al-Qasrein. The functional and formal persistence of this area, even today, is remarkable. Other facilities included banks for depositing chests of gold and silver. These tended to be located off the main thoroughfares in the side streets. During al-Maqrizi's time in the 15th century these could be found in Khan Masrur al-Kabir, Funduq Qulumtai, Funduq Bilal, Khan al-Hagar and Khan Mangak (al-Maqrizi, 1853).

The importance of the caravan trade and in particular the pilgrimage trade to Cairo has already been mentioned. The quantities of provisions, means of transport and camping materials sold played an active role in Cairo's economic prosperity. An entire district close to the northern city gates leading to the caravan routes was dedicated to travel associated goods. Al-Maqrizi (1853) describes two markets; first, *Sūq* al-Muhayireen, specialised in litters of various designs that could be fitted on to camels. He remarks these were particularly in demand for those travelling on the *Hajj* or visiting Jerusalem. The other market, *Sūq* al-Morhaleen, specialised in caravan equipment, provisions and gear. Al-Maqrizi remarks that people from all over Egypt came to this market particularly during the *Hajj* season where one could furnish 100 camels in one day with no difficulty.

Cairenes' fascination with the cemeteries as a place for leisure and recreation is well documented (Mackensie, 1992; Rodenbeck, 1998). From the time of the Arab invasions a number of cemeteries had sprung up outside the city walls. Of particular reverence was the tomb of al-Imam al-Shaf'i (a ninth century Muslim jurist) near Fustat, however from the late Ayyubid period onwards, reaching its height during the late Mamluk period, these cemeteries became zones of extravagant mausoleums, colleges and markets (Mackensie, 1992). They were so important that they were established places of pilgrimage aided by specialised guidebooks catering to visitors from as early as the 13th century (Rodenbeck 1998). These pilgrimages also took place within the urban areas; of the most popular shrines were al-Mashad al-Hussein (the Prophet's grandson) in Cairo, and al-Sayeda Zeinab (al-Hussein's sister) south of Cairo. The dispersal of hundreds of tombs within the neighbourhoods of Cairo, both for the wealthy and the blessed, are still visited even today.

The imperialist period

The rise of popular tourism

While travel in the Middle East was still based on camel caravan for trade, pilgrimage and education, Europe during the 15th and 16th centuries was experiencing profound social changes. The emergence of a common elite culture was being driven by a succession of new ideas and thoughts: the Renaissance, the scientific revolution, the Enlightenment and the Romantic eras (Towner, 1996). Accompanying this social revolution from the mid-17th century was a growth in affluence and a subsequent demand for luxury goods, as well as a rediscovery of classical learning based on values of education, taste and refinement. From the 16th century to the early 19th century the combined effect of these factors gave rise to the Grand Tour circuit, undertaken by the wealthy in society for culture, education, health and pleasure. Thus the reasons for travel had changed based on developments of philosophy, scientific thought and the intellectual movement of humanism, which encouraged the desirability to explore and understand (Towner, 1996). Visits to countries such as Italy, Greece and the Levant, to collect and study works of art became an established feature in the education of the elite. Travellers also founded special societies, playing an increasingly important role in preservation based on the increasing awareness of the 'universal value' of important works of art and historic monuments (Jokilehto, 1999). From the mid-18th century, taste had changed from travel to examine scientific phenomenon characteristic of the 'classical tour' to a quest for the picturesque and an experience of local inhabitants and cultures, the 'romantic tour'. This change in fashion was particularly fostered by artists and writers whose images informed taste, not just reflecting them, but helping to sharpen perceptions and develop awareness (Towner, 1996).

Yet another social revolution in the later 19th century and early 20th century came in response to increased socio-economic and physical mobility. More time for leisure activities and rising incomes provided new opportunities for the wealthy to make visits to exotic destinations available on a global scale. This was supported with increasing commercial intervention by travel firms such as Thomas Cook who by the early 20th century were organising international tours for the affluent industrial/commercial upper middle class (Brendon, 1991). In 1869 Cook took his first tourists to Egypt and the Holy Land.

Imperial Cairo

Egypt was an attractive destination for 19th century tourists for a number of reasons: it was warm in winter, had thousands of years of antiquities, and possessed the natural life and beauty of the Nile Valley. But most importantly, it captured the imagination of the exotica and mystique of the Orient, and Cairo, the city of the 'Arabian Nights'. To the tourists visiting Cairo in the late 19th century, the city was very different from the previous century. Modern Cairo was modelled on Parisian-style wide boulevards, *rond-points* and European style buildings further west of the walled city, including the rising hotel district, in particular the Shepheard Hotel along the Nile.

The extensive building programme and the modernisation policies of Mohammed Ali and his successors, in particular his grandson, Khedive Ismail, had changed the face of Cairo. Modernisation became synonymous with Westernisation marked by a shift to European values and a rejection of the architectural heritage of the past. Abu Lughod comments on the change in architectural values (1971: 94):

> . . . the order was issued making it illegal to enhance new buildings with *masharabiya*, those delicately turned wooden lattice windows which for centuries had graced even the dullest and least attractive buildings. . . . In place of the Mamluk and Arabian styles, a mixed southern European and Turkish style was gaining ascendancy.

A revolution in the time to transport people and goods from Europe to the Orient, and from Alexandria to Cairo, was made possible through the construction of the railway and Suez Canal. As a result, European goods flooded the Egyptian markets marginalising the trades of the walled city. British control over Egypt in 1882 and the influx of even larger numbers of Europeans simply transformed a 'Western-influenced' model of urban development to a 'Western-dominated' one (Stewart, 1999).

The impact these changes had on the walled city was profound. Modern Cairo had in effect stripped the walled city of its economic base and merchant class, isolating it from mainstream development. Many of the commercial buildings and old mansions were divided and subdivided in order to accommodate small-scale manufacturing handicraft industries and to shelter the poor and low-income groups who had started to migrate from the countryside to Cairo seeking job opportunities (Fakhouri, 1985). These factors expedited the process of urban decay coupled with the deteriorating condition of *waqf* property, especially commercial property that had lost most of its custom, and could not generate sufficient funds needed for the upkeep of bequeathed buildings. Despite the changes in class structure, the style of life in the walled city had undergone little change. Staffa (1977) links this to a 'stubborn conservatism' and basic cement founded upon social, economic, political and religious mechanism. Popular aspects of lifestyle were preserved such as the trade corporations, *sufi* brotherhoods and the ecological distribution of trades within the city (Baer, 1964). A number of unconcerted efforts to improve both accessibility in and to the walled city resulted in the removal of the traditional shop benches – *mastabat* – that had encroached onto the streets, and the construction of two wide streets, al-Muski and al-Azhar, cutting across the dense urban fabric divisively interrupting the continuity of its urban pattern.

Despite government indifference, two important works during this era must be accounted for. First, Ali Pasha Mubarak's *Khitat al-Tawfiqqiya al-Jadida*, written in 1888 in which he records first-hand data on developments in Cairo under Ismail, with sections devoted to an historical and topographical description of the walled city. His views, however, did not favour the preservation of this heritage, but rather his work appears to have been written for the purpose of recording this information for the collective memory of future generations. The second work is that of the *Comité de la Conservation de l'Art Arabe* in 1881. Modelled on its European counterparts, the *Comité* consisted of a small group of the cultured Egyptian and European elite, entrusted to survey, index and restore Islamic monuments. This was an effective, vigorous and serious professional body enjoying a high reputation for the conservation of Islamic art and architecture. The work involved an extensive selection process of culturally-worthy buildings that were then added onto an index of monuments. From that moment the *wikalas, khans, madrasas, khanqas, hammams,* even palaces and houses, were centralised and controlled by the *Comité,* separating them from their endowments and from their integral role in the urban fabric. In many respects, the *Comité*'s role has been seen as a way of constructing an exotic theme park, a 'Disneyesque' world designed to bring the 'Arabian Nights' fantasy to life (cited in Ahmed, 2000: 7). The system of monument restoration operated reasonably well as long as the *Comité* received adequate funds from central government, however, monetary crises under British rule created obstacles to effective work.

The semi-preserved sanctity of the walled city provided a unique opportunity for Europeans to experience the 'old world', the world portrayed in the fictitious tales of the 'Arabian Nights'. This imaginary narrative became part of the mindset of travellers and artists to Cairo, sending home romantic depictions of a medieval world that had long since disappeared in Europe (Ahmed, 2000). Writers such as Edward Lane (1936) published detailed accounts of this medieval world in his book *An Account of the Manners and Customs of the Modern Egyptians*. Similarly, artists such as David Roberts, Carl Werner and Walter Cyndale, captured Oriental images of the traditional markets featuring crowded streets, and merchants wearing *gallabiyas* and turbans. These romantic visions encouraged Europeans to explore the East. Thomas Cook was quick to exploit these opportunities, holding a virtual monopoly on tourism to Egypt from 1880. Part of this exploitation was his own form of image-making represented in the numerous guidebooks that he produced, focusing more on the natural scenic beauty of the Nile, its traditional *dahabeah* sail boats and modern steamers, rather than on Cairo, which featured as a brief stopover in Cook's intense itinerary. Tourists in Cairo stayed in the somewhat lavish surroundings of the European-colonial style Shepheard Hotel, taking short excursions to the Pyramids at Giza and the Oriental bazaars – a mixture of 'culture' and 'nature', which European travellers had become accustomed to (Brendon, 1991).

The success of European tourism to Egypt was the result of the pervasive nature of Western-centric image manufacturers, best summarised by Gregory (2001: 132):

> This sense of enframing – of 'traditional' Egypt as a succession of framed pictures or a moving panorama – was an exceedingly powerful organising trope, but its power derived not only from enduring cultural convention but also from their mobilisation within a new actor-network.

The actors, of course, were travellers themselves whose accounts (imagined or real) described the different manners and customs of these strange cultures, the artists who provided visualisations of the tourist experience unlike anything in Europe, and finally, the tourist firms who provided safe, fast, reliable and comfortable means of travel. As for the walled city of Cairo, despite its decline, the policy to create a 'European' city had extraordinarily preserved its urban form relatively in tact. But the walled city was no longer a self-sustained entity, it had become a spectacle whose tradition was being consumed by the European tourist thirsty for the experience of the 'old' and the 'different'. Thus Cairo's physical heritage was monumentalised and its social and economic heritage reduced to the tourist gaze.

Post-revolution period

Mass tourism

The shift from popular tourism to mass tourism corresponds to a shift from a qualitative to quantitative notion, based on the proportion or volume of tourists participating in the tourist activity (Vanhove, 1997). The distinction is also made in the standardisation of the holiday package: the collective organisation of travelling, accommodating and integrating the tourist in a rigid and inflexible itinerary marketed to an undifferentiated clientele en masse (Vanhove, 1997). Thus the changing face of tourism in the late 20th century and the 21st century is better described as one of a change in degree rather than kind from the previous century. Greater wealth, shorter working hours and the provision of paid holidays have permeated to all social classes extending the leisure culture into patterns of global dimensions. The recreational and leisure needs of the tourist industry have created distinct leisure functions both within an urban and rural context. The recognition is that leisure is not only capable of creating the landscapes of resorts and theme parks, but also has an increasing potential to transform landscapes at a much wider scale, such as the conversion of rural areas for recreational purposes dominated by commercial values over conservation values. The same can be said with tourist-historic cities in which the concept of heritage tourism as a consumer product carries with it several biases to conservation based on a selection process restricted by the choice, fashion and taste of international organisations involved in the marketing of the heritage product, and the consumers.

The conscious move to protect the heritage product by the international community marks a double-edged sword for historic cities. The 20th century marked a number of important milestones formally constituting the protection of cultural heritage by organisations such as UNESCO, ICCROM, ICOM and ICOMOS. The concept of cultural heritage has been broadened to include historic monuments and works of art in both urban and rural settings (Jokilehto, 1999). Of particular importance, the 'World Heritage Convention' of 1972 outlined the need for the 'Protection of the World Cultural and Natural Heritage' by means of assessing whether cultural heritage sites were worthy to be inscribed on the UNESCO World Heritage List. But what did designation imply? To heritage sites it meant two things. First, governments were obliged to adhere to the recommendations and guidelines in the Venice Charter related to different aspects of safeguarding cultural heritage. More lucratively, inscription also guaranteed directed funding for conservation projects. On the other side of the balance sheet, sites placed on the World Heritage List became immediate targets for international tour operators interested in capitalising on this status-defined marketing tool. Thus many cities witnessed a dramatic rise of tourism once they had been officially inscribed as a 'World Heritage Site' posing an environmental threat to the very heritage protection for which is sought.

Cairo – World Heritage Site

The historic core of Cairo was internationally recognised as being of prime cultural significance only after its inscription in 1979. This event coincided with a politically motivated 'open-door' policy allowing for the first time, since the revolution of 1952, large numbers of foreign tourists to Egypt. As a result, package holidays to Egypt became readily available worldwide, luring tourists through a reinvention of the colonial past as depicted in tourist exhibits (Gregory, 2001: 141):

> . . . these guidebooks and brochures imply that we are not 'too late' – that we can steal a march on the anguish of 'belated Orientalism' – and that we can do so, ironically enough, by imaginatively transporting ourselves back to its definitive period. By accepting this invitation, responding to its visual interpolations, and situating ourselves as late Victorian and Edwardian tourists, we are assured (and, I think, reassured) that it is possible to regain an intimacy with a 'timeless' Egypt and – by virtue of the privileges that are attached to this subject-position – to guarantee the authenticity of this 'Orient'.

This quotation reflects a distinctive interpretation of Egypt fashioned by the tastes of tour operators and the modern tourist, undoubtedly colouring the way in which the state manages the image-building process.

Cairo's image is based on its physical heritage dictating to a large extent the spatial pattern of tourist attractions. However, state intervention in conservation and development policies constrains the tourist activity and limits its spatial boundaries (Nasser, 2000). Two antagonistic, yet compounding, forces are influencing the increasing segregation between tourist space and community space within the historic core: first, the impact of state policies, and second, the economic pressures arising from tourism. In tandem these forces are inducing spatial transformations undermining the continuity of the traditional urban fabric, as well as the balance between social needs and economic imperatives.

Cairo's urban landscape owes its appearance to the multitude of speculative developments by members of the ruling class responding to local opportunities and national economic cycles. The location and financing of growth depended largely on the effectiveness of commercial endowments to generate the necessary funds to maintain buildings that fostered cultural identity and socio-economic needs. The integration between development goals and conservation aims established a complex interdependence between the various urban components (Nasser, 2002). In today's context, conservation and development are controlled by two separate bodies: the Supreme Council of Antiquities (SCA) (originally the *Comité*), and the Ministry of Planning. Partner to these authorities, the centralised Ministry of Awqaf still remains the largest landowner in the walled city. The absence of a designated conservation area, and the sole reliance on the *Comité's* index, has further segregated the walled city into two components: the monuments and the urban fabric. The former is protected by an administrative layer, further protected by the Monuments Domain Decree (1980) prohibiting the renovation or development of buildings in proximity to monuments. The Decree stimulates the deterioration of adjacent buildings, in effect divorcing the monument from its urban milieu contrary to the traditional compact morphological structure characterised by groups of buildings clustered together (Nasser, forthcoming). The latter, on the other hand, is vulnerable to uncontrolled urban transformation.

The commercial potential generated by tourism underpins many of the state's restoration projects. Monuments located within the tourist trail are given priority, geographically distributed around the Khan al-Khalili bazaar area accessible from the major route al-Azhar Street, and Bein al-Qasrein. This concentrates the tourist activity within a well-defined district leading to the progressive domination of tourist service functions, particularly the specialisation of shops selling tourist goods, traditional cafés, restaurants and parking facilities on the al-Hussein Square. Attempts for rehabilitating monuments have been slow, hampered by bureaucratic barriers between the SCA in a restoration role and the Ministry of Awqaf as landowners. This explains the hiatus. Those monuments successfully rehabilitated are owned by the SCA. Wikalat al-Ghuri, for example, has been restored and converted into a cultural and handicrafts centre, charging entrance fees for tourists. The SCA has reserved the right to the revenues generated, failing to recycle benefits to the local community, breaking with the past method of cross-subsidisation that ensured commercial revenue supported the socio-cultural milieu. *Waqf* properties pose a different problem. The majority of registered monuments are owned by the Ministry of Awqaf, whose interest lies in their real-estate function. However, enforced low fixed-rents and the poor state of preservation have severely undermined their profitability. In many cases, buildings are let out to small-scale manufacturers and squatters. Religious buildings are in less danger of demolition because they are still an integral part of daily life; however, *wikalas* are threatened by demolition due to the loss of their original function. As a result, many *wikalas* have been removed from the register, and the land converted to freehold tenure. This has a significant impact on Cairo's historical plot pattern, which has been preserved largely by the pervasive nature of *waqf* boundaries.

Unregulated changing land-uses are simultaneously destroying traditional forms. Land values are one indicator of land-use patterns determined by ease of accessibility and the financial profitability for development. The distribution of land values in the walled city corresponds to the tourist district, reaching its highest values in the Khan al-Khalili and decreasing proportionately from the centre. The value of land in the bazaar area has become the highest priced in Cairo encouraging property owners to demolish their unprofitable houses and sell the land or redevelop it to commercial uses. The gradual displacement of residential buildings by commercial functions is creating an imbalance in land-uses. Historically, the clustering of commercial and cultural buildings consistently had a residential dimension, whether it was for the foreign merchants, the proletariat or the elite. Functional conversion is leading to a loss of mixed land-use and the appearance of new building types. Meyer (1990) reported a 'new type' of high-rise *wikala* on the periphery of the Khan al-Khalili district specialising in workshops producing mainly simple consumer goods to meet the growing demand of the tourist industry. Changes in the socio-economic profile of the merchants has resulted in the conversion of crafts once demanded by the local population becoming the province of the tourist only, establishing Khan al-Khalili as the centre of the retail trade. Retail prices in Khan al-Khalili are too high for the local population, goods are unaffordable, but also land prices have increased sharply, displacing traditional retailers with outside investors (Meyer, 1990). The quality of many of the new peripheral developments bear no reference to their historical context, neither in form, height or volume further eroding the area's historicity. The distortion of the character of the area and the creation of an 'outsider' zone has marginalised the local community from participating or benefiting from the tourist activity. In essence, the tourist activity has separated the community from its physical heritage. This has created a major imbalance in the relationship between the place, its users and the activities it harbours.

Conclusions

This chapter has traced the way in which the changing nature of tourism has impacted on the evolution of Cairo. On the global scale, Cairo's rise and fall has been mostly influenced by the shift from a Middle Eastern-centred position during the Islamic era to a peripheral position in relation to a strengthening Europe. This European-centred stance placed Cairo in a different category, that of the 'Orient', featuring less and less as an integrated trade partner, but rather a commodity catering for European-colonialist leisure and taste. This phenomenon was aided by the appearance of the steamboats and railways which gradually eroded the caravan traffic that had characterised travel in the region.

On the regional and local scale, Cairo's colourful history – trade monopolies, military campaigns, plagues and famine – all contributed to cycles in Cairo's growth and prosperity. The *khans, wikalas* and *madrasas* give testimony to their patrons, powerful rulers, *amirs* (knights), their wives and daughters, and wealthy merchants, who over centuries transformed Cairo's urban landscape contributing to its cultural heritage. Not just a physical heritage, but also a social and economic heritage that can still be seen today. The heritage is based on a complex relationship between social and physical planning. The urban elite were the keystone in this relationship, not just in their capacity as major urban landowners, but more importantly in their role as patrons of social welfare, which they exploited through the *waqf* system. Spatially, these activities were concentrated in the public domain, a feature common to many city-types based on land value distribution; nevertheless in Cairo this played an increasingly important role. In a large part, Cairo owes its development to its Fatimid heritage, which influenced the spatial development of its public domain, of which political values associated with the great palaces provided the impetus of growth in this way. Growth and contraction came in response to changes in Cairo's position in the global economy, markets were created, buildings adapted and residential buildings replaced by commercial land-uses, in the process changing Cairo's urban landscape. Most importantly, the *waqf* system contributed substantially to the sustainability of Cairo's urban form in three ways. First, it provided an internal means of financing development and conservation projects through cross-subsidisation. Second, profitability of commercial *waqf* was underpinned by the economy and the land market, which influenced its distribution within the city. Third, the pervasive nature of *waqf* property law safeguarded the traditional plot pattern. What is pertinent, however, is that buildings, spaces and activities were sufficiently integrated to fulfil the needs and aspirations of the local community by underpinning their livelihood and sustaining their cultural heritage. In short, tourism was a socio-economic activity engaging regional and local people.

The commodification of tourism in Cairo showed that space was becoming segregated; tourism was claiming space for the consumers (and the producers of consumer products). These spaces tend to overlap with areas selected for the tourist activity based on a number of factors. First, state conservation and development policies are based on building-selectivity. The first selection process singles out the monuments from their urban milieu. A second selection process provides a handful of 'showcase' monuments for conservation and development. Second, the selection is also influenced by ease of accessiblity to the main artery, al-Azhar Street. Third, tourism has become the city's exclusive economy placing tremendous pressure on landowners, craftsmen and retailers to cater for the demand in tourism, thus leading to functional conversion.

In conclusion, the symbiotic relationship between the physical, social and economic environment that Cairo enjoyed before the 19th century has been disrupted by the way the tourist activity has fragmented these components. Tourism has raised the economic potential for the walled city and can provide the vehicle for urban regeneration and conservation. The keystone is a reunification of social and physical planning by:

(1) Recycling revenues generated from viable activities such as those associated with tourism to the conservation and rehabilitation of historic buildings, but also for the development of other community buildings and activities.
(2) Uniting the historic fabric with the rest of the walled city to be considered for conservation and development *in toto*.
(3) Safeguarding the traditional urban texture through property laws, guidelines and the promotion of the robust building type characteristic of the area.

In this way, tourism becomes an internalised and local activity, helping to sustain the social activities, cultural needs and the built heritage.

References

Abu Lughod, J. (1971) *Cairo 1001 of the City Victorious*. Princeton: Princeton University Press.

Ahmed, H.F. (2000) The making of a Cairo: The city of the one thousand and one nights. In M. Robinson *et al.* (eds) *Developments in Urban and Rural Tourism* (pp. 3–19). Conference in Sheffield, 2–7 September 2000.

al-Maqrizi, T. (1853) *Al-Mawa'iz wa al-itibar fi khitat* (2 vols). Cairo: Bulaq Press.

Ashworth, G.J. (1995) Managing the cultural tourist. In G.J. Ashworth and A.G.J. Dietvorst (eds) *Tourism and Spatial Transformations: Implications for Policy and Planning* (pp. 265–85). Wallingford: CAB International.

Ashworth G.J. and Tunbridge, J.E. (1990) *The Tourist Historic City.* London: Belhaven.

Baer, G. (1964) *Egyptian Guilds in Modern Times.* Jerusalem: The Israel Oriental Society.

Brendon, P. (1991) *Thomas Cook: 150 Years of Popular Tourism.* London: Secker & Warburg.

Dietvorst, A.G.J. (1995) Tourist behaviour and the Importance of time-space analysis. In G.J. Ashworth and A.G.J. Dietvorst (eds) *Tourism and Spatial Transformations: Implications for Policy and Planning* (pp. 163–83). Wallingford: CAB International.

Eickelman, D.F. and Piscatori, J. (1990) Social theory in the study of Muslim societies. In D.F. Eickelman and J. Piscatori (eds) *Muslim Travellers: Pilgrimage, Migration, and the Religious Imagination* (pp. 3–29). London: Routledge.

Fakhouri, H. (1985) An ethnographic survey of a Cairene neighbourhood – the Darb al-Ahmar district. *Journal of the American Research Centre in Egypt* xxii.

Gellens, S.I. (1990) The search for knowledge in medieval Muslim societies: A comparative approach. In D.F. Eickelman and J. Piscatori (eds) *Muslim Travellers: Pilgrimage, Migration, and the Religious Imagination* (pp. 50–69). London: Routledge.

Gregory, D. (2001) Colonial nostalgia and cultures of travel: Spaces of constructed visibility in Egypt. In N. AlSayyad (ed.) *Consuming Tradition, Manufacturing Heritage: Global Norms and Urban Forms in the Age of Tourism* (pp. 111–152). London: Routledge.

Hoexter, M. (1998) *Endowments, Rulers and Community, and Waqf al-Haramayn in Ottoman Algiers.* Leiden: Brill.

Ibn Khaldun (1951) *At-Tarikh bi-Ibn Khaldun wa Rihlatuhu Gharban wa Sharqan* (M. Ibn Tawit al-Tanji, ed.), Cairo.

Jansen-Verbeke, M. (1997) Urban tourism: Managing resources and visitors. In S. Wahab and J.J. Pigram (eds) *Tourism, Development and Growth: The Challenge for Sustainability* (pp. 237–57). London: Routledge.

Jansen-Verbeke, M. and Wiel, E. van de (1995) Tourism Planning in urban revitalisation projects: Lessons from the Amsterdam waterfront development. In G.J. Ashworth and A.G.J. Dietvorst (eds) *Tourism and Spatial Transformations: Implications for Policy and Planning* (pp. 129–47). Wallingford: CAB International.

Jokilehto, J. (1999) *A History of Architectural Conservation.* Oxford: Butterworth-Heinmann.

Lane, E. (1936) *The Manners and Customs of the Modern Egyptians* (1st edition of 1908 as reprinted by J.M.). London: Dent.

MacKensie, N. (1992) *Ayyubid Cairo: A Topographical Study.* Cairo: American University in Cairo Press.

Meyer, G. (1990) Economic and social change in the old city of Cairo. Paper presented to the *24th Annual Meeting of the Middle East Studies Association of North America*, Texas.

Mubarak, A. (1888) *Al-Khitat al-Tawfiqqiyya al-Jadeeda li-Misr was Muduniha wa Biladiha al-Qadimah wa al-Mahrusah* (20 vols). Bulaq: Mataba'a al-Kubra al-Amirriyya.

Nasser, N. (2000) Urban design principles of a historic part of Cairo: A dialogue for sustainable urban regeneration. Unpublished PhD thesis, Birmingham, University of Central England.

Nasser, N. (2001) A study in Islamic urban morphology: The case of Cairo. Paper published in the proceedings of the *International Seminar on Urban Form* (pp. 141–44), September 2001, Cincinnati.

Nasser, N. (2002) Can traditional urban design principles be reconciled with the contemporary needs for sustainable urban regeneration? Paper presented at the conference on *Conservation and Regeneration of Traditional Urban Centres in the Islamic World: Learning from Regional Experiences and Building Partnerships*, January 2002, Amman, Jordan.

Nasser, N. (forthcoming) Reconciling conservation and tourism – the challenge for urban continuity in the historic part of Cairo. In R. Zetter and G. Butina-Watson (eds) *Designing Sustainable Cities in the Developing World*. London: Asghate.

Newby, P.T. (1994) Tourism – support or threat to heritage? In G.J. Ashworth and P.J. Larkham (eds) *Building a New Heritage: Tourism, Culture, and Identity* (pp. 206–29). London: Routledge.

Pearson, M.N. (1994) *Pious Passengers: The Hajj in Earlier Times*. London: Hurst.

Raymond, A. (1993) *Le Caire*. Paris: Fayard.

Raymond, A. and Wiet, G. (1979) *Les Marchés du Caire*. Cairo: Institut Francais de Archaeologie.

Rodenbeck, M. (1998) *Cairo: The City Victorious*. London: Picador.

Sims, E. (1978) Markets and caravanserais. In G. Michell (ed.) *Architecture of the Islamic World: Its History and Social Meaning* (pp. 97–111). New York: William Morrow.

Staffa, J. (1977) *Conquest and Fusion: The Social Evolution of Cairo AD 642–1850*. Leiden: Brill.

Stewart, D. (1999) Changing Cairo: The political economy of urban form. *Internal Journal of Urban and Regional Research* 23, 128–46.

Towner, J. (1996) *An Historical Geography of Recreation and Tourism in the Western World 1540–1940*. Chichester: Wiley.

Vanhove, N. (1997) Mass tourism: Benefits and costs. In S. Wahab and J.J. Pigram (eds) *Tourism, Development and Growth: The Challenge for Sustainability* (pp. 50–78). London: Routledge.

Chapter 3

From One Globalization to Another: In Search of the Seeds of Modern Tourism in the Levant, a Western Perspective

XAVIER GUILLOT

Introduction – 'Traveling in the Orient': The Codification of an Itinerary

In the last third of the 20th century, international tourism in the world had undergone spectacular development: it became the first industry of the world in the revenue it generates every year. Although the progress of this industry in the Middle East was slowed by the instability of the regional political situation, it did not entirely miss out on this economic opportunity. The cases of Egypt, and more recently, countries of the Bilad El Sham, the historical region previously known as Greater Syria, and today covering Syria, Lebanon, Jordan, the Occupied Palestinian Territory and Israel – are examples of nations that are nowadays part of the global tourism industry.

In this respect, some authors have pointed out conflicting situations accompanying the development of this industry, which is mainly generated and managed by western firms (Lanfant, 1995; Robinson, 2001). To accommodate the growing number of travelers, cities have undergone major transformations. This is particularly obvious with the growth of high-rise five-star hotels in large cities, managed by international chains, which have become modern urban icons. Transformation has also occurred in rural areas. In this domain other authors have denounced the misuse of local culture, whereby specific patterns (i.e. the nomadic Arab culture) rather than others are marketed in order to please the western traveler (Daher, 1999; Shoup, 1985). These transformations are to be associated with the structural changes that have occurred in the economy and society over the last 30 years, and which are also representative of the emergence of a so-called 'global culture' (Featherstone, 1996).

However, despite the importance of the physical, social and cultural changes associated with global tourism, these changing patterns are not entirely new, nor is the process behind it. For centuries the Middle East has been a destination for western travelers with assorted motives. Traders, writers, pilgrims and simply the curious were attracted by the 'mysterious Orient' and the religious historical background that characterized this part of the world. Already, in the late 19th century, the Bilad El Sham could be considered as a 'prime cultural tourist destination' in a modern sense. In 1930, *The Handbook of Palestine and Transjordan*, published by Macmillan and Co. in London, presented Palestine literally as 'a tourist resort' (Luke & Roach, 1930: 140).[1]

This 'early modern period of tourism' did not occur without significant local 'adaptation' to meet the demands and comfort of western travelers. It generated important transformation in local economies and societies. As tourists' numbers increased, one sees the emergence of a new set of facilities and infrastructures allowing this population to move around easily and to settle temporarily in a region that was largely unknown to them. Looking at this early phase of modern tourism leads us to put international mass tourism into perspective as a long-term cycle evolving industry, and to evaluate its current development patterns more objectively.

Indeed, if progress made in transportation and telecommunication since the Second World War (air transport, satellite communication, in particular), marks the beginning of the current global and mass tourism phenomena, this progress should not overshadow those which occurred a century earlier, and which have similarly revolutionized human transportation and communication at the world scale. For example, following the opening of the Suez Canal in 1869, the entire Orient was connected to the west by the telegraph. In 1870, Jerusalem was connected to Europe – the same year as Singapore. At the same time, steamers were crossing the Mediterranean Sea and regular lines were already operational. In fact, already in the last third of the 19th century, traveling to the Orient had become a relatively easy and schedulable enterprise, whether by sea or by land.

This chapter is about this 'travel revolution' that occurred during the last third of the 19th century and at the turn of the next century. It is about the construction of an idea as well as a new industry that took place at the same time as the 'first globalization'.[2] It aims to understand the birth of this industry and its development by identifying four crucial agents or 'operators,' which until now have been concomitant with the 'functioning' of this industry in its most recent version: transportation, accommodation, specialized literature and package tours.

The 19th Century Transportation Revolution: Making the Journey to the Orient 'Schedulable'

Transportation and progress linked to the industrial revolution, is the first operator to be examined. Until the middle of the 19th century, traveling to the Middle East was largely an individual adventure, greatly depending on the weather (if sailing), or security, if traveling by land. In both cases, it was a long and dangerous journey. Being blocked in harbors for several weeks due to weather conditions was common. It is known that Chateaubriand spent more time waiting for favorable winds to sail out of Egypt than in visiting the country itself. Traveling to the Orient was also an expensive journey. One needed strong motivations to travel on such a visit. Chateaubriand spent almost 50,000 francs on his travel, while Lamartine spent double this amount for the expedition he organized in 1832–3. Volney dedicated all the money he inherited to finance his enterprise (Berchet, 1985).

The development of the steam engine and the improvement of security on the Mediterranean after the end of the conflict between Greece and Turkey, revolutionized traveling conditions between Europe and the Middle East. In the spring of 1833, the steamship *François 1st* was given the green light. She embarked on an experimental cruise to Greece with 50 guests of King Othon. At the end of the decade, the Messageries Françaises of the Austrian Lloyd already had regular lines, in particular for the postal service between Europe, Turkey, Greece and Egypt. Regular lines multiplied after 1840, for instance between Constantinople and Beirut, through Smyrna, Rhodes and Cyprus.

River transport has also played its part in facilitating tourism growth. After the Paris Congress of 1866, which regulated international traffic, it became possible to travel to the Middle East by cruising the Danube River to the Black Sea, from which it was then possible to reach Istanbul by land. From this time on, travel become a 'schedulable trip.' In *The Fellah*, Edmond About declares with pride that 'the fast train could carry you from Paris to Marseille in 16 hours, and the postal ship of the Messagerie put Alexandria at 6 days sailing from Marseille' (Berchet, 1985). This timing would not change until the First World War and until the first commercial flights started operating.

In addition to steamships, the invention of the steam engine is also associated with rail transport, which was another important means of transportation, both in accessing the Middle East from the west, and for movement within the region. It first appeared in 1850 in Egypt with the Delta Network, and later in the Bilad El Sham. At the turn of the century most of the large cities were connected to each other by railway: Jerusalem was connected to Jaffa, and Damascus to Beirut and Mecca by the Hijaz railway. From Europe, in 1884 it was possible to access the Black Sea with the Wagon Lits Company, which operated the Paris–Varna line. In 1890, the famous Orient Express reached Istanbul from where it was possible to access other parts of Bilad El Sham. The last great enterprise in this domain was the construction of the railway to Baghdad from Istanbul, via Aleppo, which was completed in 1914.

Improved traveling mechanization and increased speed mobility not only occurred on long distance transportation. It is also seen at the 'local level' within the cities. As early as 1904, in Damascus, the Société Impériale Ottoman de Tramway et d'éclairage Electrique de Damas was contracted by the Ottoman government to build tramway lines and to produce and distribute electrical power. In 1907, two lines of 3 km and 2 km were operating and were later extended. In Beirut in 1906, an Ottoman Company had the same type of concession as in Damascus and, as early as 1914, three lines were already operating. Parallel to the beginning of the tramway, the automobile appeared in cities in the 1920s, and in the same decade, all the gates of the city of Damascus had been adapted to fit the use of the automobile.

It is in this highly competitive context, at the turn of the century that travel to the Middle East became fast, easy and schedulable. It is from this revolution in the material condition of transportation that modern tourism was born.

Settling Temporarily in the Middle East: from Basic Accommodation to Modern Hotels

Being able to access distant destinations rapidly and in comfort is not the only operator in the development of tourism. Upon arrival at his/her destination, the tourist needs specific facilities to make the visit feasible. Among them, accommodation is a priority. Until the middle of the 19th century western travelers were accommodated in places that were not tourist hotels as such. Travelers of special status, such as government officials, writers or scientists would stay at the consul house of their own country. Pilgrims would naturally stay in religious communities.

If travelers did not fit into the above-mentioned categories, they would have to rely on what the local culture offered. Outside cities, they relied on the hospitality of local families, or improvised in tents. In cities, they often stayed in monasteries that were primarily used by pilgrims. The monastery of Mont Carmel at Jaffa was well known for providing accommodation when European travelers reached the Levant for the first time. Beirut also had such places. Inland, Jerusalem had several hostels linked to religious communities that welcomed all kinds of travelers, such as the Franciscan Casanova and the Austrian Hospice. Built in the mid-19th century, these hostels still operate with the same status as being a place for both pilgrims and cultural tourists.[3]

Khans, also called caravanserai, represented another popular alternative. The word khan, from the Turkish, means hotel. It is a specific building type that developed in cities of Muslim influence from Central Asia to the Atlantic. Its design is generally characterized by a rectangular courtyard distributing rooms at the periphery that were used for trade or sleeping. Because of its enclosed shape, the building had a capacity of isolation from the exterior life, but because of its commercial function it was connected to the city life. This double aspect welcomed foreigners while keeping them away. There were many of these khans in cities such as Damascus, Aleppo or Beirut, which were major trading centers in Bilad El Sham.[4] In Beirut, a major point of arrival for travelers coming from the west, one could find two types of khans: the khans for trading composed of two stories, and khans for travelers, some of them more often used by western travelers.[5] Comfort in khans was, however, very basic. There was no furniture. Usually, travelers had to bring their own carpet for use as a bed, their *machlah* (coat) as a blanket, and their own provisions (Guys, 1847).

The first move towards lodging providing western standards of comfort can be traced through the construction of *locandas*: an Italian word that was often used to refer to hotels or pensions for western travelers. Usually *locandas* were owned by entrepreneurs from Malta, Italy or Greece. The first *locanda* in the region was built in 1843 by Antonio Bianchi. It had the appearance of an old house surrounded by a garden. Georges Robinson (1837) writes in his diary: 'the 20 September 1830, I found here what I was not ready to find in the region, that is an excellent pension managed by a Maltais whose name is Giuseppe. It is, I think the only place to stay in all Syria that deserves this name.' For a lot of travelers, staying in a *locanda* was like being back in their own country. John Durbin, the former director of Dockinson College in Pennsylvania, writes: 'our guide brought us to the Hotel Baptista where there were comfortable rooms in comparison to what we found since we left Cairo, and again, we heard language and found the manner of Europe. The arrival in Beirut was a bit like coming back home' (Durbin, 1854: 48–9). In the second part of the 19th century, these *locandas* started to adopt names other than that of their owners, in order to recall hotels found in the west.[6] But despite these new names, these hotels were rather rudimentary comfort-wise. In fact, they were old oriental houses adapted to accommodate travelers. Hotels specifically designed and built to accommodate foreigners did not yet exist.

The first modern-style hotel that offered some of the comforts of Europe, was opened in Jaffa in the 1850s by Kopel Blatner and Sons. Tourist accommodation improved further when Cook opened his office in Jaffa in 1870. Built at the same time in Beirut, the Grand Hotel d'Orient was probably the first building designed and built as a hotel.[7] The Grand and the Hotel Bellevue – where Cook opened his second office – were the two famous hotels in the district of Zeitouneh (Borgi, 1995).

However, up until the First World War, these types of hotels were rare. It was during the Mandate period that hotel construction increased and spread to more remote areas. Henceforth it was possible to find hotels in culturally interesting areas, such as archeological sites, which also became more accessible. These same hotels are today heritage sites. Despite this increase in number, no specific innovations were noted during this period.[8] Changes were more quantitative than qualitative.[9] In cities, besides khans, a mix of different types of western facilities was to be found: convents, hospices, *locandas* and hotels. Jerusalem, a major pole of tourist attraction, if not the most visited by western travelers, is outstanding because of the telescoping of different types of hotels and the different types of travelers they represent. This 'telescopage' is still present today.

The Publication of the First Tourist Guide and the Invention of a 'Levantin Space'

In addition to safe, fast travel, with comfortable accommodation, there is a third type of requirement by the traveler: information regarding destination. Indeed, both in order to make a decision, and once having arrived, the traveler needs to decide where to go and how to get there. In response to this need, a special type of literature appeared in the middle of the 19th century: the tourist guide.

Publishers of tourist guides benefited from the large heritage literature written by western travelers to the region over the centuries. Because of its strong connection with religion, this region had been a prolific source of inspiration for travelers since the Middle Ages, reaching a peak in the 18th and early 19th centuries. Besides religion, the Middle East was an important field of research for scientific missions, in particular in the field of archeology.[10] It is therefore not surprising that the content of the first tourist guides was built on both sources of knowledge, mixing ethnographic data randomly gathered by travel writers, and more historical and geographical information reported by scientists on specific missions. It is also not surprising that the first publication of tourist guides was the work of one of these scientists.

It was in England that the tourist guide made its first appearance, with the publication of Murray's *HandBook* in 1840, and translated into French in 1846, under the name *Le guide en Orient de Quetin*. One should recall that in the early 19th century, tourism in the Middle East was primarily a British interest because of its world domination after 1815. As Berchet (1985) reminds us, before the Suez Canal construction, the Nile delta was on the route to India for families, as well as for military. One disembarked at Alexandria, to re-embark in Suez after having visited the Pyramids. In this way, traveling in this region became popular: one saw the first groups in Palestine in the form of tourism pilgrims.

For two decades, the Murray guide remained the only reference until Joanne (French), and Baedeker (German) publishers released their own original guides in France and Germany. The first edition of the 'Guide Joanne' was published in 1861 and entitled: *Un itinéraire descriptif, historique et archéologique de l'Orient* (*A Descriptive, Historical and Archeological Itinerary of the Orient*). It was a volume of more than 1100 pages.[11] In Germany, the first edition of the Baedeker guide, published in 1882, was based on the work of the famous orientalist Albert Socin from Bale. Following editions kept in line with its original scientific data, as from 1891, it was regularly revised and augmented by Dr I. Benzinger who lived and had extensively traveled in the Middle East.

At the end of the 19th century, the Murray, Joanne and Baedecker guides had become major references for English, French and German tourists. Their influence in shaping and homogenizing traveling patterns deserves special mention. Indeed, approaches to introducing this region were rather similar from one guide to another, and eventually the Baedeker was translated into French and English. Although scientific knowledge was a high priority, it was always balanced by chapters dedicated to practical information. Each of these guides was more or less used the same strategy and gave three types of information, as follows:

(1) Practical information covering all types of data, and reflect the modernization of the region. E.g. accommodation, transport, currency, food, climate, language, etc.
(2) Itinerary – suggested routes and timings, descriptions of places of interest.
(3) Detailed maps of countries and cities.

These three guides largely contributed to what Berchet called the creation of a 'Levantin Space' (Berchet, 1985). Indeed, until the end of the 18th century, travelers, and in particular scientists, used local travelers' caravans and were more or less guided by fate. As one entered the 19th century, travelers were becoming less adventurous. Progressing in time, itineraries followed by writers went through a reverse transformation to that of the scientific traveler. The idea of 'Travel in the Orient'[12] became codified and travelers no longer risked leaving the main well-traveled routes.

Suggested itineraries presented in tourist guides were in fact largely influenced by itineraries elaborated by 19th century travel writers. Travels by Flaubert, Maxime du Camp or Chateaubriand, for instance, offered the 'model of an ideal trip': Egypt, Palestine, Lebanon, Constantinople and Greece. It was this 'circular itinerary' (Berchet, 1985) copied again and again that the 'Guide Joanne' codified, with some alternatives and some recommendations, such as winter in Egypt, Easter in Jerusalem, etc.

The publication of Cook's *Help Book* was largely inscribed in this process. As with previous guides, it suggested a specific itinerary for exploring the region and gave all practical advice to achieve it.[13] Cook's *Help Book* reinforced this process by bringing it a step further in terms of information provided for the tourist's visit to the region. In addition to cultural facts and practical information (such as best time of traveling, cheapest ways, etc.), one could find an additional section called the *Help Book* advertiser: a list of hotels, shops, transportation companies recommended by Cook, and responding to the standard demands of the 'Cookies.' What is remarkable with Thomas Cook's contribution to the emerging tourism industry is that he was not only a publisher, but also an entrepreneur. Indeed, Cook symbolizes the transformation of leisure traveling into a specific industry through the implementation of a network of services advertised in his publication, and at the same time through the implementation of a new approach to traveling – the 'organized tour.'

Traveling in a 'Suitable Social Environment': The Invention of the Organized Tour

After several years of investigation, Thomas Cook decided, in 1869 (the year in which the Suez Canal opened) to launch the first tour of 10 travelers (led by him personally) through Palestine and Egypt. Between 1869 and 1883, organized tours by Cook brought about 4500 travelers to Palestine, which according to him, accounted for approximately two-thirds of the total number of tourists arriving from the west.[14]

Although the role of Thomas Cook in popularizing organized tours in the Middle East is indisputable, the idea of designing and selling such tours was not originally his. Religious groups and pilgrims from Europe had invented the concept earlier. Tours had been organized in the early 1850s by Roman Catholic groups from Italy, traveling by the Lloyd Triestino steamship line, and from France, tours were organized by the order of St Vincent de Paul, starting from Marseille twice a year, at Easter and in August. There were also tours from the United States. Ruth Kark (2001) recorded an organized 'leisure trip' to Palestine in 1867, initiated by Henry Ward Beecher's Plymouth Church. It was an important package tour for 150 Americans, and comprised a visit to Europe and then to Egypt and Palestine.

Thomas Cook followed in the footsteps of these religious tours. By combining piety with commerce, Cook's Eastern Tours helped transform Palestine from a *Terra Sancta* for pilgrims, as it had been for generations, into a destination for tourists who were not ready to spend time preparing their travel, or to accept unpredictable travel conditions. This is the very fundamental of mass tourism that Cook was the first to exploit: targeting an English and American middle-class Protestant clientele, with no experience in traveling far from their home, by offering them ready-made and safe travel. It should be noted that Cook's Eastern Tours, although group tours, were not cheap. A trip to Palestine in the 1860s averaged 31 shillings a day, including accommodation, dragoman, military escort and provisions imported from Britain.

Almost everything was paid in advance, reducing the risk of robbery. In 1873, for the journey to Palestine, Cook used the railways to Genoa and Trieste, or the Danube Steam Navigation to Varna on the Black Sea. From the Mediterranean ports, steamers took travelers to Alexandria, Port Said, Jaffa and Beirut.

To make the tourist's journey successful, Cook created a 'suitable social environment' by offering comfortable hotels, hygienic food and water, and finding a reliable dragoman, etc. It was reported that Cook acquired a house and grounds in 1875, near the Jaffa Gate of Jerusalem, and threatened to concentrate business in this house if local contractors and hoteliers 'do not treat our travelers and ourselves as they and we ought to be treated' (Kark, 2001). At the end of the century, however, many new hostels and hotels were built. Several hotels such as the Jerusalem, Mediterranean or the New Grand agreed on arrangements with Cook's travel agency. In 1903, Cook had three offices in Palestine (in David Street, Jerusalem, the German Colony in Jaffa, and near Hotel Carmel in Haifa) (Kark, 2001: 166). Simultaneously, other tourist agencies such as Tadras, Clark, Hamburg, Barakat and Nasir and Farjalla, were found besides Cook's, as competitors in the market. From now on, touring the Orient entered a new era because of the economic and cultural implications of the presence of western travelers.

As traveler numbers increased, the local activity and economy developed. Commissioners could be hired to help passengers disembark, release luggage from customs, and secure lodgings, horses and carriages. Ferrying and wagon services were available, as well as hundreds of porters, guides and escorts. Local firms proliferated. Restaurants and cafés multiplied: in Jaffa there were 64 restaurants and 81 coffeehouses in 1905 (Kark, 2001). This deployment of human activity demonstrates that one century ago social, economic and cultural implications at the local level linked with the development of tourism at the international level was already in place. Because of the profit to be made by western firms, a profession was born, as well as an industry, which is now the most profitable in the world.

Conclusion: The Legacy of the 19th Century in Today's Tourism Industry in the Middle East

Since Thomas Cook and his son first lead tourist groups to the Holy Land, and globalization entered a new phase, the tourism industry has also entered a new phase in its evolution. In the second part of the 20th century low-cost travel enabling access to virtually all parts of the world, has developed, and international hotel companies offering western standards can be found in all main cities. Tourism has entered the mass media. Travel literature and tourist guides have become an industry. Simultaneously, the concept of international mass tourism has emerged in developing countries with, in many cases, irreversible consequences on space and societies. Yet, although the 'tourism production system' has radically changed qualitatively and quantitatively, the operators that we have identified in our review of the growth of tourism in the Middle East remain valid. What has changed from 'one globalization to another' is the reinforcement of a culture of tourism and international mobility with the transformation of some of the features that characterized modern tourism during its first period.

(1) The first characteristic is the process of 'individuation' that charac- terizes modern tourism patterns. 'It involves specific cultural practices governing what is seen, how it is seen, the composition of tour groups, the behavior of individuals and the group during the tourist experience, and so on' (Feiffer, 1985; see also MacCannell, 1989). With the birth of modern transport, comfortable hotels and regularly updated travel guides, traveling to the Orient became schedulable, comfortable and safe. Package tours are nowadays increasingly designed to satisfy particular individual choices, be they cultural, sport or health oriented. Furthermore, business and leisure are increasingly linked with travelers' motives. Organized tours by Cook were a stage in this process that tends to satisfy individual choices, as well as using economic scale advantages. As Britton says,

> there was a long-term trend in Western society towards recog- nizing the individual as distinct from the group. This in turn has facilitated: (a) a corresponding differentiation and specialization of leisure pursuits; and (b) the linkage of personal status of 'indi- vidual identity' (with corresponding differentiation of life-styles and experiences) through the consumption of commodities. (Britton, 1991: 460)

(2) The word 'commodity' associated with tourism leads us to the second characteristic of today's tourism patterns. In the second globalization, tourism has become a commodified product. In one way, Cook initiated the process with his organized tours, combined with his handbook, and by incorporating an advertising section, making the organized tour a true commodity. In its most recent development, the novelty is that leisure activities have become increasingly commodi- fied as a 'culture of consumption' has evolved (Featherstone, 1990). As Britton pointed out,

> the expansion of deepening of commodity markets has witnessed the transfer of the logic and rationality of commodity production to the sphere of consumption and culture. This process comple- ments, yet subverts, the trend towards individuation of leisure, with the personalization and differentiation of leisure products expressed in market niching, cosmetic design, variations, and

advertising disguising the industrialization and mass production of such products. (Britton, 1991: 461)

(3) In the individuation of leisure, there is an important paradox: as people become more and more individualistic in traveling choices, simultaneously they become more and more dependent on a larger set of facilities and infrastructures, such as transportation and communication networks (Gras, 1993). Until the First World War the nature of this individuation-dependency relationship remained relatively stable. After this date, it evolved significantly as globalization entered its second phase of development. Modernity and individuation of daily life during the 20th century relies on the presence and the use of what Giddens called 'expert systems' and 'symbolic tokens' (Giddens, 1990), which interfere in every part of our daily lives : large sets of infrastructures, facilities, such as cars, money, etc.

Newly formed Arab nations that once composed the Bilad El Sham have not been exempt from modern tourism patterns, although it has not yet reached the magnitude of other parts of the world. First Lebanon in the 1950s and 1960s, then Jordan, and more recently, to a certain extent Syria; these three counties are nowadays equipped with the 'basic modern infrastructures,' such as highways, airports, international hotels, to mention a few, that are associated with international mass tourism.

This evolution did not occur without significant impact on places visited by tourists and local communities inhabiting these places. In Petra (Jordan), for instance, camping as it was established by Cook[15] in the midst of the Nabatean city was naturally part of history. Within the last 30 years, Wadi Musa, the adjacent village has developed into a stop-over town for tourists, and comprises a range of accommodation including renowned international hotels, such as Movenpick and Marriott. Nowadays, Petra is on the backpackers' trail as well as on the map of all kinds of organized tours, including those *wonders of the world* for fortunate corporate travelers who visit the so-called World Heritage Sites in minimum time.[16] In the middle of the ruins of Palmyra (Syria), the small stand-alone structure Hotel Zanobia, built in the early 20th century, witnesses another era of tourism. Once part of a settlement that had grown randomly within the ruins, and otherwise famous during the Mandate period for its eccentric French female manager,[17] it has become today an isolated structure, since the ruins were cleared of the local population and habitat. Tourist hotels are located farther removed in the town of Tadmore.

Although Petra and Palmyra represent emblematic examples of the evolution of tourism practice – the individuation and consuming pattern as mentioned above – it is nevertheless significant of the very selective process that accompanies the growth of international cultural tourism, and of the focus that some sites deserve more than others. One should notice that some specific sites are very well known and placed on a world tourist map (such as those belonging to the World Heritage List by UNESCO) and others are not.

One of the implications of the growth of international cultural tourism is the process of 'hygienification' of cultural sites that is occurring at the same time – cultural sites are isolated from the local domestic life and treated as special social and economical entities. This separation is a process that accompanies the implication of new players in the development, in particular in cultural tourism and the so-called management of cultural sites. As international cultural labels are given, such as the 'World Heritage' of UNESCO, local authorities must comply with specific norms, in term of restoration and tourism management. Simultaneously, touring the Orient is now becoming an integrated industry that is heavily controlled by strong organizations, which are not only in the hands of individuals and private entrepreneurs, but also under the control of international private corporations and public and semi-public organizations.

Gaining access to this status has become a prime concern for local communities and nations because of economic implications in terms of tourism. This normative international labeling system, and the technical and political struggle to comply with it, is perhaps the new type of operator that has emerged over the last few decades, and that is representative of the evolution of the tourism industry in the second globalization, marking its difference with the first.

Notes

1. 'Palestine as a resort for tourists possesses unique attractions, religious, historical, climatic and archeological, which need to be enlarged upon here. . . . By the quickest route, under normal conditions, Palestine is reached from London in six to seven days and from Cairo in fifteen hours. The best season to visit Palestine is from January to June' (Luke & Roach, 1930)
2. In using the expression 'First globalization,' I refer here to a discussion I had in Amman in June 2003 with historian Henry Laurens specialized in the Middle East, and quote him. Laurens refers to various technological events that occurred in the mid-19th century and ended with the First World War. He also refers to specific writings, which express this idea of the world becoming more accessible because of the improvement of transportation and communication, such as Jules Vernes (*Around the World in 80 Days*). These more than century-old technological events – and their economic and social impact – are one of the features of what is called the 'first globalization.'

3. See Kark (1990).
4. In Beirut, most of the khans were demolished either because of the redevelopment of the city or by the war. This is not the case in Damascus or Aleppo where many of these buildings remain.
5. In his doctoral thesis, Elias Khoury drew up a map of Beirut in which he identified 31 khans. In this period one can distinguish two types of khan: the khan for trading composed of two storeys and the khan for travelers.
6. 'Nous regagnâmes le port, sur lequel nous rencontrâmes le signore Battista, propriétaire de l'Hôtel de l'Europe,' wrote Ch. De Pardieu while traveling to Beirut (De Pardieu , 1851: 325). It was mentionned in the Baedecker tourist guide that in 1893 there were two large hotels in Beyrouth: l'Hotel de l'Orient (called Locanda Bassoul) and l'Hotel de Bellevue (called Locanda Andrea) and five hotels of a lower category: l'Hotel d'Europe ou Darricarère, l'Hotel d'Angleterre, l'Hotel de Paris, l'Hotel de l'Univers and l'Hotel Allemand.
7. Built by Nicolas Bassoul, it contained 20 rooms. The same family managed the hotel for a century until it was damaged during the war in 1976, and finally demolished in 1995. This hotel was the only one in Beyrouth to have gone through a century of welcoming travelers, tourists and VIPs who visited Lebanon (Khoury, 1999).
8. After the Second World War tourism accommodation standards took a new step and the use of the khan as a place for tourists declined. The Baedecker guide of 1912 mentions the presence of three lodging possibilities: the western hotels, the convents and hospices, and the khans. Two decades later, the two latter possibilities are not mentioned.
9. In 1923, the names of the most important hotels of Palestine, Syria and Lebanon were listed in the *Guide de la Société de Villegiature au Liban*, which was published in Cairo.
10. The scientific approach/description of Palestine and countries of the Bilad El Sham was not born in the 19th century. It developed through both progress made in philology and archeology. Already, Pierre Belon, apothecary of the Cardinal de Tournon, published in 1553 a book on 'plusieurs singularité et choses mémorables trouvées en Grèse et en Orient.' But it was later, through the work done by the Royal Society of London that scientific knowledge in the west made significant progress. The reports by English travelers of the 18th century contain remarkable information on the language, geography and architecture of Palestine (Henry Maundrell, Thomas Shaw and Richard Pococke). The event that would be the landmark was the Egyptian expedition of Napoleon, crowned by the philology work of Champollion, and marking the last step of the decipherment of hieroglyphs. The west was shaken by the work of Bopp and Burnouf on the Sanskrit language, and then by Edgar Quinet who announced a second Renaissance: an Oriental Renaissance. On 'Renaissance orientale' see Laplanche (2000). This interest for the Orient was marked by the creation in situ of various specialized institutes and, in Germany, by the creation of many research seminars in universities.
11. It was later published again from 1873 to 1882 in three volumes of 800 pages, the last volume being entirely dedicated to Syria and Palestine. Being the work of an 'erudite,' the Doctor Emile Isambert, the Joanne guide was a real encyclopedia of the Orient where one can find all practical information dealing with hotels, transportation, local guides (called dragoman), including average

daily expenses : 40 to 50 francs. The guide declares the travel 'open to any budget' for those willing to travel deck class during the warm season, that is to travel 4th class.

12. The formula 'Travel in the Orient' seems to have appeared in 1772 through the French translation of the book of R. Pococke, *A Description of the East* (London 1743–5).

13. The first publications of the Cook's *Help Book* covered a larger geographical area (Egypt, Palestine, Turkey, Greece and Italy). In the later publication, specific volumes were dedicated to each of these countries.

14. By comparison, French Roman Catholics organized 35 caravans between 1853 and 1873 – which carried only 618 pilgrims – still vastly outnumbered, of course, by Eastern pilgrims from Russia, the Balkans and the Near East. His importance is attested to by the fact Cook brought four-fifths of all British and American tourists who visited the country between 1881 and 1883.

15. Quote the story of the Nazzal family who owned the Amman-based Philadelphia Hotel and who organized the excursion from there with Thomas Cook.

16. As it was described by the General Manager of Movenpick in Wadi Musa who organized the accommodation package, and would access the site by Concorde (when still flying) and having no clue of what the rest of the country looked like (except the road between nearby Aqaba airport and Wadi Musa).

17. Marga d'Andurain manager of the l'Hotel de la Reine Zénobie from 1930 to 1932 (see Marie-Cecile de Taillac, 1994).

References

Berchet, Jean-Claude (1985) Introduction. In *Le voyage en Orient. Anthologie des voyageurs français dans le Levant au XIXème siècle* (pp. 3–22). Paris: Robert Laffont.

Borgi, Georges (1995) Hotels et Hoteliers de Beyrouth au XIXème siècle. In *Kalimat Al-Balamand. No.2* (pp. 57–85). Université de Balamand.

Britton, S. (1991) Tourism, capital, and place: Towards a critical geography of tourism. *Environment and Planning D: Society and Space* 9, 451–78.

Burns, Reverent Jabez (1870) *Help-Book for Travelers to the East: Including Egypt, Palestine, Turkey, Greece and Italy.* Thomas Cook.

Daher, Rami (1999) Gentrification and the politics of power, capital and culture in an emerging Jordanian heritage industry. *Traditional Dwelling and Settlement Review* X (11), 33–45.

De Pardieu, Charles (1851) *Excursion en Orient.* Paris.

de Taillac, Marie-Cecile (1994) *La comtesse de Palmyre.* Paris: Belfond.

Durbin, John (1854) *Observation in the East* (Vol. II). New York.

Featherstone, Mike (1990) Perspectives on consumer culture. *Sociology* 24 (1), 5–22.

Featherstone, Mike (1996) *Global Culture, Nationalism, Globalization and Modernity.* London: Sage.

Feiffer, M. (1985) *Going Places: The Ways of the Tourist from the Imperial Rome to the Present Days.* London: Macmillan.

Giddens, Anthony (1990) *The Consequences of Modernity.* Cambridge: Polity Press in association with Basil Blackwell, Oxford, and Stanford University Press, Stanford.

Gras, Alain (1993) *Grandeur et Dépendance. Sociologie des macro-systèmes techniques.* Paris: Presses Universitaires de France.

Guys, H. (1847) *Relation d'un séjour de plusieurs années à Beyrouth et dans le Liban, E.I.* Paris: Taylor et Reglems.

Kark, Ruth (1990) *Jaffa – A City in Evolution, 1799–1917.* Jerusalem: Yad Izhak Benzvi.

Kark, Ruth (2001) From pilgrimage to budding tourism: The role of Thomas Cook in the rediscovery of the Holy Land in the nineteen century. In Sarah Searight and Malcom Wagstaff (eds) *Travellers in the Levant: Voyagers and Visionaries* (pp. 155–74). Durham: Astene.

Khoury, Elias (1999) L'évolution des complexes touristiques balnéaires et de montagne au Mont Liban. Doctorate thesis in geography, under the supervision of professors Sarkis Tabar and Michael Davie, Université Libanaise et Université François-Rabelais, Tours.

Lanfant, Marie-Françoise (1995) International tourism, internationalisation and the challenge to identity. In M.-F. Lanfant, J.B. Allock, and E.M. Bruner (eds) *Internatinal Tourism, Identity and Change: Sages Studies in International Sociology* (Vol. 47) (pp. 24–43). London: Sage.

Laplanche, François (2000) A travers les récits de voyage en Terre Sainte (XVIe-XIXe): Le dévot, le curieux, le savant. In *Bulletin du centre CNRS de Jerusalem.* Autumn.

Luke, Harry and Roach, Keith (eds) (1930) *The Handbook of Palestine and Transjordan.* London: Macmillian.

MacCannell, D. (1989) *The Tourist: A New Theory of the Leisure Class.* New York: Shoeken Books.

Monmarché Marcel (ed.) (1932) *Syrie – Palestine –Iraq – Transjordanie.* Librairie Hachette: Les Guides Bleus.

Robinson, Georges (1837) *Three Years in the East: Journal of an English Gentleman who Traveled and Resided in Greece, Egypt, Palestine, Syria and Turkey.* Paris.

Robinson, Mike (2001) Tourism encounters: Inter- and intra- cultural conflicts and the world's largest industry. In Nezar Al-Sayyad (ed.) *Consuming Tradition, Manufacturing Heritage: Global Norms and Urban Forms in the Age of Tourism* (pp.34–67). New York: Routledge.

Shoup, John (1985) The impact of tourism on the Bedouin of Petra. *The Middle East Journal* 39 (2), 277–91.

Chapter 4

Digital Spatial Representations: New Communication Processes and 'Middle Eastern' UNESCO World Heritage Sites Online

SCOTT MACLEOD

Introduction

'Middle Eastern' UNESCO (United Nations Educational, Scientific and Cultural Organization) World Heritage web sites and related Internet web sites suggest a new kind of marking or inscription process related to 'Middle Eastern' cultural and historical sites, which enchase a chronicle of site inscription. Consequently, UNESCO conceptions of 'World Heritage' and World Wide Web (WWW) technologies are articulating with 'Middle Eastern' historical and cultural sites to create new forms of representation of 'Middle Eastern' heritage with global implications. UNESCO's formulation of 'World Heritage' is expressed both as part of a concept of 'local' heritage administered by the state and as part of a worldwide system of 'common heritage,' now accessed through the Internet. UNESCO's designation, in combination with the new Internet technologies, marks and transforms the representation of these 'World Heritage' sites by inscribing a layer of 'representation' accessible around the world and by many different audiences and individuals. Specific local histories and archaeologies come together in the context of UNESCO and information technology to shape a concept of 'World Heritage,' which complements, supports and rearticulates concepts of local heritage. 'Middle Eastern' UNESCO World Heritage sites, such as those in Egypt, Jordan, Morocco and Turkey, are represented in new ways, now accessible worldwide, inscribing information as interactive representations, which are hypermedia-oriented, potentially immersion-based, narrative, and are integrating various forms of media (Packer & Jordan, 2001 xxx–xxxi). The Internet then makes these productions accessible to computer users worldwide transforming the concept of 'World Heritage' both locally and globally.

Since its inception in 1972, discussion about UNESCO World Heritage Convention developments has focused on three distinctive decades: the first characterized by the convention taking firm root on the international scene; the second demonstrating the steady growth of the convention; and the third by the flowering of the list, plus anxiety over disparities, imbalances and global strategies (Whitbourn, 2002). These developments provide a significant background for looking at how other influences in the fourth decade and beyond, such as the role of information technology, may shape the program/register, especially in relation to 'Middle Eastern' UNESCO World Heritage sites. Academic discussions about the UNESCO World Heritage Convention also focus on the success of planning committees for working toward the common good by creating a link between the global sphere and the local communities, and bringing together the various disparate interests (Whitbourn, 2002). In addition, the analysis of the production of 'cultural landscapes' has come to play an increasingly significant role, especially over the past decade. Much discussion of UNESCO World Heritage examines the cultural production of specific World Heritage sites in relation to heritage and tourism studies. While discussions of virtual heritage sites highlight the multimedia production of specific sites, very little research has focused on their historical context or ways in which these new communication processes articulate with tourism.

Tourism

In contrast to cultural and historical tourism to physical World Heritage sites, the computer user can now visit nascent UNESCO World Heritage sites online. The Internet and information technology thus shape new tourist destinations, potentially articulating with and complementing physical World Heritage sites. Choices concerning representation, however, shape ways in which the tourist understands UNESCO World Heritage sites (Duncan & Ley, 1993). MacCannell (1976), Urry (1990) and Thurot and Thurot (1983) inscribe a tradition of interpreting tourism in the contexts of modernity, post-modernity and advertising/industry discourses. This tradition attempts to explain tourism first as a search for authenticity in response to alienation, a condition of modernity, then as a game in which the tourist knowingly and willingly participates, and then as the production of touristic desire and experience by an elite group of advertisers/early tourists (micro-milieu). In this chapter the author suggests that modernity yields one interpretation of touristic experience, post-modernity may construct another, and Thurot and Thurots' interpretation of advertising discourse produces yet another. Tourism, now, in the context of the development of the Internet and information technology supersedes and incorporates these previous analyses and produces other interpretations of tourism.

In the context of information technology, this author suggests that online UNESCO World Heritage site web surfing is a form of tourism shaped by multimedia developments. Tourists can now visit 'Middle Eastern' UNESCO World Heritage sites online from any computer with an Internet connection. The UNESCO World Heritage site list both organizes the sites into nations and regions, and acts as a gateway for online visitors to a variety of sites. The tourist is thus able to surf the UNESCO World Heritage site list to find particular web sites in any country, which are produced by local, state or national institutions. Schätze der Welt's (German for 'Treasures of the World') UNESCO World Heritage sites also offer online access to approximately a quarter of the current UNESCO World Heritage sites. These online sites typically include enough multimedia content to shape a nascent, cultural and historical touristic experience of the site for the online tourist, in German.

Anthropological theories of tourism especially in relation to the key concept of 'authenticity,' suggest that objective, constructive and postmodern conceptions of authenticity provide an approach to understanding tourists' motivations (MacCannell, 1976; Thurot & Thurot, 1983; Urry, 1990). More recent tourism theorists develop this tradition to suggest that 'existential authenticity' provides a useful alternative way to conceptualize touristic motivations because it emphasizes the tourist's experience rather than the arguments concerning the authenticity of the objects or sites of touristic interest (Wang, 1999: 350). Instead, Wang (1999: 365–6) suggests that 'what tourists seek are their own authentic selves and inter-subjective authenticity.' For Wang, the tourists' 'seeking' of themselves through the visiting of tourist destinations thus constitutes a form of authenticity. The online tourist's seeking of Schätze der Welt's UNESCO World Heritage sites, for example, constitutes by extension a form of virtual authenticity, where the seeking of constructed, online UNESCO World Heritage sites for the qualities of 'Middle Eastern' 'World Heritage', reflects the tourist's own authenticity-seeking self in a networked world. For the tourist, digital UNESCO World Heritage sites build in unique ways on the historical processes of heritage production.

This study of online tourism to 'Middle Eastern' UNESCO World Heritage sites examines what the tourist visits in the context of the Internet, information technology and multimedia. It also examines how these online sites were shaped by historical and 'Orientalist' processes. In relation to the concept of authenticity-seeking as a motivation for tourism (Wang, 1999), this chapter suggests that virtual authenticity-seeking serves as a motivation for the online tourist, since 'Middle Eastern' UNESCO World Heritage sites, predicated on the idea of 'outstanding universal heritage' reflect the computer user's seeking of authenticity. Virtual UNESCO World Heritage sites, entailing new forms of touristic communication processes, now influence tourism in multiple ways. Information technology-represented 'places' in the form of online 'Middle Eastern' UNESCO World Heritage sites are now transnationally accessible. The individual online computer user from the 'Middle East,' like computer users from around the world, can now visit the most comprehensive 'Middle Eastern' UNESCO World Heritage virtual sites through the UNESCO World Heritage and Schätze der Welt lists. For the tourist, nascent online UNESCO World Heritage sites thus complement, advertise and offer different kinds of information from the physical sites.

By exploring both UNESCO World Heritage web sites and other historical and pictorial representations of these World Heritage sites themselves, this chapter analyzes the significance of the relationship between historical, textual and hypertextual – 'the Internet-based inter-operability of accessing and recombining all kinds of text, images, sounds, silences, and blanks, including the entire realm of symbolic expression enclosed in a multimedia system – in our minds' (Castells, 2001: 202) – representations; this also serves as a means to examine the implications for the concept of 'World Heritage' in light of new digital technologies and the network society in an historical context. UNESCO World Heritage web sites and related web sites and technologies, as well as other UNESCO sources, are used as data. The chapter argues that the relationship between sited UNESCO World Heritage sites and their digital representations is a new form of cultural inscription articulating with and reshaping UNESCO's concept of common heritage, which both diminishes and contributes to Edward Said's construction of 'Orientalism.'

Web site production and 'World Heritage' processes inform each other in many interlinked ways:

(1) UNESCO's World Heritage Centre articulates a conception of 'World Heritage,' now shaped on the WWW through text, films, photos and interactive technologies.

(2) UNESCO structures the concept of common heritage through its register, which, along with other UNESCO-oriented institutions, not only represents 'Middle Eastern' sites in a Saidian sense, some in ways which are and some not 'Orientalist,' but also relates them one to another in the context of common heritage.

(3) While UNESCO attempts to serve as a bridge between local, regional and global heritage productions, in reality, the 'Middle East' is often represented in specific ways, which belie the term 'Middle East.'

(4) UNESCO's mission, forms of representation and pragmatic factors, shape the editorial choices of multimedia digital texts, photographs, sound and video representations, which in turn shape production, in relation to the term 'Middle East.'

(5) UNESCO 'World Heritage' thus creates a nascent form of virtual reality entailing new forms of touristic interactivity representing the 'Middle East' in specific ways.

Integration, Interactivity, Hypermedia, Immersion and Narrativity

Packer and Jordan (2001: xxx) argue that integration, interactivity, hypermedia, immersion and narrativity characterize novel communication processes resulting from the development of information technologies. While not all of these processes yet operate in relation to Egyptian, Jordanian, Moroccan and Turkish UNESCO World Heritage web sites, aspects of these processes are beginning to shape their production.

Integration refers to 'the combining of artistic forms and technology into a hybrid form of expression' (Packer & Jordan, 2001: xxx). For example, Schätze der Welt's web sites include video, text, interactive maps, and links to other sites, images, sound files and an image book index to each video.

Interactivity refers to 'the ability of the user to manipulate and affect [his and] her experience of media directly, and to communicate with others through media' (Packer & Jordan, 2001: xxx). While UNESCO-based chat rooms and messaging programs aren't yet available, on the UNESCO Turkish 'Hattusha' web site (UNESCO World Heritage Centre, 1986), the link to the 'Die Ausgrabungen in Hattuscha' (Deutsches Archaeologisches Institut, 2001), one can link through to many web pages describing the archaeology of this ancient capital of the Hittite Empire, work interactively with various site maps, and also email people related to this site. Schätze der Welt's web sites' image books links one directly to specific starting points in each film. UNESCO World Heritage Centre's site map is newly interactive.

Hypermedia refers to 'the linking of separate media elements to one another to create a trail of personal association' (Packer & Jordan, 2001: xxx). In browsing UNESCO web sites, the end user can choose, create and recreate a multiply number of trails of personal association both with UNESCO and non-UNESCO sites. This process of a user forming his or her own Internet-based path of association in relation to the Internet reflects a process, which Castells (2001) calls hypertextuality (nonlinear Internet-based interactions). In examining 'Middle Eastern' World Heritage web sites, the end user's hypertext and 'cultural' experiences interact with multimedia representations to shape a series of associations, which are inscribed as 'World Heritage' in the context of the global context of the Internet.

Immersion refers to 'the experience of entering into the simulation of a three-dimensional environment' (Packer & Jordan, 2001: xxxi). The UNESCO Great Pyramid at Giza web site (UNESCO World Heritage Centre, 2002b) uses Apple Quicktime technology to give the viewer a three-dimensional experience of the inside of a tomb. The viewer can scroll 360 degrees around, as well as zoom in and out. Bandwidth still significantly limits the immersion experience.

Narrativity refers to 'aesthetic and formal strategies that derive from the above concepts, and which result in nonlinear story forms and media presentation' (Packer & Jordan, 2001: xxxi). These technologies shape narratives, incorporating the above processes, which have the effect of creating hypertextual (nonlinear) story lines and multimedia shows. Through their UNESCO designations, UNESCO World Heritage web sites shape narrative strategies.

UNESCO's World Heritage web sites presently number 23 in Egypt, Jordan, Morocco and Turkey (UNESCO World Heritage Centre, 1972–2001) and offer useful case studies for preliminary analysis of the relationship between information technology and these destinations. A look at what information technology makes possible and the forms of representation it favors, as well as the choices about representation made by UNESCO and others in constructing these sites, explores the new forms of inscription that they constitute.

As WWW source material this chapter uses: (1) the UNESCO World Heritage web site, which includes not only its list on a single web page, but also regional groups of countries, web sites for individual countries, which each contain a brief description of the heritage site, as well as links to state or locally produced web sites, and a link to various committee documents; (2) UNESCO's 'virtual tours'; (3) the Southwest Germany telecommunication producer, Südwestrundfunk's (SWR) extensive UNESCO World Heritage site-related web site, Schätze der Welt, containing 15-minute movies for about 175 World Heritage sites, in German, including 10 UNESCO World Heritage sites in Egypt, Jordan, Morocco and Turkey, links to other related web sites, slide shows, sound tracks and movie texts; (4) the World Monument Fund list of endangered heritage sites' web sites; and (5) a variety of other 'local,' state and regional web sites found using search engines and while surfing the Internet.

Said's 'Orientalism'

Edward Said's *Orientalism* (1994) describes a system of inscription processes, which shaped an understanding of pan-Arabism and which the West, he argues, used as controlling processes. In selecting Egypt, Jordan, Morocco and Turkey, this chapter articulates a shifting Saidian construct of 'Orientalism' with the 'common heritage' implicit in UNESCO's designation. For Said, 'Orientalism' is a primarily European 'style of thought based on ontological and epistemological distinction made between the "Orient" and "the Occident"' (Said, 1994: 2). It is his 'way of describing it, by teaching it, settling it, ruling over it: in short, Orientalism is a Western style for dominating, restructuring, and having authority over the Orient' (Said, 1994: 3). 'The phenomenon of Orientalism as I study it here deals principally, not with a correspondence between Orientalism and Orient, but with the internal consistency of Orientalism and its ideas about the Orient ... despite or beyond any correspondence, or lack thereof, with a "real" Orient' (Said, 1994: 5). This way Said's argument can be used to examine the ways in which UNESCO and online 'World Heritage' representations are reshaped and reshaping concepts of the 'Middle East,' in relation to some UNESCO-related web sites located in the 'Middle East' that would fall within Said's description of 'Orientalist' discourse.

The 'Middle East,' 'Orientalism' and UNESCO World Heritage-related maps on the WWW

Said's conception of 'Orientalism' primarily refers to an 'essentializing,' 'man-made' idea, both cultural and geographical, of countries that contrast with 'the Occident' (Said, 1994: 5). In 'Orientalism' he examines countries and cities as disparate as Turkey, Egypt and Marrakech, Morocco as subsumed under Western conceptions of 'the Orient.' Because of Said's construction, this chapter assumes a broad conception of the 'Middle East' to include Egypt, Jordan, Morocco and Turkey to examine the ways in which some of these historical conceptions are or are not now represented online in terms of UNESCO World Heritage.

For administrative purposes, UNESCO's World Heritage Centre's organization is structured around regions, which they then define and use to maintain the online register. In doing this, they highlight a tension between global and local heritage, as well as regional and common heritage, implicit in the tension between reality and representation. Turkey is represented as part of Europe, and not the 'Arab States,' differentiating it from a broader, Saidian analysis of the 'Orient.' Morocco and Egypt are represented as part of UNESCO's 'Arab States,' and not a 'North African' region. Following Said's delineation of a Western concept of the 'Orient,' in this chapter's sample of the 'Middle East' Turkey is included, in part due to the Islamic heritage it shares with Egypt, Jordan and Morocco as well as its Ottoman history, as part of a broad historical construct of the 'Orient' to examine changes relative to and argue against Said's treatment. Similarly, Morocco and Egypt are also treated as part of a broadly defined conception of the 'Middle East.' By including Turkey, Egypt and Morocco as part of the 'Middle East,' Said's analysis of a geographical and cultural Western construct of the 'Orient' can be utilized to examine some of the ways representations of UNESCO 'Middle Eastern' World Heritage sites on the Internet relate to Said's 'Orientalism.'

Conceptions of the 'Middle East' are incorporated and inscribed with emphasis on their contributions to World Heritage sites based on UNESCO's list. The scope of UNESCO's World Heritage Convention, which now encompasses more than 120 countries out of roughly 183 nations in the world, utilizes a pragmatic, regional approach where regional 'commonalities' and 'histories' are used for classification. Although disclaimed by UNESCO, 'Delineation of national boundaries are for reference purposes, and do not represent an endorsement by the World Heritage Committee, UNESCO, or any UN agency' (UNESCO World Heritage Centre, 2002c), UNESCO's mapping choices may loosely perpetuate a form of 'Orientalism' by identifying a pan-Arab region based on the regional commonalities of a similar language and Islamic history in relation to other regions, especially 'Western Europe,' which has played a significant role in shaping UNESCO.

Technologically, some of these online maps are created as 'image maps,' which are 'hot' images where the end user can click on a place on the map to hyperlink to another related web page. For the web author such as UNESCO, 'image maps' are 'objects' inserted into the hypertext markup language (HTML) of a page, all of which is then 'parsed' as a web page by a browser such as Opera, Microsoft's Internet Explorer, or Netscape Navigator and 'read' by the end user. UNESCO also uses JavaScript (UNESCO World Heritage Centre, 2002c), a scripting language that enables interactivity with dynamic content (for example, JavaScript can be used to create a dynamic clock in a web page with hands that move) to display maps. In UNESCO's usage of JavaScript all of their 582 maps are part of the same program, which allows the end user more ways of selecting maps and getting information than image maps; JavaScript is more interactive than image maps and utilizes dynamic content. Spatial representations of 'Middle Eastern' heritage sites are thus reshaped by information technologies such as JavaScript.

UNESCO's map

UNESCO World Heritage has both historically and administratively (e.g. through its Paris-based 'Arab States' division) grouped together North Africa and the area east of the Mediterranean and south of Turkey as part of its 'Arab States' region, e.g. the Paris-based 'Arab States' division. 'Such locales, regions, geographical sectors as "Orient" and "Occident" are man-made' (Said, 1994: 5). While UNESCO's 'Arab States' regional grouping may emerge from an 'Orientalist,' Western legacy, UNESCO World Heritage Centre's attempt to rewrite these 'Orientalizing' processes, however, lies both in its historical mission and its program to identify a common heritage of all people as well as its intent to fairly represent this heritage. 'Middle East' heritage therefore can be reshaped in relation to the idea and practice of developing a common heritage.

Schätze der Welt's map

For Schätze der Welt's web site – linked to from the German UNESCO web page 'Wichtige Links' (UNESCO Deutsche UNESCO-Kommission e.V., 2002) – 'die Turkei's' heritage sites are represented in 'Europa,' 'Jordanien's' in 'Petra' (SWR Schätze der Welt – Erbe der Menschheit, 2002g) and 'Q'useir Amra' heritage sites in 'Asien' (Asia), and 'Aegypten' and 'Morokko's' heritage sites in 'Afrika.' The region called 'Asien' is a nominal expression of 'Orientalism,' and reflects a German/European structure of understanding the Orient, which Said assails. The use of three different regions, however, in which to categorically organize heritage sites, which in Said's sense have all been part of a colonial construction of the 'Orient' reflects his understanding of the variety of traditions and countries that make up the 'Orient' as distinct.

In terms of UNESCO World Heritage sites' online mapping for UNESCO and Schätze der Welt, Said's 'Orientalism' seems to articulate only slightly with these spatial depictions, which for him might be understood as 'Orientalist' geographical constructs.

Proportional Numbers of On-the-ground Sites on UNESCO's List: 'World Heritage' Nomination Processes' Imbalances

While 'Orientalism' may play little role in online mapping, the proportional lack of on-the-ground 'Arab States" sites in the UNESCO register suggests a misrepresentation that may reflect Said's analysis. During the 1994 UNESCO World Heritage Convention, 'Arab states" incoming heritage site nominations represented a mere 3% of all incoming nominations in contrast to European 'World Heritage' nominations at 51%. At the 1994 convention UNESCO, in developing a 'Global Strategy,' reported that it intended to redress this imbalance:

> It is therefore hoped that with the work on the global strategy, the upcoming regional and sub- regional meetings and the possible future development of regional and sub-regional World Heritage focal points ('Centres') this imbalance may finally be redressed. (UNESCO World Heritage Centre, 1994a)

The global strategy grew out of an attempt to plan for the development of the concept of 'common heritage.' In 1999, the UNESCO World Heritage Centre asked that states with proportionally large numbers of heritage sites on the register voluntarily restrain themselves from making more nominations (UNESCO World Heritage Centre, 1999). While the proportional imbalance may seem to reflect a form of 'Orientalism,' member states, however, nominate their sites for consideration by the convention. Any imbalance would thus reflect state nominating procedures rather than UNESCO processes.

While some critics have suggested that several sites in the 'Middle East' and elsewhere have not qualified for the UNESCO World Heritage list because of rigid Eurocentric conceptions of what qualifies as 'World Heritage,' some UNESCO World Heritage officials suggest (personal communication) that the cultural list itself, with about 563 cultural sites, is 'diluted' in terms of reflecting authentic 'outstanding universal heritage,' in contrast to the natural World Heritage list, with about 144 sites. These UNESCO World Heritage officials, moreover, suggest that countries that do not meet the UNESCO World Heritage criteria sometimes receive a site designation for reasons other than meeting the criteria of 'outstanding universal value.' For example, some countries maintain that they should have at least one site simply because they are a signatory to the UNESCO World Heritage Convention. While the relatively few 'Middle Eastern' UNESCO World Heritage physical sites, compared with relatively large numbers of European sites on the online World Heritage list, may reflect an historical Eurocentric bias concerning 'outstanding universal value,' this historical legacy may be best understood within the context of shifting pressures on the decision-making process of the states' convention and register.

Inscribing 'Orientalist' Stereotypes

One of the main information technologies used to represent online 'Middle Eastern' UNESCO World Heritage sites presently consists of video that is streamed over the Internet to local computers and displayed in small video/sound display programs such as 'Real Player,' 'Windows Media Player,' or Apple's 'Quicktime.' Panoramic movies are also used, where 360 degrees of a landscape, hall or a space can be shown all around. Musical and voice sound tracks can also be independently streamed. Macromedia's 'Flash' animation movies can likewise be used to create interactive movies and animations, which can incorporate photos, sound and other kinds of objects (SWR Schätze der Welt – Erbe der Menschheit, 2002f).

Technologically, web sites and groups of web pages with a common theme are typically organized around a main page, which contain hyperlinks to more related pages and media, and links to any other site on the web, as well as a search engine and other forms of information technologies including databases. The main page or any other page can also be linked to by any other web page on the Internet. For example, Schätze der Welt's main page (SWR Schätze der Welt – Erbe der Menschheit, 2002i) contains five links to five distinct 'continent' web pages each listing the Schätze der Welt World Heritage sites on that continent, alphabetical listings of countries or heritage sites' pages, and a search engine.

UNESCO's representations of 'Middle Eastern' online 'World Heritage' provide a brief description and a picture of a particular site, with links to various related web sites. They also provide access to the World Heritage list and its associated links from any Internet-connected computer in the world, thus enhancing ways in which people can gain access to information about UNESCO's register while interacting with it as well as engaging with UNESCO World Heritage.

Schätze der Welt's 'Middle Eastern' web sites provide 10–15 minute-long Internet-streamed movies (SWR Schätze der Welt – Erbe der Menschheit, 2002i) originally produced as part of a German television series that focuses solely on UNESCO World Heritage sites. The German UNESCO website posts a link to this German television company World Heritage web site with unique World Heritage content. Schätze der Welt also posts a photographic slide show, links to academic and other informative web sites about the particular heritage site, a brief chronology and history of the site, and an interactive map showing where the site is located. Each individual Schätze der Welt World Heritage site web site is linked to the other roughly 175 related Schätze der Welt 'Denkmäler' (World Heritage sites). There is also a transcription in German of the video's script, the soundtrack from the video, and an 'image book,' which allows the user to click on one of the images to begin the video at that point.

In contrast to UNESCO's online descriptions and links, some of Schätze der Welt's online UNESCO World Heritage videos engage in a form of 'Orientalism.'

Jordan

The Schätze der Welt 15-minute video on 'Q'useir Amra,' a remarkable 8th century structure in the present-day Jordanian desert, uses music, a poetic soundtrack, a female Arabic dancer behind the veil, an Arab prince, and camels to shape its 'Orientalist' image. It depicts a blatant form of 'Orientalism' where an uninhabited structure and its former inhabitants in conjunction with simulated village life are artistically represented as exotic, as potentially culturally backward, peculiar and unchanging in the context of modernization. The opening music, an eerie, ethereal wall of high tones overlaying video of timeless dessert in the heat of the day suggests an exotic other world. The text begins by invoking 'Fata Morgana,' a mystical characterization of mirage. A narrator reads in German:

> Nothing is what it appears to be, and where something appears, there is nothing. Fata Morgana, like molten glass, flies through the air over the hot glowing earth. Grace, O God, for Death follows us. Neither mother nor sisters – no one mourns us – and he comes closer, unseen, Death in the desert. Past and present merge, and everything appears deceptively – Fata Morgana – Reality, 300 Horsepower strong – 12 tires carry as much as one hundred hooves, the treasures of today,

machines and oil. (Scott MacLeod's translation, SWR Schätze der Welt
– Erbe der Menschheit, 2002h, 'Der Filmtext')

Against the soundtrack of this mystical incantation, powerful trucks
emerge in the video carrying goods and equipment of today. In juxtaposition to these trucks, camels are then shown. The viewer next sees Q'useir
Amra, an extraordinary building in the desert. The narrator invokes
images of 'a thousand and one (Arabian) nights,' 'dreams,' 'Princes,' 'the
Caliph,' and 'the harem.' In this dramatization of a dream, a 'traditionally' dressed female dancer, probably from Jordan, moves before the
camera's lens as a prince looks on. Subsequent images and text continue
to dramatically represent this site as 'Oriental' as the narrator relates the
history of Q'useir Amra. Dramatization, narrator's tone and the confla-
tion of history and myth highlight this process of 'Orientalism.' The web
production, an online representation of an UNESCO World Heritage site
produced by SWR thus inscribes 'Orientalist' stereotypes on an assem-
blage of ancient structures, thus underscoring Said's argument.

Fez, Morocco

Fez is similarly portrayed by Schätze der Welt as exotic and unchanged
by modernization, as a kind of living 'oriental' museum, as if the
producers had never visited the area that lies just outside the old city.
The video depicts the 'traditional' clothing of people from Fez. The text
begins 'Foreigner, when you come to Fez, watch out . . . blue is the color
of Fez and green is the color of hope . . . if you follow the color of blue,
you may go crazy' (Scott MacLeod's translation, SWR Schätze der Welt
– Erbe der Menschheit, 2002a, 'Der Filmtext'). The viewer is warned that
danger lies ahead. The viewer hears a call to prayer, and religious music
of Fez. A boy drinking water out of a spigot in a tiled wall is depicted.
The viewer sees 'Oriental' rugs hanging from balconies, a labyrinthine
market place, and the view upon entering a mosque. The video itself
attempts to represent a journey into and out of a labyrinth. Online representations of this UNESCO World Heritage site articulate with
'Orientalist' images described by Said (SWR Schätze der Welt – Erbe der
Menschheit, 2002a).

Marrakech, Morocco

Similar to the SWR's Fez video's use of 'Orientalist' representations, Marrakech's video ends with a haunting fairy tale of a prince, his

love nest and his quest for virgins (SWR Schätze der Welt – Erbe der Menschheit, 2002e).

Turkey

The Schätze der Welt web site presents four 'Turkish' UNESCO World Heritage videos on Göreme-Cappadocia (SWR Schätze der Welt – Erbe der Menschheit, 2002b) Heirapolis-Pammukale (SWR Schätze der Welt – Erbe der Menschheit, 2002c), Troy (SWR Schätze der Welt – Erbe der Menschheit, 2002d), and Istanbul (SWR Schätze der Welt – Erbe der Menschheit, 2002j). While UNESCO's World Heritage register lists nine World Heritage sites in Turkey, SWR's selection of four sites may reflect their relative fame, but may also reflect the significance of these sites to the West. These four videos focus almost exclusively on the Greek, Roman and Christian histories of these World Heritage sites, making almost no mention of subsequent or concurrent other regimes or traditions. Only in the Istanbul video is Ottoman history explored in the context of its articulation with Roman and Christian histories. The Göreme video emphasizes the Christian history in shaping cultural structures there. The Heirapolis-Pammukale video focuses on the Roman and natural history, which shaped this area. The video on Troy emphasizes its extraordinary Greek history. Both the choice of which World Heritage sites to represent as well as the content of each production suggests an 'Orientalist' bias.

The selection criteria adopted by UNESCO World Heritage together with the types of heritage sites selected by them, as in Turkey, for example, reinforces Said's 'Orientalism' in an indirect way and is a manifestation of the biases in the selection process. Only a very few sites from the Ottoman period are selected in comparison to several sites from pre-Islamic periods even though the Islamic periods in Turkey are extremely important and relate specifically to a 'local' understanding of heritage. Also, and in addition to the biases in the selection process, the inscription of the concept of 'common heritage' marginalizes local histories and traditions. Consequently, this chapter considers this an indirect 'Orientalist' discourse that adheres to the 'timeless paradigm' that the West had conceptualized and constructed about the 'Middle East'. In the timeless paradigm, the 'Middle East' is constructed as unchanged since antiquities, contrary to the reality of urban heritage, social history of cities, education and urban development.

While Schätze der Welt's online representations of the 'Middle East,' utilizing new forms of communication including interactivity, narrativity, integration and hypermedia, do engage in a form of 'Orientalism' through use of stereotypic images, myths, music and narratives, as well as the choice of content, the videos and web content at the same time also treat local histories and places individually belying the Saidian argument in relation to UNESCO World Heritage sites.

Local 'Middle Eastern' World Heritage web site productions, which are hyperlinked through the UNESCO World Heritage register, also shape experience of 'World Heritage' for the end user. The 'Safranbolu City' web site (Safranbolu City Web Site, 2002), linked to from UNESCO's 'City of Safranbolu's' web site (UNESCO World Heritage Centre, 1994b) offers 'local' interpretations of history, architecture, cuisine, music as well as photos, travel links, a map and news. They thus produce for the WWW a 'local' representation of a UNESCO World Heritage site. In doing so such sites present alternative representations to 'Orientalist' constructs.

Historical Configurations and Discourses of Inscriptions

Several historical layers of representation including local, state and 'Middle Eastern,' shape the portrayals of UNESCO World Heritage sites in Egypt, Jordan, Morocco and Turkey. UNESCO's World Heritage Centre's designation process for the 'Middle East' implicitly, yet loosely, inscribes at least five interrelated historical discourses in representing these sites. By sampling web sites from Egypt, Jordan, Morocco and Turkey, they can be viewed as geographically distant, but historically distinct countries in the 'Middle East.' As examples that embody a facet of the ways in which 'Middle Eastern' heritage is broadly defined, these countries' sites also exhibit a range of different histories that are all distinct yet subsumed and preserved in UNESCO's list.

UNESCO's World Heritage program, originating in 1972,

> seeks to encourage the identification, protection and preservation of cultural and natural heritage around the world considered to be of outstanding value to humanity. This is embodied in an international treaty called the *Convention concerning the Protection of the World Cultural and Natural Heritage,* adopted by UNESCO in 1972. (UNESCO World Heritage Centre, 2002a)

UNESCO's designation process identifies a set of varied, historical sites originating independently over a wide variety of time periods and out of many different traditions. State regimes and regional formations subsequently received and shaped understandings of the historical sites. UNESCO's World Heritage program, building upon UNESCO's mission to further intercultural cooperation and build peace in the minds of people (UNESCO, 1946), articulates with state and regional discourses to shape and promote a common heritage expressed through their World Heritage program.

This chapter uses UNESCO World Heritage Centre's project as a starting point to briefly identify a series of historical configurations over which UNESCO has palimpsestically inscribed the concept of common heritage via its present day World Heritage program and web sites. In doing so, it can be argued that UNESCO World Heritage online web material's emphasis on 'common heritage' acts as a process of representation that incorporates and articulates with previous forms of representation highlighting these sites' local and global representations in terms of common heritage. Thus, previous forms of representation presented now online de-emphasize Said's 'Orientalism.'

By briefly examining and analyzing a number of key historical factors which shaped these sites, I want to examine forms and discourses upon which UNESCO's register builds. UNESCO and, later, UNESCO's web sites inscribe these sites using a set of criteria, which identify the sites as part of a common heritage.

Local, historical inscription

UNESCO World Heritage sites in modern Egypt, Jordan, Morocco and Turkey reflect a very heterogeneous array of historical developments and traditions. In Egypt, ancient Egyptian, Islamic and Christian monuments predominate as examples of 'World Heritage'. Jordan's two sites represent Nabataean and 8th-century structures used by Umayyad caliphs. Moroccan sites include Islamic, Roman, Almoravid Berber, Christian and European traditions. Turkish sites include Hittite, Persian, Islamic, Lycian, Hellenic and Roman historical constructions. The local historical processes give rise to sites and monuments from diverse backgrounds, which are then subsumed under the rubric of a common heritage. They invoke questions of the way inherently different heritages are reinscribed as common legacies (Omland, 1997). The construction of common heritage through a designatory process, which ideologically can unite disparate local histories, also ideologically can shape the way places are remembered and heritage can be rewritten. Local sites with specific histories are joined into a concept of 'World Heritage' in the UNESCO register. The shaping of global heritage out of local place understandings thus reflects UNESCO's intention to forge a conception of a common heritage.

States: Egyptian/Jordanian/Moroccan/Turkish

State formations shape a unified conception of heritage in these respective countries. Ministries of Culture and Education ideologically unite what were once historically distinct traditions in the setting of political, religious and economic regimes, many of which benefit from tourist revenues. Heritage sites are often used by state regimes to shape identities based on an imagined past rooted in such sites.

In some 'Middle Eastern' countries, what are now considered heritage sites were often legacies of colonialism, and often too costly to maintain; later, they were seen as sources of tourist revenue. In some countries where religious ideologies prevailed over secular ones or where 'nation building' occurred fitfully, historical and cultural sites were often either ignored or disregarded.

These 'Middle Eastern' states today now actively promote a broad concept of 'common heritage' to shape national communities linked together by a common past and to bring in tourist revenues. By developing and shaping a common, national heritage, states actively use heritage as an historical basis, thus inscribing the sites as state productions.

On UNESCO's World Heritage list, Turkey, Morocco and Egypt have state sponsored web sites that utilize photos and text to describe their World Heritage monuments. UNESCO World Heritage site listings for Egypt's World Heritage monuments provide hyperlinks to web sites sponsored by Egypt's Ministry of Tourism, which in turn provide hyperlinks to services provided by hotel and tour operators. Three of Morocco's seven UNESCO World Heritage listings have links to Morocco's Ministry of Communication. And Turkey's nine sites have links to the Turkish Ministry of Culture. Unlike the other three countries, the two UNESCO World Heritage site listings for Jordan do not post links to any state ministry.

Regional/'Middle Eastern'

As it has been pointed out, regional and 'Middle Eastern' identities shape heritage sites and processes in this region, corresponding to the ways in which one defines the 'Middle East.' Islam and the Arab language articulate with the modern state to create tensions between religion and the state. Said's 'Orientalism' in reference to heritage potentially represents still another way that the 'West' delineates a 'Middle Eastern' identity. Tourist's visiting a region of the world also often visit sites in adjacent countries. UNESCO's attempt at defining 'common heritage' articulates with, contests and contributes to shaping this concept.

UNESCO and related World Heritage mappings for the 'Middle East' as discussed above demonstrate a very loose, non-uniform regional association through web representations. These web sites also primarily emphasize the historical significance of these destinations and thus do not emphasize a common background based on tradition but rather only a broader one based on UNESCO criteria.

UNESCO

UNESCO, an agency of the United Nations' Economic and Social Council, was begun in 1946 to encourage collaboration in the areas of science, education, culture and communications and thus was intended to promote universal respect for justice, laws, human rights and fundamental freedoms. The organization's launching statement declares that 'peace must therefore be founded, if it is not to fail, upon the intellectual and moral solidarity of mankind' (UNESCO, 1946). In 1972, UNESCO created the World Heritage Committee to identify and preserve the world's cultural and natural heritage. UNESCO's World Heritage Centre soon after began to implement its register of sites around the world and the criteria inherent in this list structured a conception of common heritage and a program 'to encourage the identification, protection and preservation of cultural and natural heritage around the world which are considered to be of outstanding value to humanity' (UNESCO World Heritage Centre, 2000b).

The criteria for inclusion in the register as a cultural site, which are periodically rewritten presently read as follows (see Table 4.1).

For 'Middle Eastern' heritage sites, such criteria lessen the significance of local, state and 'Middle Eastern' heritage inscriptions and inscribe instead a common heritage. UNESCO's inscription process therefore may universalize inscriptions that otherwise have more significance in a more local context.

States themselves, which are party to the UNESCO World Heritage Convention must nominate sites for inclusion in the register. The World Heritage Committee, which meets annually, decides which sites should be included based on technical evaluations. Two advisory institutions, the International Council on Monuments and Sites (ICOMOS, 2002) and the World Conservation Union (ICUN, 2002) provide independent evaluations. The International Centre for the Study of the Preservation and Restoration of Cultural Property (ICCROM, 2002), which is a third advisory body, provides expert advice on restoring monuments and also organizes training courses. Once a site is selected, its name is listed in the register.

Table 4.1 UNESCO criteria for selection

The criteria for selection
To be included on the World Heritage List, sites must satisfy the selection criteria. These criteria are explained in the *Operational Guidelines for the Implementation of the World Heritage Convention* which, besides the text of the Convention, is the main working document on World Heritage. The criteria have been revised regularly by the Committee to match the evolution of the World Heritage concept itself.

Cultural properties should:	*Natural properties should:*
i. represent a masterpiece of human creative genius; or ii. exhibit an important interchange of human values over a span of time or within a cultural area of the world, on developments in architecture or technology, monumental arts, town-planning or landscape design; or iii. bear a unique or at least exceptional testimony to a cultural tradition or to a civilization which is living or has disappeared; or iv. be an outstanding example of a type of building or architectural or technological ensemble, or landscape which illustrates (a) significant stage(s) in human history; or v. be an outstanding example of a traditional human settlement or land-use which is representative of a culture (or cultures), especially when it has become vulnerable under the impact of irreversible change; or vi. be directly or tangibly associated with events or living traditions, with ideas or with beliefs, with artistic and literary works of outstanding universal significance (a criterion applied only in exceptional circumstances, and together with other criteria). Equally important is the authenticity of the site and the way it is protected and managed.	i. be outstanding examples representing major stages of earth's history, including the record of life, significant on-going geological processes in the development of land forms, or significant geomorphic or physiographic features; or ii. be outstanding examples representing significant on-going ecological and biological processes in the evolution and development of terrestrial, fresh water, coastal and marine ecosystems and communities of plants and animals; or iii. contain superlative natural phenomena or areas of exceptional natural beauty and aesthetic importance; or iv. contain the most important and significant natural habitats for in-situ conservation of biological diversity, including those containing threatened species of outstanding universal value from the point of view of science or conservation. The protection, management and integrity of the site are also important considerations.

Source: UNESCO World Heritage Centre (2000a)

The concept of common heritage inherent in this process, viewed in the context of the Internet and globalizing processes, extends the way 'common' is understood. 'Middle Eastern' sites are thus subsumed within an understanding of 'World Heritage,' which begins to accent a broader concept of common heritage and brings more specific local meanings of heritage into this wider perspective. Ownership remains local (Omland, 1997), but the significance of the inscription becomes widely shared. A list of cultural and natural criteria, which identify outstanding traditions, or sites, of universal value shapes a heritage inscription process that emphasizes the one set of criteria excluding from its discourse others. The UNESCO World Heritage list designation also works as a form of branding for the culture industry, where the benefits of UNESCO's name draws visitors and revenues, and provides a marker of authenticity for visitors.

In his paper 'World Heritage – and the Relationship between the Global and the Local,' Omland (1997) identifies 'common' heritage as embodying both shared responsibility and moral duty. The duty reflects the idea of 'global stewardship.' Shared responsibility, for example, resulting from the UNESCO designation, assumes that all nations have common interest in conserving these sites and that the World Heritage Convention is a tool of a global conservation ethic. Shared resources suggest pooling financial assets toward the goal of common heritage. Moral duty includes a respect for other peoples' heritage. A UNESCO World Heritage designation in the 'Middle East' in the interest of common heritage offers potential resources, which might not otherwise be available. UNESCO's World Heritage designation thus serves as a bridge between local 'Middle Eastern' and global heritage productions. UNESCO's 'Middle Eastern' online productions then come to represent a link between UNESCO, the 'Middle East,' the individual countries, and some local producers.

UNESCO and the Internet

The Internet opens many new possibilities for the inscription of 'common' heritage. The UNESCO World Heritage Centre has utilized a number of new web technologies to inscribe and make accessible heritage sites via the Internet. Information about 'Middle Eastern' sites thus becomes accessible from anywhere in the world where Internet–computer connectivity exists.

The UNESCO World Heritage Centre first published its register of sites online in the mid-1990s. Prior to that time, the list was only available in print. As Internet usage and the number of UNESCO World Heritage sites have increased, online sites and resources related to World Heritage sites have also increased. As it has been pointed out, UNESCO's 'Middle Eastern' World Heritage sites have utilized multimedia technologies such as digital texts, photographs, sound, interactive animations/movies and video to represent 'World Heritage' in a number of new ways. In addition, the online UNESCO register has provided the opportunity for other locally produced World Heritage sites to hyperlink and be accessed from UNESCO's site, thus creating the possibility of using the online World Heritage list as a forum for 'World Heritage.' Sites in Egypt, Jordan, Morocco and Turkey thus provide access to other related sites, which extend the concept of online 'World Heritage' to non-UNESCO representations and inscribe an understanding of online 'World Heritage' as potentially virtual.

Where UNESCO and other web producers create virtual representations of online 'Middle Eastern' 'World Heritage,' these nascent online productions suggest the possibility of online World Heritage destinations distinct from on-the-ground World Heritage sites. Multimedia Internet technologies, while still developing rapidly, offer new possibilities of representation. Packer and Jordan's (2001: xxx–xxxi) five interrelated processes, describing a new cultural pattern, conjoin to shape a new form of communication about 'World Heritage.' UNESCO's online inscription of World Heritage sites thus are not only reflected in accessibility of the list but in a new mode of communication.

Information technologies reshape 'World Heritage' in manifold ways. UNESCO's concept of 'World Heritage' and its expression on the WWW moves away from Said's construct of 'Orientalism,' while Schätze der Welt, engaging in 'Orientalist discourse' in its videos and choice of content, confirms Said's 'Orientalist' construct.

The development of nascent, online UNESCO World Heritage sites thus make accessible the common heritage of 'outstanding, universal' 'Middle Eastern' heritage sites to a worldwide group of tourists and computer users at the expense of 'local' understandings. Information technology thus transforms UNESCO World Heritage sites into a series of emerging 'places' with new groups of visitors, constructing novel ways of interacting with them.

Conclusion

For the authenticity-seeking online tourist, web surfing for online 'Middle Eastern' UNESCO World Heritage sites is now shaped by interactive digital representations that are reinscribed through a worldwide network of new communication processes. These inscription processes include integration of artistic and technological forms to shape hybrid mediums, interactivity (direct manipulation of and communication through media), hypermedia (personal trail of association created by the linking of separate media elements), nascent immersion (experience of three-dimensional environment) and narrativity ('aesthetic and formal strategies that derive from the above concepts, and which result in nonlinear story forms and media presentation') (Packer & Jordan 2001: xxx–xxxi). While online UNESCO World Heritage-related sites do not represent the 'Middle East' as a whole, the possibility of viewing 'Middle Eastern' web sites on the Internet, through the inscription of a layer of 'representation' accessible around the world nevertheless shapes for the computer user and heterogeneous representation of the 'Middle East' in contrast to Said's 'Orientalist' construct.

In addition to this novel form of inscription process, the Internet shapes UNESCO 'Middle Eastern' 'World Heritage' in a number of other ways. Besides access to and from a worldwide network, one of the Internet's most fundamental characteristics is change. Not only are the technologies in flux, but also the way they represent 'Middle Eastern' 'World Heritage' is in flux. In addition, the speed at which this is occurring impacts on the way 'World Heritage' is represented.

The Internet, in addition, also affords chance or serendipitous interactions with 'World Heritage' in ways distinct from on-the-ground experiences, reshaping Said's 'construct.' The Internet provides the possibility for an easily accessed and growing quantity of content unlike any other mediums. The Internet also creates a more direct connection between 'Middle Eastern' online web productions and the end user. The Internet amplifies or magnifies the concept of 'World Heritage' by making it very quickly accessible, spanning large geographical distances in a growing number of ways. The UNESCO World Heritage Centre's inscription process for the 'Middle East' is thus significantly changed by all of the above processes, the manifold implications of which are still developing. In relation to the UNESCO online representations, Said's 'Orientalist' discourse consequently plays a relatively indistinct role in constructing representations of the 'Middle Eastern.' The production of UNESCO 'Middle Eastern' web content through these new communication processes and the production of a large amount of varied content, created by various web authors, thus represents a movement away from 'Orientalism.'

By examining the relation between a sample of local 'Middle Eastern' UNESCO World Heritage and related web sites and their nascent digital representations in terms of 'common heritage,' this chapter proposes that as a consequence of the rise of the Internet, the germinal expression of online UNESCO World Heritage de-emphasizes the significance of 'Orientalist' constructs and provides access to new forms of communication – UNESCO World Heritage multimedia web sites in Egypt, Jordan, Morocco and Turkey – reshaping UNESCO World Heritage itself. UNESCO World Heritage Centre's concept of 'common heritage' extends to include online representations and new forms of communication. The Internet and new technologies thus serve as a network to extend the concept of UNESCO's 'common heritage.' Online World Heritage sites become nascent touristic destinations complementing on-the-ground destinations, and changing the way travelers and tourists engage with 'local,' 'state,' 'Middle Eastern,' or 'UNESCO' representations of some online wonders of the world.

References

Castells, Manuel (2001) *Internet Galaxy: Reflections on the Internet, Business, and Society*. Oxford: Oxford University Press.

Deutsches Archaeologisches Institut (2001) *Die Ausgrabungen in Hattuscha*. On WWW at http://www.hattusa.org/. Accessed January 25, 2002.

Duncan, James and Ley, David (1993) *Place, Culture, Representation*. London and New York: Routledge.

ICCROM (International Centre for the Study of the Preservation and Restoration of Cultural Property) (2002) On WWW at http://www.iccrom.org/. Accessed May 1, 2002.

ICOMOS (International Council on Monuments and Sites) (2002) On WWW at http://www.icomos.org/. Accessed May 1, 2002.

ICUN (The World Conservation Union) (2002) On WWW at http://www.iucn.org/. Accessed May 1, 2002.

MacCannell, Dean (1976) *The Tourist: A New Theory of the Leisure Class*. Berkeley: University of California Press.

Omland, Atle (1997) *World Heritage – and the Relationship between the Global and the Local*. Cambridge University, Emmanuel College, Master's thesis. On WWW at http://folk.uio.no/atleom/master/contents.htm. Accessed March 22, 2002.

Packer, Randall and Jordan, Ken (eds) (2001) *Multimedia: from Wagner to Virtual Reality*. New York: W.W. Norton.

Safranbolu City Web Site, Turkey (2002) *Safranbolu*. On WWW at http://www.safranbolu.org/. Accessed February 1, 2002.

Said, Edward W. (1994) *Orientalism*. New York: Vintage Books.

SWR Schätze der Welt – Erbe der Menschheit (2002a) *Fes: Altstadt von Fes*. On WWW at http://www.schaetze-der-welt.de/denkmal.php?id=64/. Accessed May 1, 2002.

SWR Schätze der Welt – Erbe der Menschheit (2002b) *Göreme: Nationalpark Göreme und die Felsendenkmäler Kappadokiens*. On WWW at http://www.schaetze-der-welt.de/denkmal.php?id=232/. Accessed May 1, 2002.

SWR Schätze der Welt – Erbe der Menschheit (2002c) *Hierapolis-Pamukkale: Antike Stadt Hierapolis-Pamukkale.* On WWW at http://www.schaetze-der-welt.de/denkmal.php?id=165/. Accessed May 1, 2002.

SWR Schätze der Welt – Erbe der Menschheit (2002d) *Istanbul: Historische Bereiche von Istanbu.* On WWW at http://www.schaetze-der-welt.de/denkmal.php?id=164/. Accessed May 1, 2002.

SWR Schätze der Welt – Erbe der Menschheit (2002e) *Marrakesch: Altstadt von Marrakesch.* On WWW at http://www.schaetze-der-welt.de/denkmal.php?id=68/. Accessed May 1, 2002.

SWR Schätze der Welt – Erbe der Menschheit (2002f) *Flash 5 Animation.* On WWW at http://www.schaetze-der-welt.de/flash5_index.html/. Accessed May 1, 2002.

SWR Schätze der Welt – Erbe der Menschheit (2002g) *Petra: Ruinen von Petra.* On WWW at http://www.schaetze-der-welt.de/denkmal.php?id=135 /. Accessed April 1, 2002.

SWR Schätze der Welt – Erbe der Menschheit (2002h) *Q'useir Amra: Wüstenschloß Q'useir Amra.* On WWW at http://www.schaetze-der-welt.de/denkmal.php?id=136/. Accessed May 1, 2002.

SWR Schätze der Welt – Erbe der Menschheit (2002i) *Sdw_index.html.* On WWW at http://www.schaetze-der-welt.de/sdw_index.html/. Accessed April 1, 2002.

SWR Schätze der Welt – Erbe der Menschheit (2002j) *Troia: Archäologische Stätte von Troia.* On WWW at http://www.schaetze-der-welt.de/denkmal.php?id=231/. Accessed May 1, 2002.

Thurot, Jean Maurice and Thurot, Gaetane (1983) The ideology of class and tourism: Confronting the discourse of advertising. *Annals of Tourism Research* 11 (3), 173–90.

UNESCO (1946) *UNESCO Constitution.* On WWW at http://www.unesco.org/general/eng/about/constitution/index.shtml/. Accessed March 22, 2002.

UNESCO Deutsche UNESCO-Kommission e.V. (2002) *Wichtige Links.* On WWW at http://www.unesco.de/c_arbeitsgebiete/welterbe_links.htm/. Accessed May 1, 2002.

UNESCO World Heritage Centre (1972) *The World Heritage List: Alphabetically by State Party.* On WWW at http://www.unesco.org/whc/heritage.htm/. Update December 16, 2001. Accessed May 4, 2002.

UNESCO World Heritage Centre (1979a) *Abu Mena, Egypt.* One WWW at http://www.unesco.org/whc/sites/90.htm/. Update December 16, 2001. Accessed May 1, 2002.

UNESCO World Heritage Centre (1979b) *Ancient Thebes with its Necropolis, Egypt.* On WWW at http://www.unesco.org/whc/sites/87.htm/. Update May 28, 2001. Accessed May 1, 2002.

UNESCO World Heritage Centre (1979c) *Islamic Cairo, Egypt.* On WWW at http://www.unesco.org/whc/sites/89.htm/. Update May, 28 2001. Accessed May 1, 2002.

UNESCO World Heritage Centre (1979d) *Memphis and its Necropolis – the Pyramid Fields from Giza to Dahshur, Egypt.* On WWW at http://www.unesco.org/whc/sites/86.htm/. Update May 28, 2001. Accessed May 4, 2002.

UNESCO World Heritage Centre (1979e) *Nubian Monuments from Abu Simbel to Philae, Egypt.* On WWW at http://www.unesco.org/whc/sites/88.htm/. Update May 28, 2001. Accessed May 1, 2002.

UNESCO World Heritage Centre (1981) *Medina of Fez, Morocco.* On WWW at http://www.unesco.org/whc/sites/170.htm/. Update June 22, 1998. Accessed May 1, 2002.

UNESCO World Heritage Centre (1985a) *Göreme National Park and the Rock Sites of Cappadocia, Turkey.* On WWW at http://www.unesco.org/whc/sites/357. htm/. Update August 11, 2000. Accessed May 1, 2002.

UNESCO World Heritage Centre (1985b). *Great Mosque and Hospital of Divrigi, Turkey.* On WWW at http://www.unesco.org/whc/sites/358.htm/. Update August 11, 2000. Accessed May 1, 2002.

UNESCO World Heritage Centre (1985c) *Historic Areas of Istanbul, Turkey.* On WWW at http://www.unesco.org/whc/sites/356.htm/. Update April 18, 2001. Accessed May 1, 2002.

UNESCO World Heritage Centre (1985d) *Medina of Marrakesh, Morocco.* On WWW at http://www.unesco.org/whc/sites/331.htm/. Update June 22, 1998. Accessed May 1, 2002.

UNESCO World Heritage Centre (1985e) *Petra, Jordan.* On WWW at http://www.unesco.org/whc/sites/326.htm. Update June 22, 1998. Accessed May 1, 2002.

UNESCO World Heritage Centre (1985f) *Quesir Amra, Jordan.* On WWW at http://www.unesco.org/whc/sites/327.htm/. Update June 22, 1998. Accessed May 1, 2002.

UNESCO World Heritage Centre (1986) *Hattusha, Turkey.* On WWW at http://www.unesco.org/whc/sites/377.htm/. Update June 23, 2001. Accessed May 1, 2002.

UNESCO World Heritage Centre (1987a) *Ksar of Ait-Ben-Haddou, Morocco.* On WWW at http://www.unesco.org/whc/sites/444.htm/. Update June 22, 1998. Accessed May 1, 2002.

UNESCO World Heritage Centre (1987b) *Nemrut Dag, Turkey.* On WWW at http://www.unesco.org/whc/sites/448.htm/. Update August 11, 2000. Accessed May 1, 2002.

UNESCO World Heritage Centre (1988a) *Hierapolis-Pamukkale, Turkey.* On WWW at http://www.unesco.org/whc/sites/485.htm/. Update August 11, 2000. Accessed May 1, 2002.

UNESCO World Heritage Centre (1988b) *Xanthos-Letoon, Turkey.* On WWW at http://www.unesco.org/whc/sites/484.htm/. Update August 11, 2000. Accessed May 1, 2002.

UNESCO World Heritage Centre (1994a) *Bureau of the World Heritage Committee: 18th Session: Report of the Rapporteur.* On WWW at http://www.unesco.org/whc/archive/repbur94.htm/. Accessed March 1, 2002.

UNESCO World Heritage Centre (1994b) *City of Safranbolu, Turkey.* On WWW at http://www.unesco.org/whc/sites/614.htm/. Update March 12, 2002. Accessed May 1, 2002.

UNESCO World Heritage Centre (1996) *Historic City of Meknes, Morocco.* On WWW at http://www.unesco.org/whc/sites/793.htm /. Update June 22, 1998. Accessed May 1, 2002.

UNESCO World Heritage Centre (1997a) *Archaeological Site of Volubilis, Morocco.* On WWW at http://www.unesco.org/whc/sites/836.htm/. Update June 22, 1998. Accessed May 1, 2002.

UNESCO World Heritage Centre (1997b) *Medina of Tétouan (formerly known as Titawin), Morocco.* On WWW at http://www.unesco.org/whc/sites/837.htm/. Update June 22, 1998. Accessed May 1, 2002.

UNESCO World Heritage Centre (1998) *Archaeological Site of Troy, Turkey.* On WWW at http://www.unesco.org/whc/sites/849.htm/. Update August 11, 2000. Accessed May 1, 2002.

UNESCO World Heritage Centre (1999) *Twelfth General Assembly of States Parities to the Convention concerning the Protection of the World Cultural and Natural Heritage.* On WWW at http://whc.unesco.org/archive/whc99–205–5e.pdf/. Accessed May 1, 2002.

UNESCO World Heritage Centre (2000a) *The Convention: the Criteria for Selection.* On WWW at http://whc.unesco.org/4convent.htm/. Accessed May 1, 2000.

UNESCO World Heritage Centre (2000b) *Mission Statement.* On WWW at http://www.unesco.org/whc/1mission.htm/. Update June 1, 2000. Accessed December 12, 2001.

UNESCO World Heritage Centre (2001) *Medina of Essaouira (formerly Mogador), Morocco.* On WWW at http://www.unesco.org/whc/sites/753rev.htm/. Update December 16, 2001. Accessed May 1, 2002.

UNESCO World Heritage Centre (2002a) *Convention Concerning the Protection of the World Cultural and Natural Heritage.* On WWW at http://whc.unesco.org/world_he.htm/. Accessed May 1, 2002.

UNESCO World Heritage Centre (2002b) *Virtual Tours.* On WWW at http://www.unesco.org/whc/nwhc/pages/sites/s_f4.htm/. Accessed May 1, 2002.

UNESCO World Heritage Centre (2002c) *World Map.* On WWW at www.unesco.org/whc/nwhc/pages/sites/worldx.htm/. Accessed May 1, 2002.

Urry, John (1990) Cultural changes and the restructuring of tourism. In *The Tourist Gaze: Leisure and Travel in Contemporary Societies* (pp. 82–103). London: Sage.

Wang, Ning (1999) Rethinking authenticity in tourism experience. *Annals of Tourism Research* 26 (2), 349–70.

Whitbourn, Philip (2002) World Heritage Sites – The first thirty years. Talk delivered at London Metropolitan University, *The Politics of World Heritage Conference,* September 2002.

World Monuments Fund (2002) *World Monuments Watch List of 100 Most Endangered Sites.* On WWW at http://wmf.org/a/watchlist.html/. Accessed May 1, 2002.

Chapter 5

Visitors, Visions and Veils: The Portrayal of the Arab World in Tourism Advertising

SABA AL MAHADIN AND PETER BURNS

Introduction

While tourism is rightly considered a global industry, it takes place, or is consumed, in local situations. The geographic spread of the industry and given that even the most far-flung places are now on the tourist map means it can contribute effectively, but in complex ways to both economic and social development of visitors and the visited. This complexity has intrigued researchers with different backgrounds including social, cultural and political perspectives. Tourism's expansion over the past several decades has created further complexities in the form of unbalanced and unregulated relationships between local people and those who promote the industry through visual representations. The Islamic and Arab worlds have some sort of history in this, after all, Thomas Cook's earliest organized tours towards the end of the 19th century were to Egypt, but famously it was the Orientalist painters (Jan Baptiste Vanmour, Georg Emmanuel Opiz, Thomas Seddon, Jean-Leon Gerome, etc.) who, through their exoticized depictions of Pashas, Emirs and harems set the imaginative fever running through the Northern European mind. More recently, but just as powerfully, advertising images created by the tourism sector have continued this tradition. From an advertiser's perspective, potential tourists gaze upon constructed images of destinations and respond in various ways, depending on how that destination is being presented through printed press such as magazines and brochures, or audio-visual communications such as television, radio, news, documentaries and so on.

In the case of the Arab world, the basis of the images and ideologies used and expressed, pre-perceptions, knowledge and pseudo-knowledge of countries and cultures, is formed prior to travelling, which in turn frames the tourists' perceptions and prejudices during their stay. Three themes emerge to frame the discussion on the complex issues of tourism and culture in the Middle East, which will help structure the present chapter:

- Visions: The promotion of tourism of the Arab world through images, which symbolize backwardness, oppression and inferiority (veils, camels, 'timeless' (thus backward) tribal peoples) are adopted icons of tourism in order to effect tourists' travel decisions and perceptions about those countries. In other words, we will be looking at how the iconography of tourism to the Middle East can shape the knowledge and discourses about the region. In the words of Rana Kabbani visions of the Orient 'produced myths that were merely apt reflections . . . one more example of a Westerner's delusions of grandeur in the East' (1986: 112).
- Veils: Will be discussed throughout the chapter since they represent very interesting yet challenging media objects and are a key symbol of media discourse on the Arab Muslim world and Western ideology (within the framework of Orientalism). In so doing, we are borrowing Foucault's notion of an 'archaeology of knowledge' to uncover such practices in the tourism sector where they have been used to produce knowledge about the Arab world. Travelogues such as one from the 1950s describe veiled women in Morocco 'Arab women, whose eyes, peering just above their veiling, have always been so provocative' (Capote, 1981: 110–11).
- Visitors: Urry (1990) has made his mark by developing the essentially visual theme of tourism, what Franklin (2003: 103) refers to as 'post-modern visualism' whereby the tourists' visual and cultural 'beach-combing' consumes and spits out both objects and their meanings that are in turn recycled by the next group of tourists. Commercial visual images then, are a key component in the success or failure of a tourist destination, in Franklin's words (2003: 103): 'The tourist industry knows only too well how appropriately framed visual representations of tourist objects work their magic on consumers.'

The discourses surrounding visions, veils and visitors, of which Said's Orientalism is one, and the knowledge produced lead to a practice of power. In this way, the chapter contributes to cultural resistance by unearthing such power/knowledge mechanisms. The figures used in the chapter form a sort of Foucauldian 'genealogy of knowledge', which hopefully brings together Said's version of Orientalism with Foucault's sense of discourse to address a contested relationship within the tourism industry: that of viewer and viewed thus making further contribution to the understanding of tourism's complex relationships (not only between so-called hosts and guests, but between a complicated web of power relations and stakeholders). These three aspects, each of which will be explored further in the body of the text, together with a final section to bring the threads together into some cohesive conclusions, form this chapter on how the Arab world is portrayed for tourism.

Visions

From at least the time of the Crusades, the West has shown interest in the East driven by a range of theopolitical, geopolitical and cultural interests much of which was intertwined with the history of colonialism. The West's interest has created well-established travel flows to that part of the world and the publishing of many articles reflecting Western perceptions and concepts. Furthermore, these publications have formed a certain vision about the East in the Western mind: in essence, Orientalism. Edward Said (1978: 2–3) defines Orientalism as 'a style of thought based upon an ontological and epistemological distinction made between the Orient and (most of the time) the Occident'. However, many writings regarding the East, its lifestyles, ways of thinking, fatalism and so on, have been based on the perceived distinctions between the West and the East and captured for example in Samuel Taylor Coleridge's *Kubla Khan*, which 'provided a vivid contrast to the practical, industrious and technological age of nineteenth-century Europe' (Verrier, 1979: 2). In more recent times this distinction, this same narrative has been played out with the backward, irrational, emotional and unprogressive Arabs being portrayed as cowardly terrorists or fundamentalists unable to be governed with recourse to unelected theocracies or the guiding (but hidden) hand of the West: the same stereotypical images ingrained deeply into the psyche of Western thought. In terms of tourism we can see the visual narrative in the reduction of the number of directly Arab or Middle Eastern cues in advertising discourse. In the case of the Emirates' advertising very few images of Arabs are used (see http://www.emirates.org/tourism/ for example). Jordan's official 2003 tourism pages (http://www.see-jordan.com/photo.html) show 27 images in its photo gallery of which only one shows a clearly defined Jordanian, and this is a posed fashion shot shown as Figure 5.1.

As well as artistic and literary interpretations of the East, Orientalism (in the way that Said defined it) also includes anthropological work and

Figure 5.1 Traditional costume.

the reports and writings of (in the case of the British) Colonial and Foreign Office officials who emphasized their knowledge of and their power over the East. Images and perceptions of the East have become solid, and as Said (1978: 2) argued, defined the West through its 'contrasting image, idea, personality, experience'. Knowledge of the East has been the West's justification for ruling over and handling the East's affairs and this justification is reflected in the 'contrast' (opposite) image of the Orient. The search for 'exceptions, exclusions, incongruities, contradictions' as Kabbani, citing Italo Calvino's 1974 book *Invisible Cities* puts it (Kabbani,

1986: 113). Yet, such knowledge involves the writer as 'human subject in his own circumstances' (Said, 1978: 5) whereby the writer might approach the East with a mindset acculturated and politicized by social identity and modalities of feelings constructed and concretized by cultural conditioning.

The relationship between the West and the East is characterized by power and dominance. The West has regarded itself as superior, First World; the 'I' as opposed to the East, which, by its fatalism and exoticism, is inferior, Third World, and uncivilized 'Other'. This process of Othering has created a dichotomy whereby the superior 'I' has the moral task of civilizing the 'Other' in the form of direct colonization and later economic imperialism. The paradoxical nature of this relationship when confronted with the modernizing forces of economic change is well illustrated by tourism and its promotion of the past and past ways. The following extract is from an exclusive tour operator (http://www.worldsapart. org/index.htm) providing adventure/cultural tours in the Middle East and Iran:

> We seek the most authentic cultural encounters, the best balance between quality and quantity, and a relaxed pace that allows deeper cultural contact as we travel. We want you to get the feel of a place, to touch it, and to come away with memories and experiences that cannot be found elsewhere. We have been traveling to Iran since 1987, to both Oman and Yemen since 1990 (the year North and South Yemen unified) and we lived in Saudi Arabia for more than 10 years. We are the pioneers of adventure travel to Saudi Arabia and the only company currently allowed operating desert travel in 4 wheel drive vehicles in Kingdom.

The use of the phrase 'authentic cultural encounters' is at the core of the product on sale here and goes back to the idea hinted at by Kabbani (1986) about the desire to seek out contradictions to 'ordinary' lives through (for the purpose of the present chapter) touristic adventures which, in effect, can only take place in undeveloped regions of the world. Harris (1987: 18) has argued that the label 'Third World' itself was a post-war invention that was originally coined by Alfred Sauvy and was modelled on the Third Estate in the French revolution. As it has always been the case, the West's ideology has contributed to the post-war Third Worldism with little, if any, attention to what the populations of these countries want or perceive of themselves (Mehmet, 1995: 57). The binary oppositions mentioned by Kabanni (1986: 113) are at one level as simplistic as any such oppositions tend to be (lacking in nuance and so on) but they do point out that the West continually defines itself by highlighting what it is not, and thus lays the foundation for its civilizing mission; a point made time repeatedly by Said (1978). Based on this, the West takes responsibility for taming and educating this Third World population, or as aptly demonstrated in Thesiger's (1959) disappointment in changing Bedouin life, admonishment for abandoning old ways (Kabbani, 1986: 115):

> Towns rather than the desert were now centers of the new [oil] activity, and to these the Bedouins went, diminished, no longer the free spirits of the desert, unable to make use any longer of 'the qualities which once gave them mastery' [here Kabbani is quoting Thesiger's work].

Thesiger's view is the classic European one: the Western traveller, coming from a milieu of comfort and knowing he would soon be returning to it, could well afford to voice conservationist sentiments. The Arab, that ' "sometime Noble Savage" [Thesiger's sentiments expressed in the words of Tidrick (1981)] was picturesque in his environment.' In more modern times, sentimentality still pervades. Electronic media such as television news coverage and travelogues, film documentaries, and so on, represent a more recent and post-modern aspect of Orientalism, which the West (through the agency of the global travel corporations and their local agents) tends to use to emphasize the images, set by them about the Orient. These images have become more of standard 'molds' (Said, 1978: 26).

As can be seen from the above, various discourses have been used to produce knowledge about what it means to be Eastern or Western. Said's Orientalism falls within this category of revealing the practices that have given rise to the mould of the Orient as it was constructed by the West. Such moulds have had the unfavourable effect of creating particular forms of knowledge, which explain what is Oriental, and to reinforce the Western dominance. Therefore, the examination of any phenomenon has to fall within the domain of such forms of knowledge because change and resistance should start with uncovering such practices: be it the tourism sector or any other form of social exchange. So far as the Orient is concerned, standardization and cultural stereotyping have intensified the hold of the 19th-century academic and imaginative demonology of the 'the mysterious Orient'. For example, destinations are being stereotyped and labelled with certain images such as acts of terrorism, hijacking, instability and insecurity, which of course, being conveyed in such a manner will (understandably) have a negative impact on tourism. As a result, these countries are perceived in the West as being dangerous and unstable; therefore, Western tourists are sometimes warned through official travel advisories not to travel there fearing the potential for terrorism or violence, which might be of a threat to their own safety and security.

Images, signs and symbols contribute effectively to people's decisions and attitudes towards certain things and places creating the contested space of tourism such as when traditional areas (town squares, back streets, *sūq* and markets) become colonized first by itinerant tourists then by commercial business ventures and global franchises that follow the tourist-trail Starbucks and McDonald's being classic examples that have (on one hand) the possibility to alienate locals from their traditional spaces, but on the other (and one should not be naive or idealistic here) the paradoxical ability to give some youthful vigour to run-down areas in need of economic regeneration. Tourists, at one level, look for authenticity (though MacCannell is now backtracking somewhat on this position, cf. MacCannell, 2001) and that is why they tend to relate to certain places in a special way that could in return provide them with a genuine feeling regardless of what these places actually present. Travelling is a heartfelt and sensational experience in the sense that some places represent mystery to tourists, and such mystery adds up to the simple definition of travelling, paves the way for imagination, and attaches visitors with the contested representations of those places.

One of the most common images of the East (from the Afghan war to Saudi Arabia's attempts to open up to tourism) is the veil. The following section will briefly address the issue of veil and its relation with Islam and in doing so will also contribute to the debate on how '*hijab*' (modest Islamic dress, essentially the veil) is perceived in the West and the symbolic meanings of the veil.

Veils

As Leila Ahmed (1982: 149) has observed, the discourse of the veil became part of the Orientalist construct, as 'the peculiar practices of Islam with respect to women had always formed part of the Western narrative of the quintessential otherness and inferiority of Islam'. The Orientalist imagery permeated writings, paintings, postcards and photographs, allowing observers to penetrate women's privacy in Arab societies, and showing them behind the walls and barred windows. Photography was one instrument that, by what Graham-Brown (1988: 70) calls a 'leap of imagination', gives the illusion of revealing the hidden and forbidden, while creating 'the mythology' that Edward Said (1978) calls an 'orientalized Orient' (El-Guindi, 1999: 37). This emphasis is perfectly reflected in three examples. The first is a postcard from the 1920s (see Figure 5.2).

Figure 5.2 The exotic postcard (*c*.1920).
Sources: Kabbani (1986); Malek (1986).

Egypt – native girls

This card is undated but was probably produced in the 1920s (the colour of the paper and type of print font used and the girls themselves have an air of the 'flapper' about them). At this time, it certainly would have not been sent through the post, so probably constituted a 'collector's piece' a kind of soft pornography of the type seen in *National Geographic* in the 1950s. It is difficult to discern any sense of reality from this image: the jewellery looks authentic in a vague Bedouin style, shells and coins set in beaten silver, but as to the rest . . . ?

The image is like those to be found in Alloula Malek's *Colonial Harem* (1986), a book that explores the lascivious portrayal of Arabic women in the first part of the 20th century (1900–30). The image is fairly typical of (not quite) veiled and bare breasted: '*haram/hallal* (illicit/ licit)' as Malek describes it. Kabbani gave a typical description of colonial-era attitudes towards Eastern women from the literary Orientalist E.W. Lane:

> The women of Egypt have the character of being the most licentious in their feelings of all females who lay claim to be considered as members of a civilized nation . . . things are named, and subjects talked of by the most genteel women, that many prostitutes in our own country would probably abstain from mentioning. (1986: 52).

The second is an advertisement placed by Yemenia (Yemen's national airline) on the inside cover of the magazine Islamic Tourism (issue 2, winter 2002) 'A Quarterly Magazine of Tourism in the Islamic World' (see Figure 5.3). The final, third, example is from printed advertising material produced for the Yemen Ministry of Tourism in 1996 (see Figure 5.4).

This image of women (Figure 5.4) in Sa'ana, the old capital of the former North Yemen is typical of the type used in promoting Arabic destinations. In fact, it is also a typical image of Sa'ana, there is nothing faked

Figure 5.3 Yemeni advertisement (2002) showing the icons depicting Yemen: ancient buildings with a veiled woman. The message in Arabic reads 'Under a cool veil of mystery . . . a warm smile of welcome.'

Figure 5.4 General tourism brochure featuring the Yemeni city of Sana'a.

or contrived about what is seen. But it could also be argued that there are few accidents in advertising and selecting images for promotional purposes. The content of the picture is a market scene comprising two subjects: *abeya*- and *burka*-clad Yemeni women walking past what appears to be the gates to the *sūq* in the old part of the city. They are carrying their shopping comprising greens for dinner. The image-maker has taken a direct approach, yet there is the feel of documentary comment about the image. Thus we may speculate that the purpose of the image is to record and show daily life. However, as Wang (2000: 163) reminds us, 'Tourism brochures employ an underlying visual code that structures and organizes image making. This code can be termed "visual inclusion and exclusion".' He goes on to note that the selection and display of touristic images by tourism companies is a sort of ritual 'whereby features that are culturally desired are highlighted, amplified, and strategically placed'. What seems to be shown here then is a complex set if ideas, but can be summarized as either exotic Other or Orientalist. Cultural curiosity is aroused and reinforces the idea that tourism thrives on polarities or 'opposite states'. So, another reading of the image might be along the lines of: *here is Yemen. See how primitive and exotic it is. Regard the opposite to your own lives: veiled women, mud houses, alien architecture.*

In the news media, the veil is often treated with hostility disguised in 'humanism, feminism or human rights' (El-Guindi, 1999: xi). This was especially prevalent as part of the justification for the recent Afghanistan war, where veiling and women's rights were at the forefront of the moral crusade by the West. Muslim women are presented as caged, inaccessible and imprisoned behind walls and bars, hidden from men; yet, as the two examples above show, travelers, explorers, artists and scholars had produced an enormous volume of paintings, photos, postcards and writings depicting these women in detail (though admittedly not all were based on objective portrayal): the painter 'Richard Parkes Bonington never traveled further than Venice' (Verrier, 1979: 2). Hasib (1996), conveying a Muslim woman's view, clarified the misrepresentations about Islam and Muslims as an 'attitude of hostility prevalent in the West towards Muslims' and claims that 'Muslim women are strangely looked at an unusual sexual objects by the West, more so than other women in the World'. She adds that this approach was due to the challenge Islam represented at political and military levels to Europe's Christianity during the Middle Ages and the Renaissance. The veil, as a cultural icon, is rich in the way that it conveys social and cultural understanding. It also symbolizes an ideology, whether to Christianity represented in Roman Catholic perceptions of womanhood and holiness, or in Islam as a form of resistance, identity reinforcement and power.

Ernest Crawley (1931: 76) wrote: 'a Muslim woman takes the veil, just as does a nun' the veiling of the two women having equivalence. Yet, there is a noticeable difference between them that lies in what the veil means, represents, its ideology, the concept of womanhood, and the idea of 'sexuality'. Sherif Abdel Azim argued that the veil in the three religions – Jewish, Christianity and Islam – differs in its meaning and representations. The Jewish veil reflects a high social status and nobility, while in Christianity, women's cover is a symbol of men's power over women because men are regarded as the 'image and glory of God'.

Finally, the Islamic dress is an indication of modesty and self-protection: that is, women's protection.

Within Islamic societies, the well-being and the shared characteristics of women are the grounds on which same-sex intimacy and closeness are found. Relations do not exceed that because of the way women in Islam are educated and brought up in a manner that allows them to understand differences of relations with people from the same sex as opposed to those with the opposite sex without losing or consuming either kind of relations. Relations are protected and controlled by the Islamic regulations, which allow freedom of relations yet within limits. This 'protective freedom' is characterized in the dress code by the word '*hijab*' the root of which is '*hajaba*' meaning to hide from view or conceal. The Holy Qur'an says:

> Say to the believing man that they should lower their gaze and guard their modesty; that will make for greater purity for them; and Allah is well acquainted with all that they do. And say to the believing women that they should lower their gaze and guard their modesty; and that they should not display their beauty and ornaments except what must ordinarily appear thereof; that they should draw their veils over their bosoms and not display their beauty except to their husbands. (The Holy Qur'an, *Surrat al Nour* 24, *Aya* 30–1)

A pamphlet from the Institute of Islamic Information and Education (Ali, n.d.) describes this passage as 'having two injunctions: a woman should not show her beauty or adornments except what appears by uncontrolled factors such as the wind blowing her clothes, and the head covers should be drawn so as to cover the hair, the neck and the bosom'. Ali goes on to write:

> A Muslim woman who covers her head is making a statement about her identity. Anyone who sees her will know that she is a Muslim and has a good moral character. Many Muslim women who cover are filled with dignity and self esteem; they are pleased to be identified as a Muslim woman. As a chaste, modest, pure woman, she does not want her sexuality to enter into interactions with men in the smallest degree.

Rana Kabbani (1986: viii) shows how Western feminists, with their own ideology of veils perceive them as an 'aspect of patriarchies and a sign of women's backwardness, subordination, and oppression', and a weakness as opposed to the superiority of the Western culture. Western culture desires to free Muslim women and civilize them through unveiling.

Veiling is a cultural tradition introduced long before Islam. Covering the body has always been a cultural tradition rather than a religious requirement. Dress in Islam symbolizes as El-Guinidi (1999) shows.

- Modesty: It is about covering certain parts of the body to hide nakedness, prevent shame and people's gaze. Helen Watson (1994: 143) defines modesty, based on the Qur'an, as '*sitr al-'aura*', which provides the basis for regulation of behaviour, the segregation of the sexes and proper dress'. Akbar Ahmad (1992: 192–3) adds that 'Islam is specific about modesty in both men and women'; a dress that is tight on the skin is against this restriction;
- Privacy – of space and body: The concept of privacy in the Arab and Islamic world is quite different. It is more than just having one's own secret space; it is about woman and family. For women, it is a 'right and an exclusive privilege which is shown in dress, space, architecture and proxemic behaviour'. A woman is 'guardian' of the holiness that is essential to the society. A married woman becomes 'the lady of the home' (El-Guindi, 1985) and a senior, which again shows her role as a guardian. Therefore, privacy is not about individuals or isolation. It has to do with relations and people;
- Identity: Dress survives undermined borders to convey messages about identity and to serve as a personification of the memory of the group. Dress 'serves as a sign that the individual is linked to a specific community, simultaneously differentiates the same individual from all others; it includes and excludes' and this also applies to groups (El-Guindi, 1999: 1). This code of dress emphasizes an Islamic identity: fairness, society, identity that rejects Western materialism, consumerism and commercialism. That code disapproves of the 'exaggeration' of dress and acts, which was there before Islam. That means that it is not about particular time in history but something that can take place anywhere at any time. Therefore, societies do change and develop, in terms of understanding of dress and behaviour, as part of the whole process of 'renewal' of identity.
- Resistance: Veil as a movement (El-Guindi, 1999: 129). Dress has had a crucial role as a custom, political and symbol. The code has reflected a way of behaviour and ethnicity. Islam has fought to place itself in relation to the Islamic veil. As a result, the seculars and feminists have responded in a manner that reflected the extent of the threat of such 'ritual' to their ideologies and perceptions. Reziq (1983) explains how European efforts to prevent the wearing of the *haik* in Algeria resulted in having it as a sign of resistance.

- Social status: Women have role in the community, and their veils have never been an obstacle; on the contrary, the veil has helped pave the way for them to understand life and to work effectively in their communities. Furthermore, veils have given them a sense of belonging to certain community where they have gained respect, power to make a change in the sense that women were identified by their contribution to their community. Garments and mode of dressing reflect a person's socio-economic standing (El-Guindi, 1999).

In Islamic communities, dress links aspects of gender, sexuality, sanctuary and sacred privacy. They are all cultural constructions and social phenomena. As a material, there are two classifications: first, clothes to cover the body for modesty and protection purposes as well as for artistic reasons such as decoration; second, clothes and dressing style connote Islamic values of morality, respect and general humanness.

When God created men and women as a couple, it proves that both share certain rules related to obedience to God and neither is excluded from following this set of rules including the necessity of dressing in a certain way. El-Guinidi (1999: 76) draws the following conclusions from studying the creation of male and female:

- Both male and female, as a pair, were created (simultaneously) and treated equally in moral and behavioral responsibility;
- Neither female nor male was singled out in the disobedience, such in Christianity, known as the 'fall,' that was caused by Satan's deception – it is Satan who is sinful;
- Dress plays a fundamental role in their origins, their ultimate state of mortality and human morality;
- Dress is used in its material sense and in a symbolic sense; that is, to cover the body as form of protection and symbol of modesty;
- *Libas*, the Arabic Islamic word for dress, in its material form functions for clothing, protection and adornment; and
- *Libas* is a symbol of interdependence between the sexes, gender mutuality, and a cultural notion of 'respect' and privacy.

Hijab in general and veiling in particular have become potent symbols of Islam because this dress code provides a public display of social and cultural identity and religious affiliation and belief. A Muslim woman is expected to commit to *hijab* as a reflection of faith, which gives her honourable, respectable and dignified life. In one respect *hijab* is a tool to liberate and gives a feeling of respect whereby women are appreciated for their mind and personality 'not for their beauty or lack of it' and not as sex objects (Chopra, 2003). The dress code gives the woman the freedom to be whom she is from within, and protects her from the looks of the opposite sex as if she is just a sex object. It is liberation from the gaze of men and in being objects of sexual lust. They are equal to men and share the same rights within different social contexts.

This leads us to the next section in which we explore how media are used to carry ideologically constructed messages and images, the language used to serve such purposes, and the underlying intent of such communication.

Visitors

As MacCannell (2001) reminds us, the normative version of the tourist gaze is framed by tourist infrastructure and institutions; a straightforward desire to have visual and experiential contrast to normal, routine daily life, 'it is aligned with commercialized entertainment'. People tend to look for adventures and explore new destinations with different cultures. Tourists' perceptions of destinations and cultures are created through exposure to media: both printed and audio-visual in the form of advertising, editorial, news and travelogues. Such information will be framed by various sets of language in order to express certain thoughts; in other words: discourse.

Norman Fairclough (1995) provides a definition of discourse that links particularized social practice and the construction of power and knowledge. The world is presented in particular ways through the language used in media, in addition to identities and social relations representations (for instance, particular representations of Arabs, or the economy). Use of language is most likely to constitute of (1) social identities; (2) social relations; and (3) systems of knowledge and belief (corresponding respectively to identities, relationships and representations) (1995: 55).

Ideologies are used to serve power. They contribute to the production of certain power relations and dominance. They may be implicit, for instance, in the presuppositions (taken-for-granted assumptions) of texts. Ideologies are also implicit in the naturalized ways of organizing particular types of interaction. To show that meanings are working ideologically it is necessary to show that they do indeed serve relations of domination in particular cases. Returning to MacCannell, while not referring to ideology directly, he notes another type of tourism gaze in which 'seeing is not believing. Some things will remain hidden from it . . . The second gaze [an alternative to Urry's] turns back onto the gazing subject [i.e. the tourist] an ethical responsibility for the construction of its own existence.' In this case, MacCannell seems to be suggesting an ideology of the tourist, if so, then some progress is being made in theorizing at least some of the problems outlined in this chapter by placing much more responsibility on the tourists for their behaviour rather than seeing them as passive consumers of images and other signifiers.

The discourse for Arabia and the Middle East (including the Eastern Mediterranean) is firmly set in exoticism and Orientalism such as the following passage from Thesiger writing of his journey through the so-called 'Empty Quarter' of the Oman/ Saudi border:

> It was a bleak morning with a cold wind blowing from the north-east. The sun rose in a dusty sky but gave no warmth. Bin Kabina set out dates and fragments of bread, left over from the previous night, before calling us to come and eat. I refused, having no desire for food, and remained where I was, crouching behind a rock, trying to find shelter from the cutting wind and eddies of driven sand. I had slept little the night before, trying to asses the dangers and difficulties which lay ahead. (Thesiger, 1991: 222)

This 'Boys Own' style of writing about desert adventures with the white man firmly in control, reinforced the national psyche of the UK, already well prepared on a diet of other travel writers such as Freya Stark who, in telling of her travels to 'The Southern Gates of Arabia' in 1936 wrote:

> So far I had met only three of my Bedouin, Sa'id and Salim his nephew, and Salim's ten-year-old brother Muhammad, a skinny little boy with hair like rat's tails and a smile always ready on his frog-like little face . . . Said was a gay [happy] little bearded man with full lips and a straight nose and low forehead, horizontally wrinkled, from which his woolly curls were tied back in a girlish way with a broad, ragged band round his head. He was active and solid, like a figure of some lesser Roman god not of the best period, but inclined to the baroque. He had an ingratiating way of talking with his head on one side, and large spaniel eyes, very friendly and brown in the indigo of his face . . . His nephew, Salim had heavy lids, like a cat when it pretends to be sleepy, and a pouting, full upper lip; he was quite young and I thought he looked difficult to deal with. (Stark, 1945: 51)

The references to spaniels and cats, domestic pets in most countries together with the proprietarily use of the phrase 'my Bedouin' make it quite clear which traveller is both superior and in charge. Words like 'girlish', 'pouting' and 'difficult' all make excellent examples of Said's version of Orientalism. These days the patronizing language (to be frank, perhaps 'insulting' language is a better phrase) has moderated but remains, as can be seen from Figures 5.4 and 5.5 both taken from a 2004 up-market travel brochure (Kuoni Morocco) marketed at the UK visitor. In general, this is a fascinating brochure as visitors are (with the exception of one image by a swimming pool, and a series of action shots on the two-page spread on golf in Morocco) totally absent. Instead, Moroccans are presented in a variety of generally respectful situations going about their business in aesthetically pleasing or exotic places such as isolated mountains and busy *sūq*. The message here for any would-be visitors is that of exclusivity, away from the normal round of tourist trappings, of visitors who are cultured and appreciative.

Figures 5.5 and 5.6 both show the visitor an unthreatening and unchallenging cultural environment bounded by history and not of the present, complex world but rather as an example of less complex times.

On the other hand, in Panorama's 'Summer Sun Morocco' brochure for 2004 (a UK-based tour operator with a focus on family holidays) visitors abound and local people are hardly to be seen except where they provide

Figure 5.5 Relaxed and friendly people. Handsome smiling Arabs under the caption 'warm and friendly people' greet potential Kuoni 'World of Morocco' customers placing these non-threatening males in a neutral context.

Figure 5.6 A friendly welcome. Not quite veiled, but perhaps 'ethnic chic', a smiling, pretty face bedecked with Bedouin costume jewellery, as remote from everyday lives.

a little local colour. Here, the visitor is seen relaxing and being pampered; signifiers of the 'opposite' way of life from the busy existence in post-industrial UK, whereby 'individuals can choose types of travel that contrast distinctly from the types of behaviours and activities partaken in everyday life. This type of inversion can be linked not only to theories of dissonance . . . but also the role of inversion through tourism' (McCabe, 2002: 72).

Curiously both brochures feature water sellers (Figures 5.7 and 5.8). These highly mobile water carriers move effortlessly from brochure to brochure. In talking about the images provided in brochures that help tourists' choose their holiday destination, there is a danger of ignoring

Figure 5.7 The water sellers of El Fina Square (Panorama brochure).

Figure 5.8 Water bearers of Casablanca (Kuoni brochure).

media constructs. Even so, travelling is a personal choice, but ironically the choice is based unconsciously on what the media is constructing and is offering to its audience. Tourism, just like any other industry, has its own rules and implications, and is highly effective depending on how the countries are presented in the media.

The picture (Figure 5.9) of a mosque featuring its minaret can be considered typical of images portraying the Arab world. At first glance, it may seem 'just a picture,' but here we have Islam on show, not as the threatening purveyor of Jihad often seen in the Western press, but as non-threatening and backward. The mosque is probably 17th century and the minaret is framed by an entrance arch thus containing the image. The old man is stooped with age and the burden of living in a non-modern culture. Age has emasculated him so unlike his sons, he is unlikely to be a terrorist. Other than him, the courtyard is empty, so there are no 'hordes' to be seen. One reading of Urry's work interprets the scene as a 'romantic gaze' in the sense that 'solitude, privacy and a personal, semi-spiritual relationship [is] emphasised (2002: 150). In Dann's (1996) frame of reference the image is 'Paradise contained': a safe view of exotic other.

Conclusion

Underpinning this chapter, though not directly referred to in an overt way, is the idea that tourism is more than just receiving tourists, bringing in foreign exchange or even offering job opportunities. Tourism is a hybrid affair, with complex social, economic and political factors, which, from a political perspective, can be examined within the following three categories suggested by Richter (1989: 3–18).

(1) International relations: The increase or the decrease in the number of tourists between two nations can be used as a reference to the nature of the relation and shows the extent of their international collaboration. The issue of travel advisories issued by national governments and the extent to which these are political in nature is an area that is worth examining here. Relationships are, as noted above, characterized by power and dominance. In the case of the Middle East, the relationship between it and the West has been skewed by the politics of oil. The calls for democracy (especially by the US and the case of South America) have been strangely muted in the case of oil-rich countries that remain, for the most part, undemocratic in character. Discourse about tourism reflects these political international relations and remain draped in the 'Other' discourse of Orientalism.

Figure 5.9 Minaret.

(2) Public administration: Tourism is related to the public sector and interests. While governments are paying more attention to training and development programmes there are areas that are being neglected such as social impacts and consequences of tourism that can be ameliorated through awareness campaigns and public administration that gives agency to its constituents. As noted directly above, the real need is for democracy that enables constituents to influence the presently disputed spaces and representations promulgated through tourism: the need here is for accountable public administration.

(3) Policy studies: Tourism is not a mere economic or social activity. Policy is supposed to be somehow 'public' policy and as such should be democratically arrived at or at least have some kind of transparency about policy decision-making and implementation. Emphasis here is on how tourism can be used as a tool in building partnerships to create a more responsible society built around the values of accountability, democracy and sustainability.

To paraphrase the traditional Chinese proverb, 'we live in interesting times' and US aggressive action and attitudes in the Middle East and its dominance in global media (thinking here of Fox and CNN news channels, though the rise of Al-Jazira TV has been fascinating to watch) leads to the conclusion that there is no escaping the fact that Arabs and Islam are now perceived as political issues. Said (1978: 27) gives the following explanations:

> The history of popular anti-Arab and anti-Islamic prejudice in the West, which is immediately reflected in the history of Orientalism ... The struggle between the Arabs and Israeli Zionism, and its effects upon American Jews as well as upon both the liberal culture and the population at large, the almost total absence of any cultural position making it possible either to identify with or dispassionately to discuss the Arabs or Islam ... The Middle East is now identified with Great power politics, oil economics, and the simple-minded dichotomy of freedom-loving, democratic Israel and evil, totalitarian, and terrorists Arabs, the chances of anything like a clear view of what one talks about in talking about the Near East are depressingly small.

The paradox is that even within this geopolitical framework, and even given the increasingly complex versions of tourist motivation, the East itself and Arab world in particular represent a kind of authenticity that tourists and visitors hope to experience when they set out on their journeys. Their experience allows them to be in close touch with what they have read, seen and heard. From a Western visitors' point of view, veils are more than a body cover or religious dress, veils are what the East is all about: Orient, backwardness, oppression, inferiority. Travelling for the West is more than relaxing; they are after the mystery of the Orient and the authenticity of the place, which also gives some explanation for the appropriation of the veil by the travel industry to promote its products.

An important outcome is that despite the mobility across nations and accessibility to different cultures through tourism and other movements, which has resulted in the visible presence of veiled women in Western cities, the veil is still considered a sign of backwardness and oppression. The veil as an Islamic icon and identity actually liberate women and allows them to be present in public places while preserving their cultural and religious modesty. It can be argued that the veil has given women respect for who they are and not for what they wear.

To understand the Muslim society, the media should work more effectively. Such portrayal of the Arab Muslim world has a negative impact on promoting rational ideas about the Orient, and in effect discourse by the travel trade is a form of post-Orientalism. Visitors attracted to the region based on such images and portrayals will be confused and thus disappointed: the search for authenticity in the 'opposite' state of your own being by the fake time travel of tourism is not sustainable and is not helping the maturation of politics in the region: given the rich cultural and natural heritage of the region it is, at least, unfortunate that tourism promotion relies so heavily on experiencing the Otherness, which has been the de facto label for Third World.

References

Ahmad, Akbar S. (1992) *Postmodernism and Islam: Predicament and Promise*. London: Routledge.

Ahmed, Leila (1982) Western ethnocentrism and perceptions of the harem. *Feminist Studies* 8 (3), 521–34.

Ali, M. (n.d.) *What is Hijab?* Chicago: Institute for Islamic Information and Education. On WWW at http://www.usc.edu/dept/MSA/humanrelations/womeninislam/whatishijab.html. Accessed 10/10/2003.

Capote, T. (1981) Tangier notes. In M. O'Brien (ed.) *Travel in Vogue* (pp. 110–12). London: Book Club Associates.

Chopra, S. (2003) *Liberation by the Veil*. On WWW at http://www.islam101.com/women/hijbene.html. Accessed 12/11/2003.

Crawley, E. (1931) *Dress, Drinks, and Drums: Further Studies of Savages and Sex*. London: Methuen.

Dann, G. (1996) The people of the tourist brochures. In T. Selwyn (ed.) *The Tourist Image* (pp. 61–82). Chichester: John Wiley.

El-Guindi, F. (1985) The status of women in Bahrain: Social and cultural considerations. In J.B. Nugent and T.H. Thomas (eds) *Bahrain and the Gulf: Past Perspectives and Alternative Futures* (pp. 75–95). Sydney: Croom Helm.

El-Guindi, F. (1999) *Veil – Modesty, Privacy and Resistance*. Oxford: Berg.

Fairclough, Norman (1995) *Media Discourse*. London: Arnold.

Franklin, A. (2003) *Tourism: An Introduction*. London: Sage.

Graham-Brown, S. (1988) *Images of Women: The Portrayal of Women in Photography of the Middle 1860–1950*. London: Quartet Books.

Harris, Nigel (1987) *The End of the Third World: Newly Industrializing Countries and the Decline of an Ideology*. Harmondsworth: Penguin.

Hasib, L. (1996) *Exotic Western View of Muslim Women*. On WWW at http://www.muslimedia.com/archives/special98/women.htm. Accessed 10/10/2003.

Kabbani, R. (1986) *Europe's Myths of Orient*. London: Pandora.

McCabe, S. (2002) The tourist experience and everyday life. In G. Dann (ed.) *The Tourist of the Social World* (pp. 61–75). Oxford: CABI.

MacCannell, D. (2001) Tourist agency. *Tourist Studies* 1 (1), 23–37.

Malek, A. (1986) *The Colonial Harem*. Minneapolis: University of Minnesota Press.

Mehmet, Ozay (1995) *Westernizing the Third World: The Eurocentricity of Economic Development Theories*. London: Routledge.

Richter, Linda K. (1989) *The Politics of Tourism in Asia: Thailand Sri Lanka India Bhutan Bangladesh China Philippines The Maldives Nepal Pakistan*. Honolulu: University of Hawaii Press.

Reziq, I. (1983) Women's role in contemporary Algeria: Tradition and modernism. In B. Utas (ed.) *Women in Islamic Society: Social Attitudes and Historical Perspectives*. London: Curzon Press.

Said, Edward (1978) *Orientalism*. London: Penguin Books.

Stark, F. (1945) *The Southern Gates of Arabia*. London: Penguin Books.

Thesiger, W. (1991) *Arabian Sands*. London: Penguin Travel Library.

Tidrick, K. (1981) *Heart-beguiling Araby*. Cambridge: Cambridge University Press.

Urry, John (2002) *The Tourist Gaze* (2nd edn). London: Sage.

Verrier, Michelle (1979) *The Orientalists*. London: Academy Editions.

Wang, N. (2000) *Tourism and Modernity: A Sociological Analysis*. Oxford: Pergamon.

Watson, H.E. (1994) Why fundamentalism? *Government and Opposition* 28 (4).

Chapter 6

The 'Islamic' City and Tourism: Managing Conservation and Tourism in Traditional Neighbourhoods

AYLIN ORBAŞLI

Introduction

Although it is not possible to make generalisations on historic cities in the Middle East, or on their present state or condition, many are at a time of significant and complex change. Not only are the older quarters in urban areas being rapidly replaced by new 'developments', but also changing rural practices, better communication and transportation networks are changing the nature of small villages and impacting on vernacular traditions. In many instances the rapid loss of the urban heritage and traditional settlements can only be counteracted with the new appeal of these places as potential tourist destinations. Today the economic development benefits of tourism are being seen as a key opportunity for area-based conservation by both conservationists and developers (Orbaşlı, 2000). Tourism can also be an important catalyst in attaching value to the urban heritage and increasing its appreciation by local communities.

The concept of the 'Islamic' city has long been debated, but it is undeniable that a distinct urban tradition has developed in the Middle East, around the Mediterranean and into the Balkans (Bianca, 2000). Two key characteristics of the urban form, the separation of public and private space, and the social value attached to privacy and protection can present serious challenges for tourism development. The idea of visiting historic towns or settlements is one imported from the west and its adaptation in the Middle East must recognise the differences of the physical urban form and the social values that are inherent in the morphology.

Furthermore, for the communities involved, one of the greatest reasons for the abandonment of historic areas has been the aspiration for better

161

and 'modern' living conditions and a communal desire for participation in the modern economy (Kuban, 1978, Warren & Fethi, 1984). There is often an inherent conflict between the desired 'experience' of the tourists, the reality of a destination and the aspirations of the local population. This chapter looks at the case of 'Islamic' cities in the Middle East as tourist attractions and the implications of tourism for the conservation and continuity of traditional urban patterns.

Historic Cities and Conservation

Tradition, spatial form and character

Islam has dictated a certain urban pattern in the Islamic world, part of which is derived from the strictures of the Holy Quran. It would, however, be impossible to make stylistic generalisations on Islamic architecture; there are a variety of styles and forms ranging from the Balkans to Malaysia, through a variety of climatic regions with differing cultural and environmental influences. The laws of Islam have been interpreted and implemented differently in each region and the structure of an Islamic city differs in Iran, in Anatolia, in the Maghreb and other places (Kuban, 1980). Regional variations have also been influenced by the availability of materials and climatic differences as well as the influences of colonialisation and post-colonial political ideologies. In many Islamic countries urban form derives from a combination of belief, national identity and local tradition. Social lifestyle has strongly influenced urban form and in many cases continues to do so.

Nevertheless, in many places Islamic ideology has played a role in shaping towns, particularly human behaviour and movement within the towns, defining public and private spaces. Bianca (2000) points out that Islam embeds religious practice in the daily life of the individual and society, which then correlates to physical patterns in the urban environment. According to Abu Lughod (1980: 64) the Islamic city is a 'unique pattern of spatial organisation' reflecting an underlying ideology that each part of the city is a whole within itself, locking into a street and open space pattern and becoming part of the overall whole of the city, defining the togetherness of man and his environment within the city.

Organic formation and growth are the main characteristics of the Islamic city where the absence of a geometric land division system has often resulted in a network of winding streets and culs-de-sac (Kostof, 1991). Societal or sectoral ownership, by taking over areas and privatising streets has contributed to the characteristics of narrow and winding

streets and in general an absence of formal open public spaces (Madanipour, 2003). 'The organic character was further enriched in the Islamic
towns through surprise vistas at every corner of the street and every bend
of the road, a characteristic which can be identified today as part of the
Islamic heritage in human settlement' (Aga Khan Trust for Culture, 1980:
36). These characteristics are by no means incidental and play a role in
maintaining privacy and counteracting the climate. They are also some
of the characteristics that appeal to tourists.

Another common characteristic relates to the age and therefore style of
the buildings. While the underlying urban morphology was maintained,
the individual buildings within it were more frequently renewed, since,
unlike major monuments and public buildings, the 'humble' residential
dwellings were often built out of perishable or low-quality material
(Küçükerman, 1985). Even in Istanbul few houses date further back than
the 18th century (Goodwin, 1992) and those that have survived for over a
century are likely to have been intended for a mere 50-year lifespan.
Unlike European historic cities, with buildings spanning several centuries,
the Islamic city presents a greater stylistic homogeneity (Cerasi, 1999).

The two key components of traditional cities in the Arab world are
the public and the private areas (Raymond, 1984). Thus the traditional
city constitutes a succession of transitions between open, semi open and
closed places, which are also linked to the social hierarchy of public, semi
public, semi private and private spaces within the urban structure. The
public city was the centre of religious, administrative and economic
activity with the wider streets connecting the centre to the urban boundaries. Not unlike Christian medieval towns, the commercial area formed
a second centre to the town and craft trades were grouped together in
streets. The *sūq* or bazaar, unlike the medieval market place, however,
was a linear development of small cells and often colonnaded units. Open
spaces as well as some of the main streets became the venues for weekly
markets. Other commercial buildings, including the *han* (or *Khan*), served
businesses and visiting traders.

In the private city, the house was the starting point of privacy: each
unit defined by the, often extended, family with its own public and
private areas. This pattern, to a greater extent has been dictated by the
male–female relationship in Islamic and Middle Eastern society and such
divisions continue to influence house building in some areas still today
(Madanipour, 2003). The residential areas often form a concentric pattern
from the centre with an irregular street network and closed neighbourhoods. Traditionally, self-contained quarters were occupied by different
ethnic, trade or craft groups; regulation in this manner makes the Islamic

tradition stand apart from the western pattern (Berque, 1980: 52). Each quarter, known as *mahalle* centred around a mosque or a place of worship according to the religion of the inhabitants, a *hamam*, the bath house, and probably a bakery. Surrounded by walls and the gates, the *mahalle* could also be secured at night.

Colonialisation, industrialisation and 'modernisation'

Globally the growth of urban populations is impacting on the survival of historic quarters. In developing countries rapid urbanisation coupled with aspirations to modernity poses a serious threat to the future of historic quarters. In the Middle East development pressure for growth has often been at the expense of the urban heritage. Malik (1993: 65) describes the urban structure of most contemporary cities in Muslim countries as being made up of

> a few select areas designed and shaped by the few professionals and experts trained almost anywhere, in any language, culture and history except their own, and in marked contrast, vast un-planned areas of physical and environmental decay and deprivation built anyhow, anywhere and by anyone.

He continues by defining the dominant urban model, backed today by policy and decision makers, having three distinct sectors: the inherited city (the historic city); the new city; and the slum city (Malik, 1993: 68–9). Of the three sectors, the historic areas have often come to represent a transition zone, between the planned new and the sprawling squatters, and between civilised and undeveloped, at times disappearing altogether at the intersection of this conflict.

In Isfahan in Iran owners were encouraged to sell their plots in the old city to make way for multi-storey apartment developments (Fethi, 1993), while only a few timber houses survive today in Istanbul's up and coming districts. In Mecca and Medina, expansion of the two holy mosques and their supporting infrastructure has been at the expense of the Aghawat quarter in Medina and the equally valuable domestic and monumental heritage of Mecca. Both Fethi (1993) and Bianca (2000) point out that the richest Arab countries were the first to destroy their historical quarters.

But, lifestyles are also changing. Today only a small portion of urban dwellers continue the urban lifestyle patterns from which many of the traditional quarters grew. Warren and Fethi (1984: 74) note that 'in the city of old the family was a nomad in its own house, migrating around the dwelling to obtain the greatest advantage of shade, shelter or winter sun, according to circumstances and season'. Not only has the introduction of modern commodities such as air-conditioning, changing sanitary provision and the pressures on land and space obliterated this practice, but also traditional houses in their traditional form are no longer suitable for the new smaller family size and modern lifestyle. Meanwhile, contemporary western styles in architecture are frequently being replicated with few modifications to incorporate local cultural, climatic, heritage or building tradition values. The Aga Khan Trust for Culture (1980: 32) refers to this attitude as a 'barrenness of spirit' that creates 'irrelevant and inefficient' environments.

Yet, for many, the old cities and their way of life are deemed outdated and irrelevant (Malik, 1993). As a result, in many places, the old quarters are disappearing, through decay and lack of maintenance (see Figure 6.1). Even though monuments are often being cared for and restored,

> the great bulk of buildings constituted by vernacular architecture are being wantonly destroyed, because their cultural and symbolic, even economic values are not subordinated to the exigencies of new life patterns, to the status of new forms and materials and speculative profits of staggering dimensions. (Kuban, 1980: 10)

In many instances close proximity to commercially viable land has often been at the expense of the historic core (Bianca, 2000). In spatial terms too, the layout of the traditional cities was seen to be confusing to the modernisers, and an obstacle, especially for the needs of cars and new infrastructure projects. The new public places that emerged 'were similar to the modern spaces of their western counterparts: dominated by the cars rather than pedestrians, losing much of their meaning and role in social life' (Madanipour, 2003: 213).

Where the upper and middle classes have left the older neighbourhoods for the modern suburbs, the larger houses have been divided up by the poor, increasing inner-city population densities, detracting from the architectural qualities and reducing the privacy the inner courtyards once provided. In the case of larger cites the older neighbourhoods have frequently deteriorated into slums or totally disappeared. In Ankara in Turkey, the neighbourhoods around the citadel, having provided housing for the new administrative elite in the 1920s, with the shift of the commercial centre further eastwards, have rapidly deteriorated into poor accommodation housing migrant workers and a transitionary population (Günay, 1988). However, with less pressure on development and change, historic quarters in smaller towns have often had a better chance of survival, as again can be illustrated in places such as Kütahya, Afyon or

Figure 6.1 Traditional houses, such as this one in Kula, Turkey, are abandoned in favour of new and 'modern' dwellings. But will
tourism fit comfortably with the traditional way of life maintained in the neighbourhood?

Source: Author's own photograph (1993).

Amasya in Turkey. Another example is Salt in Jordan, where the high level of survival of the historic fabric can be attributed to its location on a border zone and therefore 'out of the way' of development and with it inward investment (Daher, 1999). Nevertheless, aspirations towards western styles of living are rapidly spreading from the larger centres to smaller towns and rural areas, threatening the survival of traditional quarters.

The traditional commercial centres are also under pressure from development and competition from new commercial developments. While many continue to thrive economically, they are physically decaying. Although the smaller units tend to be occupied, the larger ones, such as the *han* which are often under single ownership, are more likely to be in need of substantial investment. Many have been abandoned because they are beyond repair that is feasible to the commercial community. In some places the old commercial complexes have gained monument status in their own right and the covered bazaar of Istanbul or the *sūq* of Damascus have become tourist attractions today. In other cases, however, this important aspect of the urban heritage is still fighting for survival against the pressures of new commercial development and rising land values. The last remaining Ottomon *sūq* in Hofuf, Saudi Arabia, also an important centre for craft trades, has been under constant pressure for redevelopment, and was substantially damaged by a fire early in 2002 (see Figure 6.2).

In rural areas, changing agricultural practice, availability of new construction materials and new transportation networks are also resulting in the abandonment of traditional lifestyles. The more 'modern' yet often characterless style of buildings that are appearing is impacting on the character of the landscape and from a tourism point of view also detracting from the appreciation of the setting and natural environment.

Urban conservation in practice

Compared to the European urban conservation movement, recognition of the heritage value of historic quarters and associated rehabilitation initiatives are relatively recent in the Middle East. Against desires for 'development', common problems facing conservation have been a lack of funding, lack of expertise and the absence of quality control.

The dilemma between old and new exists in both western and eastern cities (Larkham, 1996, Tiesdell *et al.*, 1996). However, in the east there is less understanding of historic continuity and more emphasis on the activity of development and status of the modern (Kuban, 1980: 6).

Figure 6.2 Although the Qaysariya *Sūq* in *Hofuf* in Saudi Arabia is a unique example of a place where craft traditions continue to thrive, it has recently been threatened by fire.

Source: Author's own photograph (2002).

Conservation, particularly as it is seen in Western Europe, can become an exaggerated concern to keep everything as it is, which may not be possible or desirable in another cultural context. Heritage understanding is different for each community and the communal value of a neighbourhood may be seen as more important than the heritage value of individual buildings. Aestheticism, historical continuity and materialistic wealth are predominantly European values and are not necessarily values other communities identify with. In other societies symbolic, religious and naturalistic values may be greater reasons for conservation (Oliver, 1982: 3). 'Conservation is not only a scientific issue but also a social one' (Hodjat, 1995). As Butt (1988: 1) points out, 'people attach considerable value to aspects of their immediate environment . . . which give them a sense of identity and pride of place'; in many instances lived-in surroundings are rarely identified as heritage.

Referring to the Arab Medina, Warren and Fethi note that it

cannot effectively be conserved in part. If important individual houses are to be saved, they cannot be isolated, to be left standing as individual monuments with bared party walls, in reversal of the original condition. The Medina is a complex matrix like a honeycomb and the whole of the fabric must be brought into repair and upgraded coherently. (Warren & Fethi, 1984: 76)

Yet, conservation concerns and programmes are rarely able to consider the whole and many proceed with little social concern.

Further compounding conservation efforts is the fact that the traditional city form was developed for the use of pedestrians and animals only, making vehicular accessibility a major consideration in the preservation and rehabilitation of Muslim towns. Antoniou (1981: 87) notes that 'the fabric of a traditional Islamic settlement is much less able to withstand the pressures of intrusion'.

Privacy of residential units, human scale, physical and social intervention, interaction between buildings and enclosed spaces, linkages between housing, markets and social facilities are essential assets of the historic city, which need to be carefully balanced against the advantages of better vehicular accessibility. (Bianca, 2000: 180)

Economic interests and political preference is also decisive in the conservation of urban areas. Overall urban planning and measures on conservation areas are often not considered together, and may even be administered by completely separate state departments. Much depends on which national and local bodies have control. While departments of antiquities are responsible for the protection of historic buildings, building activities within urban areas are often controlled directly by municipalities. For many of these overworked and under-funded departments, historic buildings are only an item on a protection list rather than a cause for action. In many cases there is a lack of qualified or expert staff and insufficient resources needed to carry out or even control conservation. Poor administration is a known problem and heavy bureaucracy for the simplest intervention is common to most places, hampered by constraints to policy implementation in the current market-led political climate. In efforts to avoid a lengthy and expensive process, owners and occupiers of houses in historic areas continue to repair, change or demolish properties without official consent.

Tourism in Historic Cities of the Middle East

The historic city as a visitor attraction

On the subject of visiting historic monuments in the Islamic tradition, Hodjat (1995) points out that it is not uncommon to visits monuments and public buildings, which he refers to as 'relics', as they are seen as the greater thing whereas human settlements, regarded as 'humble', are less likely to be considered as a relic, and therefore visited or revered in the same manner.

Historic urban areas and traditional settlements can be cultural tourism attractions, and for many historic towns in Europe, tourism has become a major economic sector. For local authorities, tourism represents a new and 'clean' economy, where the urban fabric constitutes both the asset and the investment. Thus, cities, towns and villages become 'products' for the tourism sector, where they are marketed as 'destinations' with little consideration for the urban realities or future sustainability of these places.

Tourism is potentially a catalyst for the safeguarding of historic fabric and the initiation of conservation on an urban scale. Appreciation of the historic environment by visitors not only becomes a reason for conservation but also increases local interest in the environment. Although tourism is not a direct financial resource for conservation, indirectly it opens up previously unavailable development finances. The restoration and reuse of redundant buildings encourages other environmental improvements, adds life and activity to a place, provides an example of conservation, and may boost the economy to a level that will enable other small-scale improvements to happen (Orbaşlı, 2000). Community awareness of the benefits of conservation increases local involvement and demand for conservation. Experience shows that where an organised initiative has been introduced, results and public engagement have been successful, whereas in the absence of guidance results have been mixed.

For tourists, the attraction of historic towns and settlements for tourism are:

- the physical attractiveness of the buildings, streetscape, townscape, views and vistas;
- the human scale lost in the modern metropolis;
- their walkable and explorable characteristics;
- the life within them;
- the small industry and crafts trades that are part of their life and character;

- the opportunity for visitors to become temporarily part of urban life;
- intangible values such as atmosphere and sense of connection with the past.

Sustainable or responsible tourism may be unlikely labels to attach to visiting historic towns and settlements, but much of the use and activity in traditional settlements can be environmentally considerate. The reuse of an area, the reuse of existing buildings, the lower energy demands of existing buildings or the pedestrian scale that encourages walking are just some aspects. Added to this is the reduction of pressure on fragile natural and urban environments for new developments.

There are three distinct aspects of urban tourism that need to be carefully considered in relation to the conservation of historic quarters. The first is the political dimension and associated decision making process that influences the ways in which tourism develops and how historic quarters are conserved. The second is the economic dimension that involves the servicing of tourism though retail, catering and accommodation facilities. Finally, and most importantly is the social dimension, involving the interaction between the visitor and the host community (Burkart & Medlik, 1974). Each creates different conflicts between tourism and historic areas, and between tourists and local inhabitants.

Tourism, conservation and urban form

In many cases political and commercial interests are guiding historic town conservation towards quick turn-around projects and recreated façades to generate tourist interest and associated commercial gain. The notion that tourism will bring money and that historic buildings are desirable have lead many owners to hasty and often damaging 'restorations'. Middleton and Hawkins (1998) refer to a common attitude of 'jumping on the tourist band wagon' in coastal regions of Turkey and Greece. Hastily activated conservation and tourism development is likely to be short-lived, especially where buildings and environments are irreversibly damaged in the name of conservation. Once the sought popularity is achieved, there is an immediate threat of over-development and subsequent devaluation.

Tourism interest has in places triggered off some examples of 'show piece' conservation, through the isolated 'restoration' of historic houses to appeal to visitors. In some cases this may form a focus for both tourism activity and for further restoration projects. Istanbul's Soğukçeşme Street restoration is no more than a multi-coloured façade clad onto a concrete frame building set on a mock street adorned with 'heritage' style street lamps, which are a common feature in many of Europe's historic towns (Orbaşlı, 2000). This practice nevertheless continues to be seen as a valid approach in Turkey and more recently a section of traditional houses in Konya adjoining the much visited Mevlana Museum were redeveloped as a new commercial centre. The project, incorporating shops, restaurants and offices clearly deviates from the original form and morphology of the area. In order to be able to accommodate the needs of the new functions, the architecture has been substantially altered and a number of the houses replaced with new buildings built in new materials an historic 'pastiche' style with interiors that are unapologetically contemporary. Outside, gates separate ownership while defying the logic and character of the former street patterns.

In the residential quarters of Islamic settlements, the ground level is used for access, storage or for animals while the upper levels are for living. It is commonly the case that high walls on the ground floor ensure privacy in houses while openings emerge in the first floor level where the living quarters are. Penetration into the ground floor walls, as a result of demands of new commercial activity, not only damages the physical fabric but is also a wholesale intervention to townscape and character (see Figure 6.3). This has been the experience in many of Turkey's coastal historic towns. Antalya, once one of the best-preserved historic quarters in Turkey, today has increasingly little to offer as a historic town as extensive retail use of the quarter has replaced the tranquillity and quality of the former residential quarters (Orbaşlı, 2000). Uncontrolled development in the 1990s resulted in an unprecedented growth in commercial activity in the residential core. Shops, restaurants and guesthouses have overwhelmingly taken over the residential buildings, radically transforming them in the process. Although the street network has been maintained, the experience has been completely altered as buildings have been poorly restored, incorrectly rebuilt and modified to accommodate the new uses. The opening up of ground floors for shops has completely altered the visual character and authenticity of the whole, while the growing number of new building 'replacements' of the old, has diminished the group value of the traditional buildings. Subsequently the character of the walled city has changed from a lived-in residential quarter to a poorly restored and altered tourist commercial zone, which has already started to loose its value as an attractive place for visitors.

Here other common characteristics of the Islamic city should be noted. While a neighbourhood street is best expressed in tranquillity, the *sūq* or commercial centre comes alive with the presence of people. From a social

Figure 6.3 This traditional house in Ankara, Turkey, is a typical example of a commercial restoration, where the proportions of the ground floor have been altered to make way for the restaurant entrance.

Source: Author's own photograph (1995).

point of view tourists can be more easily absorbed and become part of a busy marketplace, but the same is not always the case in the 'private' neighbourhoods.

Conflicts arising from tourism

> Tourists at various times occupy places which 'belong' to others and which carry cultural meanings for the host community.
>
> Robinson, 2001: 48

Most principles on the conservation of historic cities have been developed in Europe and are based on the European context, which is not always responsive to the cultural differences and socio-economic realities of other cultures. The approach to conservation, particularly of urban areas, is often different and will not necessarily comply with the western ideas of historic towns and their picturesque qualities, nor will local populations necessarily tolerate tourism in towns in the same manner. While it is tradition to be hospitable and welcoming towards guests, when this is exploited by tour operators and excessive numbers, many feel their privacy and lifestyle is invaded and become hostile or start seeing tourists purely as an element of economic gain. In the village of Şirince, close to Turkey's western coast, low-scale rural tourism from nearby coastal resorts was rapidly turned into a major tourist operation, which in the course of 10 years has not only seen physical developments of car parks, shopping areas and other associated tourist services, but also social change and commercial rivalry within the village. Village hospitality has been replaced by an unprecedented level of commercialism, while the character of the village has been irreversibly changed and its attractiveness is likely to be short-lived (see Figure 6.4).

Carrying capacity extends to the number of shops, hotels and other services provided, as a balance must be retained with the size and character of a place, and oversupply avoided. Commercial exploitation and overcrowding rapidly overwhelms and devalues historic quality. With the spread of tourist commercialism there is a tendency to spread the commercial activity into the neighbourhoods. Where residential gives way to commercial, then the social balance, the spatial characteristics and most importantly the sought after character will be lost.

A historic city as a tourist destination undoubtedly attracts commerce, and this is more likely to be at a local level, which could simply be the continuation of the existing tradition. In existing commercial areas, there

Figure 6.4 Aggressive commercialism has overtaken the once peaceful and picturesque village of Şirince. Increasingly imported and generic souvenirs are replacing local products.

Source: Author's own photograph (2000).

is often a delicate balance between local commercial activity continuing and the market being directed towards tourist commercialism. Where increased economic activity is allowed to exceed its capacity then 'the character of the town will be altered – at best compromised and at worst ruined' (Worksett, 1989: 2). Once the market function is converted to the benefit of the tourist industry, the informal sector and the economy of the inner city that related to its inhabitants may be lost (see Figure 6.5). As tourist functions spread out from the centre to the neighbourhoods, inhabitants will also leave the area, or if they are too poor they will be driven out not only for not complying with the tourist image, but also because they can no longer to afford to live there. For poorer economies, moving people out of areas has even greater social consequences (Habitat, 1984). In many cases the procedure is seen as one of providing alternative housing, not as a social issue. Removal of inhabitants not only cuts off social ties and vital links to the centre for jobs, but it is also a loss for the inner-city economy and vibrancy.

Figure 6.5 The old *khan* and covered bazaar of Kayseri in Central Anatolia
             competes with modern shopping malls and office buildings
             that surround it today.

Source: Author's own photograph (2000).

Opening historic areas to tourism involves presenting the historic town or quarter as a 'product', in which authenticity becomes an important component of the so-called visitor experience. Urry (1995) points out that much of tourism consumption is not in the actual purchase of a hotel room and the like, but the incidental, which he describes as that which is gazed upon, be it objects, places or people. Visiting historic towns in the Middle East is most likely to generate interest amongst western visitors. For many of them there is a distinctively romantic image of travelling to the east or the notion of the 'orient' suggesting exotic and mystical experiences that are also being emphasised through travel literature. Gregory (2001) links this to colonial nostalgia, referring to expectations of being served, and of seeing a lesser culture where camels and veiled women are considered part of the scenery. In the west, there is also a romantic image attached to dilapidation: 'The taste for decaying mud walls is a Western one, deriving from our passion for the romantic and the picturesque' (Lewcock, 1978: 73). What is seen as old and dysfunctional to residents comes to be seen as 'picturesque' to the visitor.

Much of this creates a conflict between the desire of local people for modernisation, which is often seen as westernisation, and the visitor's search for a lost oriental 'authenticity'. Furthermore while visitors search for the 'real' life, residents are demanding modernisation and better sanitation. The social carrying capacity is even more important than the physical carrying capacity of an urban area. Daher (2000: 111) refers to an example in Amman, where the conversion of a historic house into an internet café has resulted in an 'intrusion into this calm residential neighbourhood . . ., producing alienation and discomfort among the local community and intensifying the separation between the neighbourhood and its architectural heritage'. The privacy the urban pattern provides often continues to be valued by those living in traditional quarters. The neighbourhoods of the Islamic city, with their many culs-de-sac and few communal open spaces, are not physically formed to accommodate large numbers of tourists, but the explorative nature of tourism may also result in intrusion into the privacy of local inhabitants.

Privacy, particularly for the family, is an important component of both Islamic and Middle Eastern culture. Expectations for privacy in the neighbourhoods can be a challenge to tourism initiatives that are trying to develop a historic town or settlement as a whole for tourism. Cities, rural settlements and houses within them have been designed or developed to safeguard this privacy. Although part of the sought-after experience of visiting traditional settlements will be to see the traditional way of life, within the prevalent culture of the Middle East, it cannot be expected for villagers to randomly permit visitors into their houses. In places where settlements have been totally abandoned this is not an issue, though such distinctions should be communicated through interpretation.

There are strong arguments that tourism will bring change to otherwise conservative communities, particularly with younger generations aspiring to western influences (see also Murphy, 1985; Negi, 1990; Smith, 1978). Change, nevertheless, is inevitable and any form of tourist development will bring change to towns and communities. There will also be a process of change that is a natural outcome of modern development and progress, which will inevitably impact on local urban and social patterns. In an era of globalisation and communication most communities are experiencing some degree of change and this is likely to occur with or without tourism.

Heritage/tourist villages

Another emerging trend is the concept of so-called 'craft' villages. Created as part of an urban settlement or isolated in a rural location, they often bring together disappearing building and craft traditions often with a financial motive. Many result in bland and artificial environments and they may not necessarily be the best means of safeguarding a craft tradition. The Hatta village in the United Arab Emirates (UAE) is a typical example of a village rebuilt 'to serve as a spot of tourist interest and place of heritage' (Dubai Municipality, 1996: 15), most of the time devoid of human life (see Figure 6.6). While there are times when the creation of a 'park' environment is the only solution for the preservation of certain building types or techniques, the authenticity of these approaches must be questioned.

Another, frequently quoted example of remodelling the vernacular heritage for tourism purposes is the Taibet Zaman Hotel near Petra in Jordan. The project appears to be the reuse of the village houses as hotel accommodation. Nevertheless, in order to achieve five-star standards, new buildings have been constructed, a swimming pool added and the original houses substantially altered including concrete ceilings and under-floor heating (Jamhawi, 2002). More significantly the hotel complex has become isolated from the village and its community. Daher (2000: 111) notes that tourists are being presented with an 'image' of the distant past, rather than being given an opportunity to interact with the 'dynamics and realities of the present', and states for the case of Jordan: 'Very few projects attempt to sustain a living environment, most projects end up museumizing and commodifying historic environments' (Daher, 2000: 113).

Figure 6.6 Hatta village, UAE, a rebuilt 'traditional' village.
Source: Photograph by Simon Woodward (1997).

Craft traditions are dying across the Middle East, with a decline in demand and an improvement in work conditions. Newly made hand-woven carpets, for example, are more expensive than antique ones, and for many countries importing textiles and metalwork from Asian countries is a cheaper option. Similarly, nomadic traditions are also disappearing or changing their appearance, and the nomad tents have started appearing as permanent fixtures in tourist parks, whether it is *yörük* tent in western Anatolia or the Bedouin tent 'camps' along the Red Sea. However, any collection of traditional dwellings, however authentic, if unlived in will only offer the visitor a museum experience.

Responding to Tourism

Heritage, when considered at a national level, often relates to monuments and ancient sites and very rarely concerns itself with urban environments and the people who inhabit them. National policies for development may also overpower the interests of the smaller communities and the economies that support them. As Butt (1988: 1) notes 'attachment to historic buildings and townscapes is stronger among local residents than among administrators and politicians whose job it is to oversee environmental matters'. While national governments are keen to support conservation, interests are more likely to be in furthering development and increasing revenue, for which tourism is seen as a prime resource.

Tourism in cities, towns and rural areas

The approach to planning and the benefits derived from tourism can be very different depending on the size of a settlement. While the centres of large cities can easily absorb the impacts and fluctuations of tourism, the impact is much greater on the smaller towns, which have a more traditional way of living. A successful example of heritage tourism development in a large city is Old Jeddah, in Saudi Arabia, where local initiatives towards preserving the old town have also turned it into a pleasant place to visit. In other parts, Jeddah is considered a thriving commercial city, including other leisure attractions such as the Corniche. The restored former governor's house, Beit Nasif, acts both as a visitor centre and a focus for the protection and development of the old town. In many other cases though centrepiece restorations have generated grand projects that involve new buildings, some of which are not even faithful to the original design intention or construction techniques.

In Dubai, better known as a business hub and for the shopping facilities it offers in the Gulf region, the vernacular heritage is being rejuvenated as the tourism base is expanded. Tourism promotion includes cultural excursions to traditional wind tower houses, local *sūq*, spice and gold markets (Laws, 1995). Much of the promoted wind tower houses have in fact been rebuilt or reinstated partly in response to the developing tourism potential (Dubai Municipality, 1996). Gabr (2000: 204) describes the Basktakia district as 'a historic resource of potential value to tourism', and argues that the 'restored' area will complement other types of tourist attractions of the city. Nevertheless, and notably, the area is being restored as museum, with a view 'to reinvent the image and character of Dubai in general and to target historically sensitive and culturally sensitive tourists' (Gabr, 2000: 204).

One of the most important characteristics of the Islamic city was that it was a living city with continuous change and replacement. A spatial organisation can only be preserved if it is functional. Order is the definition of the city and disorder that of the crowds that keep the city alive through their movement. Even noise is an important aspect of the city with the *muezzins'* call five times a day, shopkeepers' competition, street sellers, etc. When this everyday life is replaced by a bland commercialism and showcase restoration the very essence of the city, what makes it attractive, is lost. Gabr (2000) notes the limited tourist interest in the Bastakia district of Dubai and questions the authenticity. To him the district is authentic and therefore 'real', but the absence of 'life' and continuity will test whether the proposed 'aggressive promotional campaign' (Gabr, 2000: 204) will achieve the desired goal of an 'authentic tourist experience'.

In many small and medium sized towns, where many residents have been born in the area, there continues to be a stable population and social cooperation. The medium sized or small town, it could be argued, will derive better benefits from tourism potential than large cities or rural settlements. There is less pressure for development, more likely continuation of a traditional lifestyle and often the greater need to benefit from successful tourism. Also most conflicts that need to be addressed including the ones for development are not as great as they are in the larger centres. For the case of the smaller towns it can be said that:

- Domestic architecture has been very utilitarian and a response to climate rather than with any stylistic concern; therefore continues to grow and change in response to changing family structure and social values.
- Society has experienced lesser change and the dominating features of public and private spaces continue to some extent to be part of the communities' concern, and privacy is regarded as important within the strict boundaries of the neighbourhood.
- Even though new trade patterns are being introduced, there continues to be a thriving informal sector occupying the small shops along the narrow streets in the more traditional commercial centre.

There remains a wealth of historic centres in the smaller towns, which are being given a new lease of life by becoming tourist attractions. With government budgets hardly ever stretching to conservation, tourism may become the only option for the preservation of heritage and urban development. An important point to consider while preserving old quarters is whether they will continue to be functional and relate to present-day urban problems and ongoing social changes. Successive tourism development plans for Salt in Jordan have failed to acknowledge its unique character as an 'Islamic' city and its social realities. Amongst various proposals for tourism development have been suggestions to establish cultural centres, new commercial zones for traditional crafts and the introduction of heritage trails, none of which fit comfortably with the existing social profile of Salt and indeed community needs (Orbaşlı, 1994).

With the need to work within tight budgets conservation has to be about 'the careful planning and management of limited and selected resources. It is a conscious process to control and manipulate change to a minimum – to a rate that ensures the survival of cultural heritage over a long time' (Fethi, 1993: 161). There is potential through tourism for the reuse of redundant buildings for the tourism-related functions. Visitors have the benefit of a genuine setting, a local building is restored and community life enhanced. Projects by the Turkish Touring and Automobile Association in Istanbul and Safranbolu have set an example by restoring redundant mansions and using them for tourist accommodation. In the Kariye project in Istanbul it was possible for a mansion to be converted into a hotel while the surrounding houses were restored and rented back to the original tenants. Since the Touring Club was operating as a not-for-profit organisation, it was able to divert some of the income from a tourist development towards upgrading housing.

Although rural settlements may also become destinations in their own right, they are not always able to offer the diversity of services available in urban settlements. The need to adapt to changing agricultural practices as a means of livelihood is also rapidly changing the shape and character of these settlements. Some are being abandoned altogether for a more convenient location, dictated by a transportation network for example. The picturesque village of Dhi Ain in Saudi Arabia makes a perfect poster image. The village itself however is rapidly decaying as it has been left abandoned. Unfortunately its biggest attraction for tourism is its picturesque image and setting, which could only be maintained at a high cost with very little return. In other places there are examples of abandoned villages that have been successfully turned into 'tourist villages'. Moreover, where there is a living population, the physical and social pressures of tourism are most felt in small settlements.

Planning and management of tourism

Tourism should not be the *only* solution for the protection and conservation of the urban heritage. Indeed, not every historic place is suitable for tourism development. Ease of access, proximity to other attractions (historic, leisure or commercial) will play an important role in developing tourism potential. Furthermore, the extent of survival of historic buildings, the level and appropriateness of modern interventions and the overall character of a place will determine its success as a 'destination'.

Close proximity to another similar and better preserved attraction may discourage tourism, but through careful planning and marketing the two could be linked for added value.

Nevertheless, tourism can become a vital tool in enabling the continuation of historic neighbourhoods as living environments for their inhabitants. To achieve this, patterns of urban tourism, the types and interests of the visitors need to be precisely understood. Part of a quality-based approach is to understand the types of visitors that a place is receiving and determine visitor patterns that produce the least impact on the locality and most benefit to the local economy. From this perspective it becomes possible to plan for both development and conservation at a local level that will attract this type of tourist. For example tourists travelling independently can be much better 'customers' for local establishments, even though they represent a smaller proportion in numbers. In Bergama, a medium sized town in close proximity to Turkey's western coast, backpacking type travellers and other independent groups bring greater benefit to the town than the hundreds that pass through each day on coach tours visit the ruins of the nearby archaeological site of Pergamon. Small-scale local businesses have been established running guest houses in the historic quarter, while local restaurants and shops benefit from the evening trade (Orbaşlı, 1994).

The availability of several attractions, possibly of a different nature, and a pleasant atmosphere inclusive of locals will encourage visitors to stay longer, and foster integration with the local community and lifestyle. Visitors appreciating and frequenting towns will provide long-term benefits for tourism growth, historic appreciation and urban development. At the same time, visitors themselves are becoming more demanding of destinations, the facilities on offer and the quality of the experience. Urry (1995) draws attention to a dropping trend in repeat visits to places, thus increasing competition for new custom in the cultural tourism marketplace.

Governments, with little experience of the tourist industry, will continue to try and attract as many tourists as possible rather than turn them away. It is also common for authorities to concentrate funding on historic monuments and sites that are perceived to have tourist appeal, thus creating a disproportionate distribution of already scarce conservation funds. Although large numbers impose pressure on fragile environments, control and management of numbers may be partially dependent on distant national policy.

Visitor management is not only a matter of traffic or pedestrian flow management, but also involves imaginative solutions to enhance the visitor experience, maintain a favourable reputation for the destination, while at the same time ensuring a high-quality environment for residents to live and work in, and visitors to enjoy. Chosen visitor strategies have to respond to specific needs and remain appropriate to the local culture. A thorough understanding of the urban situation, morphology, space and associated socio-economic factors is essential.

In the Islamic city maintaining the differentiation between the private and the public city could become more attractive to tourists and could be used to feed expectations. The hustle and bustle in the crowded markets contrasts with the calm retreat the 'private' residential areas can provide. There will always be a limit to the number of houses that can be converted into guest houses and it is more practical to use houses on the outskirts of a neighbourhood, and areas with better links to the commercial centre for such purposes. This will leave the private areas for the residents and continue to group tourist commercialism with the commercial centre. Nor should local activities be separated from those presented to tourists. For many visitors, visiting a local fruit and vegetable market and feeling part of it is seen as far more desirable as just looking at cheap tourist stalls. The attraction of visiting historic towns and quarters is the certain qualities offered to the visitor, including a lifestyle that is essentially not exploited by tourist commercialism.

Conclusion

Following the example of western historic cities, there is a growing awareness in the Middle East in preserving and developing historic quarters and traditional settlements for tourism. It must however be recognised that such developments are taking place at a time of significant change, transition and complexity within the physical and social context of the so-called Islamic city. To this end, conservation of the urban realm must recognise that culture is not a reminiscence of the past, but an essential part of human life within a city. Although tourism is seen as a vital tool for economic development in many of the worlds historic towns, 'progress has come to be identified with improvement in quantitative indicators; these concern mainly economic processes, seldom social, hardly ever cultural' (de Kadt, 1990: 9). As Rogers (1982: 15) points out, 'we must realise that maintaining structures means maintaining the desirability or continuity of a culture – we are in fact conserving cultures not buildings'. It is the people and communities living in historic neighbourhoods that create the sought-after 'character' and it is through improvements to the local needs that will encourage continuity of the historic cities.

The conservation and continuation of the urban heritage will be largely dependent on successful tourism management, achieved through an integrated approach accommodating and balancing the physical, spatial and social needs and concerns of both the community and of visitors. Tourism, however, cannot be the only solution to urban conservation in the Middle East. Where tourism development as a growth industry is possible, it can only be successful as long as economic benefits are penetrated into the community as provider, where the historic environment is appreciated and identified with by the resident community, and where visitors are given the opportunity to become part of urban life rather than remain superficial spectators.

References

Abu Lughod, Janet L. (1980) Preserving the living heritage of Islamic cities. In Renata Holod (ed.) *Toward and Architecture in the Spirit of Islam* (pp. 64–75). Philadelphia: The Aga Khan Awards.

Aga Khan Trust for Culture (1990) *Architectural and Urban Conservation in the Islamic World* (Vol. 1). Geneva: The Aga Khan Trust for Culture.

Antoniou, Jim (1981) *Islamic Cities and Conservation*. Switzerland: The UNESCO Press.

Berque, Jacques (1980) An Islamic Hieropolis. In Renata Holod (ed.) *Toward and Architecture in the Spirit of Islam* (pp. 87–99). Philadelphia: The Aga Khan Awards.

Bianca, Stefano (2000) *Urban Form in the Arab World: Past and Present*. London: Thames and Hudson.

Burkart, A.J. and Medlik, S. (1974) *Tourism: Past, Preset and Future*. London: Heineman.

Butt, Richard (1988) Auditing your heritage assets. In *Heritage and Successful Regeneration*. Strasbourg: Council of Europe.

Cerasi, Maurice M. (1999) *Osmanli Kenti: Osmanlı Imparatorlğunda 18. ve 19. Yüzyıllarda Kent Uygarlığı ve Mimarisi* (trans. into Turkish by A. Ataöv from Italian original). Istanbul: Yapı Kredi Yayıncılık.

Daher, Rami F. (1999) Gentrification and the politics of power, capital, and culture in a Jordanian heritage industry. *Traditional Dwellings and Settlements Review* X (2) 33–45.

Daher, Rami F. (2000) Dismantling a community's heritage 'heritage tourism: conflict, inequality, and a search for social justice in the age of globalisation'.In M. Robinson *et al.* (eds) *Tourism and Heritage Relationships: Global, National and Local Perspectives* (pp. 105–28). Sunderland: Business Education Publishers.

Dubai Municipality (1996) Traditional architecture of Dubai. *Arts and the Islamic World* 27 and 28 (special supplement).

Fethi, Ihsan (1993) Conservation in the Islamic world: Current practice and critical lessons. In Sultan Barakat (ed.) *Architecture and Development in the Islamic World*. Unpublished.

Gabr, Hisham (2000) Heritage and architectural preservation for tourist development: Reflections on the historic Bastakia district of Dubai, UAE. In M. Robinson *et al.* (eds) *Tourism and Heritage Relationships: Global, National and Local Perspectives* (pp. 197–209). Sunderland: Business Education Publishers.

Goodwin, Godfrey (1992) *A History of Ottoman Architecture.* Oxford: Thames and Hudson.

Gregory, Derek (2001) Colonial nostalgia and cultures of travel: Spaces of constructed visibility in Egypt. In Nezar AlSayyad (ed.) *Consuming Tradition, Manufacturing Heritag: Global Norms and Urban Forms in the Age of Tourism* (pp. 111–51). London and New York: Routledge.

Günay, Baykan (1988) Ankara: A case study. Paper presented at the *Salzburg Congress on Urban Planning and Development*, Salzburg, 6–9 May 1988.

Habitat (1984) *Upgrading of Inner-City Slums.* Nairobi, Kenya: Habitat.

Hodjat, Mehdi (1995) Cultural heritage in Iran: Policies for an Islamic country. Doctorate thesis, Institute of Advanced Architectural Studies, University of York.

Jamhawi, Monther M. Al-Dahash (2002) Conservation and tourism: Jordan's post 18th century architectural heritage. Unpublished doctorate thesis, Oxford Brookes University.

de Kadt, Emanuel (1990) *Making the Alternative Sustainable: Lessons from Development for Tourism.* London: Institute of Development Studies.

Kostof, Spiro (1991) *The City Shaped.* Boston: Bulfinch Press.

Kuban, Dogan (1978) Conservation of the historical environment of cultural survival. In Renata Holod (ed.) *Conservation as Cultural Survival* (pp. 1–8). Istanbul: The Aga Khan Awards.

Kuban, Dogan (1980) Toward an understanding of architectural symbolism. In Renata Holod (ed.) *Toward and Architecture in the Spirit of Islam* (pp. 32–41). Philadelphia: The Aga Khan Awards.

Küçükerman, Ö. (1985) *The Turkish House: In Search of Spatial Identity.* Istanbul: The Turkish Touring and Automobile Association.

Larkham, Peter (1996) *Conservation and the City.* London and New York: Routledge.

Laws, E. (1995) *Tourism Destination Management.* London and New York: Routledge.

Lewcock, Ronald (1978) Three problems in conservation: Egypt, Oman, Yemen. In Renata Holod (ed.) *Conservation as Cultural Survival* (pp. 66–76). Istanbul: The Aga Khan Awards.

Madanipour, Ali (2003) *Public and Private Spaces of the City.* London and New York: Routledge.

Malik, Ayyub (1993) Contemporary cities in the Muslim world. In Sultan Barakat (ed.) *Architecture and Development in the Islamic World.* Unpublished.

Middleton, V.T.C. and Hawkins, R. (1998) *Sustainable Tourism: A Marketing Perspective.* Oxford: Butterworth Heinemann.

Murphy, Peter E. (1985) *Tourism.* New York: Methuen.

Negi, Jagmohan (1990) *Tourism Development in Resource Conservation.* India: New Delhi Metropolitan.

Oliver, Paul (1982) Cultural issues in conservation implementation. In Roger Zetter (ed.) *Conservation of Buildings in Developing Countries.* Oxford: Oxford Polytechnic.

Orbaşlı, Aylin (1994) Historic towns: Tourism, conservation, development with particular reference to Turkish towns. Unpublished doctorate thesis, Institute of Advanced Architectural Studies, University of York.

Orbaşlı, Aylin (2000) *Tourists in Historic Towns: Urban Conservation and Heritage Management.* London and New York: Spon Press.

Raymond, André (1984) *The Great Arab Cities in the 16–18th Centuries: An Introduction.* London: New York University Press.

Robinson, Mike (2001) Tourism encounters: Inter and intra-cultural conflicts and the world's largest industry. In Nezar AlSayyad (ed.) *Consuming Tradition, Manufacturing Heritage Global Norms and Urban Forms in the Age of Tourism* (pp. 34–67). London and New York: Routledge.

Rogers, P. (1982) Conservation and implementation. in R. Zetter (ed.) *Conservation of Buildings in Developing Countries.* Oxford: Oxford Polytechnic.

Smith, Valene, L. (ed.) (1978) *Hosts and Guests.* Oxford: Blackwell.

Tiesdell, Steven, Oc, Taner and Heath, Tim (1996) *Revitalising Historic Urban Quarters.* Oxford: Architectural Press.

Urry, John (1995) *Consuming Places.* London and New York: Routledge.

Warren, John and Fethi, Ihsan (1984) *Conservation of Traditional Houses, Amanat al-Assima, Baghdad.* York: Coach Publishing.

Worksett, R. (1989) Managing tourism: Achieving a balance between commercial development, tourism requirements and historic preservation. *Tourism in Historic Towns*, 6th European Conference of Historic Towns, Cambridge, 20–2 September 1989. Strasbourg, Council of Europe.

Chapter 7

Development of Community-based Tourism in Oman: Challenges and Opportunities

BIRGIT MERSHEN

Destination Oman

The discussion about greater local participation in decision-making processes in tourism development and in the economic benefits from tourism has increasingly become an issue in global tourism literature, and includes Arab countries from Morocco to Jordan. What distinguishes Morocco, Tunisia, Egypt or Jordan from the Gulf States in general and from Oman in particular is their relatively longer tourism experience.

It was in the mid-1990s only that the Sultanate of Oman emerged as a new tourist destination in the European travel industry. Yemen, due to its rich archaeological and cultural heritage as well as to its natural attractions, had by then become an established destination for the Middle East traveler. Dubai on the other hand was aggressively promoting the United Arab Emirates (UAE) as a haven for shopping, business, conference and sun-sea-sand tourism.The Sultanate gained popularity as a politically safe, yet 'largely unknown tourist destination in the Orient, combining adventure and comfort, solitude and urban life, diversity of landscapes and cultural attractions' (translated from Kabasci & Franzisky, 1996: backcover). The shores of this new destination (see Figure 7.1), in the south east corner of the Arabian Peninsula, cover a distance of around 1700 km, from the Strait of Hormuz in the Arabian Gulf over the Gulf of Oman and the Indian Ocean to the borders of Yemen. With a population numbering only about 2.7 million inhabitants, the Sultanate occupies the large area of more than 300,000 sq. km. This area includes different types of terrain, from plains, to highlands and mountains, intersected by wadis, and a great variety of natural and man-made landscapes, ranging from sand deserts and gravel plains to the woodlands on Jabal al Akhdar and

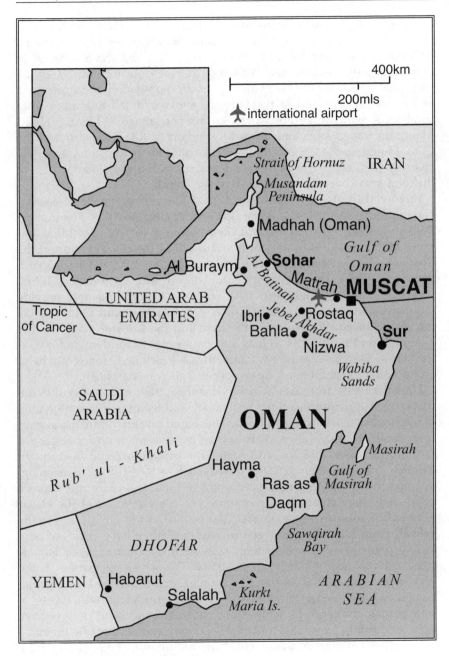

Figure 7.1 'Sultanate of Oman' – map.

the monsoon-affected escarpment of the Dhofar Mountains, and the man-made oasis gardens. Oman's economic backbone is in the coastal Al-Batinah plain overlooking the Gulf of Oman and the Salalah plain overlooking the Arabian Sea. Although they account for only 3% of the total landmass, today more than 50% of the population is concentrated in the capital area and in the Batinah, and continued migration from rural areas will furthermore increase this percentage. While the Hajjar Mountain Range stretching from Musandam to Ras Al-Hadd, and the Qara Mountain Range in Dhofar make up 15% of the total area, the sparsely populated gravel and sand deserts with approximately 82% of the total area cover the largest part of the country.

Promoted by its geographic location at the intersection of three zoo-geographical regions: the West Palaearctic Region; the Afrotropical Region; and the Oriental Region; Oman offers a variety of wildlife and flora. Mountain areas in the north and south of the country support the existence of populations of rare animals such as the Arabian tahr, leopard, ibex, and others. But even the central desert with its plains of Jiddat Al-Harasis, an extremely arid area, where only fogs and dew provide moisture, sustains a rich wildlife, such as the Arabian and Rhim gazelle, the reintroduced Arabian oryx, the hare and the fox and many smaller mammals and reptiles, as well as a many species of resident and migratory birds. Oman's marine environment has a rich occurrence of whales and dolphins, five different turtle species and corals and fish.

Until the 1970s, around 80% of the Omani population lived mainly from oasis based agriculture, animal husbandry and fishing, or a combination of these subsistence strategies. Settled life based on agriculture has always been confined to certain pockets, where the two main prerequisites for farming i.e. cultivable soil and water for irrigation could be brought together. Since the emergence of towns, such as those of the archaeological sites in Bat, Hili and others, around five thousand years ago, Oman's main oasis settlements are concentrated in the piedmont of the Hajjar Mountain Range. Cities along the coast of the Gulf of Oman, and in the Salalah plain have been engaged in sea-trade, they have their archaeological predecessors in pre-Islamic sites such as Sumhuram, or Islamic sites such as Sohar, Qalhat, Sur, Al-Balid. The settlement pattern at the higher altitudes is characterized by smaller spring-irrigated oasis settlements as well as the temporary and semi-permanent settlements of transhumant pastoralists, while the vast gravel and sand deserts have only been thinly populated and exploited by pastoral nomadic tribes.

Since the renaissance under His Majesty Sultan Qaboos bin Said the country's rapid modern development has not been confined to the capital area. Oman's rural areas and interior settlements took their share in the process of modernization, in terms of infrastructure, education, capital inflow and migration of people to the cities. Agriculture no longer plays an important role in the rural economy, and is now carried out mostly by elder family members or hired laborers from the Indian Subcontinent. Hundreds of traditional settlement quarters have been abandoned for new ones with modern facilities, which now stand in mute testimony to their past and if preserved, managed and interpreted have the potential to add to the cultural and archaeological attractions of the destination Oman (Mershen, 1998: 201).

The tribal organization of Omani society 'has produced characteristic features in the landscape of settlement. The quarter is a spatial unit which encloses dwellings and communal structures belonging to one tribe and groups affiliated to it' (Mershen, 1998: 201). These quarters are located inside the oasis or, to save cultivable terrain and for strategical considerations, along its fringes, typically on an elevated position on mountain slopes or wadi banks, overlooking the date gardens. Urban development in the oasis towns often took the form of fortified settlements or settlement quarters with many defensive elements, such as forts, city walls and gates, fortified houses and watchtowers. Up to the present these have remained a prominent feature of the Omani landscape. An oasis town usually had a whole series of towers, located on the surrounding hilltops, while the larger towns had their own forts. Most settlement quarters were walled and accessed only through fortified city gates, shut at sunset. The quarters were strictly residential in nature, with markets located outside their perimeters. Communal space, such as that constituted by mosques, meeting halls, religious schools, falaj-related installations such as washing and bathing facilities, communal ovens to roast the meat during the Eid, grain mills and so on, were generally located close to the city gates or along the main streets, so as not to disturb the privacy of the dwelling quarters.

Settlements were built in stone or sun-dried mud-brick architecture, the choice depending upon the local availability of building materials. In the settlements along the coast and in the Bedouin camps in the desert palm-frond, houses and huts (*arish*) were a traditional form of dwelling.

Much remains to be done if the genuine character of Oman's oasis towns is to be preserved for the future. Paradoxically, the sudden pace of change in the Sultanate may be regarded as an ally for preservation efforts. In other Arab countries, development at its far more gradual pace has gone unnoticed for long. As a result, by 1969, when the concern for preserving the national heritage heightened, a great part of these countries' cultural landscapes and traditional architecture had already vanished. The delayed advent of modernity in Oman, however, coincided with an increased concern for preserving the national heritage. There is a potential for the tourism industry, if properly managed and developed, to fill the economic gaps left by the declining importance of agriculture in the oases (Mershen, 2000: 115).

Tourism in Oman – a Recent Phenomenon

> Tourism, the fastest growing industry in the world, has become the centre of attention of most countries in the Gulf. Banking on their natural, cultural and traditional heritage, these countries are all set to strengthen the tourism industry and make it the largest after oil. Oman is not lagging in the initiative either. (Erikson & Erikson, 2001: 18)

Aiming at economical diversification, the Sultanate had since the late 1980s cautiously opened its gates to selective tourism, thereby closing one of the last remaining blanks in the tourism landscape of Arabia. Until 1970 Oman was basically closed toward the outside world and only little was known about the land and its people. Although Muscat was frequently visited by European ships, few people had until then traveled to Oman's interior. Travel accounts from explorers such as Wilfried Thesinger in the 1940s, who holds the record of being the first European to ever have traveled the Wahiba Sands, differ little from those of the earlier travelers such as Wellsted, S.B. Miles and others (Ward, 1987) in that they describe adventurous journeys through unknown lands.

While there were no hotels in the 1970s, Oman by the mid-1980s 'boasted a number of luxury hotels in Muscat which businessmen alone could not fill. In 1987, a cautious welcome began to be extended to suitable tourist groups, and to individual tourists' (Oman Infoworld – Tourism, www.inforamp.net/ emous/oman/tourism.htm), although in the beginning mainly tourists on expensive package tours were allowed in. From 1997 to 1999 the number of hotels had almost doubled from 52 to 102, most of them located in Muscat, along the Batinah coast and in Salalah.

Having cautiously been initiated in the late 1980s, tourism in Oman is a recent phenomenon, which since the mid-1990s is gaining some momentum. The Sultanate's tourism development policy, which strives for quality rather than mass-tourism, is revealed in the building of prestigious five-star hotel projects, such as the Al-Bustan Palace Hotel opened in 1985 to house the Arab Gulf Cooperation Council (AGCC) Summit, and other luxury hotels, such as the Intercontinental, Crowne Plaza, Crowne Plaza Sawadi Resort, Holiday Inn, Holiday Inn Beach Resort, Grand Hyatt, Sheraton, or The Chedi. All of those are part of multinational companies, of which 'Six Continents', with six of the mentioned hotels, is clearly dominating the market.

It has been claimed that there is a 'selective strategy aimed at attracting the more affluent tourists from Europe and Asia, thus avoiding the negative impact of mass tourism' (Ministry of Information, www.Omanet. com/ comm_ind_tourism.htm). The Omani authorities are aware that an invasion of tourists, ignorant of the customs of the country, could have a disturbing effect. 'We are looking for quality rather than quantity' remarked Muhammad Ali Said, Director of Tourism in the Ministry of Commerce and Industry.[1] 'We are not out to sell Oman on her fine beaches but rather to attract visitors interested in our heritage, history and archaeology' (Oman Infoworld – Tourism, www.inforamp.net/ emous/oman/ tourism.htm). In fact, the government has always stressed the importance of keeping up the country's cultural traditons and maintaining its natural resources.

The cultural tourism track so far has been focusing mainly on restored forts and fortresses, completely refurbished traditional markets (such as in Muttrah, Nizwa and Salalah), or on various forms of staged cultural heritage, such folklore shows, camel- and horse-races, and fairs presenting traditional craftsmen, Omani cuisine and the like, in addition to some of the better-known archaeological sites.

In this context it should be mentioned that cultural and archaeological sites are not yet sufficiently managed and interpeted, a lack that is now being realized and has led the Ministry of Heritage and Culture to the commission a Heritage Management Plan for the World Heritage Site of Bahla Oasis, and the initiation of planning for archaeological parks. It has likewise led the Ministry of Commerce and Industry, Directorate of Tourism to the creation of 'The Forts and Castles Development Project' and the initiation of the Misfat Al-Abriyin Restoration and Rehabilitation Project.

Eco-tourism – this term in Oman often being mentioned interchangeably with nature tourism or environmental tourism (Ministry of Regional Municipalities and Environment, n.d.) – as an internationally growing sector of tourism, came to be a key concept in the country's aspiration to develop a strategy towards 'quality' tourism (which in this context may actually be interpreted as sustainable tourism). Already at an early stage, the Sultanate had imposed strict laws to protect wildlife and set up nature reserves to prevent destruction of the natural habitat of animals such as leopards, hyenas, oryx, gazelle, tahr, ibex, desert foxes, antelope and wild cats, as well as turtles, through population pressure and modern development.

Located in the Jiddat Al-Harasis, which is inhabited by the nomadic pastoralist Harasis tribe, is the Arabian Oryx Sanctuary. It is home to the Arabian oryx, which was reintroduced to the wild in 1982. But the reserve's rich wildlife also includes Nubian ibex, caracal, Arabian gazelle, sand gazelle, sand cat, the last wild breeding population of the Houbara bustard in Arabia and a great number of other animals. The sanctuary furthermore includes many important geological features, and archaeo-logical sites dating back to the Palaelolithic and the last two millennia BC (Ministry of Regional Municipalities and Environment, n.d.), and an information resource center at Ja'looni, in close proximity to the sanc-tuary. Some of the local tribesmen have found employment as guards and rangers. Now, that tour operators have started to organize guided tours to the sanctuary since 1998, it is anticipated that this traffic might generate some income for more local residents through sale of food and drinks and local crafts (Al-Salmani, 2000: 5).

A much more frequented nature reserve is Ra's al Hadd Turtle Reserve, aiming at the protection and study of the endangered green turtle. The reserve covers an area of 120 sq. km of beaches, coastal land, seabed and two khawrs. Annually 6000–13,000 green turtles nest and hatch at its beaches. Within the reserve there are many archaeological sites of great importance, which are currently under excavation and study. Encour-aging eco-tourism is one the objectives of the reserve. On the main turtle-watching beach of Ras Al-Jinz the building of a scientific center and museum is currently being planned to enhance visitor facilities and to increase control over natural resources and to better manage turtle-watching practices. Also under study are different 'tourism options which benefit the local people, without causing damage to the biological res-ources, are addressed' (Ministry of Regional Municipalities and Environ-ment, n.d.). If eco-tourism and rural tourism are to promote sustainable development, there has to be local participation and economic benefits. The crucial role of local participation in eco-tourism and rural tourism (Erikson & Erikson, 2001: 20–3; cf. Brand, 2001 for the Wadi Rum Reserve, Jordan).

A number of further nature reserves have been proclaimed in the north and south of the Sultanate. These include woodland, mountain, and island reserves, as well as the 'khawr' reserves – seawater inlets fed by fresh springs. In Dhofar several famous archaeological sites, such as the early Islamic city of Al-Baleed or pre-Islamic Sumhuram are situated on the banks of khawrs. With their rich mangrove and other vegetation and abundance in fish they are used by more than 200 species of migratory birds (Erikson & Erikson, 2001).

The great eco-tourism potential of Oman's resident and migratory birds is now being 'recognized by international bird tour companies. Consequently, foreign birdwatchers are arriving here in increasing numbers. Right now many birdwatchers consider Oman one of the best kept secrets in the birding world' (Erikson & Erikson, 1999: 1).

Current Trends of Large- Versus Small-scale Tourism in Oman

Initially the growing tourist numbers seemed to indicate that the 'high-quality tourism' strategy worked out as anticipated. As a new destination that previously had been closed to the Western market, Oman obviously had a special bonus in attracting tourism. Visitors to the Sultanate often were people who had traveled a lot and now sought to fill one of those last remaining gaps on their map of destinations.

Gradually the situation is changing. With tourism's contribution still accounting for less than 0.4% of GDP, and the notion of tourism as 'the golden alternative of oil' (Al-Hayat newspaper, 6/6/2002) being but a vague vision for the future, the advance laurels seem to have been used up. An official report on The Fifth Five Year Plan acknowledged that its 'objective of turning tourism into one of the most important economic sectors in Oman had not been achieved' (Al-Markazi, 2001: 32).

According to the Priority Action Plan report not only

> high quality accommodation was limited and complimentary services and facilities scarce. Many of Oman's unique natural and heritage attractions are either not supported by adequate road access and other infrastructure, or do not have facilities such as suitable accommodation, eating and dining facilities of an acceptable quality. (Al-Shaybany, 2001)

In addition to this, there is the almost complete lack of management and interpretation of such sites. Because tourism growth and revenues have not developed as hoped and expected, the Priority Action Plan now suggests a new strategy that focuses on 'four product groups that are most likely to be accepted by Oman's primary markets. Special interest; touring/city tours; Sun, Sand, and Pre and Post Commercial Tours' (Al-Shaybany, 2001). Currently a particular emphasis is given to the development of coastal resorts, not only catering to the upper market segment, but also to the families on budget holidays (*Oman Observer*, 25/06/2001). 'In future, Oman will be hoping to cater to families on budget breaks as well as tourists demanding five-star luxury which is evident in the plans drawn out by many of the planned resorts that have a range of three to five star accommodation to offer' (*Oman Observer*, 25/06/2001). Most noteworthy among these planned resorts are the Shangri-La Asia Ltd's US$ 200 million Barr Al Jissah Resort spread over 124 acres of secluded rocky shore line, 15 km east of Muscat. Other large-scale tourism projects are the Sawadi Beach Resort (US$ 300 million) 100 km north of Muscat, which is to be managed by an international consortium and the recently launched 'The Wave' mega-project on a 7 km-long strip of coast within the capital. The ambitious tourism development plan is to be achieved through the private sector, thus the attraction of large-scale investment in particular from foreign investors is one of the current priorities.

As for the cultural tourism track, it has already been mentioned that officially projected cultural destinations, such as archaeological sites and traditional architectural ensembles, often lack sufficient development in terms of tourist infrastructure and heritage management and interpretation.Until recently the emphasis of conservational measures has been on the visually prominent military architecture of the 17th through 19th centuries. In fact an impressive number of forts have been restored over the past decades. Currently the 'Fort and Castles Development Project' is starting to implement measures to manage, interpret and revive these historical buildings.

Otherwise the architectural heritage, whether in form of archaeological remains, as traditional settlements, or as industrial or agroeconomic installation, which reflects millennia of development and man's interaction with the environment, has been accorded less attention. If left unmanaged or even unattended, hundreds of oasis settlements, abandoned by their residents since the 1970s when moving into new housing areas or into the capital, will fall into disrepair and eventually face complete destruction. This means the loss of cultural heritage and of potentially invaluable tourist attractions. The lack of heritage management also is one of the reasons to be blamed if tourists engage in culturally and socially unacceptable activities and behavior, which in turn results in adverse effects on local acceptance and tolerance of tourism. Namely the inappropriate intrusion into the private sphere of living quarters and homes in villages, usually without local guides who could act as interpreters and cultural monitors, causes a lot of disturbance for the local population, only aggravated by the fact that it is not linked to economic benefits.

With visa regulations eased, a rapidly developing excellent road network and increasing numbers of self-drive tourists reaching previously more secluded settlements, it has become more difficult to control the flow of tourists into areas with little tourism infrastructure and hence a more limited tourism carrying capacity, such as the wadis and mountain settlements of the Hajjar Mountains. The scenic mountain village of Misfat Al-Abriyin exemplifies some of these problems related to tourism. Located within easy reach from the main traffic axis Muscat–Nizwa–Bahla at a distance of about 2.5 hours from Muscat, and connected to the main road by a tarmac road accessible by salon car, it has come to be one of the best-known and most visited mountain villages. A combination of factors, including its topographical setting perched on a steep slope above the wadi, its falaj meandering through the narrow terraces of palm trees, bananas and lime trees, the almost intact traditional stone architecture and the fact that the old village is still inhabited to a large extent, make it a very attractive and popular destination. International as well as domestic tourists, groups as well as individuals, visit and spend some time strolling through the shaded plantations and the intricate network of narrow village alleys, or picnicking at the side of the irrigation channels. They will leave the village without having been able to spend money even on a cup of tea, because of the entire lack of tourist facilities: there is no accommodation facility, no local guides, not even coffee-shops or shops selling postcards or handicrafts. At the same time visitors frequently cause disturbance to local residents, as they are unaware of the unwritten local code of behaviour, and are not properly guided so as to distinguish between the semi-public alleys leading through the village and those leading straigh into the privacy of dwellings or areas reserved for female use only. Visitors ignorant of the fact that it is the falaj channel from where women fetch the drinking water have been causing pollution and thus forced the villagers to do a long walk to the source of the falaj to obtain their daily water supply.

Such negative impact of tourism upon the village community might be amended to some extent (cf. Robinson, 1999: 17) if the residents are given the opportunity to participate in decision-making, to operate tourism projects and to generate income from their village as a tourist destination (cf. the recommendations of Daher (1999: 56) for similar proposed tourism projects in Jordan). 'No longer imposed, tourism will then be accepted as an opportunity to show off one's culture and at the same time to earn income' (Barree, 1996: 8).Within the joint Omani-German research and documentation project on 'Oasis Settlements of Oman in Transition,' Misfat Al-Abriyin had since 1997 been architecturally and to some extent ethnographically surveyed and documented (Oasis Settlement in Oman Documentation and Research Project, Pilot-Study 1999–2000, unpublished report). The results of this research led to investigations how to realize the rehabilitation of the village, the restoration of its architecture and a cautious and community-oriented development of small-scale tourist facilities in uninhabited houses. A range of possible facilities and house re-use options have been identfied, such as bed-and-breakfast type accommodation, craft-workshops, small museums, souvenir shops, coffee-shops and restaurants. Furthermore the village has a potential for organized and guided mountain trekking, donkey-riding facilities and the like. The management and operation of the larger part of such facilities and businesses should be through local entrepreneurs, in particular through families. It is anticipated that such an approach will not only result in a more authentic tourist experience but will also minimize risks of alienation and disassociation of the resident population, which is inherent in architectural conservation projects (Daher, 1999). As a result of growing awareness both about the need to preserve historical settlement quarters and traditional architecture and about their tourism potential, the proposed 'Misfat Al-Abriyin Restoration and Rehabilitation Project' in the beginning of the year 2003 is being realized within the Directorate General of Tourism, Ministry of Commerce and Industry.[2]

The 1990s saw the first signs of a developing small-scale tourism sector through local residents in different parts of the Sultanate. Until recently this occurred quite independently from governmental incentives[3] and on a track parallel to the official tourism strategy. A growing trend toward microenterprise development has been crystallizing basically in areas that hitherto had been lacking tourist infrastructure. This trend is most evident in the central Sharqiyah region, albeit not in village settings, but along the northern fringes of the Wahiba Sands. Here several tourist microenterprises owned and run by local Bedouins or residents of nearby villages offer Bedouin-style camp facilities and other services.

Development of Local Small-scale Tourism Enterprises in the Wahibah Sands

The Wahiba Sands represent a relatively small (15,000 km^2) isolated desert that has been repeatedly described as a 'perfect specimen of a sand sea'. From 1985–7 it had been the subject of a major multi-disciplinary research project by the Royal Geographic Society. The geomorphological, archaeological (Edens, 1985/6), biological and ethnographic findings of the investigations (*Journal of Oman Studies*, special Report 3) confirmed the uniqueness of the Sands. The pastoral population of the Sands in 1985 had been estimated at 450–500 households belonging to different tribes of nomadic goad and camel herders, who through seasonal migrations make use of the Wahiba Sands' different ecological zones and respective resources (Webster, 1985: 6).

In the pre-modern period the economic activities of the Sharqiyah region had been dominated by the exploitation of the agricultural and maritime resources and the transportation and exchange of produce and other goods (Hoek, 1998: 63). The modern development of the Sultanate has had a strong impact upon both the settled and the nomad populations' ways of making a living. Although oasis cultivation continues to be carried out in the villages along the northern and north eastern margins of the Wahiba, its economic significance has reached a marginal level due to the fact that there is no more demand for the traditional export of dates to India, which formerly constituted a major source of income for the region.

The Bedouin way of life since the 1970s and 1980s has changed profoundly, one of the reasons being the development of road and communication infrastructure and mechanized transport, which deprived them of their traditional occupation and role in transportation and safeguarding of transit roads, that is the role of the rafiq (Webster, 1988: 461–72). In the mid-1980s it was stated that although some Bedouin families in the Sands seemed able to subsist by herding alone, the income derived from livestock appeared to be small. In fact, it was increasingly supplemented, respectively substituted by remittances from family members working in the army and police forces of UAE, Qatar, Kuwait and Bahrain (Webster, 1988: 469). When the obstacle of illiteracy was overcome, new employment opportunities in the Omani army and police opened up to the Bedouins of the Sands. At present many families have either settled or have become less mobile and tend to spend much of the year close to the towns bordering the Sands where their children attend the schools. In such cases, herding and (in many cases motorized) movement of herds to new pastures is attended to by individual members of the families. This leaves the rest of the family more free time to engange in other economic activities, such as labor migration and in casual entrepreneurial activities (Webster, 1988: 462).

The tourism potential of the Sands had already been highlighted in the reports on the Wahiba Sands Project: 'The Sands are of such striking beauty and interest that there is clearly scope for local and international tourism' (Munton, 1988: 571). In order to protect the fragile environment from disturbance of the wildlife, such as the gazelle, destruction of vegetation and rangeland through proliferation of roads and tracks, as well as the local people and their livestock from disturbance, and finally the visitors from potential dangers, it has been argued that there needs to be 'careful management of the sands under a tourist regime to safeguard the resources of the sands and the livelihood of the people who live in them.' It was further suggested that a monitored tourism development would both provide for some local employment, and could benefit from the indigenous knowledge. The local people 'have an intimate knowledge of different parts of the Sands and could usefully contribute to tourism by working as guides' (Munton, 1985: 6). Entrepreneurial incentives of such kind do actually tie up with more traditonal occupations, such as caravan business, and guiding and escorting strangers (i.e. the role of *rafiq* mentioned above) through difficult or hostile terrain.

In the 1990s this vision of local residents engaging in desert tourism started to materialize on an albeit limited scale and completely independent from any monitoring tourism regime. The only tourism development project in the area of the Wahiba Sands had so far been a small – and at that point state-owned – resthouse in Al-Qabil, now several micro-scale tourist enterprises owned and partly operated by local families came into being within the limited geographical area of the Wilayets Ibra and Biddiye in the northern part of the Sands (Al Qabil, Al-Wasil, Al-Mintirib). The successful establishment of the first tourist camp in 1990 was an incentive to other families to follow the example and set up camps of their own.[4] Permits to establish a camp or a tour operating company were relatively easy to obtain from the Ministry of Commerce and Industry, as this does not require the proof of special qualifications. As a consequence, in 2002 there were six tourist camps located within the fringes of the Sands, in addition to a further camp located a little north east of the Sands the outskirts of Ibra town. The ownership of these camp facilities reflect the tribal diversity of the area with major tribes such as the Al-Wahiba, Al-Hagri and Al-Harthi represented. These camps, mostly set up amidst scenic dunes, offer accommodation in palm-frond huts, the traditional Bedouin accommodation also used by the villagers as summer huts.

Differences between the camps relate to their number of accommodation units (between 10 and 70 units), to technical equipment and sports facilities, and furthermore to owners' and operators' respective social and environmental attitudes and approaches to desert tourism. Some camps are equipped with generator-powered electricity. As opposed to the traditional *arish* huts, the accommodation units in more luxurious camps consist of tents or small prefabricated rooms, concealed behind palm-frond huts, or even small chalets, equipped with individual bath-rooms. However, the outward appearance of palm-frond architecture or palm-frond facing, campfire and camels amid sand dunes is very similar and as stereotyped as the tourist activities on offer. Drawing upon the local resources and attractions they package visits to Bedouin families, the opportunity to buy local crafts products, and folklore performances with camel-riding around the camps, and four-wheel drive dune bashing, sand sliding and skiing. Some operators seek to surpass the thrills of this standard program by renting four-wheel drive motorbikes and dune buggies.

The Wahiba camps target both the expatriate (Europe and Subconti-nent) and the European inbound market segments, as well as the domes-tic market, although the individual camps may put a slightly different emphasis on these market segments. They either have business links to inbound tour operators or form part of such a company. Marketing is done either through these tour operators, or through the local press and inter-net websites. Contacts are also sought to be established with the European tourist market, in particular with Germany (IT Berlin) and England.

In order to get a better understanding of the dynamics and the inherent problematic of this newly evolving type of tourism in Sharqiyah, the case of the 'Nomad Desert Camp,' which may be considered quite successful in terms of sustainability, will be presented in greater detail.

The Nomad Desert Camp (see Figure 7.2) was the first tourist camp that came to be set up in the Sands in 1990 by Rashid bin Muhammad bin Hamoud Al-Mughayry and his family. The Mughayry are a small pastoral sub-section of the Al-Hagri tribe and are herders of goats and camels. Rashid's family also owns a few sheep, as well as chickens. Both the tourist camp and the family's camp are located close to the village of Al-Wasil. Rashid is a young man in his mid-twenties. He is married, but as is custom with many tribes of the area, his wife continues to live in her father's camp for the first few years of marriage . When he is not engaged in the tourism camp or in related business he either stays with his wife and her family, or with his own extended nuclear family's camp (see Figure 7.3). The latter is inhabited by his parents, his unmarried younger brothers and sisters, his married sister and her child and his grandfather. The camp is composed of several *arish* huts, a larger one for reception of guests, smaller huts for sleeping, fenced open areas for cooking and family life. The family even has a battery-powered TV. Around the huts are water tanks, fodder troughs and pens for chickens and the lambs and kids.The young animals, including the camels, are kept at the camp day and night. The adult animals are returned for the night, except for those

Figure 7.2 Nomad Desert Camp – general view.

Figure 7.3 Rashid's family camp with youngster welcoming guests.

that have been moved to pastures further in the desert. The family owns 29 camels and around 150 goats and sheep. This camp is located midway between the tourist camp and Al-Wasil, from where it is a 15 minutes drive. Whereas in the past the family used to move the campsite according to availability of rangeland, today the camp has become their permanent place of residence, as the children attend the school in Al-Wasil. In winter parts of the family migrate further into the Sands in search of new pastures, whereas the rest of the family stays in the permanent camp. In summer the family, in order to escape the heat of the desert, spends the daytimes in Al-Wasil, where they own a cement-block house and a small number of date palm trees. For the night, they do, however, return to the desert camp.

While it was Rashid, the eldest son, who set up the Nomadic Desert Camp, the father Muhammad (who in 2002 was in his late fifties), back in 1987, had started the family's venture in tourism. At that time he was a pastoral nomad with no other occupation, no school education and no knowledge of English. In 1987, he came to the aid of a British expatriate, who had got stuck in the desert.This man conveyed him the idea of employing his knowledge of the Sands to conduct guided tours through the desert. Rashid, who helped his father during school holidays, became interested in this type of work. Once he had finished his schooling, he set up the tourist camp at a distance of a few kilometers from his family camp, in a shallow depression surrounded by dunes. His family, although not owning the land, had always held traditional rights of camping on this land. According to the family, everybody in the area knows that nobody else is entitled to use this land. In fact in the immediate vicinity of the tourist camp several other residential camps of Rashid's uncles are located. The government acknowledges such traditional land-use rights, as long as no permanent structures are erected. In such a case, the land would have to be leased from the government.

The Nomadic Desert Camp was built according to Rashid's plans and design, which was based upon the huts used by his family. The building materials for the huts are palm-fronds, which he purchased from the Batinah coastal plain and palm-trunks he bought from Al-Wasil. The construction of the huts (see Figure 7.4) was carried out by Rashid and his family. The 10 guest huts, each equipped with two beds, are set up in a semi circle along the perimeters of the camp. The common room 'Majlis' is a long hut open to the front (see Figure 7.5), its back wall being protected from the wind by carpets and blankets. The floor is covered with carpets, matresses and cushions. A long table with chairs, set up at one short side of the tent, constitutes the breakfast area. The Majlis is also

Figure 7.4 Individual *arish* hut in Nomad Desert Camp.

Figure 7.5 Nomad Desert Camp – close-up of Majlis, fireplace and huts.

the place where the camp owner and his assistants sleep at night. In front of the Majlis a fireplace surrounded by plastic chairs has been built. A little apart from the Majlis two huts both equipped with running water from tanks accommodate a Turkish-style porcellain toilet sink, respectively a wash-basin and a shower. To the other side of the Majlis a small kitchen room has been built from mudbricks. Amongst other equipment such as a gas cooker, this room accommodates a gas-operated refrigerator. The mudbrick room was constructed by a traditional builder from Al-Wasil. The campsite is fenced off to avoid disturbance by camels, whether those used by the camp for tourist entertainment, or other camels that are freely roaming in the area. The camp's facilities are completed by a four-wheel drive vehicle and a pick-up to transport water tanks and other supplies.

The camp is operated on a family basis, i.e. everybody assisting Rashid with hospitality, further customer service and maintenance of the camp facilities is from his close relatives. In addition to his nuclear family, parents and siblings, he draws upon the help of his grandfather and his maternal uncle. During peak tourist seasons whenever a shortage of manpower does occur, more distant family members join forces. Rashid objects to employing staff from outside his family. He feels that, dealing with family members only, is his best insurance for proper customer service quality, as family members behave more responsibly than strangers. At the same time Rashid is aware that his main capital is the local knowledge and desert expertise of his family elders, and his far-reaching network of family and tribal connections. These are the prerequisites that enable him to provide his guests with an 'almost authentic' experience.

There is, however, clear division of camp-related labor within the family. Rashid is the director and operator. He welcomes the guests at a meeting point along the main road, guides them to a coffee reception at his family's camp and then further into the desert to the tourist camp. He entertains them and cares for their well-being. He helps in the preparation and serving of breakfast and dinner and related activities. Abdallah, his younger brother, prepares breakfast, serves dinner, does the dishwashing and takes care of the water and other supplies. Hmud, Rashid's maternal uncle, takes care of the camels, which are fetched from the family's herd every evening for the entertainment of the guests and upon guests' arrival at the camp, and takes the guests on short camel rides around the camp site. Muhammad, Rashid's father, is considered the family's camel specialist. Upon customers' requests he organizes and guides several day-long camel safaris through the desert. Rashid's mother and his sisters are responsible for the preparation of dinner, which is cooked at the family camp and delivered to the tourist camp, whereas his young brothers and nephew welcome and entertain guests upon their arrival for a coffee-break at the family camp. The family of Rashid's wife gets involved only when there is a need for additional camels during peak tourist season.

Accommodation at the camp is booked in advance and the all-inclusive rate of around Omani Rial 24 (c. US$ 60 at the time of writing) includes pick-up at the main road in Al-Wasil around 4 p.m., coffee-break at the family camp, arrival at camp, serving of Omani coffee and dates, half-hour camel ride on the dunes surrounding the camp, dinner in the Majlis, entertainment around the campfire. The next morning breakfast is served around 8 a.m. and is followed by a four-wheel drive ride through the surrounding dune landscape where guests are shown how to descend high dunes. Around 10 a.m. the guests are guided back to the main road.

Rashid is running the camp within his own small Muscat-based tour operating company 'Nomadic Adventure and Tours,' which is managed by his partner, a Western expatriate tourism professional and personal friend of his. Besides the camp they organize and operate a whole array of tours through Oman. Among others, these include camel safaris through the Wahiba Sands and off-road tours to the Oryx Sanctuary in the Jiddat Al-Harasis, where contacts with families from the Harsusi tribe have been established, and tourists are taken for coffee-breaks in their encampments, as well as tours along the coast to the southern region. To operate such tours the company has to rent cars and drivers. They furthermore undertake mountain trekking in the Eastern Hajjar Mountains and then cooperate with transhumant mountain pastoralists for provision of donkey-transport of camping equipment and supplies.

The camp and the company is the family's main source of income. A small additional income is from the occasional sale of animals. At one point Rashid had sought to get into the business of breeding racing camels for sale to the UAE market. This is another high-profit promising industry many Bedouins from Sharqiyah like to invest in. Rashid finally refrained from involvement when realizing that the risks are proportional to the high investment costs into fodder and vetinerary care.

Rashid had set up the camp with a permit from the Ministry of Trade and Industry. He neither received governmental assistance in form of soft loans or grants nor did he take bank loans. Instead, he financed the camp through money borrowed from members of his family. Self-financing through the families was also the case with some of the other camps. Many young small-scale entrepreneurs appear to be reluctant to approach the authorities out of fear that their proposals will be rejected and their ideas possibly realized by others with more experience and/or easier access to governmental assistance.[5]

Except for the money going into purchase of food supplies from Muscat-based companies, there is minimal leakage and most of the profits gained from these small tourist camps remain within the area. Direct and indirect benefits from the camp and the related increase in tourist numbers for the local population are derived from salaries to local employees, the building of the camps through local craftsmen, to some extent the sale of local crafts products through Bedouin women, as well as increased demand on general local services such as petrol stations, shops and restaurants.

The Nomad Desert Camp mainly targets the European tourist segment, many of them expatriates living in Oman who will come with visiting friends or family members. The total number of camp visitors has been 1600 from September 2001 to early May 2002. The majority of visitors were European expatriates. Although the total number has remained almost constant compared with the previous year due to an increase of individual visitors, the effects of the September 11 events resulted in the decrease of international tourism in the form of group travels, which in other years accounted for around 60% of the visitor total number.

Marketing is done through 'Nomadic Adventures and Tours,' through the internet and occasional book advertisements and through participation in the IT Berlin. But many of the expatriate customers come by way of word-of-mouth propaganda. And there is a number of guests who come back regularly with their visitors. A Dutch guest asked for the reason of her repeated visits to the camp remarked that, of all the Wahiba camps, Rashid's camp was closest to basic, that he was an excellent and creative host, and that the intimate contact with the Bedouin family was delightful. It was furthermore felt, that in the absence of electicity there was a real desert experience much like self-camping, but requiring less organizational effort on the part of the camper.

This unobtrusive, cautious approach toward desert tourism is not followed by all other camps in the vicinity. Many have gone for an increased accommodation capacity, others want to offer more modern comfort, or more thrilling attractions. Often they work on a different operational basis, as for example the 'Golden Sands Camp' (see Figure 7.6) located at a distance of about 2 km from the 'Nomad Desert Camp.' This camp was built in 1998 by a member of the local Al Hagri tribe, living in Muscat. The camp is operated by Indian employees, and the owner is only occasionally present at the camp. It is comparatively more comfortable as it is composed of a series of cement-block chalets, each with two

Figure 7.6 Golden Sands Camp – approaching the entrance.

rooms in Omani-style decoration and a bathroom. The chalets are set in a circle around an open breakfast bar. The entrance to the camp is through a traditional wooden entrance door giving way to a built Majlis reception room and into the plastered courtyard flanked by the chalets. The camp is equipped with electricity from a generator and has its own water well. Palm trees and other trees are planted within the camp and along its fringes. Two years after its establishment the camp was extended beyond its original perimeters to accommodate a series of *arish* huts around a large reception hall built from palm-fronds. A black goat-hair tent completes the enlargement. 'Golden Sands' receives a lot of Omani, regional Arab and both Indian and European guests. It is furthermore booked for company outings of up to 50 people.

Another camp located 20 km south west of Mintirib has almost grown into a camp city with its 70 *arish* huts, 8 built accommodation rooms, Majlis, covered cafeteria, kitchen and sanitary units. The owner, who is from a local village, operates the camp with the assistance of Indian employes. Catering for up to 200 guests, it nevertheless promotes itself as destination to 'experience the authentic Bedouin lifestyle.' This end is meant to be met in a full-days' activities package, which offers dune driving and a motorbike show on the dunes, besides camel rides, dune climbing, dune sliding and a Bedouin folklore show. In addition guests may rent dune buggies and four-wheel drive motorbikes.

Discussion of Challenges, Difficulties and Opportunities Relating to Tourism in the Wahiba Sands

Evaluating the difficulties, challenges and opportunities of recent tourism development in the northern Wahiba Sands, one is faced with a rather equivocal situation where benefits and costs for community and environment have to be weighed against one another. Clearly positive is the fact that almost all the camps are local establishments. Although only one owner is actually Bedouin, they are (with just one exception) local residents. In general the camps use architectural styles that reflect the local architecture and blend in well with the desert environment (cf. Al-Husni, 2000: 65). The extent of community outreach of economic benefits of the camp tourism is more questionable, as there seems to be little concerted action on a communal level. Some income is generated for local residents, who are not members of camp owners' and operators' families, or employees. The group who profits most seems to be owners of riding camels, who rent their camels to tourist camps and perform camel tour-guiding upon request. Local folklore groups performing folk-dances and women carrying out henna-painting in the camps, or selling their crafts products are benefitting on a more limited scale. A minor additional income is made by Bedouin families arranging with tour-operators for tourist group coffee receptions at their homes. A further group of local people benefitting from the Wahiba Sands tourism is constituted of craftsmen from the surrounding villages who benefit through the constructing and maintenance of camp facilities. Other beneficiaries are car- and other repair-shops, gas stations and general stores. Communal benefits from tourism could certainly be increased if the local community was involved in the planning and decision-making processes of the local tourism development. So far, however, no institutional body such as a non-governmental organization exists, which could facilitate this involvement.

All the other camps, which followed the initially founded camp in rapid succession, and partly by way of imitating the original project, were established within less than 10 years. They are positioned in strategic settings, which take advantage of both the particular desert ambience and the fact that they are located within easy reach of the main road from Muscat to Sur, as well as of the settlements acting as supply centers for water, fuel, food and other items. With seven such facilities offering very similar services, and distributed over less than 400 km², there appears to be an over-supply of the same product in a very small geographical area. As a consequence of over-supply's negative effect upon visitor numbers, aggressive competition has arisen between the individual camps.[6] As tourist camps are going into unfair and detrimental price-wars and attempt to snatch each others customers, in particular group travels, more far-sighted camp operators feel that they are ultimately ruining each other. In response to this situation a permit-stop for further Wahiba camps has been put into effect by the Ministry of Commerce and Industry.

The desert camps as tourism products reflect the entrepreneurs' intentions to present their cultural and natural heritage, readapted and transformed according to tourist expectations respectively to entrepreneurs' perception of such (cf. Butcher, 2000: 53 on this phenomenon). Ultimately, the final product, sold as the 'authentic' Bedouin desert camp experience, in too many cases does represent the commodified version of a rather romanticizing and standardizing Western model of 'the Bedouin,' which is a result of the fact that 'the host society adapts to the presence and imported cultural models of tourists' (Jafari, 1996: 45; Parris, 1996: 49). The apparent trend toward commodification of heritage and the growing import of environmentally disruptive motorized activities, raises the question whether the tourist development in the northern parts of the Sands is starting to outgrow the carrying capacity of the area (cf. Al-Husni, 2000: 70) both in environmental terms and with regard to the host society (cf. Moulin, 1996: 66), and whether it soon will be reaching a phase where it is locally no longer acceptable.

A desideratum would be greater diversification and specialization on particular tourist products, and increased concern for sustainability, which will have to include moves to overcome the stereotype vision of desert tourism. Many of these young entrepreneurs lack the indigenous knowledge[7] that has proved such a crucial basis for earlier generations' succesful coexistence with the harsh and resource-scarce environment.[8] A prerequisite for eco-tourism, as appropriate form of sustainable tourism in the Sands would thus be environmental education and training of the operators. In order to do so efficiently local knowledge has to be recorded and documented. Its transmission to the young generation could possibly be achieved through communal channels of communication. The creation of communal channels would be a useful tool for conflict-solving and would help small-scale entrepreneurs to reach agreements about pricing policies and diversification. Individual camps' specialization on special interest themes (archaeology, nature, culture, animals, etc.) could facilitate developments that are complementary rather than competitive.

It would allow individual camps to target particular market segments and would enable larger segments of the local population benefit economically from tourism. This however would have to be achieved through supra-family and supra-tribal cooperation and arrangements on the community level. The current situation is characterized by the perpetuation of traditional inter-tribal[9] animosities on the level of commercial rivalry.

Conclusions

The importance of local people's participation in tourism and their sharing of the profits has been stated earlier. But the presented observations on the developing local tourist industry in Sharqiyah also prove that meeting solely this one requirement will not provide a sound basis for a tourist development that is both environmentally and culturally sustainable.[10] Local individuals' entrepreneurial incentives should evolve in a more community-oriented approach. To develop sustainable tourism and eco-tourism in Sharqiyah, whether through micro-scale enterprises, the activties of the larger domestic and international tour operators, or through other future tourism projects, there will have to be more involvement of local communities in planning and decision-making processes (cf. Barkin, 1996; Weaver, 2001: 137–8). There also is a need for qualified training of those involved in local tourism, both in industry-related issues and in issues related to the natural and social environment, to local historiography and to archaeology. Communal advisory bodies, cooperatives and non-governmental organizations could constitute the appropriate institutional framework, provided that there is coordination and concerted action with the public sector and with research institutions.

Notes

1. Until the creation of the Ministry of Tourism in June 2004, a Directorate General of Tourism as part of the Ministry of Commerce and Industry was in charge of tourism.
2. The negotiations on project definition and mission, and how authorities and residents and / or house-owners could interact in ways that are satisfactory for both sides, are an ongoing process, occasionally slowed down or disturbed by family- and tribally-based contrasting points of view. That this should not be viewed as alarming, and that community-based tourism requires a slow process of community-building, has been aptly demonstrated by M. Reed (1997: 587 for a small community in British Columbia, Canada).
3. Since 2003 the Directorate of Tourism has shown interest in supporting smaller tourist businesses through leasing of land and provision of planning

or architectural design expertise. A small eco-tourism accommodation project owned and operated by a local family is presently under construction on the Seeq Plateau of Jabal Akhdar.

4. Entrepreneurial incentives linking tribes from more remote areas of Oman into the modern economy are a phenomenon that is not without precedent. Bedouin tribes in Oman have a repeatedly proven ability to adapt fast to changes in their natural, administrative, social and economic environment. The case of the Harasis tribe in Oman is presented by Chatty (1996: 27, 93).

5. This is corroborated by Webster (1988: 466), who reports that Bedouin families in the Wahiba Sands 'often rely on loans from relatives and friends, and banks report that bedu seldom make us of "official" credit facilities.' Hoek (1998: 94) also demonstrates that up to 1990 there had been little response from Sharqiyah small-scale entrepreneurs to soft loan schemes of banks.

6. Comparable tribal conflicts have been analysed in Wadi Rum, Jordan, by L.A.Brand (2001: 579–80).

7. The Royal Geographic Society's research

> team studying the people of the region [Wahiba Sands] found that they have evolved an economic and social way of life in keeping with their environment and have adopted environmentally-sound ways ofexploiting local resources. However in recent years, the advent of oil wealth has brought change and diminishes the inhabitants' dependence on local resources with a consequent lessening of interest in using them with traditional skills and wisdom. (Royal Geographic Society, www.rgs.org)

8. This, in fact, is a widespread and recurrent problem, which in Oman has also been reported for the Oryx Sanctuary in Jiddat Al-Harasis and the Harasis tribe in the early 1980s.

> Early during our fieldwork in 1981, it became obvious that a camel, gazelle, or when required, an oryx could be tracked with great skill by the generation in their thirties and forties. The younger group of men in their late teens could not, as a rule, follow animal tracks with the same ease, but could identify and follow a car track out of a maze of tens of hundreds of tracks ... What is unfortunate is that some of the younger generation are not building upon the survival skills of their elders, but merely developing those they find important or interesting. In the harsh and extreme environment of the Jiddat, a motor vehicle breakdown in an isolated location could spell death for someone who no longer had the skills to deal with the environment without the mediation of a modern technological device. (Chatty, 1996: 111)

9. In the Jiddat Al-Harasis tribal competition for employment facilities in the nature reserve, which led to the problem of poaching, goes back to the early oil exploitation in the 1950s and is based on an antagonism from the 1930s concerning territorial rights (Chatty, 1983: 158). Weaver (2001: 121) reports of a case in Papua New Guinea where 'a successful project by members of one particular clan led to inferior copycat iinitiatives and exacerbated inter-clan jealousies and animosity' and where eco-tourism thus led to destabilization of social conflict control mechanisms among clans.

10. That local control is not necessarily a guarantee for communally acceptable tourism development is illustrated by Weaver (2001: 122), reporting of socially destructive eco-tourism reinforcing existing inequalities as dominant families, clans or tribes seeking to increase their dominance through tourism.

References

Al-Husni, Izz al-Din (2000) *A Strategy for the Development of Sustainable Tourism in the Sahara* (Arabic translation). Paris: UNESCO.

Al-Markazi (2001) Tourism in Oman – the way forward. *Al-Markazi* (bi-monthly publication of the Central Bank of Oman) April–May , 26 (2), 30–6.

Al-Salmani, Yahya (2000) The return of the oryx. *Man and Environment* (periodical magazine issued by the Ministry of Regional Municipalities and Environment) X (5).

Al-Shaybany, Saleh (2001) Oman's tourism potential all but untapped. On WWW at www.arabia.com/oman/business. Accessed August 27 2002.

Barkin, David (1996) Ecotourism: A tool for sustainable development. On WWW at *www.planeta.com*/planeta/96/0596monarch.html. Accessed June 5, 2006.

Barree, Herve (1996) General introduction to the debates. In UNESCO/AIEST, *Proceedings of Round Table 'Culture, Tourism, Development: Crucial Issues for the XXI Century'* (pp.5–13). Paris: UNESCO/AIEST.

Brand, Laurie A. (2001) Development in Wadi Rum? State bureaucracy, external funders, and civil society. *International Journal of Middle East Studies* 33, 571–89.

Butcher, Jim (2000) The 'New Tourist' as anthropologist. In M. Robinson *et al.* (eds) *Reflections on International Tourism – Motivations, Behaviour and Tourist Types* (pp. 45–54). Sunderland: The Centre for Travel and Tourism and Business Education Publishers.

Chatty, Dawn (1983) The Bedouin of central Oman: Adaptation or fossilization. *Journal of Oman Studies* 6 (1), 149–62.

Chatty, Dawn (1996) *Mobile Pastoralists – Development, Planning and Social Change in Oman.* New York: Columbia University Press.

Daher, Rami F. (1999) Gentrification and the politics of power, capital and culture in an emerging Jordanian heritage industry. *Traditional Dwellings and Settlements Review* X (11), 47–59.

Edens, Christopher (1985/6) *Oman Wahiba Sands Project, Rapid Assessment Document* (Chapter 3.3).

Erikson, Hanne and Erikson, Jens (1999) *Birdlife in Oman.* Muscat: Al Roya Publishing.

Erikson, Hanne and Erikson, Jens (2001) Banking on nature. In Salih al-Zakwani (ed.) *Tribute* (pp.18–24). Muscat: Apex Publishing.

Hoek, Corien W. (1998) *Shifting Sands – Social-economic Development in al-Sharqiyah Region, Oman.* Nijmegen: Nijmegen University Press.

Jafari, Jafar (1996) Tourism and culture: An inquiry into paradoxes. In UNESCO/ AIEST, *Proceedings of Round Table 'Culture, Tourism, Development, Crucial Issues for the XXI Century'* (pp. 43–7). Paris: UNESCO/AIEST.

Kabasci, Kirstin and Franzisky, Peter (1996) *Oman: Geheimnisvolles Sultanat zwischen Gestern und Übermorgen.* Hohentann: REISE KNOW-HOW Verl. Därr.

Mershen, Birgit (1998) Settlement space and architecture in South Arabian oases – ethnoarchaeological investigations in recently abandoned settlement quarters in inner Oman. *Proceedings of the Seminar for Arabian Studies* 28, 201–13.

Mershen, Birgit (2000) Oases of life. In Salih al-Zakwani (ed.) *Tribute* (pp. 102–15). Muscat: Apex Publishing.

Ministry of Regional Municipalities and Environment (n.d.) *Guide to Oman's Protected Areas*. Sultanate of Oman.

Moulin, Claude (1996) Host communities, culture and tourism: Local strategies. In UNESCO/AIEST, *Proceedings of a Round Table 'Culture, Tourism, Development, Crucial Issues for the XXI Century'* (pp. 65–7). Paris: UNESCO/AIEST.

Munton, Paul (1985/6) *Oman Wahiba Sands Project, Rapid Assessment Document* (Chapter 10.2).

Munton, Paul (1988) A system for the evaluation and management of the Wahiba Sands. *Journal of Oman Studies* (special report) 3, 565–72.

Oasis Settlement in Oman Documentation and Research Project (1999–2000) Pilot-study. Unpublished report, Department of Archaeology, Sultan Qaboos University.

Parris, Ronald G. (1996) Tourism and cultural interaction: Issues and prospects for sustainable development. In UNESCO/AIEST, *Proceedings of a Round Table 'Culture, Tourism, Development, Crucial Issues for the XXI Century'* (pp. 48–52). Paris.

Reed, Maureen (1997) Power relations and community based tourism planning. *Annals of Tourism Research* 24 (3), 566–91.

Robinson, Mike (1999) Cultural conflicts in tourism: Inevitability and inequality. In M. Robinson and P. Boniface (eds) *Tourism and Cultural Conflicts* (pp. 1–32). Oxford: CABI Publishing.

Ward, Philip (1987) *Travels in Oman – On the Track of the Early Explorers*. Cambridge and New York: The Oleander Press.

Weaver, David (2001) *Ecotourism*. Milton: John Wiley & Sons Australia, Ltd.

Webster, Roger (1985/6) *Oman Wahiba Sands Project, Rapid Assessment Document* (Chapter 8.1).

Webster, Roger (1988) The Bedouin of the Wahiba Sands: Pastoral economy and society. *Journal of Oman Studies* (special report) 3, 461–72.

Chapter 8
From Hajj to Hedonism?
Paradoxes of Developing Tourism in Saudi Arabia

PETER BURNS

Introduction

Within the psyche of Western European thought, the word 'Arab' in general and the name 'Saudi Arabia' in particular has, in the past, connoted multiple meanings. On the one hand, there are the mythologies of Lawrence of Arabia's and Wilfred Thesiger's 'noble savage' version of the Bedouin, but on the other, and intentionally less flattering, notions of tribalism, anti-progress and a duplicitous nature have been expounded. At a level of scholarship and intellect, Edward Said (1978) has successfully demolished these views in his work on Orientalism as colonialist-inspired instrument of cultural repression. Ranna Kabbani (1994) has also worked towards confuting the cultural mythologies through her analysis of Orientalist images. Said's work has been described eloquently by Salman Rushdie (Said, 1995; this essay first published 1986) as an analysis of 'the affiliation of knowledge with power' and how the carefully manufactured social construct of 'the Arab' was used to provide the 'justification for the supremacist ideology of imperialism' in yet another example of binary divide, not so much Lévi-Strauss' 'raw and cooked' but more as a form of van der Ploeg's (1993: 210) scientific knowledge vs. 'art de la localité' (wherein Western power is bounded by 'proper' or rational knowledge and that of the East is perceived as folkloric and superstitious). The history of Saudi Arabia is intertwined with British colonialism, the US' blind allegiance to Israel and the geopolitics of oil (and increasingly, water). It is the US-Israeli axis of course that has enabled new forms of Orientalism to arise – witness Western, especially CNN, media coverage of the Israeli-Palestinian conflict of April 2002 and the virtual non-coverage of the obscene wall being built (at the time of writing the present chapter, July/August 2003) by the Israelis partly on the Palestinian homelands. The central paradox of neo-Orientalism is eloquently captured by Said:

> If Orientalist scholarship traditionally taught that Muslims were no more than fatalistic children tyrannized by their mindset, their *ulama* and their wild-eyed political leaders into resisting the West and progress, was it not the case that every political scientist, anthropologist, and sociologist worthy of trust could show that, given a reasonable chance, something resembling the American way of life might be introduced into the Islamic world via consumer goods, anti-Communist propaganda, and 'good' leaders? The one main difficulty with the Islamic world, however, unlike India and China, it had never really been pacified or defeated. For reasons which seemed always to defy the understanding of scholars, Islam continued to sway over its adherents, who, it came regularly to be argued, were unwilling to accept reality or at least that part of reality in which Western superiority was demonstrable. (1995: 61; this essay first published 1980)

This somewhat lengthy but useful quote helps clarify some of the difficulties encountered when writing about the Arab world. Moreover, in his book on *Islamic Identity and Development* Mehmet identifies a major paradox about the very concept of a nation state and Islamic values:

> Nationalism . . . is a [worldview] built on ethnicity and territoriality, ideas incompatible with Islamic universality . . . The nation-state seeks to shift allegiance from God to the state. In return, it promises its citizens the benefits of socio-economic development in this life. Here too the nation-state conflicts with Islam. For it is precisely in the area of development that Islam has failed to evolve an ethos, to mobilize the masses for improving the quality of life. (1995: 1)

While on the surface this appears a seductive (if somewhat simplistic) explanation for the lack of democracy in the region, there is a distinction to be drawn between Islam on the one hand and concepts of culture and tradition on the other with the state's version of Islam a third form for debate (Rami Daher, personal correspondence). In Saudi Arabia there is a mixing of *Sharia* and the tribal customs of the *Bani Saud*, which leads to the need to emphasize the distinction between Islam, the official rhetoric of Islam as promulgated by the official national discourse of Saudi Arabia, and development. It could be argued that the house of Saud uses Islam as a means of constructing and confirming its legitimacy as rulers in perpetuity. In his description of the 'complex early history of the region'

Geertz talks of rulers reinforcing 'the distinction between *bled al makhzen* (the land of government) and *bled al siba* (the land of insolence) (1993: 298). To complicate matters even further Findlay (1994) reminds us that Saudi Arabia celebrated its sixtieth year of nationhood (1932–92) under the slogan 'Sixty years of Progress without change' and the illustration of the official poster claimed that in the case of Saudi Arabia

> the discovery of one of the world's biggest oil reserves in the Eastern Province of the Kingdom in 1938 helped fuel the development of the country at an unprecedented rate. In particular during the last two decades [1970s–1980s] Saudi Arabia has been transformed into one of the most prosperous and dynamic of world economies. Infrastructure and the welfare of the people have been developed to match the best anywhere. Yet, the Saudis have remained constant and true to their traditional values and Islamic beliefs. They have progressed beyond recognition, but have remained unchanged! (Ministry of Information cited in Findlay, 1994: 192)

The meaning behind this curious mix of hyperbole, naivety and schizophrenia is better and more humanely expressed in the words of the late King Feisal who was assassinated in 1975:

> Our religion requires us to progress and advance and to bear the burden of the highest tradition and best manners. What is called progressiveness in the world today and what reformers are calling for, be it social, human, or economic progress, is all embodied in the Islamic religion and laws. (Cited in Mansfield, 1992: 364)

The seemingly conflicting views are a reflection of what has been described as the 'difficulty of reconciling the development goals of what was [at the start of the twentieth century] a relatively poor state with the puritanical beliefs of the religious movement [*Wahabbism*], which had bought the *Saud* family to power' (Findlay, 1994: 40).

This brief foray into the literature has suggested that the notion of tourism, described by Rami Daher, editor of this volume, as part of the 'new modes of post-modern consumerism and consumption that centers on culture and entertainment' (personal correspondence) that tourism and Saudi Arabia's self-image as the guardian of authentic Islamic culture are not easy bedfellows.

So, within the socio-political context described above, this chapter will attempt to examine three paradoxes of developing tourism in Saudi Arabia. First, that the Kingdom is the guardian of the Holy Mosques and has a special duty to keep those sites from the sight of unbelievers and non-Muslims. Second, the underlying motivation for developing a service industry comprising large numbers of semi-skilled jobs in a seemingly oil-rich economy and finally, the political underpinnings (such as promoting national identity) for developing a sector of which large sections seem to be at odds with some core values within Islam.[1]

Cultural and Political Economy of Saudi Arabia

To link the introduction to this chapter with the present section on cultural politics, a very significant illustration will be used shown as Figure 8.1.

Drawing on semiotic analysis, it can be seen that here we have a photomontage from the official Saudi Arabia government website that summarizes the Kingdom's official view of itself. The most prominent image is that of the King Fahd, unsmiling, stern yet looking the camera (and thus the viewer) directly in the eye. Behind his right shoulder is a military jet of US origin, emphasizing power and military might. Next comes a picture of what is probably Masmak fortress, in effect a most potent signifier – reaffirming the house of Saud as supreme rulers over the Kingdom. The dark cone-shaped building is al-Faisaliah Tower (a prestigious office/hotel/shopping complex), which was financed by one of the royal princes thus linking 'modern' commerce with the royal family. At the centre of the image is a multicoloured graph and two small illustrations of oil-related activities – a well and some pipelines, which signify modernity, technology and the foundation of Saudi Arabia's wealth. Finally, and one could say most importantly (though not most prominently) comes the image of the Ka'bah in Mecca, the absolute

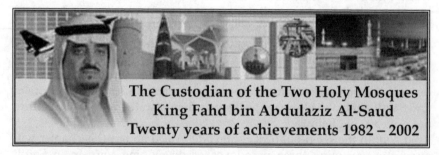

The Custodian of the Two Holy Mosques
King Fahd bin Abdulaziz Al-Saud
Twenty years of achievements 1982 – 2002

Figure 8.1 The official image of Saudi Arabia.

Source: www.saudiarabia.gov.sa

spiritual centre of Islamic faith (though if the picture is read from right to left, as is Arabic script, then the Ka'bah becomes the first image). The words in the image speak for themselves in linking the King directly with Saudi identity. Here we have it then: royal family, military might, tradition and history, commerce, technology and oil, underpinned by unswerving faith. However, as can be expected, while the picture does denote a particular story, the iconography connotes how official Saudi discourse, dominated through the power of the ruling family, reaffirms its own legitimacy and links itself inextricably with Islam.

In relative terms, there is little doubt about Saudi Arabia's wealth, though it is not as great as in the 1980s. At the end of 2000, Saudi Arabia's stock market was valued at about $70 billion making it then the twelfth-largest market in the world. However, even with an estimated post-September 11 value of $80 billion, there are signs of financial shortcomings as the global economy seeks recovery (http://www.mebn.org/saudi.html). The financial profile of the country is further complicated by, as the *Economist* puts it, 'the cosy patriarchies that currently siphon off much of the region's vitality' (*Economist*, 2002), which, in the case of Saudi Arabia, refers, in part, to the 5000 princes and their families who have 'cradle to grave welfare' (*Economist*, 2002) with ease of access to jobs and business opportunities.

Social and Employment Issues

In common with the richer of its oil-producing neighbours (notably those countries in the Gulf Co-operation Council (GCC)) Saudi Arabia has a heavily distorted population profile with large numbers of immigrant workers in all sectors of the economy. By the end of 2000, the population stood at around 22 million, 3.1% up on the previous year. Saudi nationals made up approximately 73% (16.2 million) with foreigners, mostly Asians and other Arabs, making approximately 26% (5.8 million). Given an annual projected population growth rate of something under 3.5% by 2010, the total population is likely to be some 30 million. A highly significant factor is that in the recent past, between 1982–9 and 1992–2000, the population grew faster than the economy. These data reveal one of the most pressing social problems facing the Kingdom: productive employment for nationals. While official data on unemployment do not exist, one authoritative source (Saudi American Bank, 2002) reckons that 'unemployment among Saudi citizens was an estimated 14 per cent, and 20 per cent among workers aged twenty to twenty-nine years old'. This situation was recognized officially with one pro-Saudi web page (http://www.hrw.org/wr2k1/mideast/saudi.html) reporting the Interior Minister Prince Nayif bin Abdelaziz's comments on the Kingdom's high population growth rate and the large number of job-seeking graduates as representing 'an economic, social, security and cultural problem'. Table 8.1 gives a summary of population and employment data from a variety of sources.

The high levels of unemployment present what must be a unique paradox in the light of the millions of workers and their families in Saudi Arabia from various poor Arab and Asian countries, many skilled and professional, but about half unskilled. The foreign workers include some 1.2 million Egyptians and 1.2 million Indians and a number of undocumented, illegal workers including those who remain after entering the country to perform *Hajj* or *'umrah* (terms described later in this chapter), and those who stayed after the expiry of their official work permits.

The converging phenomena of rapidly increasing population and decreasing growth make social unease, not to say unrest, almost inevitable. Cultural attitudes towards jobs and employment have not been

Table 8.1 Summary of population and employment indicators

Population and national labour force: key indicators	
Total population	22.1 million
Saudi population	16.2 million
Foreigners	5.8 million
Population growth	Slowing from 4.7% (1980–97) to 3.3% (1997–2010)
Age structure	60% under 20 years old
Labour market	7 million *of which* 3.1 million (45%) are Saudi
Total female employment	15% of total labour market
Saudi female employment	2% of total labour market
Unemployment rate	14%, increasing to 20% in the 20–9 year age group
New entrants	100,000 nationals enter the job market each year
Labour demand	Projected to increase by 0.9% per annum over DP7 period (1999–2004)
97% of all new growth is projected to be in the private sector	

Sources: KSADP6 (1994); KSADP7 (1999); World Development Indicators (WDI) database, July 2001[2]

helped over the past few decades by government policies that simply created relatively undemanding white-collar jobs in the bureaucracy. It was an easy option that derogated the acquisition of skills as something for foreigners and one that is recognized as unsustainable. Moreover, public-sector, white-collar job-creation for Saudi nationals has also tended to denigrate technical (even highly skilled) occupations. In a sense, an unsustainable culture has been created whereby families expect the government to provide such jobs, and individual government officials are often under pressure to create work for the children of friends and relatives. In the past such pressure has been gladly accepted in the sense that the 'giving' of jobs was another form of power through social control: if success in obtaining a government job was framed by largesse rather than formulaic criteria and merit, then families that want their children to have jobs had better behave and show respect to those in power. The government's 6th and 7th Development Plans (KSADP6 and KSADP7) go some way in recognizing that government cannot continue creating jobs and in KSADP7 it was publicly stated that through a process of Saudiization and encouraging new business ventures, private-sector job-creation was to take priority. The *Washington Post* (generally pro-Saudi) put it this way:

> In fairness to policy makers, the Saudi government has been conscious of this population explosion and its impact on the job market and unemployment. Of all government policies, Saudiization and job creation is rated the most important. From this standpoint has flowed the rest: accession to the WTO, the liberalization program, reform, training, skills assessment – all these stem from the government's consciousness of the perils of unemployment, poverty and social discontent. (Washington Post, 2001)

By most economic indicators, Saudi Arabia is a developed country, but the population shows the characteristics of a developing country in terms of high birth rates, surprisingly high illiteracy rates (see Table 8.2) and, for cultural rather than economic reasons, extremely low female participation. As mentioned above, a central paradox in the socio-economic development of Saudi Arabia is the very high unemployment rate amongst young Saudi males. At present, families tend to support these young men until an appropriate position transpires but increasing financial pressure (including cost of living) has made the practice unsustainable. The social problem is being further pressured as the very high numbers of children born in the 1980s are now entering the job market in increasing numbers.

Table 8.2 Population and literacy data 1996, 1999 and 2000

	1996	*1999*	*2000*
Assumed total population, total (million)	18.7	20.2	20.7
Urban population (% of total)	83.4	85.1	85.7
Illiteracy rate, adult male (% of males 15+)	18.6	16.5	15.9
Illiteracy rate, adult female (% of females 15+)	38.7	34.1	32.8

Source: WDI database, July 2001 (these data vary a little from other sources, but the value of the information gained is not compromised))

Three major themes merge together to form an inevitable negative consequence for future socio-economic development and the role of young Saudis in society:

(1) Social and cultural perceptions of what does and does not constitute 'worthwhile' employment for Saudi nationals, *which in part has led to . . .*
(2) The huge number of foreign workers and their families, which has created a dependency situation that underpins (3) (below) and strengthened (1) (above) . . .
(3) The almost total absence of appropriate technical education including apprenticeships and formal trades training for Saudi nationals.

Inevitably, few Saudis have the necessary skills to replace foreign technical and blue-collar workers, though efforts are being made to address this issue. Collectively, the data reveal a malfunctioning labour market. For example, a fact that illustrates a number of social and cultural issues is that there are over 500,000 chauffeurs employed by private households 'for the simple reason that women are not allowed to drive' (Economist, 2002: 15). Arguably, the two biggest labour force issues facing Saudi Arabia are:

- the existence of a dual economy where there are in effect two labour forces; and
- that women in general and Saudi women in particular face almost insurmountable practical and cultural difficulties in taking up employment.

On the first issue, the dual workforce comprises Saudi nationals that have social and economic expectations associated with an oil-producing country including high salaries. On the other hand, there is a vast pool of cheap labour from South and East Asia where the expectations are tied to the economic misfortunes of those regions. This dichotomy is not unique to Saudi Arabia, but perhaps the difference between the Kingdom of Saudi Arabia (KSA) and her immediate GCC countries is the sheer size of the population. On the issue of Saudi women's employment, some progress has been made, but there is real and continuing resistance from some conservative quarters.[3] Again, a paradox arises because the opportunity for women's education has increased quite dramatically over the last decade of the 20th century. The government has made it clear that it cannot and will not continue with public-sector job creation to accommodate the increasing numbers of young Saudis coming into the workforce. Given that in 1996 only 7% of the private-sector workforce was Saudi (EIU, 1996), KSADP7 makes it quite clear that the private sector has to meet this challenge, mainly through Saudiization and expansion: hence the drive for, among other things, tourism.

Tourism and Saudi Arabia

Given that King Fahd, the ruler of Saudi Arabia, is first and foremost the guardian of the Holy Mosques and has a special duty to maintain the Holy sites, enable the Faithful to perform their *Hajj* obligation and keep those sites from the view of unbelievers and non-Muslims as required by the Qaran, no discussion about tourism in Saudi Arabia can take place without reference to the Islamic pilgrimages of *Hajj* and *'umrah*. In Arabic, the word *Hajj* literally means going to a place for the sake of visiting. However, its usual and normal use refers to the act of going to the *Baitullah* in Mecca to observe the necessary devotions related to pilgrimage. According to the Islamic *Sharee'ah* (religious law) the ritual of *Hajj* is performed in the month of *ZulHijjah*, the twelfth and last month in the Islamic lunar calendar year. Mecca is of course the birthplace of the Prophet Mohammed but his religious fervour forced him to flee to Medina where he continued to preach and convert. Less than a year before his death in 632 AD, his teachings became pre-eminent and he made a pilgrimage back to Mecca and thus established the principle of *Hajj*.

Unlike most other pilgrimages, *Hajj* is not an option for Muslims but a fundamental obligation, and this element of compulsion makes it difficult to define as tourism proper. Men and women who are physically capable and economically able have a religious obligation to perform *Hajj* at least once in their lifetime. Each year, pilgrims from all over the world perform *Hajj* enabling them to interact with other believers. The command concerning the *Hajj* is found in several Qaranic verses, among them Al-Hajj: 26–7:

> And when We assigned to Ibraheem the site of the Sacred House (*Ka'bah*), saying 'Do not associate with Me anything, and purify My House for those who circumambulate the *Ka'bah*, and those who stand up and prostrate and bow in prayer. And proclaim the Pilgrimage among men, and they will come to you on foot and mounted on every kind of camel, lean on account of journeys through deep and distant mountain highways.

Besides this annual ritual which, with its 1.36 million pilgrims in 2000, is one of the largest gatherings on earth, there is a lesser *Hajj* known as *'umrah* that can be performed at any time during the year. In 2000, there were some 2.27 million *'umrah* visitors. The word *'umrah* is derived from *I'timar*, which means a visit. However, *'umrah* technically means paying a visit to *Ka'bah*, performing *Tawaf* (circumambulation) around it, walking between *Safa* and *Marwah* seven times. The Saudi government has expanded the *'umrah* season to ten months (Shakiry, 2002: 6) so as to encourage Muslims in their religious duty (as opposed to obligation) and enhance the socio-economic activity of the country.

Placing the definitional complexity of *Hajj* and to a lesser extent *'umrah*, to one side, there has been no international leisure tourism in the KSA as defined by most academic observers (Burns & Holden, 1995; Smith, 1989). However, this does remain a contentious issue because the World Tourism Definition of tourist (people travelling for holiday, leisure, business and religious purposes) would clearly include *Hajjees* even though their travel was an obligation (or perhaps aspiration) rather than a free choice; as illustrated by the fact that the Kingdom remains one of very few countries not to issue tourist visas, though group visas for guided tours are available. In some ways, a comparison could be made with the official travel agency of the former Soviet Union, 'In tourist', in that foreigners allowed into the country would have to be carefully monitored so that they did not spread morally/politically unacceptable ideologies such as freedom of speech, democracy or atheism.

The first official position of Saudi Arabia on tourism and the stated rationale for its development are to be found in the KSADP6, which talks of *domestic* tourism services as being 'an effective means of preserving the unique values, traditions and identity of Saudi society' (1994). This announcement came as something of a surprise to some observers within and outside the KSA. Placing tourism on the economic (and therefore political) agenda reflected the growing anxiety (seen and dealt with a decade earlier in most other GCC members) about the need to diversify the economy and create a much wider range of employment opportunities. The theme of domestic or 'internal' tourism was continued at an official level, as the Cabinet notes for May 1999 reveal:

> Turning to domestic affairs, Prince Sultan spoke of the development of internal tourism in various parts of the Kingdom, pointing out that the country, endowed with security and stability in addition to a good climate, natural scenic beauty, and an advanced transportation network, has become an attractive tourist destination not only for Saudi citizens, but also for those of the other GCC member states. He went on to praise the positive role being played by the private sector in developing internal tourism and reiterated the support of the state to investment in this sphere. He noted that development of internal tourism conforms to the major economic development plans that aim at diversification of the economic base and boosting sources of income. (www.saudiarabia.gov.sa)

Interestingly, given that the tourism being planned for was to be primarily for domestic rather than foreign tourism, the usual arguments about using national resources to support the leisure activities of foreign tourists did not apply. Moreover, it could be argued that given Saudi Arabia's state capitalism approach to development (despite the rhetoric of free markets and the pre-eminence of the private sector) such investment and development approaches are expected by civil society. The measures stated above took place within a very clear development objective, namely: 'to develop tourism and recreation areas in a manner which does not conflict with protection of the Kingdom's natural resources, historical sites and social traditions' (www.saudiarabia.gov.sa). This conforms with the KSA's own (official) description of itself as being 'based on the institutions of a free market economy and guided by the teachings of the true faith of Islam' (KSADP7, 1999: 15). For both the preceding points, the use of language proves interesting. Analysis reveals an unacknowledged acceptance of international tourism on the basis that the domestic sort, undertaken by citizens who 'know the rules' so to speak, is unlikely to cause social disharmony (though it could be argued local tourists are as capable as any other sort in causing socio-environmental damage).

Tourism policies in the Kingdom were summarized in KSADP6 (1994) as follows:

- The expansion of diverse tourism facilities and the provision of recreational services in the tourism development areas will continue to be encouraged.

- The facilitation of private-sector participation in the development of tourism win be continued.
- Tourism-related agencies will co-operate in the active promotion of domestic tourism and the provision of high-quality services.

Official institutional arrangements for policy-making, planning and, to some extent, implementation are the responsibility of a relatively new body, the Supreme Commission for Tourism (SCT) based in Riyadh. The SCT was formed in April 2000 with a mission to 'develop, promote and enhance the tourism sector in the Kingdom and facilitate the growth of such sector, which is deemed to be an important resource for the national economy' (Ministry of Planning, 2000–4). The SCT's biggest achievement to date is the development of a complex and comprehensive tourism master plan, which was approved by the Council of Ministers in June 2002. In addition, Provincial Councils and local Chambers of Commerce in regions that have some sort of tourism potential also have the potential to co-operate and take something of a lead in facilitating private-sector expansion and investment in tourism and tourism projects.

It is clear that the KSA does have certain attributes that could be counted as tourism assets. Among them good internal communications and a variety of cultural and environmental features such as coral reefs along the Red Sea coast, mountainous areas and natural springs. Such attributes are particularly attractive to GCC citizens (mentioned above and who have highly simplified visa arrangements) who feel they can travel in a manner appropriate to their faith and culture, which includes attractions, restaurants and accommodation suitable for Muslim families to move around without undue exposure of women to the gaze of outsiders. While it is a little ironic that the two sites likely to provide most interest to visitors, the holy cities of Mecca and Medina are off-limits to non-Muslims, the KSA does have a number of other cultural assets and potentials that could be linked together to form tourist attractions[4] such as:

- Pre-Islamic civilizations including the Nabataeans (for whom the 'carved' city of Medain Saleh was the second most important city after Petra in Jordan).
- The frankincense and other trade routes including the historic oasis town of Najran (following the Asian example of 'the Silk Road').
- The life and times of the Prophet including parts of the pilgrimage routes (excluding holy sites for non-Muslims).
- Jeddah, as the 'gateway' to the two holy cities, has an array of vernacular architecture and traditional *sūq* such as *Sūq* Al-Alawi.

- (Linked to the above point) diverse urban tourism in both modern and old cities, towns and villages.
- The historic fight for Arab independence including the Saud family history, Lawrence and the Hijaz Railway.
- Ecotourism in mountainous, green areas such as Aseer and in dry regions.
- Bedouin traditions including the huge camel market outside Riyadh.

In addition, diving in the as yet unspoilt reefs of the Red Sea off the coast of Jeddah and four-wheel drive desert-adventure tourism has enormous potential. However, what remains difficult with such a list is the way in which it becomes quite clear that while heritage and the recent past could be forged together to provide a fascinating narrative of this important part of the Middle East region, the official discourse, narrations and representations have been constructed so as to glorify the present nation state rather than to provide an objective account that includes pre-Islamic times or even the Ottoman period of the region. As Rami Daher (personal correspondence) puts it: 'Many historic studies on the Ottoman period in *Bilad al Sham* uncritically lumped it into one long period and labelled it as four centuries of alien domination, neglect and deterioration.' By dismissing the period of history in such fashion, histories and cultural heritage located outside the boundaries and limitations of national identity, or that overshadow it, are somehow qualified as a sort of 'Other' history, not worthy of full recognition; the authentic 'us' as defined by ideological and genealogical discourse, in binary opposition to marginalized and fragmented 'Other'.

While there is a conflict between Saudi national discourse and pre-nation realities that leads to difficulties in how heritage sites and the past are presented, the development of the assets listed above is probably what the government has in mind when, through KSADP6 (1994), it announced a number of measures to support tourism as a sector, including:

- loans for hotel construction and development;
- the provision of physical infrastructure such as roads, communications, telephones, electricity and fresh water in areas of touristic significance;
- establishment of gardens and parks in regions with significant tourism potential;
- development and implementation of zoning mechanisms in tourism development areas;
- organization of sportive events and cultural festivals that encourage domestic tourism.

However, with regards to culture and history, Saudi Arabia is, as Rami Daher pointed out (personal correspondence) something of a special case; the geopolitical milieu of the region and the globalized interdependence on oil (keeping industrial engines turning in the consuming countries, and oil revenues flowing in the direction of producing countries) means that realpolitiks overcome potential political dichotomies or binary ideological splits. For example, Saudi Arabia's official discourse on the US is strangely silent when it comes to matters of faith (and acquiescent on the US' pro-Israel stance) and likewise the 'freedom loving' Americans tolerate routine human rights abuses by religious and government officials in the Kingdom. While KSA was never officially colonised, its national borders and dealings with foreign states such as Britain and the US have had a colonial flavour about them whereby KSA has been supported almost as a client state of the US and the officially turned US/UK blind eye to Saudi nationals' roles in the events of 9/11 demonstrated the strange power relationships. Moreover, and returning to the theme of culture and history, it could be inferred from the physical actions of the government, such as the destruction of the *Hajj* Fort in Mecca, its refusal to co-operate in the rebuilding of the Hijaz railway, the building of accommodation and apartment blocks in Medina and Mecca on sensitive sites (and demolishing historic buildings in the process), disassociation from its far past such as the Ottoman Empire, and its relentless promotion of recent history (i.e. that of the House of Saud) over other histories that tourism itself might be used to legitimize the present ruling family.

Moving from speculation to firmer ground, KSADP7 took the policies that burgeoned in KSADP6 and developed them further, emphasizing that a main aim for tourism should be to 'develop into one of the major economic sectors capable of creating self-generating sources of income and contributing to economic and social progress' (KSADP7, 1999: Introduction). The style used here is intriguing in that the phrase 'self-generating' is coded language that reiterates the government's intention to slow the provision of public-sector jobs through shifting responsibility for employment generation to the private sector. This is an open and much stated policy, and it is interesting to see it cutting across into tourism policy. The reference to 'social progress' is also a signifier revealing the government's concern that employment, and to a lesser extent the notion of 'opening up', are two important elements in the process of modernization. International tourist arrivals by purpose of visit are shown in Table 8.3.

Table 8.3 International tourist arrivals by purpose of visit (2000)

Purpose of visit	Tourist arrivals	Percentage of total
Hajj	1,364,000	22
'umrah	2,270,000	36
Vacation/leisure	262,000	4
Visiting friends and relatives	1,096,000	17
Shopping	469,000	7
Business/conference	688,000	11
Health	101,500	2
Other	44,500	1
Total	6,295,000	100

Source: SCT (2001)

It can be seen from (Table 8.3) that over half the arrivals are religious tourists: pilgrims. And that only 4% are for vacation/ leisure. In terms of expenditure, unsurprisingly, almost half the international tourism expenditure in KSA can be attributed to pilgrims on *Hajj* and *'umrah* as seen in (Table 8.4):

Table 8.4 International tourism expenditure in Saudi Arabia (2001)

Market segment	Tourism expenditure (US$ million)	Percentage of total
'umrah	655	19
Hajj	961	28
Vacation/leisure	58	2
Visiting friends and relatives	621	18
Business/conference	658	19
Shopping	396	12
Other	71	2
Total	3420	100

Source: SCT (2001)

Table 8.5 International tourism expenditure by item (2001)

Expenditure item	Expenditure (US$ billion)	Percentage of total
Shopping	1395	41
Accommodation	827	24
Food and beverage	477	14
Transport	418	12
Recreation	167	5
Other	136	4
Total	3420	100

Source: SCT (2001)

Table 8.5 shows expenditure by category and illustrates that 'shopping' takes first place with accommodation coming in second. Food and beverage revenues differ in Saudi because of the complete ban on alcohol, and given the relatively high mark-up by hotels and restaurants on wines and other alcoholic drinks, this has a tendency to decrease revenue. The transport item is relatively high because the most favoured form of internal travel is by air. While these 'normative' data are interesting, the purpose of this chapter has been to explore the qualitative implications of tourism development. Several socio-cultural factors arise that are discussed in the next section.

Separation of men and women outside the family environment

This places many constraints on employment opportunities for both men and women, though this has, to some extent, been overcome by, for example, dividing restaurants into appropriate sections (family, men and women). However, service encounters still arise where such a system is too clumsy to work such as at the reception of a hotel or on an aircraft during both ground-handling stage and in-flight. The whole cultural concept of keeping women away from the gaze of strangers and the polite requirement on the part of men not to look at women from another family means that there is no simple solution to avoiding or overcoming cultural clashes in the workplace.

High population growth rate and high proportion of young people

KSA has rightly identified tourism as an engine for employment growth. These demographic trends mean that more jobs and a broader productive capacity are essential ingredients of a stable society. Tourism growth and development fit the spatial location of the population to large degree. Interestingly, in a discussion on Saudiization, evidence suggests that social expectations are becoming 'more realistic' and that 'the government can't deliver a career ... on a platter'. The growing number of youngsters will need employment, especially in the private sector. However, as a family choice, Saudis do not take up employment in the hospitality sector, because, as mentioned above, it revolves around face-to-face service encounters.

Women and the labour market

While women comprise around 15% of the total labour force, only a tiny minority of this percentage is made up of Saudi women. Women are restricted to jobs where they are unlikely to deal directly with men, or are completely separated from men. In some cases, video conferencing technology is used to avoid men and women being in the same room at work. This may have implications for Saudiization in the sense that many white-collar jobs in tourism involve service encounters. If women are not allowed to deal with such situations then the Saudiization programme will be operating with only 50% of the potential workforce.

Developing cultural tourism in KSA

KSADP7 and subsequent reports are very positive about the role of tourism in cultural revival and enrichment. One report in particular speaks of a revival for crafts, arts and tradition but rather ominously within the context of 'factual interpretation'. The quality of these traditions can be further protected by training in arts and crafts as well as developing the necessary human resources to protect and interpret physical culture sites and monuments (including guides). However, the problem remains that young Saudis and their families do not value the employment aspects of crafts and arts even if they value the material products. Most craft work is undertaken by foreigners and traditional transfer of skill from one generation to another has more-or-less been broken. In effect, the Saudis have excluded and marginalized themselves from the practical skills needed for craft-making.

Attitudes to employment in tourism

This is central to the challenge of developing tourism and has been mentioned several times above. There appears to be a difference between what Saudi nationals say in response to surveys and opinion polls and what they actually do. While surveys indicate a fairly neutral attitude towards tourism employment, in 2001, only 7% of the hotel employees were Saudi, the rest were foreigners. Hotel and tourism employment represents considerable problems for Saudis: dislike of commercial hospitality/ service; mixing of males and females outside the family environment; confused and negative attitudes towards commercial 'pleasure' (for example, cinemas are forbidden in the Kingdom). To be fair, negative attitudes towards tourism employment is not a uniquely Saudi proposition; many countries (including Britain and Australia for example, have suffered from the same phenomenon). What makes Saudi Arabia different is the composition of the workforce with its dual nature and wages geared to the poor countries of Asia.

Conclusions

Both KSADP6 and KSADP7 cite various aspects of 'culture' as part of the assets that can be mobilized for tourism. This aspect of so-called 'product development' invokes an argument about whether culture and people should be enmeshed in corporate marketing strategies (Burns & Holden, 1995) or provide the backdrop for amusement and recreation for tourists. The complexity of tourism's social and economic dynamic, both as act and as impact, means that it should not be perceived as an integrated, harmonious and cohesive 'whole' and yet it is a complex system. As can be seen above, the relationship between culture and tourism (including cultural dynamics, and systems and structures) makes meaning between visitors and the visited possible. In Saudi Arabia, this approach is important for at least three reasons:

(1) Culture (especially culture that is understood to be unique or unusual by actors including marketing specialists and planners) can be seen as a commercial resource.
(2) Such understanding might help deflect or ameliorate negative change to a host culture occurring through the act of receiving tourists.
(3) Tourism literature rarely acknowledges the world as a system of relations wherein the properties of a 'thing' (in this case, culture) derives meaning from its internal and external relations.

These three items are reflected in Wood's (1993) perspective on the issue of culture, tourism and impacts. His analysis of culture and tourism relies on identifying and understanding systems, in discussing tourist and development discourses. He argues that 'the central questions to be asked are about process, and about the complex ways tourism enters and becomes part of an already on-going process of symbolic meaning and appropriation' (Wood, 1993: 66).

What the complex example of Saudi Arabia re-affirms is that place and space are inexorable elements of culture that cannot be separated from the natural environment where they develop. Under most circumstances, the extent to which components of culture are adapted by the local population and offered to tourists for consumption is likely to be framed by at least two factors. First, the relative difference and thus the relative novelty between cultural components of the visitors and the visited, and secondly, by the type and number of visitors. However, for Saudi Arabia the problematic nature of religious purity is an added factor in the complex relationship between the visitors and visited. After all, this is no easy population that will be persuaded to accept foreign visitors as a matter of economic imperative. Quite the opposite perhaps. For example, an observer of the KSA, Howard Schneider reported that it is considered a national responsibility to maintain 'careful distinctions ... between Muslims and non-Muslims' going on to cite a school textbook telling Saudi school children that:

> Sharing the joy of atheists and expressing your condolences is also inappropriate because it indicates an alliance with them and increases good feelings which puts them in a higher position ... Also it is prohibited to initiate a greeting when meeting them or to start making way for them on the streets. (Schneider, 2001: A15)

While such attitudes may not be the direct experience of foreigners living in or visiting Saudi Arabia, it makes for an extraordinary socio-cultural setting to start thinking about the development of tourism involving non-Muslims. These cultural attitudes are shocking to Muslims from other countries that do not recognize such exhortations to shun non-believers as any part of *Sharia* or their faith, which teaches peace and harmony. Saudi Arabia differs too, in that for the most part, the usual argument about superior economic wealth of tourists is not appropriate. However, there are still pockets of poverty in Saudi Arabia and youths confused by the conflicting demands of duty to their religion and the temptations of modern conspicuous consumption create instability and make for socially vulnerable youths such as the unemployed, bored or restricted, ripe for manipulation by extremist political elements – a phenomenon distinctly demonstrated by the high number of young Saudis involved in the events of 9/11.

The title of this chapter 'From *Hajj* to Hedonism?' is a play on words that highlights the paradoxes and dilemmas facing Saudi Arabia as it embarks on a sustained programme of tourism development. On the one hand, as noted above, the Kingdom is the guardian of Muslim values even to the extent that it believes its own 'version of Islam is the "true" Islam' (Schneider, 2001: A15). On the other hand, the government is promoting an economic sector based on the commercial (not spiritual) consumption of time, space, culture and Western-inspired values of secular vacation time, in short: hedonism. The underlying motivations remain unclear.

This chapter has identified several paradoxes not least of which seems to be that the political underpinnings, such as the linking of national identity with the House of Saud for developing a sector of the economy in which large sections seem to be at odds with the some core values of Islam. However, there is no getting round the fact that touristic developments, even those discussed in the somewhat bullish terms in the KSADP7 are taking place in a very paradoxical politico-cultural situation. It can be seen that national demographic, regional economic and global political forces are combining to place enormous pressure on the existing polarity of modernization vs. ultra-conservative norms. Saudi Arabia is an arena where the cultural values of old and modern, Self and Other, are struggling to find common ground. For all its problems, tourism may be able to make a positive contribution to the struggle.

Acknowledgement

I would like to acknowledge the detailed reading and helpful advice from the editor of this volume, Rami Daher. I have integrated many of his ideas directly into the text and his guidance has, with no doubt, constructed a much richer chapter than the earlier drafts would have had me believe. A colleague who lives in Saudi Arabia and who did not wish to be identified shared valuable insights especially with regard to business practices and religion. He also identified al-Faisaliah Tower in the photomontage.

Notes

1. Rami Daher pointed out to me that concepts of travel and tourism are not at all alien to the Islamic world and that the Holy Quran contains several verses

that encourage people to 'see the world': 'travel through the earth, and see what was the end of those who rejected truth' (Al Imran: 3:37). 'Do they not travel through the land so that their hearts (and minds) may thus learn wisdom and their ears may learn to hear?' (Al Hajj: 22:46).

2. I thank Kevin Millington, director of Acorn Consulting for assembling these data.

3. This is putting it mildly. The treatment of women in Saudi Arabia provides a major dichotomy for all but the most ardent cultural relativists and these issues deserve a book on their own.

4. These ideas for attractions were drawn together by Simon Woodward (personal communication).

References

Burns, P. and Holden, A. (1995) *Tourism: A New Perspective*. Hemel Hempstead: Prentice Hall.

Economist (2002) Time travellers: A survey of the Gulf. *The Economist*, March 23–9.

EIU (1996) *Country Report: Saudi Arabia, No. 4*. London: Economist Intelligence Unit.

Findlay, A. (1994) *The Arab World*. London: Routledge.

Geertz, C. (1993) *The Interpretation of Cultures*. London: Fontana.

Kabbani, R. (1994) *Imperial Fictions – Europe's Myths of Orient*. Glasgow: Pandora.

KSADP6 (1994) *Development Plan (1995–1999)*. Ministry of Economy and Planning. On WWW at http://www.saudi-un-ny.org/ch9–6pln.htm. Accessed December 2001.

KSADP7 (1999) *Development Plan (2000–2004)*. Ministry of Economy and Planning. On WWW at http://www.planning.gov.sa/PLANNING/Drive_A/7CONTe. htm. Accessed December 2001.

Mansfield, P. (1992) *The Arabs* (3rd edn). London: Penguin.

Mehmet, O. (1995) *Westernizing the Third World: The Eurocentricity of Economic Development Theories*. London: Routledge.

Ministry of Planning, KSA (2000–4) *General Objectives and Strategic Bases of the 7th Development Plan (Decree No. (58) of 28/3/1420)*.

Said, Edward (1978) *Orientalism: Western Concepts of the Orient*. London: Routledge Kegan Paul.

Said, Edward (1995) *The Politics of Dispossession: The Struggle for Palestinian Self-Determination 1969–1994*. London: Vintage.

Saudi American Bank (2002) Directors' report. On WWW at http://www.samba. com.sa/about/pdf/Financials_EOY_2002.pdf. Accessed 9 September 2004.

Schneider, H. (2001) For many in Saudi Arabia, a fundamental conflict: After Sept. 11, questions deal with tension between ultraconservative culture and influences of modern world. *Washington Post*, 8 November, p. A15. On WWW at www. washingtonpost.com/ac2/wp-dyn/ A58716–2001Nov7?language=printer.

Shakiry, A. (2002) Cultural tourism and its civilised aspects. *Islamic Tourism* 2 (Winter).

Smith, V. (ed.) (1989) *Hosts and Guests: The Anthropology of Tourism* (2nd edn). Philadelphia: University of Pennsylvania Press.

Van der Pleog, J.D. (1993) Potatoes and knowledge. In M. Hobart (ed.) *An Anthropological Critique of Development: The Growth of Ignorance* (pp. 209–27). London: Routledge.

Washington Post (2001) Population growth: Training and a growing economy are vital to creating jobs for a young and rapidly expanding workforce. *Washington Post*, 3 November. On WWW at http://www.washingtonpost.com/wp-adv/specialsales/spotlight/saudi/art12.html.

Wood, Robert (1993) Tourism, culture and the sociology of development. In M. Hitchcock, V.T. King and M.J.G. Parnwell (eds) *Tourism in South-east Asia* (pp. 48–70). London: Routledge.

Chapter 9

Touristic Development in Sinai, Egypt: Bedouin, Visitors, and Government Interaction

DAVID HOMA

Introduction

Egypt has been a tourist destination for thousands of years. The Nile valley is the central focus for those venturing to see the ancient wonders that Egypt has to offer. During the past two decades the Egyptian government has been attempting to shift part of the touristic influx to other priority zones including the Mediterranean coast, the Red Sea coast, the Gulf of Aqaba, Upper Egypt, and the western desert area (Wahab, 1997: 36). Developing additional tourist zones will help distribute tourists throughout a wider area of Egypt in addition to the potential economic benefits associated with the tourism industry. There are deleterious effects of tourism with any touristic influx into new areas. Egypt must expand its tourist destinations while balancing expansion with the need to protect areas from the long-term effects of tourism. This chapter will specifically address tourism development in the Sinai Peninsula focusing on the Gulf of Aqaba coast, the impact of this development on Bedouin living in the Sinai, visitors to the Sinai, and the role of the Egyptian government in the various stages of touristic development.

Three key variables play vital roles in tourism development in the Sinai. Numerous Bedouin tribes have lived in the Sinai for centuries. Sinai Bedouin have had minimal say in the development of the Sinai; however, sustainable tourism in coordination with the Egyptian government makes the future of the Sinai Bedouin a viable possibility. The next variable of tourism development is the tourist or traveler. (A distinction between traveler and tourist will be used to differentiate between the locations each type of visitor prefers to patronize. The word 'visitor' will hence forth be used to mean both traveler and tourist, if no specific distinction is necessary between either types of visitor.) Visitors seek out different experiences while traveling. A better understanding of what each visitor is looking for will also help tourism development in the Sinai. Wahab states: 'It may be safely said that the tourist product of Egypt is multi-faceted and affords multiple tourist typologies appealing to a wide range of overseas visitors' (1997: 32). The final variable is the Egyptian government which implemented the Sinai Development Project in 1994. This project, slated for completion in 2017, deals with multi-level development, tourism being one part of the overall plan.

Current and future tourism development in the Sinai is centered on three key areas. First, the Egyptian government has its tourism develop-ment plan for the Sinai focused on the wealthier tourist and the idealistic beach paradise. Second, tourists and travelers seek out their own concept of Sinai development affecting the Sinai's metamorphosis over time via tourism. Tourists are looking for the idealistic beach setting that the government wishes to provide. Travelers are looking for a relaxed atmosphere with an underlying idealistic Bedouin theme providing the travelers with a sense of authenticity. This is not to say that tourists do not seek out their own authentic experience. Finally, Sinai Bedouin also desire a role in Sinai development beyond the relatively limited allowance offered by the Egyptian government. Bedouin deal with issues of authen-ticity and how their future of 'Bedouinness' will play out in relation to Sinai development.

Bedouin of the Sinai

The current population of Bedouin living in the Sinai walks a fine line between touristic perceived tradition and the reality of the condition in which Bedouin actually exist. Whereas visitors seek out what they believe to be Bedouin of the desert, Bedouin are looking for ways to better their lives within the confines and limitations placed on them by the Egyptian government. Multiple meanings come into play for Sinai Bedouin intro-ducing the conundrum of 'what the differences are between cultural expressions . . . designed for outsiders [i.e. the Egypt government and visitors], as opposed to those designed for the people themselves' (Bruner, 1986: 29).

Sinai Bedouin are not a homogenous group who share the same initia-tory arrival date. The current tribes present in the south Sinai range in time of arrival from the 6th century to the 20th century. The oldest tribe, the *Jabaliyyah*, are said to be descendants of a small group of Macedonian soldiers brought to defend the monks of Saint Katherine's Monastery, whereas the *Huweitat* arrived in the early 20th century from the Arabian Peninsula. Those unfamiliar with when Bedouin arrived in the Sinai assume they are viewing Bedouin *in situ* thus placing Bedouin in an awkward position. Do Bedouin play to their perceived role for the touristic element or do they ignore this element and go in the direction their own culture takes them?

The traditional or, more accurately, stereotypical view of Bedouin is of a desert dwelling, nomadic people wondering from oasis to oasis. The reality is quite different for the majority of Sinai Bedouin. It is true that in the past certain Sinai Bedouin tribes did follow a migratory pattern or *rihla*; however, this pattern would be better labeled semi-nomadic. Certain visitors who come to the Sinai seek out an 'authentic' Bedouin experience such as camel treks led by Bedouin through the interior of the Sinai. Bedouin have been willing to grant visitors their wish to have an authentic Bedouin experience even if the trek is removed from the reality of Bedouin existence.

Bedouin role in Sinai development

What role should Bedouin play in touristic development of the Sinai and, more importantly, how should Bedouin represent themselves to those visiting the Sinai? Each variable involved, the Egyptian government, visitors, and Bedouin have a stake in the ultimate future of the Sinai.

The Egyptian government implemented The National Project for Development of the Sinai in 1994. A key component of the project is the relocation of nearly 3 million people from the Nile valley to the Sinai. The majority of population influx will be concentrated in the north Sinai with approximately 500,000 people living in south Sinai. The goal is to reduce the continuing population pressure being placed on the Nile River. The completion date is set for 2017 with the project costing an estimated £E 75 billion. One area of potential employment for the people relocating to the Sinai will be in the tourism sector.

Egyptians own nearly all aspects of the tourist sectors in the Sinai. (Sinai Bedouin do not always consider themselves Egyptian thus a distinction will be used to differentiate between Sinai Bedouin and Egyptians or, as Bedouin call them, *el-wadi*.) The Egyptian population in the Sinai will continue to marginalize Bedouin from the tourism sector beyond those willing to play their perceived authentic Bedouin role. The following dimensions of the Sinai Development Project do not even directly mention the current Bedouin inhabitants.

The essential dimensions of development in Sinai are (The National Project for the Development of Sinai, 1995):

- Benefiting from the characteristic locations of Sinai, which is considered a basic resource of development.
- Developing industrial activity and resettling industrial projects thus leading to an increase in the demand for educational and specialized training services.
- Due attention is given to agricultural development in Sinai by growing crops that need little amounts of water and chemical treatment.
- Due attention is given to touristic activity since Sinai enjoys numerous elements of tourist attraction such as religious, therapeutic, and conference tourism.

The Egyptian government focuses its development toward tourists not travelers coming to the Sinai. There is little evidence that any differentiation is seen between the travelers and tourists even if various accommodations are sought out. Travelers often seek out what they believe to be an authentic Bedouin experience. Tourists are generally satisfied staying within the confines of their hotel, venturing out infrequently to 'experience' the local ambiance. Travelers on the other hand will sometimes seek out an environment for the sole purpose of experiencing what they at least believe to be authentic. Though as Wang points out: 'Authenticity involves a range of different meanings, to confine it to the originals is over simplistic' (Wang, 1999: 354). Whether it is, at the least, seeing Bedouin acting the part of a Bedouin or actually experiencing a 'traditional' Bedouin experience (e.g. a camel trek through the desert), the traveler often has a preconceived vision of what they expect to encounter upon arrival in the Sinai. If only seeking a halcyon environment to relax in, travelers come to the Sinai with a preconceived notion of what they will experience. The current scenario does not take into consideration of what Edgerton believes:

> It is mistaken to maintain . . . that if a population has held to a traditional belief or practice for many years, then it must play a useful role in their lives. Traditional beliefs and practices may be useful, may even serve as important adaptive mechanisms, but they may also be inefficient, harmful and even deadly. (2000: 131)

Is it necessary or even desirable for Bedouin to incorporate their traditions into the tourism sector? Visitors (and certain anthropologists) may believe Bedouin maintaining their traditions to be beneficial or a topic not even up for discussion. Bedouin see the situation through their own cultural lens, as does the Egyptian government.

The Bedouin population is placed in a difficult position within the context of Sinai development and more specifically tourism development. The Egyptian government acknowledges the Bedouin population yet places them in the periphery for future development. The National Project for the Development of Sinai: Objectives, mainstays, and potentials does not even mention Bedouin. Chapter 2 states: 'Sinai is a model of national pioneer development in which new and unconventional policies of *building new societies* are implemented . . .' (emphasis added; The National Project for the Development of Sinai, 1995). Elimination of Bedouin is not directly indicated as a governmental policy though little is said in this section about allowing Bedouin to go their own direction.

Travelers have been passing through the Sinai for thousands of years. The Sinai is the only direct link between the African and Euroasian continents. Nonetheless, Sinai Bedouin have had minimal cultural interference. Israel's impact in the Sinai was relatively small during its brief occupation from 1967 until the complete return of the Sinai to Egypt in 1982. Numerous Bedouin who lived under Israeli occupation claim life was better for them. Such statements could come from Israel's lack of interest in developing the Sinai during its occupation. While also having little to do with the Sinai prior to 1967, Egypt saw potential for growth and by 1994 had implemented the Sinai Development Project.

Throughout the myriad political changes during the last five decades of the 20th century, Bedouin have had essentially little to no voice in what has occurred in the Sinai. The issue of what role Bedouin will play, if any, is moot to the extent that the Egyptian government has already begun a plan for the Sinai. This is not to say that the Egyptian government denies the existence of Sinai Bedouin or that Bedouin will not play any role in the Sinai development. Bedouin can be a tourist draw so long as they play a 'Bedouin' role. As is stated: 'The National Project for the Development of Sinai works for the urbanization of the tribal population and at the same time maintain their tribal culture as it is part of Sinai heritage' (Sinai: Location and natural resources, 1995). It will be a difficult proposition to maintain a heritage that has not included urbanization.

If Graburn is correct in saying that 'the concept of heritage requires a sense of ownership . . .' (2001: 68), how will Bedouin maintain their heritage when how they lived is taken away via urbanization? If there cannot be a Mount Fuji without the Japanese people (Grabrun, 2001: 69), how will it be possible for Bedouin to exist without the Sinai as it once was? If heritage is to be balanced along with tourism, what of the

'... tensions between tradition and modernity' (Nuryanti, 1996: 249)? Tradition is what others not of the 'authentic' group will create around said group once modernity takes hold.

Environments change and morph over time but if a culture is not allowed to change with the environment what then is a 'true' heritage? Sinai Bedouin are being placed in a situation in which they will have to balance cultural survival (i.e. heritage), cultural advancement, the outsiders view of being Bedouin, and the Egyptian government's placement of Bedouin within the greater goal of Sinai development. One major issue Bedouin face is dealing with the social and cultural differences that tourists and travelers bring with them.

Culture clashes

Cultural clashes between host and guest are as old as tourism studies itself. Bedouin follow the tenets of Islam and are faced with myriad visitors who are not Muslim. This is not to say that visitors outright reject any restrictions placed on them such as nude sunbathing, though there are those visitors who believe acting how ever they please is a basic human right regardless of the setting. Tourists who stay in tourist villages are given greater leeway since they are behind the walls of the village. Tourist villages in the Sinai fall between what Dann calls 'paradise controlled' and 'paradise confused.' 'Paradise controlled' is limited contact with locals. At least within the tourist village itself, 'paradise controlled' is the environment in which visitors exist. This is not to say that 'paradise confused' does not interact with 'paradise controlled.' Paradise confused is '[f]urther contact with locals, attempt to enter locals-only zones: natives as seducers, natives as intermediaries, natives as familiar . . .' (1996: 67).

Visitors to the Sinai will find themselves between 'paradise confined' and 'paradise confused' depending on multiple variables. Certain tourists who visit the Sinai for as few as three days to locations such as Sharm el-Sheikh fall into the 'paradise confined' category. Such a person flies into the local airport, goes to a multi-million dollar hotel complex to relax by the pool and then leaves via the same route a few days later. On the other end where 'paradise confused' is found, travelers deal directly with the 'natives.' 'Natives' in Sinai should be understood to mean Egyptian not only Bedouin. Visitors, unless directly told, might assume that the majority of people they come into contact with in the Sinai are Bedouin. Visitors will see, talk with, and even spend time with Bedouin but well over 90 to 95% of all businesses in the Sinai that visitors come in contact with are owned and run by Egyptians from Egypt proper.

Bedouin youth and visitor interaction: Dahab

One example of where Bedouin do have direct contact with visitors is along the *masbat* (a cove area) in Dahab (see Figure 9.1). Young Bedouin girls (a small number of boys also participate) ranging in age from 6 to 13 spend time selling cotton bracelets to travelers and tourists relaxing in the restaurants. The youth are not permitted to go into the hotels or the tourist villages but they are tolerated where the majority of travelers spend their time. The youth are 'tossed out' if a customer acts annoyed enough to get a restaurant worker's attention or if a large group of youths begins to congregate around visitors believed to be an easy customer for the youths.

Young girls from mainly poorer families or families where the father must find work outside of Dahab, will purchase various colored cotton thread. The morning is spent preparing pre-made bracelets for quick sale. Visitors usually begin to descent on the *masbat* around noon with the majority coming later in the day after 3 p.m. The girls use two methods

Figure 9.1 Example of where Bedouin do have direct contact with visitors along the *masbat* (a cove area) in Dahab.

Source: Photograph taken by the author.

to sell the bracelets. First is the direct method where the visitor is simply asked to purchase a bracelet. The younger girls with minimal selling and foreign language skills will use this method far less than older girls with more experience (see Figures 9.2 and 9.3).

Indirect selling is the more common and effective method used by the majority of girls. From one to five girls will wonder the *masbat* looking for the most recent arrivals or visitors with whom they have developed a relationship during the visitor's stay. The main method to hopefully force a sale is through some type of game that can be played between the girl and perspective customer. The bet is that a loss by the visitor will mean the purchase of a bracelet. Backgammon and *shishbish* (played on a backgammon board) are the most common games played. A price is generally set prior to the beginning of any game, though the price is subject to change and often entails renegotiation regardless of any set price. Whether knowingly or not the girls are able to use their position (i.e. young and female) to manipulate, within a given limit, the price of the bracelet if the visitor loses.

Figure 9.2 Young Bedouin girls attempt to sell bracelets to foreign tourists at the *masbat* in Dahab.

Source: Photograph taken by the author.

Cotton bracelets that are sold by the girls are an interesting mix of an item being authentic, inauthentic, unique, traditional, and modern all at the same time, depending on the context in which the bracelet is found. Bracelets created by Bedouin youth are authentic in that each one is handmade by a young Bedouin girl. No other Bedouin produce bracelets except for those bracelets made in the specific visitor/youth relationship. From this, each bracelet is considered unique, at least within in the context of the Middle East. Travelers who see these certain bracelets away from the Sinai are quick to note that such a bracelet must have come from the Dahab area (although during the past several years cotton bracelets are being made in multiple places along the Gulf of Aqaba coast, though still only by young girls). The bracelets are also considered inauthentic because the origin of the bracelets is said to have been brought to the Sinai by young Israelis vacationing in the Sinai who in turn had first brought similar bracelets back from South America. Prior to the mid-1980s, a small number of Bedouin youths sold 'Dahab pants', a simple, baggy cotton pant.

Figure 9.3 Bedouin girls at the *masbat* in Dahab.

Source: Photograph taken by the author.

Few if any visitors believe that the bracelets made by Bedouin youth are traditional in the same context as owning a camel or living in a goat-hair tent. On the other hand, can the bracelets be considered modern because of who is making the bracelets? Travelers and tourists alike appear to associate objects created by the guest culture as being traditional if certain variables are present. One key variable is when an object is handmade. A handmade object implies that time has been needed to develop the skill to create the object. Handmade objects also often fall under the guise of being authentic. Authenticity and traditional are not always separate concepts to those unfamiliar with the place they are visiting.

Regardless of what label is placed on cultural objects such as the bracelets made by Bedouin youths, multiple groups will label objects from their own frame of reference. And as Craik believes: 'The appeal of [cultural objects] to tourists takes second place to other motivations, experiences and appeals' (1997: 121). Thus does the labeling of cultural objects even matter to those visitors who are only passing through a touristic location? As tourism expands in the Sinai who, if anyone should decide how cultural objects are labeled? In truth, the labeling of objects can be very beneficial to the host culture. Travelers and tourists generally expect that other locations to which they visit will be different in certain ways. Even if, for example, an American seeks out a familiar place, like McDonald's, she or he is cognoscente of the fact it is a McDonald's not in America. The farther removed and unfamiliar an object is to a visitor, the better the chance of an object being considered authentic or traditional.

Authenticity: Created for the Visitor but by Whom?

Authenticity issues are not new to the study of tourism (Bruner, 1989, 1991; Chhabra *et al.*, 2003; Cohen, 1988; MacCannell, 1973, 1976; Pearce & Moscardo, 1985; Turner & Manning, 1988; Wang, 1999). Conceptually authenticity has been critically analyzed and deconstructed by academics in multiple fields. The direction of authenticity general comes from the tourist's perspective. How, though, do people dealing directly with authenticity issues understand and connect it with their situation in relation to these issues? The second consideration to include with Bedouin authenticity is what balance is it possible to reach between tradition and modernity when the Egyptian government has implemented the Sinai Development Project?

Egypt will invest in the tourism industry in the Sinai but also balance investment with realistic future goals. One possible route to achieve this is to understand what types of travelers and tourists are coming to the Sinai. The Nile valley offers millennia of history for tourists to visit. The Sinai, while certainly not lacking in history, is being developed, from a tourism standpoint as a beach paradise. The Sinai offers more than 20 'official' hotels and tourism villages. The town of Dahab on the east coast of the Sinai has more than 20 hotels if locations such as the Fighting Kangaroo and the Mohammed Ali Camp (low-end traveler accommodations) are included as hotels. Travelers seek out more authentic locations to spend time relaxing. Travelers to Dahab do not wish to be associated with tourists and thus are willing to stay in the likes of the Fighting Kangaroo. 'Tourists dislike tourists. Touristic shame is not based on being a tourist but on not being tourist enough, on a failure to see everything the way it "ought" to be seen' (MacCannell, 1976: 10). A sense of authenticity is believed to exist if it appears or is seen as though Bedouins are running an establishment or at least working in such lodging facilities.

Wang (1999) believes that '. . . authenticity is a label attached to the visited cultures in the terms of stereotyped images and expectations held by the members of tourist-sending society' (1999: 355). If this statement is correct, how then will the visited society handle those arriving with preconceived ideas? Bedouin have taken steps in their environment to deal with authenticity and tradition/modernity issues. One example is camel treks into the desert. A popular adventure with travelers and tourists alike, Bedouin combine the traveler-perceived authenticity with a dash of tradition (e.g. sleeping under the night sky and riding on camels) and the modern economic aspects brought about by the business of being Bedouin.

Authenticity and tradition are more closely assimilated in the area of cultural museums and handicrafts. The museum located near St Katherine's Monastery gives the visitor a view of how Sinai Bedouin have lived over the past centuries. In addition to a museum, handicrafts made by local Bedouin women offer, albeit minimal, economic opportunities to benefit from what visitors believe to be authentic. A distinction is necessary between authentic and unique within the context of handicrafts. Whereas, clothing items sold to visitors are authentic in the sense that certain designs, material, and colors are Bedouin, such clothing is better labeled unique. The clothing is unique in that Bedouin have not actually used what is being sold to the visitors. Thus, handicrafts that are made for visitors are essentially unique within the context of Bedouin culture.

Table 9.1 shows three types of authenticity in tourist experience. While the table is about the tourist, how do the descriptions relate to the 'visited'?

Table 9.1 Three types of authenticity in tourist experiences

Object-related authenticity in tourism   Objective authenticity refers to the authenticity of originals. Correspondingly, authentic experiences in tourism are equated to an epistemological experience (i.e. cognition) of the authenticity of originals.
Activity-related authenticity in tourism   Existential authenticity refers to a potential existential state of being that is to be activated by tourist activities. Correspondingly, authentic experiences in tourism are to achieve this activated existential state of being within the liminal process of tourism. Existential authenticity can have nothing to do with the authenticity of toured objects.
Constructive-related authenticity in tourism   Constructive authenticity refers to the authenticity projected onto toured objects by tourists or tourism producers in terms of the imagery, expectations, preferences, beliefs, powers, etc. There are various versions of authenticities regarding the same objects. Correspondingly, authentic experiences in tourism and the authenticity of toured objects are constitutive of one another. In this sense, the authenticity of toured objects is in fact symbolic authenticity.

Source: Wang (1999: 352)

The visitor falls under one of the three types listed in Table 9.1. Bedouin, in essence, are the toured object, which in turn forces them to comply whether knowingly or not with the tourist created sense of authenticity. However the government wants to control how the 'toured object' is allowed to present itself. One example of this scenario happened in 2000 as Bedouin entrepreneurship clashed with Egyptian investment.

Bedouin-run camps had been marginally tolerated by the government until the early 1990s. By the mid-1990s development had taken precedence and authorities wanted something done. Mohamed el-Khatib was a consultant for the Tourism Development Authority (TDA) at the time and decided to help the local Bedouin comply with TDA regulations. This involved forming a company on their behalf and presenting designs and technical assessments of their projects. El-Khatib helped the locals develop a viable economic opportunity including the creation of a non-governmental organization (NGO) called the Bedouin Heritage Association (Mostafa, 2004). Bedouin entrepreneurs saw what was happening and decided to build their own tourist camps. By 2000 growing interest in coastal development by Egyptians and outside investors outweighed Bedouin economic advancements in a number of locations. The government took steps to eliminate or at least minimalize the influence of tourist camps specifically those run by Bedouin. In the summer of 2000 the TDA used 200 soldiers and two bulldozers to remove bamboo huts and several restaurants in both the Bedouin Dream and Freedom Beach locations. Bedouin argued that they had the right to build camps and derive income from tourists. The government stated that '. . . the camps were unregulated, posing environmental health risks' (Beasley-Murray, 2000). Regardless of the conditions, the land had been earmarked for hotel development by a former government official. Bedouin were not going to be allowed build where outside investors saw the potential for economic development. Investors believed they knew what type of accommodations visitors to Sinai would seek out.

The type of tourist villages, hotels, and camps are reflective of which type of lodging is chosen by a visitor. The Egyptian government wants to attract those looking for an upscale environment. The entire east coast of the Sinai has been divided into five zones with each zone having priority development areas. Tourists are the focal point for development of these zones while younger travelers are not as important from a governmental perspective.

Locations such as Dahab have been seen a traveler's destination. One common source of information is the Lonely Planet guide book which states 'Dahab was once a sleepy backwater, but these days there are more pot-smoking backpackers than Bedouins, and the town has become somewhat of a lazy layover' (Egypt: Off the beaten track, n.d.). Where makeshift roofs once stood over travelers lounging along the *masbat*, the government came in during late 1996 and removed what was said to block the view of the beach. Others in Dahab believed the 'renovations' were initiated to eliminate unwanted elements such as those mentioned in the Lonely Planet guide. Of the restaurants that are found along the *masbat*, nearly all are owned and run by Egyptians not Bedouin, a fact not lost on local Bedouin in Dahab.

Travelers seeking the relaxing atmosphere of places such as Dahab also look for an authentic Bedouin setting. People staying at the Fighting Kangaroo are not so naive as to think such lodging representing anything near authentic. However, many travelers will go on a camel trek into the desert with local Bedouin men feeling some sense of authenticity. Even occasional ventures to a late-night Bedouin wedding gives a traveler the sense of an authentic experience even though the traveler was 'invited' along with several other travelers from the _masbat_. Local Bedouin recognized as far back as the late 1960s that travelers wanted a relaxing atmosphere mixed with a touch of Bedouin authenticity.

The Egyptian government is attempting to change how Dahab is viewed by visitors:

> Recent development trends suggest a move towards a more commercialized and upscale market. Backpackers, once the mainstay of Dahab's economy, are being pushed to the fringes in favor of package tourists, despite the town's lack of infrastructure to support them. (McGrath, 2002)

The changes occurring will not only affect those coming to Dahab but also those who live in Dahab. How will the government shape the physical and social landscape?

The Egyptian's Government's Role in Tourism

Egypt's antiquities have drawn tourists to their grandeur and magnificence for millennia. From Herodotus in the 5th century BCE, to the advent of modern travel to Egypt by Thomas Cook in the 19th century, to young Australian backpackers, each visitor has come for myriad reasons. Even with such a storied history of tourism: '[Today] Egypt's share of the tourist market is still smaller than might be expected considering its natural endowments and historical attractions' (Wahab, 1997: 29).

The Middle East accounts for a little less than 2% of world tourist arrivals. Recent political and social events over the past decade have only exacerbated the problem causing fluctuations in overall tourist arrivals throughout the region. Egypt's international tourist arrivals, until recently, were the largest in the Middle East. Figures from the World Tourism Organization (WTO) as of September 2003 now place Egypt third. The percentage share for Egypt during 2002 was 17.8% (4.9 million arrivals) compared to United Arab Emirates at 19.7% (5.45 million arrivals), and Saudia Arabia with the largest share at 27.2% (7.5 million arrivals) (World tourism highlights, 2003).

Events within Egypt have caused tourism arrivals to ebb and flow during the past decade. During the 1990s Egypt dealt with the Gulf war in 1991, terrorist attacks in the early 1990s, crackdowns by the Egyptian government on Islamic fundamentalists in the mid-1990s and the tourist killings at Luxor in 1997. The current decade has had its own problems. The second _intifada_ in Israel starting in 2000, the terrorist attacks in

America in the fall of 2001, and most recently the war in Iraq all have impacted on tourism in Egypt to varying degrees.

Events and their impact on tourism in Egypt and government agencies

Though the attacks on September 11, 2001 in America took place thousands of miles away from Egypt, the impact on Egypt's tourism sector was enormous. From January to June 2001, the tourism sector had taken in a record US$ 4.3 billion. In October 2001, following the attacks in the United States, Egypt saw tourist arrivals cut in half with cancellations continuing through the peak winter months (Egypt's economy, 2002: 36). Tourist arrivals declined overall in 2001 by 1.3%. This number is misleading when looked at in more detail. Tourist arrivals actually were 4.2% from January to August 2001. The last four months, however, saw an overall decline of 11% in tourist arrivals, with the Middle East being the hardest hit sustaining a 30% decline. Egypt itself saw a nearly 16% decline in the tourism sector during the last four months of 2001 (World tourism stalls in 2001, 2002).

In March of 2003 the United States and its allies went to war against Iraq in an attempt to depose Saddam Hussein. Egypt's tourist arrivals declined by 15.3% in April and by 10.1% in May. However, Egypt saw a rapid turn around in arrivals with a 5% increase in June and a 26.1% increase in July. These increases gave Egypt a year to the date increase of 6.5% (World tourism barometer, 2003: 8). In August 2003 Egypt saw a record 743,000 tourists in one month. In addition, visitors in August spent a total of more than 9 million [hotel] nights in Egypt, an increase of 121% over August of 2002 (Summer brought record tourism, 2003).

Internal and external events related to tourism are dealt with through various agencies in Egypt's government. Egypt's main overseer of the tourism sector is the Ministry of Tourism (MOT). There are four semi-autonomous governmental organizations under the MOT: the Public Authority for Conference Centers; the TDA; the Egyptian General Authority for the Promotion of Tourism; and the Tourism Academy. In addition to governmental organizations, the Egyptian Federation of Tourist Chambers represents the tourism private sector. This chamber has four chambers: the Chamber of Travel Agencies, the Chamber of Hotel Establishments, the Chamber of Handicraft Industries, and the Chamber of Tourist Establishments (Wahab, 1997: 33). Each division within the tourism sector attempts to work both independently but also in conjunction with the others to better regulate and develop the tourist sector in Egypt.

Sinai Development Project

Tourism development in the Sinai falls under The National Project for the Development of Sinai. This project, which was initiated in 1994, is slated for completion in 2017. Tourism development under this project will cost slightly over £E 8 billion of the nearly £E 75 billion projected for the entire project. The money available for tourism development ranks fourth in spending behind urban development at £E 20.8 billion, agriculture at £E 12.2 billion, and industry and mining at £E 10 billion (The National Project for the Development of Sinai, 1995). There are a total of 17 sectors listed in the development plan.

The project as a whole hopes to realize the following (The National Project for the Development of Sinai, 1995):

- The promotion of agricultural production and contributing to the enhancement of self-sufficiency at regional and national levels.
- The enhancement of the industrial sectors by using available resources in the Sinai.
- As an important sector, tourism should cope with world trends in order to attract tourists form all parts of the world. Domestic tourism is also given due attention.
- Work for the increase of the Sinai population so that the total number in 2017 will be about 3.2 million.
- The total investment cost of the project amounts to £E 75 billion from 1994 to 2017. The project aims at developing all sectors in all parts of Sinai according to available resources and fair distribution within the framework of integrated development.

Each of these objectives represents a broad perspective for the future of the project allowing room for adjustment as is deemed necessary by the Egyptian government.

The Sinai Development Project sets the stage and direction for the Sinai and also its Bedouin inhabitants. As has been previously mentioned, the main focus of the project is to relieve the growing population pressure on the Nile valley by relocating 3 million people to the Sinai. How this will be accomplished is through a multi-tiered approach incorporating industrial activity, agricultural development, and the tourism sector. Decrees issued tell of how the land will be divided ranging from 50% for investors, 15% for youth, 28% for beneficiaries, and 7% for Sinai inhabitants (The National Development Project for the Development of Sinai, 1995).

Tourism, while not the major focus of the Egyptian government, is understood to be key in bringing in money for the development project.

Within the context of the Development Project, the MOT has development priority areas, one being the Gulf of Aqaba coast. This zone is divided into five zones: Taba Sector, Nuweiba Sector, Dahab Sector, Wadi Kid Sector, and Sharm el-Sheikh Sector. Each sector is also divided into individual centers for specific development based on the issues such as topographic features. Topographical and environmental features are used for certain types of tourism developments. Sinai development also has the potential of being directed by historical and religious features (e.g. archaeological sites and Mt Sinai).

The Sinai Development Project separates tourist destinations into types including therapeutic tourism, cultural tourism, scientific tourism, safari (adventure) tourism, and religious tourism. Each type of tourism will attract those types of visitors seeking out specific travel experiences. All of these destinations are directed at tourists not young backpacker travelers. It is understood that the backpacker element will not disappear and in truth, backpackers were the first type of visitor seeking out the Sinai. Nonetheless, if these environment are not what a backpacker looks for, then fewer of this particular type of visitor will come to the Sinai.

It should be noted that cultural tourism would be better labeled historical tourism. According to Sinai development information, cultural tourism focuses on monuments and historical sites (Sector development, 1995). Nothing is said of the Bedouin inhabitants of Sinai as being part of cultural tourism. What role might Bedouin play in cultural tourism? Bedouin do have small roles within the overall context of the Sinai but are not considered an integral part of the future development. Bedouin are relegated to the periphery not unlike backpackers.

Two other important elements of tourism development are accommodation capacity and tourist investment opportunities. At the beginning of the Sinai Project there were over 4500 rooms in hotel and tourist villages (note: these numbers do not include unofficial lodging i.e. Bedouin-run camps). Current projections set the total capacity by 2017 to be nearly 43,000 (Sector development, 1995). The majority of these rooms will be located throughout the five sectors along the Gulf of Aqaba.

The entire Sinai Project is dependent on available funds. To help with funding, Egypt is encouraging tourist investment both from within Egypt and, more importantly, from outside of Egypt. The total investment cost projected for tourist development until 2017 is estimated at £E 8.2 billion (Sector development, 1995). The tourist sector initially will receive nearly £E 3 billion by 2002 (this being the fourth five-year plan). The key focus during this time period is for construction and internal infrastructure of tourist development centers (Sector development, 1995). Tourist development until 2017 will need a labor force in all sectors including construction, maintenance, and workers. Current estimates are that nearly 113,000 job opportunities will be associated with tourist development.

Dahab: A Case Study

Dahab is located 135 kilometers south of Taba and 100 kilometers north of Sharm el-Sheikh. Dahab is an example of touristic development during the past several decades. Dahab, the city, can be broken down into three different sections, though officially there are only two sections Dahab and Assalah. The first part consists of the city of Dahab, which functions mainly as the administrative center. Housing for workers (mostly Egyptian), a small number of shops, grocery stores, and restaurants are located in Dahab. The second part of Dahab is technically a separate Bedouin village though it is not always differentiated from Dahab itself. Assalah consists of Bedouin housing and a small number of shops. The third section of Dahab has an ever-growing number of tourist villages, hotels and restaurants for people visiting Dahab. The third section is often referred to as Assalah though the two sections will be differentiated here.

Dahab city (see Figure 9.4) plays a minimal role in the tourism sector for Dahab overall. Dahab city is often used by short-term visitors as a drop-off and pick-up point for transportation. The main bus station is often the only part of Dahab city that visitors ever see. Long-term visitors will sometimes utilize other facilities in Dahab city such as the post office or hospital. Once a visitor arrives in Dahab at the bus station, depending on where the visitor is staying, either someone from the hotel will pick up the visitor or it will be the visitor's responsibility to find a ride to his or her accommodation.

Numerous writings on Dahab mix and match the various areas, particularly the village of Assalah. The Egyptian government considers Assalah and surrounding tourist amenities a separate area north of Dahab city. Assalah was first developed as a Bedouin community for those Bedouin either choosing to or, in some cases, being forced to settle in permanent housing. For the purpose of this chapter Assalah will be considered separate from the tourist destinations.

Accommodations in Dahab range from the Hilton Dahab resort to the Fighting Kangaroo. As has been previously discussed, different accommodations attract different types of visitors. The five-star rated (3-star AAA rating) Hilton Dahab Resort offers one of the most expensive lodging in the Dahab area. Prices vary greatly depending on time of year and number of occupants. As of February 2004, the lowest advertised rate

Figure 9.4 General view of Dahab.
Source: Photograph taken by the author.

is US$65 for a single occupancy between the dates of December 1 through 22, 2003 and January 5 through February 28, 2004. The highest rate is US$583 for three people in one room December 31, 2003. These rates include a 19% tax. A check of availability on February 1, 2004 showed that the Hilton Dahab already had 70% of its rooms booked for the week beginning June 2004.

The Hilton offers numerous amenities to its guests. Built in 1998, it is a single-storey hotel with 163 rooms. It is located on the southern outskirts of Dahab in the self-contained Golden Beach area. Guests want for little as this hotel is meant to cater to nearly ever need that a tourist may have.

Hotel description
Overlooking the Lagoon in Dahab surrounded by the stunning view of the Sinai mountains. The resort has a private sandy beach and gardens landscaped with large shallow salt water lakes approximately 1,200 square meters of surface. The buildings are single storey with all rooms having a terrace/balcony. There is a large swimming pool and sun terrace overlooking the sea.

Room description

King room – Large room with seating area/satellite TV and Sony Playstation/Large terrace with sea view.

Twin room – Large room with seating area/ satellite TV and Sony Play-Station/Large terrace with sea view.

Facilities

24hr housekeeping, robe, mini-bar, television, desk, air-conditioning, smoke detector, safe, bathroom phone, balcony, hairdryer, sofabed.

General information

Babysitting, beach, business phone, car rental, children's menu, crib, business fax, currency exchange, gift shop, valet, location transportation, meeting facilities, multi lingual staff, parking, pets, playground, billiards, pool, restaurant, safety deposit box, scuba diving, telephones, turndown, water skiing, golf, horse riding, snorkeling, secretarial service, paddle tennis table, etc. (Hilton Dahab, n.d.)

Several other higher-end hotels and tourist villages are found in addition to Hilton Dahab Resort. In the same category a tourist could stay, for example, at the Novotel Coralia Club Bay listed as a 141-room leisure and sports resort. Sirtaki Hotel and Dive Center and Nesima Resort offer many of the same amenities as the Hilton Dahab. Perspective tourists seeking out possible accommodations for the Dahab area on the internet will be directed to higher-end lodging. A search of the internet on Google.com brought up the above mentioned hotels along with the following list: Canyon Dive Resort, Ganet Sinai Hotel, Lagona Village Dahab, Dyarna Dahab Hotel, Inmo Hotel, Nubia Touristic Village, Helnan Dahab Hotel, and Sarah Village. Each of these tourist resorts and hotels specifically cater to higher-end tourists. It is this type of tourist that the Egyptian government is hoping to attract.

Even with tourism development focusing on the tourist, travelers as previously discussed have played a role in initial tourism development going back to the late 1960s and early 1970s. Travelers have sought out a particular environment for relaxation, among other amenities, that could be found in the early years of what would become Dahab as it exists today. Early travelers to what would become Dahab were looking for beaches and cheap lodging. Initially there were essentially minimal, if any, lodgings available. In the late 1960s after the occupation of the Sinai by Israel following the 1967 war, young Israelis would travel along the Aqaba Coast (Israel calls this same body of water the Gulf of Eilat) seeking out a place to relax following or just prior to their mandatory service in the Israeli military.

The Mzenia Bedouin had long spent time along the ocean near present-day Dahab. As larger numbers of people sought lodging, Bedouin entrepreneurs quickly realized the economic value of creating traveler accommodations. Makeshift huts were erected to accommodate those looking for a cheap place to stay. Israel had minimal development in the Sinai during its occupation from 1967 until the return of the Sinai to Egypt was completed in 1982 following the Camp David Accords. Egypt did not immediately begin development in the Sinai. However, by the time the Sinai had been returned, Dahab had turned into a popular traveler destination along the lines of Goa in India or Koh Samui in Thailand. Dahab provided a 'hippy' hangout for those looking for a relaxed atmosphere and the ability to partake in a drink of choice or readily available marijuana or hashish with friends.

The Egyptian government has taken steps to change the perception of Dahab and the Sinai's association with illegal activities. In June of 2001, Egyptian police arrested more than 60 people in drug raids and seized, according to the state-run Al-Ahram, six tons of cannabis (Four foreigners sentenced for drugs, 2001). The Egyptian police in late 2003 reported uprooting 1 million cannabis plants in the Sinai. In early 2000 four foreigners were arrested in Dahab for drug use and sentenced to jail time and fines of up to $36,000. And according to the *Middle East Times*: 'A Sinai court sentenced a Belgian woman to six years in prison and ordered her to pay a fine of $7,600 for selling marijuana and other drugs' (Egypt roundups, 2003). She was arrested while working as a dive monitor in Dahab. Bedouin association with the drug trade in the Sinai is also a growing concern for the government.

Throughout the past two decades a thriving traveler community has developed along the *masbat*. At one time the *masbat* was nothing more than a place for Bedouin to camp occasionally during the year. Once visitors began to converge on this strip of land, a makeshift development began that today is a bustling hub of daily activity. Travelers arriving in Dahab city will load onto the back of small trucks and are driven to where the *masbat* begins. Here a traveler will be inundated with offers of the 'finest lodging in Egypt!' Travelers often seek out the cheapest accommodations possible. For a number of travelers, 'roughing it' is seen as a badge of honor spoken of proudly among fellow travelers. The cheaper the traveler is able to travel, the more authentic the experience.

The *masbat* offers the cheapest places to stay and eat. Though prices have gone up slightly in the past several years, it is still possible to find a bargain at £E 10 per night. £E 10 will afford a traveler a weather-beaten 1 inch mattress (sometimes including sheets) that rests on the floor of a small 8 feet square (or other shaped) room. Depending on which room you have, a small window may be included though the view is often less than spectacular. Other amenities will include any number of the following: shared toilets and showers, laundry facilities (generally consisting of a sink and clothes line), small areas to sit in the shade, bus schedules throughout the Sinai and Egypt, and a plethora of relative- or friend-owned businesses hoping to help the travelers.

Nearly all of the traveler lodgings are owned and run by Egyptians. While neither the proprietor nor the atmosphere pretends to be authentically Bedouin, the travelers associate the experience as being closer to an authentic experience than if the traveler was to stay at the Hilton Dahab. Even with minimal amenities and the occasional nocturnal cockroaches as bedmates, staying where other travelers stay is considered to be an authentic experience. The Egyptian government pays little if any attention to the traveler element. Thus the minimization or even total elimination of the traveler element, while not a stated goal, would not be considered a loss.

The final element in Dahab is Bedouin looking to be part of the tourism industry. The main source of direct income from visitors comes in the way of desert treks that are offered. A few older Bedouin men and several younger Bedouin boys bring their camels to the *masbat* to entice visitors walking along the *masbat* to take a desert journey. Camel treks into the desert are pitched to visitors as a true Bedouin experience. Resorts and higher-end hotels also offer camel treks but these treks are more luxurious than those found along the *masbat*. Travelers have stated that the camel treks taken with Bedouin along the *masbat*, while not offering the number of creature comforts the expensive hotels camel treks do, are perceived to be closer to a true Bedouin experience. The basis for this belief comes from the cost of the trek and the appearance of the Bedouin with whom they ride into the desert.

Dahab is only one example of the numerous towns, tourist villages, and hotels throughout the Sinai. Dahab shows the multiple variables that are part of the tourist sector. Each tourist areas is different in certain ways, nonetheless, Dahab shows the evolution of tourism development over several decades. Dahab should be used as a case study for future tourism development throughout the Sinai both for its positive and negative points.

Conclusion: Unveiling the Sinai

Multiple elements exist today in the tourism sector of the Sinai. This chapter has looked at only a small sample of tourism and the direction in which it will head. The key aspect of tourism development in the coming decades is placed squarely on The National Project for the Development of the Sinai. Billions of Egyptian pounds have been earmarked for development of tourism through the year 2017. Regardless of any amount of money that will be used for tourism, numerous other aspects need to be considered.

From a cultural standpoint, Sinai Bedouin have the opportunity to play a role in elements that will be associated with the Sinai beyond present developments. If given the opportunity Sinai Bedouin should utilize their heritage in such a way so as to pass on, even in only a small way, the cultural heritage they believe best suits their identity. The Egyptian government has set aside only 7% of the land for Bedouin use. Further sustainable cultural development will allow Bedouin the opportunity to create a future that they will be proud of. One way that Bedouin may be able to achieve such a goal is through intervention by NGO's or other organizations willing to help them.

One example of NGOs taking positive steps in the Sinai was the creation of the Hemaya Association started by Sherif el-Ghamrawy in 1997. The main focus of this NGO is to preserve and protect the delicate environment of the south Sinai (Sustainable tourism, n.d.). This organization includes the tourism industry and Bedouin in dealing with the growing waste management issues being generated by the enormous growth taking place throughout the south Sinai. Among the 13 stated goals at the outset, all groups will benefit from the following:

1 Creating environmental awareness among local community, visitors, tourists, and the newly established institutions;
2 Preserving endangered species and prohibiting their hunting down;
3 Conserving and managing resources;
4 Protecting the cultural heritage of the Bedouins (the nomads of Sinai) as well as assisting them in raising their standard of living through projects and events promoting the traditional making of their arts and crafts;
5 Advising and sharing experiential knowledge about environmental among individuals and institutions;
6 Providing necessary research to conduct environmental impact assessments for the area. (Sustainable tourism, n.d.)

Finally, the visitors who come to the Sinai will influence the direction of tourism development in the Sinai. Whether the visitors are the tourists the government hopes will infuse the economy with their money or travelers seeking an authentic experience, each type of visitor will need to be served in such a way that all visitors find what they are looking for during their visit. Different visitors seek out different travel experiences thus the government has the opportunity to understand what visitors are looking for and create an environment visitors will enjoy. In addition, visitors also have the opportunity not only to help Bedouin living in the Sinai to keep their cultural heritage but also to allow Bedouin culture to exist into the future.

Tourism has the potential to play an important role in the overall development of the Sinai. The government, Bedouin, and visitors will need to work together when possible to create a viable future for all groups interested in living, working, and traveling in the Sinai. The Egyptian government has the ultimate say in what direction tourism development will head. It is difficult to predict what will happen as political changes occur in the coming decade. Who will replace the current President Hosny Mubarak or how it will change the political landscape in Egypt is yet to be seen. The Egyptian pound is now worth almost half of its pervious value from only a few years ago. Nonetheless, the future of the tourist sector has the potential to benefit all people involved. The Arabic word for travel (*safar*) has an important connection to its root meaning 'to unveil.' How the Sinai will be unveiled to those involved with its future is yet to be seen.

References

Beasley-Murray, Ben (2000) The Tourism Development Authority uses environmental rhetoric to justify demolishing Bedouin-owned camps in favor of big hotels. *Cairo Times*. On WWW at http://www.cairotimes.com/content/archiv03/sinai2.html. Accessed May 2004.

Bruner, E.M. (1986) Experience and its expressions. In Victor Turner and Edward Bruner (eds) *The Anthropology of Experience* (pp. 3–30). Urbana: University of Illinois Press.

Bruner, E.M. (1989) Tourism, creativity, and authenticity. *Studies in Symbolic Interaction* 10, 109–14.

Bruner, E.M. (1991) Transformation of self. *Annals of Tourism Research* 18, 238–50.

Chhabra, Deepak *et al.* (2003) Staged authenticity and heritage tourism. *Annals of Tourism Research* 30 (3), 702–19.

Cohen, Erik (1988) Authenticity and commoditization in tourism. *Annals of Tourism Research* 15, 371–86.

Craik, Jennifer (1997) The culture of tourism. In Chris Rojek and John Urry (eds) *Touring Cultures: Transformations of Travel and Theory* (pp. 113–36). London: Routledge.

Dann, Graham (1996) *The Language of Tourism*. Wallingford: CAB International.

Edgerton, Robert B. (2000) Traditional beliefs and practices – Are some better than others? In Lawerence Harrison and Samuel Huntington (eds) *Culture Matters: How Values Shape Human Progress* (pp. 126–40). New York: Basic Books.

Egypt's economy: Lonely as a pyramid, without tourists. (2002) *Economist* 362 (8254), 36–7.

Egypt: Off the beaten track. (n.d.) On WWW at http://www.lonelyplanet.com/destinations/Africa/Egypt/obt.htm. Accessed May 2004.

Egypt roundups. (2003) *Middle East Times*. On WWW at www.metimes.com/2K3/issues2003–50/eg/egypt_roundups_font.htm. Accessed May 2004.

Four foreigners sentenced for drugs. (2001) *Middle East Times*. On WWW at www.metimes.com/2K1/issue2001–41/eg/four_foreigners_sentenced.htm. Accessed May 2004.

Graburn, Nelson (2001) Learning to consume: What is heritage and when is it traditional? In Nezar Alsayyad (ed.) *Consuming Tradition, Manufacturing Heritage: Global Norms and Urban Forms in the Age of Tourism* (pp. 68–90). New York: Routledge.

Hilton Dahab. On WWW at www.nightnight.net/eg_sharm_el_sheikh/546_hilton_dahab.html. Accessed May 2004.

MacCannell, Dean (1973) Staged authenticity: Arrangements of Social space in tourist settings. *American Journal of Sociology* 79, 589–603.

MacCannell, Dean (1976) *The Tourist: A New Theory of the Leisure Class*. Berkeley: University of California Press.

McGrath, Cam (2002) Dahab is losing its luster. *Middle East Times*. On WWW at www.metimes.com/2K2/issues2002–33/bus/dahab_losing_its.htm. Accessed May 2004.

Mostafa, Hadia (2004) Bedouin camps. *Egypt Today*. On WWW at www.egyptoday.com/issues/0402/613A/0402613Ap.asp. Accessed June 2004.

Nuryanti, Wiendu (1996) Heritage and postmodern tourism. *Annals of Tourism Research* 23 (2), 249–60.

Pearce, P. and Moscardo, G. (1985) The relationship between travelers' career levels and the concept of authenticity. *Australian Journal of Psychology* 37, 157–74.

Sector development for the National Project for the Development of the Sinai. (1995) Government publication. On WWW at http://www.sis.gov.eg/public/Sinai/html.text03.htm. Accessed June 2004.

Sinai: Location and natural resources. (1995) Government publication. On WWW at http://www.sis.gov.eg/public/Sinai/html.text01.htm. Accessed June 2004.

Summer brought tourism record. (2003) *Middle East Times*. On WWW at www.metimes.com/2K3/issues2003–37/eg/summer_brought_tourism.htm. Accessed June 2004.

Sustainable tourism development through integrated urban development, Nuewbia. (n.d.) On WWW at www.bestpractices.org/cgi-bin/bp98.cgi?cmd=details&id=20745&key=Eppyfgjbkdfdag. Accessed June 2004.

The National Project for the Development of Sinai: Objectives, mainstays, and potentials. (1995) On WWW at http://www.sis.gov.eg/public/Sinai/html/text02.htm. Accessed May 2004.

Turner, C. and Manning, P. (1988) Placing authenticity – On being a tourist: A reply to Pearce and Moscardo. *Australia and New Zealand Journal of Sociology* 24, 136–39.

Wahab, Saleh (1997) Tourism development in Egypt: Competitive strategies and implications. In Chris Copper and Stephen Wanhill (eds) *Tourism Development: Environmental and Community Issues* (pp. 29–42). Chichester: John Wiley & Sons.

Wang, Ning (1999) Rethinking authenticity in tourism experience. *Annals of Tourism Research* 26 (2), 349–70.

'World tourism barometer' (2003) *World Tourism Organization* 1 (2), 1–20. On WWW at www.world-tourism.org/market_research/facts/barometer/WTO Barom03_2_en.pdf. Accessed June 2004.

World tourism highlights: Edition 2003 (2003) World Tourism Organization. On WWW at www.world-tourism.org/market_research/facts/highlights/pdf. Accessed June 2004.

World tourism stalls in 2001 (2002) World Tourism Organization Press Releases, Madrid, 29 January. On WWW at http://www.world-tourism.org/newsroom/ Releases/more_releases/January2002/numbers_2001.htm. Accessed June 2004.

Chapter 10

Tourism, Heritage, and Urban Transformations in Jordan and Lebanon: Emerging Actors and Global-Local Juxtapositions

RAMI FAROUK DAHER

Introduction

The development of tourism in the Levant or Bilad al Sham in the second half of the 19th century is partially attributed to the business of Thomas Cook and Son who popularized mass tourism to the region (Hunter, 2003: 157). A typical journey from Europe covered Egypt's ancient monuments, the Nile, the holy sites in Palestine and prime locations in major cities such as Beirut, Jerusalem, and Damascus. Sites such as the Temple of Jupiter in Ba'albeck, Dome of the Rock and the Church of the Holy Sepulchre in Jerusalem, the Umayyad Mosque in Damascus, the ruins of Palmyra, and the rose-cut city of Petra were popular sites among tourists.

The definition of heritage of the region was confined to its classical, religious, and ancient monuments during mandate and early statehood periods in the first half of the 20th century. Meanwhile, and according to Maffi (2002: 210–11) Daher (2002), and Schriwer (2002: 197), the heritage of the recent past was marginalized by official state discourses that attempted to disassociate from the recent Ottoman past and local realities and instead to construct legitimacy for the different new emerging state systems (Jordan, Palestine, Syria, Lebanon) by creating constructing links with distant origins (e.g. Nabatean in Jordan, Phoenician in Lebanon). It is only recently and through changing state interests and semiotic shifts, but also through new emerging actors and agents, that new sites are being incorporated into the realms of heritage and the tourist. Such sites include most recently the urban heritage of secondary cities such as for example Tripoli (Trablus) and Sidon (Saida) in Lebanon, but also Salt and Kerak in Jordan. Furthermore the 'city' is being rediscovered as a site of tourism attraction, the urban scene in the region is re-emerging as a place of consumption, play, and entertainment.

This chapter ventures into the epistemology of urban conservation/ regeneration of historic cores in different cities of Jordan and Lebanon within the cultural region of Bilad al Sham. Through its various discourse analysis, the research will investigate the nature, scope, and effect of diverse groups of publics, actors, networks, and agencies (international and local) engaged in the definition, production, consumption, and regeneration of 'urban heritage' and its links to place politics, identity construction, and tourism development. The chapter will attempt to reveal the various connections, networks, and discourses operating between those publics, actors, and agencies.

Hall (1996: 155) examines how cities are being packaged and introduced as products for marketing in an age of 'New Urban Tourism,' he investigates how 'although urban centers have long served to attract tourists, it is only in recent years that cities have consciously sought to develop, image and promote themselves in order to increase the influx of tourists.' Within the larger context of the Middle East, which includes the Arabian Gulf states and parts of North Africa, one observes how, whether it was Beirut or Amman, Dubai or Manama, Cairo or Tunis, it is very obvious that cities all over the region are competing for inward business and tourism investments with considerable consequences not only for how these cities are being transformed, or how heritage and urban regeneration is being conceived, but also for how tourism, tourist products, and experiences are taking a central role in this overall transformation.

It is very obvious that tourism and its related development had played a significant role in the transformation and reshaping of cities recently. This chapter sheds light on current socio-economic and cultural/spatial transformations affecting urban centers and historic city cores within the region and identifies several significant emerging phenomena:

(1) The emergence of several urban regeneration/tourism projects within the region that stems from neo-liberal urban restructuring and circulation of surplus global capital as in the case prime cities of Beirut's Solidere Project in the downtown area and Amman's Abdali Mega Urban Project, which is represented as the 'new downtown for the City'.

(2) The emerging role of aid agencies and international donors in the regeneration/tourism projects targeting historic urban centers of

secondary cities within the region and circulating a standardized form of heritage and of place in places like Salt, Kerak, Jerash, and Madaba in Jordan, and Tripoli, Byblos (Jbeil), and Tyre (Sour) in Lebanon.

(3) The emergence of new/old actors and agents in the form of 'notable families' who reintroduce themselves in the region as patrons of culture, heritage, and history. They work to fund and patronize urban regeneration projects, adaptations into cultural tourism facilities and into heritage museums and interpretation centers. Though the impact might be minimal at the moment, in comparison to other agents of change, such families and philanthropists are reintroducing another alternative to the state's formal vision of history and of the past, furthermore, they facilitate different itineraries for tourists and visitors that rest on an informal narration of the past and an emphasis on the 'ordinary,' on the social history and matters of everyday life.

While the first phenomenon centers on the circulation of global capital and networks and city development approaches within prime cities such as Beirut and Amman, the second phenomenon centers on the involvement of donor agencies (mainly the World Bank) and the state in urban regeneration and tourism endeavors in secondary cities in Jordan and Lebanon. In the midst of global flows and circulating donor agencies' interventions emerges local actors and agents in the form of families and philanthropists from the region who attempt to reintroduce and grant voice to an ordinary local heritage and narration of history, thus contributing to a more contextual and involved cultural tourism experience.

The significance of the chapter rests on the fact that it ventures into very contemporary and recent transformations and changes within the region of the Middle East that had stayed predominantly outside the interest of researchers and scholars such as the inseparable relation between tourism and urban change. Observers of the current transformations of the urban scene in the region are likely to conclude that cities are gradually becoming business and tourism spectacles. For example, Reiker (2005) elaborates how there has been over the last decade considerable research and literature that examined neo-liberal urban projects and tourism ventures in metropolitan context in the west, but that 'much less attention has been given to these developments in the region.' Tyler (2000: 287–8) elaborated that urban tourism is about the political management of change and how tourism 'had adopted a central role in the late 20th century' in terms of the choices made concerning the nature of the changes in city form and functions. The following quotation assists in explaining such urban transformations and change and their links to tourism at a global level:

> These changes can be seen in relation to four main concepts which form two axes. First, city administration has had to market their cities in order to seek new inward investment, creating new attractive spaces within the city as part of the process. Taken together with the thesis of the Fantasy City this provides one axis for analyzing these changes in form and function. The second axis relates the contestation of space between stakeholders which leads to capacity issues and debates over the nature of tourism development. (Tyler, 2000: 287–8)

New Urban Restructuring and Emerging Actors and Agents in the Age of Tourism

In order to commence to understand current urban transformations in the region and their links to tourism, one has to reflect on the current urban restructuring, and the role of different actors and agents vis-à-vis such transformations within the region. Actors and agents range from global networks of multi-national cooperation to international donor agencies together with central governmental agencies (such as ministries of tourism) with certain *development* agendas, to philanthropists and local notable families who are also playing a significant role in such urban transformations.

It is fascinating to understand the effect of the circulation of global capital, excessive privatization, rise of new Arab elite, and circulating urban/tourism flagship projects in Jordan, Lebanon, and through out the Arab region. New emerging urban islands of excessive consumption for the chosen elite where the city is becoming a place to play signifies this neoliberal urban restructuring in places such as downtown Beirut, Abdali in Amman, and in many other places as well.

Furthermore, it is also interesting to analyze and understand the rationales behind the sudden shift to tourism as a main initiator of urban regeneration in the development plans presented by international donor agencies to secondary cities in Jordan and Lebanon such as current projects in Kerak, Salt, Madaba, and Jerash in Jordan and Tripoli, Sidon, Tyre, Ba'albeck, and Byblos in Lebanon. Finally, contrasting the global circulation of capital, of images and of heritage, it is worthy of note to also understand the role played by certain families in the region as patrons of art, culture, and heritage providing a different tourism experience as well.

Prior to embarking on understanding such transformations, it is crucial to put things in perspective and to contextualize such transformations by first understanding the interest of developing governments to invest in tourism, and second understanding the shift in global economic restructuring from modernity to neoliberalism.

Urban De-industrialization Process in the West and the Interest of Developing Governments to Invest in Tourism

More recently, and within the past 20 years or so, it was interesting to note the emergence of several global trends within the different countries of the world. One very important trend is the appeal of heritage tourism to many governments in developing countries in attempts to achieve successful economic restructuring signaling a shift to the service sector in a late capitalist era with consequences on heritage/tourism relationships and privatization dynamics (Chang *et al.*, 1996: 286–99). Robinson (2001: 40) elaborates how

> for developing economies whose natural resource base is depleted, tourism would appear to provide a rather rapid way of generating hard currency and creating employment. Indeed, utilizing the cultural and ethnic resources of a nation or region for tourism may be the only way out.

This is not a new phenomenon, it had occurred in developed countries as well. Tourism developments continue to play a major role for developed countries in their attempts to restructure and readjust from a manufacturing to a service-sector base (Robinson, 2001: 40). This is an evident in many ex-industrial and manufacturing small- and medium-size cities shifting their economy to tourism industry and the service sector.

Tiesdell *et al.* (1996: 68) elaborate how many cities in their attempts to revitalize historic urban quarters are 'attempting to attract new activities; a key new activity has been tourism and associated cultural activities.' They added that strategies for tourism or culture-led revitalization 'have encouraged the exploitation of the area's historic legacy for tourist development. Such development has usually meant a partial or extensive diversification or restructuring of the area's economic base.' The literature is full of many examples of cities in the industrial world that had witnessed deindustrialization and a shift to a service-sector economic base.

Robinson (1999: 133–4) elaborates about de-industrialization in UK smaller cities and the shift to a service-sector base saying that 'at its heart, de-industrialization is normally taken to mean the dismantling of manufacturing industry, particularly, the productive primary and secondary industrial sectors.' This dismantling process was particularly rapid in the 1970s and 1980s and included coal mining, steel production, shipbuilding, engineering, automotive and textile production. Robinson continues to explain that the outcome from the de-industrializing process is a

> political, economic and moral agenda to 'regenerate' the de-industrialized urban centers. Paradoxically, this has required a level of intervention which was at odds with the Thatcherite ideologies which contributed to decline. However, it has been an intervention of private capital; private ownership and a planning process which side-stepped traditional democratic politics. (Robinson, 1999: 136–7)

Hall (1996: 155–9) emphasizes the universality of this phenomena and its spread to different cities and water fronts all over the Western World and beyond:

> Following the deindustrialization of many industrial and waterfront areas in the 1970s and 1980s, tourism has been perceived as a mechanism to regenerate urban areas through the creation of urban leisure and tourism space. This process appears almost universal in North America, Western Europe, Australia and New Zealand. (Hall, 1996: 155–9)

Examples for such a shift are evident in many cities such as Lowell, Massachusetts (Tiesdell *et al.*, 1996: 73) and Manchester, UK (Tiesdell *et al.*, 1996: 80). In some larger cities' historic cores that were associated with steel or milling industries; there is also a major shift to a broader service-sector base centering on entertainment, tourism, and the heritage industries. In Minneapolis, Minnesota, for example, the whole milling district on both sides of the Mississippi in historic downtown Minneapolis (known as the Mills District) is shifting into very creative adaptations of industrial museums, housing in the form of lofts and apartments, and mixed use tourism-oriented and commercial activities (City of Minneapolis Planning Department, 2000). Based on research conducted by the author about urban regeneration in the city,[1] several projects and skillful adaptations emerged in the form of 'festive markets' that contributed to urban regeneration in such previously deteriorated spaces like the 'Mills' and the 'Warehouse' Districts. Fainstein and Judd (1999b: 2) sum up this process of urban transformation by adding that

> once cities prospered as places of industrial production, and then in the industrial era they were engines of growth and prosperity. On the

eve of the twenty first century, they are becoming spaces for consumption in a global economy where services provide the impetus for expansion.

Swarbooke (2000: 271) elaborates how in many communities, 'tourism has been adopted as an urban regeneration tool, almost as a last resort' as part of a strategy of desperation when there seems to be little chance of other alternatives to help regenerate the local economy. In the developing world, and with increasing economic problems and mass unemployment, tourism is gradually becoming an attractive sector to invest in because it does not demand huge investments nor does it demands high technology that is not available for most such countries.

In cities of the Middle East, there might have not been a period of deindustrialization like in the West, but it is obvious that governments of these countries are choosing tourism as a main generator of economic growth and prosperity; and in Jordan and Lebanon, the urban heritage of cities is being chosen as the new tourism product. This is manifested not only in donor agencies and governmental ministries' several projects in secondary cities but also in neoliberal restructuring in prime cities as well. As will be explained in the remainder of the chapter, these urban transformations in Jordanian and Lebanese cities are changing the nature of urban experience in a sense where cities are being incorporated into the tourism market, and are becoming a commodity and a place to play, to see and to be seen.

Tourism plays a significant role in the budgets of Jordan and Lebanon. In 1996, the tourism sector provided more than 770 million Jordanian Dinars in revenues amounting to more than 12% of the gross domestic product (GDP) of the country to the extent that it had been defined as Jordan's number one foreign exchange earner (Daher, 2000: 22). In Jordan, for example, Gray (2002: 325) believes that the main link between economic liberalization programme and tourism in Jordan is that tourism has been used to cushion some of the financial hardships caused by liberalization. It is significant to notice how certain governments in the region such as Syria, Jordan, Turkey, and Lebanon are attracted to the 'labor-intensive nature of tourism, and the hard currency that foreign tourists provide for the economy. Further, tourism is not a complex sector to develop and does not usually rely on large injections of capital or expertise' (Gray, 2002: 325).

Lebanon's whole economy was always dependent on tourism, especially inward Arab tourism from Saudi Arabia and the Gulf states. Before the civil war and in the early 1960s and 1970s tourism accounted for over

20% of Lebanon's GDP, making it one of the countries most important economic sectors. Most of the visitors came from the Arab Gulf region but also from the rest of the Arab world enjoying the cool climate in the mountains above Beirut in the summer months.

After the end of the civil war in the late 1980s, the government of Lebanon attempted to regain its position again as the region's most popular tourism destination. Lebanon's success in achieving such a goal is occasionally hampered by political unrest such as the assassination of the former Prime Minister Rafiq al Harriri in 2004, which had an adverse impact on the tourism market, and a flourishing market after the war, which the government together with private businesses are becoming gradually very dependent on. In fact, after September 11, the circulation of Saudi and Gulf capital investment, after it was no longer welcomed in the US and Europe, found its way to the Lebanese tourism market in the form of several international chain hotels such as the Movenpick of Beirut, but also the Rotana group of hotels, which is funded by United Arab Emirates (UAE) Emirs and Sheikhs.

Global economic restructuring: From modernity to neoliberalism

Change and transformation is in evidence, over the past century the First and Third World countries alike had witnessed major discursive and structural shifts from modernity to postmodernity to globalization. More recently, we are witnessing further changes and transformations affecting First and Third Worlds alike. Under the rationales of economic liberalization and privatization of the state's enterprises and investments, the world is now part of a neoliberal moment anchored by more conservative politics and excessive economic liberalization and restructuring. Such a moment was manifested in excessive privatization, the withdrawal of the state from welfare programs, the dominance of multi-national corporation politics, and as far as the Third World is concerned, the restructuring of international aid to the Third World in the form of structural adjustments and policy instead of project-oriented aid. This was coupled with the surfacing of several discursive tactics for such a neoliberal transformation such as dominance of the World Trade Organization (WTO), international gatherings such as the World Economic Forum (WEF), the North American Free Trade Agreement (NAFTA), and several similar other instances of economic restructuring at the global level.

It is evident that such major transformations of course have substantial effects not only on cities and the nature of urban and heritage tourism emerging, but also further complications on how tourism benefits and revenues are distributed and shared between the different segments of society and across national boarders where the First World–Third World divide had been even made more intertwined, complicated, and blurred. Furthermore, such neoliberal economic restructuring will also affect how and for whom such urban tourism spaces emerge and constitute, in many cases, secluded 'gated communities' intensifying issues of social equity, inclusion-exclusion, and accountability. Furthermore, and with an increasing competition between cities, they are gradually becoming places of play and commodities themselves. The following quotation from Fainstein and Judd (1999a: 261) illustrates how urban culture is gradually becoming a commodity within such cultural changes from modernity to postmodernity, and from internationalism to globalism with considerable effects on urban tourism:

> Tourism has been a central component of the economic, social, and cultural shift that has left its imprint on the world system of cities in the past two decades. Theorists have variously termed it formational mode of development, from modernism to radical modernism, from modernity to postmodernity, and from internationalism to globalism. In spite of considerable debate over the newness of the tendencies revealed and the extensiveness of the changes, there does seem to be a degree of consensus that the present epoch involves a different, more flexible organization of production, higher mobility of both capital and people, heightened competition among places, and greater social and cultural fragmentation. Within the city the unity previously imposed by a manufacturing-driven economy has disappeared, and urban culture itself has become a commodity.

Prime Capitals and Neoliberal Urban Restructuring

The chapter aims to understand the effect of the circulation of global capital, privatization, the rise of new Arab elite, and circulating urban flagship projects in Jordan, Lebanon, Egypt, all over the Arab Gulf states, and throughout the Arab region. New emerging urban islands of consumption for the elite signifies this neoliberal urban restructuring in places such as downtown Beirut and Abdali in Amman, Dreamland in Cairo (Adham, 2005), the Financial District in Manama and even in the heart of the Holy City of Mecca through the Jabal Omar Project.[2]

Middle Eastern cities compete for international business and tourism

Cities across the Middle East are currently competing with one another in order to attract international investments, businesses, and tourism developments. Cities are 'obliged' to create the right milieu, competitive business climate, and first-class tourism facilities in order to attract people to come live, invest, and be entertained. Developments in Dubai and the current urban reconstruction for the Beirut downtown area (the Solidere Project) are becoming the models to follow in such developments. Dubai had about 4.8 million visitors in 2003 in tourism through its entertainment, business, and sport tourism, and is planning to add another 100 hotels within the next five to seven years (Sadiq, 2005).

It has been estimated that the Gulf Cooperation Council has around US$80 billion in liquidity expected to be spent in real-estate, international business, and tourism investments within the next five years and especially in countries such as the UAE, Qatar, and Saudi Arabia. This vast amount of money, which before September 11 used to be invested primarily in the US and Europe, will attempt to find new markets in the region, and of course part of it had already found way into Lebanese, Syrian, and Jordanian[3] markets through multi-national hotel and real-estate investments (Sadiq, 2005).

Hall (1996: 155–7) has commented how city centers are shifting to leisure and tourism in many parts of the world. He has noted that the 'primary justification for the redevelopment of inner city areas for tourism is the perceived economic benefits of tourism.' The urban core is increasingly looked upon as a recreational environment and as a tourism resource, with one of the purposes to 'attract and retain the interest of professionals and white-collar workers, particularly in "clean" service industries such as tourism and communications' (Hall, 1996: 155–6). According to Harvey (cited in Hall, 1996: 158), imaging a city through the organization of spectacular urban space is a mechanism attracting capital and people (of the right sort), in a period of intense inter-urban competition and urban entrepreneurialism.

Competition between cities in the region of the Middle East is likely to have an effect not only on the nature of urban tourism developments, but also the type of clientele such tourism developments attract, and complexity of the investment, especially in an age where neoliberal urban restructuring and excessive capital accumulation by multi-national cooperation are the norm.

Neoliberal urban restructuring and first-class tourism development: Beirut's Solidere and Amman's Abdali projects

This section of the chapter focuses on formal discursive shifts in the creation of 'public' urban space/tourism investments orchestrated by partnerships between multi-national corporations and the state through the establishment of newly regulating bodies (such as Solidere[4] in Beirut and Mawared[5] in Amman) within the last 10 years. Several of these *neoliberal* corporate visions, blessed by the state's public discursive shift concentrating on economic prosperity and encouraging international investment in the country, are leading to urban geographies of inequality and exclusion, and spatial and social displacement of *second-class* citizens, functions, histories, and itineraries in favor of *first-class* tourism developments and real-estate ventures. In this section of the chapter, the author will attempt to compare and contrast each of these two cases in an attempt to understand the nature of such urban transformations in the different contexts of the region (Beirut and Amman). Therefore, the author will be oscillating between the two cases, rather than presenting each separately, in order to reflect on such similarities and differences between the two contexts.

The Solidere Beirut downtown reconstruction project was presented to the public as the main post-war reconstruction effort, and has been critiqued as simply being a real-estate development project where the history and heritage are simply themes incorporated through *Disneyfied* pastiche representations (Figure 10.1). The project also includes the *preservation* of older buildings and urban spaces from the traditional Lebanese and French mandate periods (Khalaf, 1998; Summer, 2005). This reconstruction is creating a collaged urban morphology that is designed for consumption by tourists and the Lebanese people alike.

The Solidere Model for neoliberal urban restructuring became the adopted approach within the region. Not only was copied in Amman through the Abdali Project, but also there are plans to transform it to other places within the region as well. This neoliberalization in the creation of public urban space circulates urban images, spectacles, and models and is gradually creating *generic* realities out of cities and is leading into the dilution of local differences and the circulation of 'corporate' urban realities and images.

In Jordan, formal state discursive shifts are gradually moving away from regional politics (e.g. emphasis on Arab nationalism and unity) and elaborate social agendas (e.g. agriculture, health case, education) into

Figure 10.1 The Saifi village is part of the reconstruction efforts in
downtown Beirut after the civil war, known as the Solidere
Project. The Saifi Village is an up-scale adaptation of existing
historic fabric into chic and expensive apartments that are
becoming very popular amongst tourists from Saudi Arabia
and from rich Arab Gulf states. The police in the picture are
not city police, but rather security guards to provide a certain
feeling of exclusiveness for this 'gated community' in the
center of the city.

Source: Photograph taken by Rami Farouk Daher (2005).

adopting neoliberal agendas of privatization and a rentier state where most vital assets and sectors had been rented or sold to the outside (e.g. water, telecommunication, power). Such formal semiotic shifts are also manifested in the creation of new 'public' urban space/investments orchestrated by partnerships between multi-national corporations and the state through the establishment of newly regulating bodies in Amman within the last 10 years. The Abdali Project represents a clear realization of such neoliberal urban restructuring efforts and is facilitated by the state's Socio-Economic Transformation Program. Blessed by the 'state's' public discursive shift concentrating on economic prosperity and encouraging international investment in the country, and by turning its back on Amman's original downtown, which is only about 1.5 kilometers away from the Abdali site, the Abdali Project is anticipated to lead to urban geographies of inequality and exclusion and spatial and social displacement of *second-class* citizens, functions, histories, and itineraries in favor of *first-class* tourism developments and real-estate ventures.

This neoliberal urban restructuring phenomenon is not new to the world. Swyngedouw *et al.* (2002: 542–3) elaborated how, and based on a study that incorporated 13 large-scale recent urban development projects in Europe, most of these projects

> accentuate socioeconomic polarization through the working of real-estate markets (price rates and displacement of social or low-income housing), changes in the priorities of the public budget that are increasingly redirected from social objectives to investments in the built environment and the restructuring of the labor market.

In Amman and Beirut, the effect of such socio-economic transformation on the creation of new public urban space produces 'a privatized public space' based on a highly selective definition of the public, thus triggering a new critical investigation of the meaning of public/private and inclusion/exclusion. Furthermore, and in Beirut, the Urban Development Corporation System (Solidere) worked to annex different parts of the downtown area to the Beirut Central District (BCD) and demarcated the BCD from its periphery (Saliba, 1997b).

Amman's *Abdali*, modeled after Solidere, in fact enjoys some of the same investors, and is promoted by Mawared's brochures, website, short video, and other promotional materials as the 'New Downtown for Amman' (Figure 10.2). New introduced functions include the American University of Amman, an IT Park, medical tourism, and different high-end commercial activities, in addition to a newly created civic 'secular' plaza bounded by the State Mosque, the parliament, and the law courts.

Figure 10.2 Billboard at Abdali, Amman's major neoliberal urban restructuring site. These images represent an *Oriental vision of the
Occident* and are the only interface and source of information about the project between the multi-national real-estate
companies financing such urban restructuring endeavors and
the public at large.

Source: Photograph taken by Rami Farouk Daher (2004).

This represents a symbolic replacement of the existing historic downtown and the current civic/urban symbols (e.g. the Historic Husseini
Mosque and specialty Ammani markets). This will intensify the socio-
economic and spatial polarization not only between East and West
Amman, but also between this new 'elitist urban island' and the rest of
the city.

In Beirut, the Solidere Project eradicated the whole concept of property
rights, divorcing the city from its social memory where it no longer
became a 'downtown' where business takes place and people of different
social backgrounds go shopping. The compensation and consolation for
ex-owners of land and property take the form of 'shares' in this newly
erected multi-national cooperation 'Solidere.' In the case of Amman, the

Abdali Project will also culminate in the displacement of the nearby existing Abdali transportation terminal, together with its drivers, informal venders, and occupants, to the outskirts of Amman away from the center of the city. The project will also definitely present fierce competition to the existing downtown that is gradually disintegrating and is already suffering from a lack of economic vitality. This is reinforced through a combination of physical, social, and cultural boundary formation processes. Furthermore, Hall (1996: 159) elaborates how the 'creation of a "bourgeois playground" in the name of economic progress may create considerable tension in the urban policy-making environment.'

After a clear observation and critical analysis of the details of the investments in Beirut and Amman, one easily realizes that the bottom line is that the state is subsidizing large-scale investment for the business elite of the region to create such flagship or mega projects of urban restructuring. Contrary to formal state discourse, which advocates an absent state in such neoliberal privatization efforts, it is very clear that in urban restructuring projects, the 'state' is not absent, but is 'there' heavily involved and there to stay. Yet, regardless of the similarities in these two mega urban projects in Amman and Beirut, forms of such subsidies differ based on each context.

In Beirut for example, the financial contribution of the state is considerable. On the one hand, it cannot cash any possible tax revenues from the development for the first 10 years. On the other hand, and most importantly, it has to compensate the private developer for the infrastructure works by allocating it 600,000 sq. m of land reclaimed from the sea, which are allowed to be developed at very high densities (Summer, 2005). In Amman, prime urban land made available for investment forms a greater part of the subsidy, but other forms of the subsidy also include taxes exemption, infrastructure provision, and elimination of all barriers and red tape in addition to special building regulations made possible for this particular development.

It is also important to compare the two cases in terms of the nature and details of the shareholding setup. In Beirut, for example, Solidere's capital initially valued at US$1.82 billion when first issued consisted of two different types of shares:

- type A shares issued to holders of expropriated property in the downtown area relative to the value of the expropriated property; and
- type B shares (with an initial stock offer of US$100 per share) issued to external investors.

Solidere's own rhetoric sugar-coats the type A shares and rationalizes their facilitation by stating that 'most lots in the Beirut Central District are owned by tens, hundreds and in some instances (the *Sūq* areas) thousands of people.' Therefore, the type A shares are being presented as the only 'just' solution for such a dilemma. Furthermore, it has been stated that 'through this approach, the property right holders would *relinquish* their rights in exchange for shares in the company while investors would provide the required capital in exchange for shares in order to finance the project' (Kabbani, 1997). Maha Yahya (2005) on the other hand elaborated on the process of 'emptying of the Center' in Beirut and how the 4000 previous residents never came back. The emptying of the center is already exerting negative consequences not only on the ownership patterns, the city's social memory, but also the overall urban experience for users and tourists alike.

In Amman's Abdali, the Abdali Investment Company (AIC) has been created and is composed of the main investors: Mawared and Saudi Oger[6] only. As a private real-estate developer, it is responsible for implementing the project, and is in charge of the management and the master planning of the project (similar to Solidere in Beirut). But the shareholder set-up in Abdali is very different. The two main stakeholders in the company are Mawared and Saudi Oger, no other company or individual is allowed to buy shares (Summer, 2005).

Regardless of the similarities between the two projects, they are different in terms of details of the investment as mentioned earlier and also in terms of the levels of public contestations. In Beirut, for example, the nature of critical debates engages a wider sector of non governmental organizations (NGOs) and critical actors, debates center on anti-globalization and commodification of the historic and built environment (an active civil society rooted in not only in technical matters but also in business and financial administration). There have been critical debates on the many places constructed during the post-war boom, which have become simply places of consumption, thus leveling the local differences and positive distinctions that might have otherwise emerged during the reconstruction process. Many actors and critical thinkers are attempting to counteract bland consumerism and commercialization in Beirut's post-war construction.

But again, this is limited to only isolated critical voices more recently. In fact, there have been several revisions for the Solidere plan for downtown Beirut reconstruction until the final version was approved. For example, one can witness the merger between old mentors such as senior architects and urbanists who had taken part in pre-war construction on one hand and a young generation of critical thinkers on the other. Such critical public groups together with different NGOs (e.g. Association for the Protection of Sites and Ancient Dwellings (APSAD) and the revived Order of Engineers and Architects) have been very active in launching campaigns to disclose the shortcomings of the different post-war recon-struction projects and schemes (Rowe, 1998: 135–9; Khalaf, 1998: 140–5). Also, in Beirut, the level, intensity, and sophistication of the 'publication' efforts on the Solidere Project and even other neoliberal urban restruc-turing endeavors is to be noted.

In Amman, critical debates are more sporadic, concentrating on 'tech-nical' matters of investment and heritage developments. In addition, and in many contexts, there is a huge overlap between the state and the public sphere represented by its various civil institutions and NGOs (which might form communication structures facilitating critical public debate). In Jordan, the border-lines between the state and civil society are very blurred. In Jordan, for example, many NGOs receive state funding or engage in state-run projects, others are very much linked to the Royal Family who patronize such civic institutions that are seen as extensions of the state where the concept of resistance becomes impossible or very difficult. The border-lines between the state and civil society are very blurred where the concept of critical resistance becomes very difficult to emerge. Publications remain very scarce, if any.

It is interesting to notice, that regardless of the similarities between the Beirut and Amman projects, how each of the projects takes shape within a completely different local context and is consequently reshaped by it. El-Sheshtawy (2004: 18–19) confirms that while certain processes in globalization may seem to come from outside (e.g. multi-national corpo-rations and the setting up of regional headquarters), yet, these are processes that are activated from the inside by local actors. Furthermore, Swyngedouw *et al.* (2002: 545) elaborate how such neoliberal urban restructuring projects are incorporated in localized settings, hence the term 'glocalization.'

Swarbrooke (2000: 275) elaborates how in certain developed countries such as the UK, for example, one can find public contestation against the use of public resources (funds, subsidies) to support such flagship projects and tourism developments. The reasons for contestation are because it is thought that it would be 'wrong for poor communities to, in effect, offer subsidies, to wealthy private companies' and that 'the money invested in tourism could be devoted to more valuable causes. It is often suggested

that in depressed urban areas it is the social infrastructure – health, education, and housing – that should be the priority for the allocation of public
funds' (Swarbrooke, 2000: 275).[7]

It is very important to understand local/global relationships vis-à-vis
latent processes of urban inclusion/exclusion and power mechanisms
embedded in such 'urban restructuring' projects and corporate visions in
Middle Eastern cities and locales such as Beirut and Amman. Therefore,
it is also important to understand the effects of such socio-economic
transformation on the creation of new public urban tourist space in such
cities producing 'a privatized public space' based on a highly selective
definition of the public (Crawford, 1995), thus triggering a new critical
investigation of the meaning of public/private and inclusion/exclusion
(Anderson, 1995). The Solidere Project is producing 'gated communities'
that are isolated from the rest of the city's participants and that are facilitated by this privatization of planning.

This notion of 'Island Planning,' where certain urban development
projects (UDP) turn their back on adjoining districts and areas, becomes
a contested reality that deserves further attention and contemplation.
For example, the issue of reconnecting BCD to its periphery is a preoccupation of planners and urban designers (Saliba, 1997a). Referred to
by Sassen (cited in El-Sheshtawy, 2004: 18) as the 'Quartering of Urban
Space,' the same problem is expected to appear in Abdali, the result will
be a 'fragmented City', a 'patchwork of discrete spaces with increasingly
sharp boundaries (gated business centers, leisure, tourism, or community
spaces).' Fainstein and Judd (1999b: 9) have added that

> carefully bounded districts have been set aside as tourist bubbles'
> isolated from surrounding areas of decay. Within these districts,
> historic and architecturally significant structures are integrated with
> new generation of tourist facilities that, instead of evoking images of
> an urban golden age, are quite contemporary.

Swyngedouw *et al.* (2002: 542) elaborate how

> large-scale urban development projects have increasingly been used
> as a vehicle to establish exceptionality measures in planning and
> policy procedures. This is part of a neo-liberal 'New Urban Policy'
> approach and its selective 'middle and upper-middle class'
> democracy. It is associated with new forms of 'governing' urban inter-
> ventions, characterized by less democratic and more elite-driven
> priorities.

AlSayyad (2001: 14) refers to the 'transfer of design and political control from local governments and citizens to large corporations and the design professionals they hire.' In Amman, and based on interviews conducted at the Greater Amman Municipality (GAM), many felt that Mawared has been created to take on the role of GAM in such sensitive projects. While previously, GAM responsibilities covered what Mawared is doing now. In both cases in Beirut and in Amman, it is interesting to notice the transfer of power to and the emergence of new regulating bodies replacing state institutions such as Mawared and Solidere.

In the cases of Beirut and Amman, underneath the rhetoric of Mawared or Solidere lies a public (state) subsidy for private real-estate development for very selective urban business regional elites from Lebanon, Jordan, and the Gulf. This conservative liberalism, according to Swyngedouw *et al.* (2002: 547):

> seeks to reorient state interventions away from monopoly market regulation and towards marshaling state resources into the social, physical, and geographical infra-and superstructures that support, finance, subsidize, or otherwise promote new forms of capital accumulation by providing the relatively fixed territorial structures that permit the accelerated circulation of capital and the relatively unhindered operation of market forces. At the same time, the state withdraws to a greater or lesser extent from socially inclusive blanket distribution-based policies and from Keynesian demand-led interventions and replaces them with spatially targeted social policies and indirect promotion of entrepreneurship, particularly via selective deregulation, stripping away red tape, and investment 'partnership'. (Swyngedouw *et al.*, 2002: 547)

Solidere's Project in Beirut is booming with tourists, especially at night, eating and drinking in its different diverse restaurants and coffee shops, tourists and local residents come to the downtown to see and to be seen, but one has to ask the question if this is the place for businesses and where the regular Beirutis go shopping or rent offices as the whole place it geared and targeting the very rich or the affluent tourist (e.g. Arab tourists from the Gulf or Saudi Arabia). One taxi driver once commented that the new downtown after the Solidere intervention is longer for the Beirutis, he longed for a time when one could really go shopping downtown or have a decent meal or even drink a cup of coffee. As a tourism space, yes, it is packed with people, but social interaction is limited confined and iconographic. The urban sense at Beirut is turning into a commodity, the downtown is transforming from a real downtown to a, and borrowing from Tyler (2000: 292–3), 'playful spectacle.' Fainstein and Gladstone (1999: 27) elaborate how 'since the tourist experience is contrived, staged authenticity replaces the genuine. At their most extreme, tourist destinations become wholly de-attached from their social context.'

In Amman's Abdali, while it is too early to judge the project as it is still under construction, similar tourists experiences are anticipated where the urban experience will be commodified and packaged in front of a passing audience. The Abdali Project has been promoted as a site for not only civic activities, educational, and medical tourism, but also as a high-end tourist destination in the form of boutique shopping and residential activities with 'a prestigious address living "above" the city' as indicated by one of the promoters of the project. One feature of the project would be the 'Ammani Street,' which is a modern shopping street modeled on Ammani urban heritage architecture in the downtown area. This pastiche replica would reduce the complexity of the real downtown experience with its details, years of evolution, and special dynamic into one *Disneyfied* moment with its kitsch postmodern fake building façades, yet chic, well-proportioned, and pretentious corporate architecture.

It is very obvious that tourism plays a major role in both case studies presented before where a staged rather than a lived city is continuously situating itself as a spectacle for tourism investments and entertainment. Cities in the region are competing for inward business and tourism investments. Mawared and Solidere are producing millions of dollars worth of billboards, short videos, websites, TV and newspaper ads with high-quality graphics and design to market and sell the cities and their new projects. Tyler (2000: 292–3) talks about the creation of the 'Fantasy City,' where the city turns into a 'playful spectacle' and elaborates on city marketing where he sees it as a reaction to economic change – a method of promoting inward investment by marketing, undertaking physical change, and image recreation:

> A major element of this process was to demonstrate to potential investors that your city was a good place to locate because of both business and lifestyle advantages. In creating the image to attract investors often city centers and waterfronts were changed out of all recognition and in some cases local communities were socially and economically excluded from the newly created tourist bubbles. City marketing, however, was essentially a boosterist approach to redevelopment believing that all investment was good investment as it created jobs

and, therefore wealth. However, as city marketing became an ever-more competitive process it evolved into a more complex movement incorporating public-private partnerships, embracing the consumer driven middle classes and youth markets of city regions and creating not just tourist bubbles but entertainment and cultural quarters in existing city spaces that appealed to those willing or able to spend money on leisure activities, but excluded those who could not. (Tyler, 2000: 292–3)

Secondary Cities and Donor Agencies' Urban Regeneration/Tourism Recipes

Jordan and Lebanon, and other countries in the region have received international funding from the World Bank and the Japanese International Cooperation Agency (JICA) to boost their national tourism strategies and development in the form of tourism and urban regeneration in secondary cities and smaller towns. Such international aid was in support of several tourism/urban regeneration projects in different cities such as Tripoli, Tyre, Ba'albeck, Sidon, and Byblos in Lebanon, and Kerak, Salt, Jerash, Amman, and Madaba in Jordan. Several of these donor agencies' projects centered on improving the tourism sector in each country.

Furthermore, the cultural urban heritage of smaller towns is starting to be the focus of such projects shifting the usual stereotypical, 'orientalist,' and later on nationalist approaches, from tourism that concentrated previously on classical and ancient ruins, biblical sites, and high-class architecture in prime 'traditional' cities such as Cairo, Beirut, Damascus, and Jerusalem to tourism where the heritage of smaller towns and the local history and culture have become incorporated into the tourism industry. It is interesting to notice how smaller towns in the *region* are attempting to diversity their economic base by locating their cultural and localized distinctive heritage as part of the objects of the tourist gaze. This is somehow gradually changing the nature of the tourism product and experience in the region.

International aid in the neoliberal age

It is important to link such socio-economic agendas and transformations and this notion of privatized planning within the city (such as the Abdali or Solidere Projects) with other neoliberal urban restructuring in the region (e.g. provision of Qualified Industrial Zones (QIZs), privatization of vital sectors such as water, telecommunications, and privatization of even tourism/heritage sector orchestrated by the World Bank and International Monetary Fund (IMF) with the blessing of the state in Jordan and Lebanon and to a certain extent within the region of the Middle East. Brenner and Theodore (2002) elaborate how in many countries of the world, the World Bank and the IMF were subsequently 'transformed into the agents of a transnational neo-liberalism and were mobilized to institutionalize this extension of market forces and commodification in the Third World through various structural adjustment and fiscal austerity programs.'

Mosley and Toye (1988) presented a critical and interesting critique of World Bank and IMF lending policies to Third World governments in general and conditional program lending in particular. They pointed to the lending trends enforced and adopted, since the beginnings of the 1980s, by the World Bank and other international development agencies. Such agencies had invested a large proportion of its resources in 'conditional program lending,' that is, in finance designed to underpin not a project but a cluster of policy changes.

> In the Bank's case such finance is known as Structural Adjustment Lending (SALs) if it applies to the entire economy, and by a variety of labels (e.g. 'sectoral adjustment lending,' 'economic recovery program,' 'expert rehabilitation loan') if it applies only to a part of it. (Mosley & Toye, 1988: 395–6)

Sharpley (2000: 5) stated that within a global economy the lending policies of the World Bank and the IMF after the 1980s (during the Reagan–Thatcher era) followed neo-classical economic paradigms that adhered to the fact that

> liberalized international trade can be a positive force in 'export-led economic development.' Reliance on the free market economy was promoted and lending conditions, through *Structural Adjustments Programs*, included mechanisms to facilitate this reliance such as the privatization of state enterprises and overall reduction of state intervention. . . . In particular, it has guided the policy of the World Bank and the International Monetary Fund (IMF) and their Structural Adjustment Lending (SAL) programs, which render loan facilities conditional on specific policy and economic structure changes in loan-receiving countries. However, such policies have attracted widespread criticism both in a general development context and in specific context of tourism. (Sharpley, 2000: 5)

The international response to the debt crises was structural adjustments that were imposed from First World countries. Structural Adjustments Programs singled a shift from project-based aid to policy-based aid. This 'liberal' rhetoric in foreign aid policies promoted liberalization policies within the governments of the Third World that took the form of liberalization and privatization of governmental agencies to facilitate control and exploitation. The responsibility of the state was to find a buyer (mostly foreign) of its enterprises and various operations including investment rights in tourism and other sectors of development. Gradually, a new form of government is emerging, one that is unaccountable, uninvolved, and faceless.

> The loss of national economic control has been accompanied by a growing concentration of power without accountability in international institutions like the IMF and the WB [World Bank], and GATT [General Agreement on Tariffs and Trade]. For poor countries, foreign control has been formalized in structural adjustments programs, but IMF decisions and GATT rules affect all countries. (Brecher & Costello, 1998: 31)

As we will see in the next section, international aid to countries such as Jordan and Lebanon concentrated on restructuring of national policies to encourage a shift to excessive and uncontrolled privatization. Tourism development, and drafting of national tourism policies received a considerable chunk of international aid, donor agencies that were involved in such projects included the World Bank, JICA, United Nations Development Program (UNDP), and US Aid and International Development (USAID).

In the case of Jordan, for example, in 1999, the IMF has approved credits totaling US$220 million for Jordan in support of the nation's 'economic adjustment' and 'structural reform program' for the period 1991–2001. Of the total US$220 million, about US$174 million is available under a three-year Extended Fund Facility[8] (IMF External Relations Department, 2001). A major portion of that fund is allocated to tourism through several World Bank-funded projects. The amount allocated to tourism is in the range of US$40 million, but this total is continuously increasing. The scope started with the First and Second Tourism Priority Projects, which addressed urban development and tourism in cities such as Kerak, Jerash, and Salt, but now the Third Tourism Priority Project is underway targeting the same cities but also Ajloun and Madaba as well. A recent (October 2005) meeting with members of the Ministry of Tourism and Antiquities

(Technical Development Department (TDD) personnel) provided information about a new World Bank project where urban tourism is the focus: the Cultural Heritage, Tourism, and Urban Development Project (CHTUD) funded by a Japanese grant through the World Bank. The CHTUD Project addresses urban architecture and tourism in selected areas within the historic cores of Kerak, Salt, and Madaba.[9]

In the case of Lebanon, the government received in October 2003 an amount of US$31.5 million from the World Bank and French and Italian governments to be spent on the Cultural Heritage and Tourism Development Project (CHTD). The project was later on renamed Cultural Heritage and Urban Development (CHUD) as will be explained later on in this chapter. The project was defined as having a major urban tourism component and its objectives were to preserve the urban cultural heritage of the selected historic city centers, encourage private sector-driven development, archaeological sites conservation and management, and support tourism facilities in the historic cores of Tripoli, Sidon, Tyre, Byblos, and Ba'albeck. The project is administered by the World Bank and a host country implementing agency, which is the Lebanese Council for Development and Reconstruction (CDR), the Directorate General of Antiquities (DGA) and the different municipalities of each town.[10]

Tourism as a preoccupation of donor agencies: Tourism/urban regeneration juxtapositions in the 1990s

The 1990s in Jordan were typified by several significant global, national, and regional events characterizing the transition from the 20th to the 21st centuries. One major event was the peace process with Israel, which affected the nature and types of developments proposed by international donor agencies and adopted by national policy makers. In addition, during the 1990s, conditional aid to Jordan concentrated on neoliberalization of different sectors of development that took the form of privatization and the opening up of Jordanian markets to global businesses. One of the main tracks for development that was emphasized by the World Bank was for Jordan to invest in, develop, and promote its tourism sector, and cultural heritage in general, and the urban heritage of Jordanian cities in particular, and for the first time in Jordan, was identified as one of the main assets for the generation of such development. Joffe (2002: xvi) stated that:

> In the context of 1994 peace treaty, tourism was seen as key to the promotion of open borders and economic cooperation that would

both strengthen peace and produce prosperity. There was, indeed, a short-term boom that, in turn, led the Jordanian state to encourage major investment in the sector. However, the necessary management skills were lacking and the centralized direction of the expansion of tourist facilities undermined initiatives towards integration with regional and global tourism strategies.

The Ministry of Tourism and Antiquities of Jordan (MOTA)[11] elaborated that this interest in the urban cultural heritage really started after the peace process in 1994, and is supported by international donor agencies taking into consideration that the topic of 'cultural heritage' is a preoccupation of the international community (e.g. World Bank, JICA). In addition, several other donor agencies, and in cooperation with the World Bank and the IMF saw in tourism and in the promotion of tourism development a venue and an opportunity not only to promote regional collaboration and stability but also liberalization of development and investments.[12]

In Lebanon, and after the end of the civil war at the beginning of the 1990s, Lebanon witnessed a remarkable post-war reconstruction boom, and the reconstruction of the severely war-damaged historic city center (the Solidere Project) became the symbol for Lebanon's new age after the war (Rowe, 1998: 135–9). In Lebanon, and in addition to this neoliberal urban restructuring in prime cities such as Beirut, the World Bank had started in 2003 to initiate, as mentioned earlier, a series of several heritage management plans and urban tourism development schemes for secondary cities and smaller towns such as Tripoli, Ba'albeck, Sidon, Tyre, and Byblos.

The International Tourism Development Institute of Japan, and through international funding from JICA, had been involved in tourism development plans and implementation strategies in different places from Jordan (e.g. the Tourism Development Plan for the Hashemite Kingdom of Jordan of 1996) and Lebanon (e.g. Tourism Sector Review by International Tourism Development Institute of Japan).[13] The production of such knowledge in the form of national tourism strategies, tourism development plans, or site management plans for certain areas or zones, had certainly put tourism as a priority on national agendas. The preoccupation of such international donor agencies' research facilitated the surfacing of different 'urban regeneration/heritage tourism' developments in places such as Amman, Salt, and Kerak in Jordan, or Tripoli, Sidon, Tyre, Byblos, and Ba'albeck in Lebanon orchestrated and funded by international donor agencies, primarily the World Bank and JICA.

In Jordan, these various projects were seen by Maffi (2002) in the frame of a 'wider plan aimed at developing international tourism in Jordan' and not so much leading to a local sustainable effort of urban regeneration and conservation of the urban heritage of the country (Maffi, 2002: 208). Tourism and tourism development had been presented to the Jordanian public by the state as one of the main 'peace rewards' anticipated to left up and nourish the Jordanian economy. Michael Lynch (1999) argues that economic rewards caused by tourism developments and waiting to be reaped by investors were more of a public sphere justification strategy or an official justification tactic than a major cause of the peace process. In reality, while it is true that tourism development in the wake of peace 'offered opportunities for some entrepreneurs in Jordan; tourism development has been difficult to sustain in the context of an increasingly complex global tourism economy without adequate public and private institutions for its promotion' (Hazbun, 2002: 331).

> Driven by unwarranted optimism and the political imperative of over-promoting tourism development as a means to capture the economic rewards of peace, state agencies and state plans lacked an accurate vision of what the tourism economy would look like from the vantage point of the individual private firms in the tourism sector. (Hazbun, 2002: 340)

Swift urban heritage donor recipes: Cosmetics urban regeneration

It is interesting to compare the scope, objectives, and details of donor agencies' projects of urban regeneration and tourism development between 1999 and 2005. Based on the analysis of the Terms of References (TOR) given for these projects, analysis reveal how similar these projects are in terms of their scope, component, rhetoric, tendering procedures, and even place details. In almost all of the projects, the TOR covers issues of physical and functional accessibility to the site (e.g. tourist trails, public spaces), improvement of infrastructure and quality of services, rehabilitation of the urban environment, community participation, and institutional capacity building at the level of municipalities. Many of these components have not been implemented, particularly the ones related to the rehabilitation and conservation of the built environment, community participation, and capacity building.

One of these projects, that was an outcome of the JICA study, was the Urban Heritage/Tourism Development Projects in the cities of Salt

(Historic Old Salt Development), Amman (Amman Downtown Tourist Zone), and Kerak (Kerak Tourism Development). The project in Salt centered on the following components: Historic Old Salt Museum (The Historic House Museum of Abu Jaber), tourist trails and steps, open plazas, panoramic lookouts, and training for tourist services. The project in Amman centered on similar components: The National Museum, tourist trails and steps, open plazas, panoramic lookouts, and training for tourist services. It is interesting to find out if such projects (see Table 10.1) emerged out of a conscious motivation and 'practice' or urban conservation/regeneration institutionalized in local and governmental

Table 10.1 Components and scope of work for the JICA-funded Urban Heritage/Tourism Development Project

Project	*Components and scope*	*Clients and agencies*
Historic Old Salt Development	1. Historic Old Salt Museum (The Historic House Museum of Abu Jaber) 2. Tourist trails and steps 3. Open plazas 4. Panoramic lookouts 5. Training for tourist services	MOTA, Greater Salt Municipality (GSM), Salt Development Cooperation (SDC).
Amman Downtown Tourist Zone and the National Museum	1. National Museum 2. Tourist street 3. Tourist trails 4. Raghdan Bus Terminal 5. Downtown Visitor Center 6. Training for tourist services	MOTA, Greater Amman Municipality (GAM)
Kerak Tourism Development	1. Kerak Castle Presentation 2. Tourist Street 3. Castle Observation Points 4. Visitor Center 5. Training for Tourism Services	MOTA, Kerak Municipality (KM), Kerak Development Cooperation (KDC)
Dead Sea Parkway and Dead Sea Panoramic Complex	1. Road construction. 2. Tourist facilities 3. Dead Sea Museum/lookout 4. Training for tourism services	MOTA, Ministry of Public Works and Housing (MPWH), Jordan Valley Authority (JVA)

policies, or if they simply emerged as 'shock treatments' with negligible outcomes and low levels of sustainability (Daher, 2005: 301–2).

Once one attempts to understand the various components and the nature of the end product of such projects in Amman and in Salt (Figure 10.3), it is obvious that they mainly concentrate on physical aspects of urban regeneration (e.g. tourist trails, pedestrianization of public plazas, and an adaptation of an old house into a heritage museum, tourist panoramic lookouts, streetscapes, and signage). The intervention in the public urban space centers on stone pavements for plazas, streets, or steps, outdoor furniture and lighting, and signage. Eventually, this is a one-time limited intervention in the form of *architectural cosmetic* on the historic urban tissue of the city without serious attempts to address the establishment of heritage tools, systems, or practices that insure the continuity of urban regeneration and community involvement in the long run.

Figure 10.3 The old core of the historic city of Salt, Jordan. This city is in the process of undergoing schemes for urban regeneration and tourism development funded by donor agencies (JICA and the World Bank).

Source: Photograph taken by Rami Farouk Daher (2000).

A new World Bank project where urban tourism is also the focus is the CHTUD funded by a Japanese grant through the World Bank. The CHTUD Project addresses urban architecture and tourism in selected areas within the historic cores of Kerak, Salt, and Madaba as mentioned earlier. Again, the focus is primarily on physical aspects of urban regeneration and tourism development such as upgrading and improving street networks and public spaces, adaptive reuse of historic buildings, and traffic and parking improvements. Yet, the project, and based on its TOR, attempts to address city center zoning and building regulations. Issues such as capacity building, building communities, helping communities to invest in tourism or other non-physical interventions are not likely to be addressed. The project calls upon eligible engineering firms to apply for the bid.

Inam (2002: 35) has elaborated how in several urban regeneration projects and heritage conservation endeavors in urban settings, the practice is manipulated by architects, engineers, and urban planners more than any other experts (such as urban sociologists and anthropologists), therefore, such a practice is 'obsessed with impressions and aesthetics of physical form; and it is practiced as an extension of architecture, which often implies an exaggerated emphasis on the end product.' Urban regeneration is as much about community building as much as it is about physical place enhancement, which these networks of projects are not succeeding in achieving.

The situation in Lebanon is a little different, but it still shares a lot of similarities with Jordan. In Lebanon, the World Bank had provided funding in the amount of US$31 million for the CHUD Project. The amount is almost similar to the one allocated for Jordan for the same group of projects. Other international donors were Agence Francaise de Development, the French government, and the Italian government. The objective was to protect, rehabilitate, and revitalize the historical and cultural heritage resources of five selected peripheral cities: Ba'albeck, Tripoli, Tyre, Byblos, and Sidon. It is interesting to note that the original name of the CHUD Project that was given to it by the World Bank was Cultural Heritage and Tourism Development (CHTD) when it was first initiated as a partnership between the World Bank and CDR. The name was then shifted to CHUD where the U refers to Urban, as some of the local consultants felt that the project needed to concentrate more on the problems of these urban historic cores rather than simply address tourism (World Bank & CDR, 2002). It is very early to judge whether the scope of the project had shifted as the name indicated as the many projects are still being implemented. Table 10.2 indicates the total amounts, including contingencies, in millions of US$ allocated for each of the five cities.

Table 10.2 The total amounts and contingencies for the rehabilitation of each of the five historic city centers and urban infrastructure improvements

Rehabilitation of historic city centers and urban infrastructure improvements (WB/CDR CHUD Project)	Total estimated cost in millions of US$ (including contingencies)
Ba'albeck	9.149
Byblos	3.079
Sidon	3.647
Tripoli	19.286
Tyre	7.433
Total	42.594

Source: WB and CDR (2002)

As indicated by a key official from the Lebanese CDR (Itani, 2005),

the project has two key development objectives: a) to create the conditions for increased local economic development and enhanced quality of life in the historic centers of these five cities; and b) to improve the conservation and management of Lebanon's built cultural heritage.

Based on 2002 Summary Progress Report for the project (WB & CDR, 2002: 1), the CHUD Project 'presents, for the first time, a strategic approach to protect, preserve, enhance, and better present the country cultural heritage, both as a focus of national identity and pride, and as a unique magnet for the cultural tourism industry.'

In February of 2002, an open workshop was held in Tripoli to discuss such urban regeneration/tourism development projects in Lebanon and Tripoli specifically. The meeting was attended by representatives of NGOs, anthropologists, academicians, and specialists and experts who worked with the World Bank consultants on these World Bank-funded projects. One particular expert from Tripoli who works with the World Bank consultants indicated that the World Bank CHUD Project is very comprehensive as seen in reports, PowerPoint presentations, and different projects documents, but in reality, and when it comes to implementation, the projects ends up becoming very modest as several initial components get deleted such as restoration of houses, addressing heritage tools within the historic cores, capacity building, and economic incentives for the local community. At the end, the project concentrated on urban beautification in the public space in the form of tiling of tourist trails and plazas, awnings and canopies, signage, and the like. He added that a lot of money is spent during a very short period, but the outcome does not match the research and the initial aspirations of the project. During the same meeting, a local anthropologist had commented that 'the same way we are sold the fast food meal; we are sold the World Bank Project.'

During a more recent visit to Tripoli in 2005, the author had observed that apart from the World Bank Project (which had not achieved considerable or physical results yet), the old city witnessed several 'local' initiatives and interventions that were well received by the local community. These local interventions included the renovation of *Sūq Bazirkan* (grain market) funded by a prominent political figure from Tripoli (Isam Fares), renovation at *Sūq al Dahab* (gold market) (Figure 10.4), funded by Tripoli Municipality and the French government; and renovation at *Sūq al Haraj*

Figure 10.4 Gold market in historic Tripoli in Lebanon. This old *Sūq* represents one example of several efforts for urban regeneration in the city by philanthropists or even international donors such as the World Bank.

Source: Photograph taken by Rami Farouk Daher (2002).

(auction market) funded by the German government. One significant person who had contributed to the success of these local initiatives is a local professor from Tripoli, Rawya al Majzoub, who teaches at the Lebanese University and directs the Center for Restoration and Conservation of Historic Monuments and Sites there. As an activist, she had succeeded in rallying local and international support for the old city of Tripoli. Now, it is true that these three interventions remained confined to specific areas within the old city and were mainly centered on urban beatification (e.g. wooden canopies, re-pointing of stone facades, provision of light fixtures), but at least they attempted to work with shop keepers and owners of cafés and other functions within the old city. Furthermore, they proceeded with local capabilities and minimum funding that was directly channeled to the conservation of the old city. Based on interviews conducted by the author in Tripoli in 2005, many local shop keepers and residents in the old city are gradually becoming convinced that such small local initiatives are more sincere and will achieve better results than the *comprehensive plans* of the World Bank, which promised a lot and ending up delivering minimal change without really addressing the problems and concerns of the old city.

Such projects in Jordan and Lebanon started with comprehensive planning at the scale of the whole historic city cores; in fact, they were seen by local politicians as the *optimum solution* to the various problems of historic city cores. Gradually, they were reduced to very modest outcomes (action projects) centering on open space beautification and architectural 'cosmetics.' Even such action projects and urban cosmetics attempts, and through the donor agencies constrains and regulations, were very limited and did not target private properties, façades of buildings or street façades that are privately owned.

This reality becomes an issue for public contestation when one attempts to take into consideration the nature of such projects (comprehensive planning at larger scales) and significant funding levels (tens of millions of dollars, a great portion of which would end up accumulating foreign debt). Such funds have been channeled (during very short periods of time) and through very complicated donor agencies' tendering procedures, complicated methodologies, and complex network of agents, governmental officials and central agencies, and experts involved in these urban regeneration/tourism projects. Gradually, and once these projects are implemented, a certain reality would emerge in the region's historic city cores. These urban regeneration/tourism projects rarely attempt to establish a sustainable practice of urban regeneration and heritage conservation in such communities; nor do such practices end up in putting in place urban management heritage tools that might engage the local authorities (e.g. municipalities).

Furthermore, such projects, and due to the fact that local actors (e.g. municipalities of such smaller towns) in most cases were not fully involved in either the decision making process or implementation of the projects, lack strong sustainability indicators. They represent a one-time intervention, a *shock treatment* with not enough consideration as to how such urban places will function after the intervention is over. Daher elaborates about the nature of the relationship between the local actors and central governmental agencies (MOTA) in Jordan and adds that 'it was very obvious right from the beginning that these projects were initiated and progressed and will be implemented, throughout the same patriarchal types of relationships between the Municipality and the Central Government' (Daher, 2005: 296). A Project Management Unit (PMU) was established for all JICA-funded projects in Jordan and was mainly housed in Amman and was composed of mainly MOTA personnel with minimal decision making powers at municipal levels. In an interview with MOTA personnel, it was elaborated that the rationales for the creation of the PMU was to facilitate mechanisms and contacts between the various agents of the project (MOTA, municipalities, JICA, and others). All contacts and decisions are done through the PMU, which in return is directly linked to the Secretary General and to the Minister of Tourism (Daher, 2005: 296).

In Lebanon, a PMU was also created for coordination purposes at CDR; it is responsible for monitoring progress against agreed-upon performance monitoring indicators. The PMU prepares in addition to the progress reports, detailed mid-term reports to serve as a basis for project reviews. Similar to Jordan, the municipalities in general are peripheral actors within this overall process and usually this is rationalized due to the lack of staff and expertise at the local municipal level. In certain Lebanese cases (e.g. Saida), municipal implementation units were added, but their ability to make decisive decisions remains minimal. Both the PMU and CDR will be jointly responsible for different aspects of the project. The following quotation by Daher (2005: 297) explains the mechanisms leading to embedded central government authoritarianism in the practice of tourism/urban regeneration processes in Jordan:

> The researcher would argue that the various mechanisms of power (such as, but not restricted to, the establishment of a sub central government agency like the Project Management Unit) shaped and reshaped the types and patterns of contact between central and local governments regarding the Projects under research and emphasized

a patriarchal structure of Central Governmental Agencies (MOTA) regarding urban regeneration/heritage tourism developments that characterized the relationship between the Center and the Municipality. This patriarchal structure reflects embedded central government authoritarianism in the 'practice' of tourism/urban conservation and management in Jordanian cities.

The practice of urban regeneration and tourism development in secondary cities in Jordan and Lebanon, through the different international donor-funded projects, is tied up and linked to sporadic agents of power that have generated, so far, *shock treatments* in these towns and small cities and very modest outcomes in the form of architectural cosmetics rather than an institutionalized practice. These projects lead to the circulation of different forms of urban and heritage projects and of a prototypical tourist experience within the region. Gradually, not only is local difference between the different cities disintegrating, but also the tourist experience is confined to consuming the same manufactured concept of heritage and to gazing at the same urban furniture detail, lamp fixture, or floor pattern. Furthermore, these projects are not designed in a way to help local communities develop their tourism investment potentials at grassroots levels (e.g. help entrepreneur individuals realize certain development dream, help families start their own small- or medium-size bed and breakfast or other tourism business); on the contrary, the level of the interventions is simply physical and centers mainly on the beautification of the historic environment in the form of urban cosmetics as indicated earlier. The communities, and based on several interviews in the different cities, feel disengaged from this tourism development endeavor even though interested to participate in and benefit from this cultural industry.

By looking at these different donor agencies' projects in secondary cities in Jordan and Lebanon, one can form a better understanding of current transformations in the production, manufacturing, and consumption of heritage and urban space. These transformations are leading to a very generic realities of urban space, heritage, and of tourist experience where not only local differences disintegrate, but also where a 'new' system of visioning the city emerges. Robinson (2001: 49) has elaborated on how the

> tourism industry is also open to criticism for its growing legacy and export of 'international' styles of functional, postmodern blandness. Resort areas, waterfront developments, hotels, and attractions have all evolved with little or no concession to environmental setting, local traditions, and the nuances of local culture and ethnic difference.

Comparing the different urban heritage details in urban tourism and heritage projects mentioned above (such as wooden canopies, pergolas, signage, lamp posts, and even manhole covers) leads to the conclusion that the postmodern blandness that Robinson refers to reflects the production of certain 'franchise' forms of heritage and place.

Projects of urban regeneration and tourism development funded by donor agencies can be viewed as a manifestation of neoliberalism. Such urban transformations affect the type of tourism development and experience prevailing within these secondary cities and smaller towns of the region; they lead to the circulation and definition of place, tourism experience, and of heritage-diluting local specificities and the distinctiveness of each locale. Yet, these projects are contributing to the fact that a newer tourist product (urban and social heritage of secondary cities within Bilad al Sham) is being incorporated into the tourism industry. This is a major shift from previous Orientalist visions that had confined the tourism product in the region of Bilad al Sham to classical and ancient ruins, biblical sites, and high-class architecture in prime 'traditional' cities such as Damascus, Beirut, or Jerusalem. Regardless of the limitations of these projects, it is interesting to notice how smaller towns in the region are attempting to diversity their economic base by locating their cultural and localized distinctive heritage as part of the objects of the tourist gaze. This is somehow, gradually changing the nature of the tourism product and experience in the region.

Notable Families as New Emerging Local Actors and the Rewriting of History

In the midst of neoliberal urban restructuring and donor agencies' urban heritage/tourism recipes emerges a local voice that attempts to rewrite history, re-define heritage, and re-position itself within such grand socio-economic and territorial transformations in our cities today with considerable consequences on the rewriting of local history, redefining of heritage, and emerging new tourist product and experiences within the region. This local voice is embodied in either:

(1) contemporary local politically or economically influential families in the region; or
(2) notable families from the 19th century who used to play a considerable role during Ottoman periods as mediators between the central government in Istanbul and local regional authorities within each of the Ottoman provinces (Manna', 1992: 70–1) and whose role had

subsided during mandate period in the first half of the 20th century and the creation of nation states in the region during the second half.

Whether it is al Hariri, Debbane', or Audi in Lebanon; Shoman, Tell, Bataineh, or Bisharat in Jordan; Toukan, Khouri, Qattan, or Husseini in Palestine; or Ayidi, Jabri, or Azem in Syria; many of Bilad al Sham's notable families and cultural and political elites are re-emerging and reintroducing themselves on the public scene as patrons of art, heritage, and culture. Family estates, historic mansions, and heritage places are being conserved, rehabilitated, and adapted into centers of culture, history/heritage museums, art galleries, and themed restaurants that are appreciated by a wider spectrum of society, especially the youth or adults between 35 and 45 years of age who share a sense of belonging and an appreciation to these historic parts of towns and cities (Daher, 2004). These *heritage patrons* are reclaiming their position in different places of *the region* through the appropriation of heritage and through an appeal to culture, art, and the intelligentsia. It is very interesting to notice how part of these heritage patrons are the same urban elite who emerged in Bilad al Sham in the 19th century (and were defined by the term 'notables' by scholars and historians), are reinstating their position within society as active supporters of culture and critical public debate within civil society.

Sidon in Lebanon represents a perfect example where local families are involved in the local cultural scene. While the Debbaneh family are restoring and adapting their old residence into the new Debbaneh Palace and Saida History Museum; other notable families in Saida such as the Audi family, had also adapted their old residence into a Soap Museum and had been involved heavily through the Audi Foundation into urban regeneration activities in the city (Figure 10.5). The Debbaneh Palace was built in 1721 by the Hammoud family, and was acquired in 1800 by the Debbaneh family. Then, it underwent several periods of restoration; and especially after the war in 1999 when the descendants of Raphael Youssef Debbaneh set up the Debbaneh Foundation, which established the Debbaneh Palace and Saida History Museum. The objectives of the museum are to represent and shed light on the city's urban, socio-economic, and political history. With the aim of constantly renewing the visitor's interest in the city, the project will not only include artifacts from the past, but it will also focus heavily on the societies that produced them. This will involve explanations and extracts from people's daily lives, family social structures, and political circumstances, not to mention construction, architecture, and town planning.[14]

Figure 10.5 Interior of the adaptation into the Soap Museum of one of Saida's historic complexes by the Audi Foundation in Saida, Lebanon.

Source: Photograph taken by Rami Farouk Daher (2002).

Endowed by the Audi Family in Saida, the Audi Foundation transformed the old family residence (the old soap factory) into the headquarters of the Foundation and into a thematic museum of handmade soap. This thematic museum seeks to relate the history of soap to the region at large stretching between Trablus (Lebanon), Haleb (Syira), Nablus (Palestine), and Salt (Jordan) and to show the various stages of its manufacturing and the diversity of its shapes. Furthermore, the family's involvement in the city included the renovation of the facades of the neighboring historic El Chakrieh Street and the rehabilitation of various traditional housing units in the same historic neighborhood.[15] The work of both families (Audi and Debbaneh) adds to their prestige and sense of identity in addition to strengthening their relationship with their hometown. The Soap Museum marks one of the early examples of such projects, of which several have started to appear in Lebanon such as the Bsous Museum, which narrates and displays the heritage of the silk industry in the country (Dahdah, 2004).

Another type of family patronage, which is more political in nature and takes the form of major charitable work and foundations, is the work of the Harriri Foundation founded by the late Lebanese leader and ex-prime minister Rafiq al Harriri. The Harriri family, native to Saida, has concentrated on the restoration of major heritage monuments within the city such as the Omari Mosque (a significant 12th century historic mosque that was shelled by Israeli planes in 1982) and Khan el Franj (an historic urban hotel and inn supporting business and trade from the 17th century). The urban heritage of Saida town captured the interest of such political elite. Reasons for such patronage could be multiple, but it is also linked to creating legitimacy for such a powerful family and also strengthening its elite networks and political power. The Harriri Foundation also supported the upgrading of major streets through development of their infrastructure (e.g. water and sewage) in the old city.[16]

It is interesting to notice that the extensive work and involvement in heritage/tourism projects of both cultural and political elite families in Saida had encouraged the World Bank to reduce the amount of money allocated to this city for its CHTD (and later on CHUD) Project. Based on Table 10.2 the share of Saida is US$3.647 million in comparison to Tripoli (US$19.286 million), or Sour (US$7.433 million).

The Abdul Hameed Shoman Foundation, established by the Arab Bank in Jordan, is another example of family/corporate philanthropy in the region that supported the change and transformation in contemporary Arab cultural discourse. The Shoman Foundation, and through its different cultural activities such as the Shoman Forum (a series of public lectures by local Arab social critics and critical thinkers), provided a different alternative voice for the sake of dialogue in a time of crises. The Foundation had been extensively involved in the conservation and protection of the architectural heritage of the city of Amman through the Darat al Funun Project: an old deserted house/complex built on ancient ruins and converted into a nexus of art and culture accessible to all groups of society and serving the Jordanian public. In 1993, the complex was adapted in a way that allowed a panoply of cultural events and historical layers (ancient Roman, Byzantine, and early 20th century Amman) to coexist. The project had attempted to connect with the community both physically, through its architecture and overall layout within the neighborhood, and spiritually, through its transparency and accessibility (Al-Asad, 1997; Daher, 1999).

The Tell family of the Jordanian poet Arar, in Irbid, had been a continuous supporter of local art and of a rich cultural life in northern Jordan. They were the patrons of several heritage conservation and cultural projects in the city of Irbid such as the rehabilitation of their old *madafa* (a communal place for hosting family gatherings and events and for receiving guests and travelers). The family also adapted the old house of the Jordanian poet Arar (Figure 10.6) into a cultural center that was offered as a gift to the city.[17]

These family-patroned heritage projects work to, first, re-define heritage by concentrating on marginalized local and regional realities that had been previously subjugated and disguised by the formal state discourse on heritage and history. Second, these projects tend to concentrate on issues related to everyday life such as soap production, silk, commerce, *madafas* (architecture of hospitality), and urban social history. This presents a completely new experience of the region for tourists that supports the diversification of the tourism product and the development of cultural tourism.

In the Middle East, and mostly in places such as Jordan and Lebanon, as in most of the developing world, local public financing mechanisms

Figure 10.6 Arar House in Irbid, Jordan. This historic house where the famous Jordanian poet, Arar, used to live has been granted as a gift from the Tell family to the city of Irbid.

Source: Photograph taken by Rami Farouk Daher (1999).

are minimal. Furthermore, funding provided by the state for urban regeneration or heritage conservation and site management is almost nonexistent. In Jordan and Lebanon, the 'state' is busy venturing into private/public neoliberal urban restructuring projects in prime locations such as in downtown Beirut or Abdali in Amman. The urban cultural heritage of smaller towns or the ordinary history of everyday life stays predominantly outside the interest of the state. In similar conditions, philanthropy in general and the work of such families in particular, becomes of crucial importance, as in some cases, it represents the only alternative to a different reading of history, of heritage, and of place.

Tiesdell *et al.* (1996: 74–5), for example, elaborate about economic restructuring and economic and cultural conservation of Lowell, Massachusetts and addresses the availability of local funds and the supportive infrastructure for heritage conservation. At Lowell, funding was acquired from the Great Society Model Cities Programme to create a national Historic Park, and also, as early as 1966, funding was provided through Federal Environmental Education money. More recently, and in the late 1970s and early 1980s, and after the designation of Lowell as an Historic District, Lowell Historic District became eligible for federal grants under the national Historic Places Trust and also through various tax benefits and incentives, Commercial Development Block Grants, and several revolving funds.

The different examples presented so far are a testimony to how such notable (elite) families of Bilad al Sham are attempting to rewrite themselves into history and into today's society in a global time of emerging different groups of 'publics' and 'counter publics' active in civil society. These families definitely represent an old/new group of 'publics' that is reintroducing itself in the region through not only the patronage of heritage projects, the arts, and culture, but also through socio-economic and political public life as well.

Urry (1990: 84–5) has elaborated, when addressing cultural changes and the restructuring of tourism in a shift from modernity to postmodernity, on the notion that while modernism involved *structural differentiation*, '[p]ostmodernism, by contrast, involves de-differentiation where borders between *high* and *low* culture, between scholarly or auratic art and popular pleasures, and between elite and mass forms of consumption' are dissolved. Now, one witnesses the celebration of the ordinary and of the everyday culture. One can easily situate the phenomenon of emerging patronages of art, culture, and heritage of the everyday life by notable families in the region (e.g. museum of soap or silk production in Lebanon, or a house that celebrates a life of local poet in Jordan), as part of this mode of postmodernism, which is anti-hierarchical, and opposed to such vertical differentiations.

Yet, and most important of all, these local family heritage projects produce an important opportunity and a new accessibility for the re-reading of history and memory of the recent past in *the region*. This is part of a recent paradigm shift in scholarly Arab historiography in the region that is characterized by a shift from focusing on the *grand narratives* of national/formal history to focusing on the local, and granting voice to social and urban history, the ordinary, and the everyday life. These projects offer an ethnographic approach to the understanding of local history and the role of different families and foundations and provide the chance to investigate and research intersections and mediations between state and society today. Finally, these projects not only represent a form of assertion of the role of such families and foundations in the public sphere, but also grant voice to re-articulated memories at a regional scale, that is Bilad al Sham focusing on patterns, interconnections, regional motilities, and moments of change and transformation.

Notes

1. The author had conducted in 1991, while a graduate student at the University of Minnesota, extensive research on the current transformations of the Mills District in Minneapolis and the different adaptations such as 'Riverplace' and the 'Milwaukee Road Depot.' Such adaptations in the form of 'festive markets' contributed significantly to the processes of urban regeneration in the city.
2. www.jabalomar.com. Accessed April 23, 2005.
3. *Al-Rai'* newspaper. May 19, 2005. 'Saraya Project in Aqaba.' No. 12659, p. 13. Amman, Jordan. *Al-Rai'* newspaper. May 21, 2005. 'New projects in Amman.' No. 12661, p. 17. Amman, Jordan.
4. Solidere (Societe Libanaise de Developpement et de Reconstruction).
5. Mawared (National Resources Investment and Development Corporation).
6. Saudi Oger (Oger Jordan) is an international developer. Saudi Oger entered the partnership as main investor and also brought the expertise of its alien-ated master planners (Millennium Development, Laceco).
7. Studying and comparing the levels of contestation against such flagship projects and neoliberal restructuring in the different contexts of Amman and Beirut is of extreme value and can be discussed in future research.
8. The Extended Fund Facility (EFF) within the IMF was established in 1947 to provide medium-term assistance in particular to members with (1) an economy suffering serious payments imbalances relating to structural mal-adjustments in production and trade where price and cost distributions have been widespread; or (2) an economy characterized by slow growth and an inherently weak balance of payments position, which prevents pursuit of an active development policy. The length of an EFF arrangement is typically three years and disbursement is conditional on the borrower meeting specified

performance requirements, including structural reforms (IMF External Relations Department, 2001).

9. *Al-Rai'* newspaper. October 5, 2005. 'Second priority tourism development projects implemented by the Ministry of Tourism of Jordan.' No. 12798, p. 3. Amman, Jordan.

10. http://www.gwutourism.org/tpf_sampe_case.htm. Accessed October 19, 2005.

11. Interview with Director for the Tourism Second Priority PMU, MOTA, Amman, Jordan. July 11, 2002.

12. On August 6, 1997, the government of Jordan and the World Bank signed a loan agreement for US$32 million to finance the Second Tourism Development Project as part of the growing interest in expanding the tourism industry in Jordan. Part of this loan was allocated to the Aqaba Regional Authority, at that time, as a grant for the development of the Wadi Rum area. The project objectives specifically concentrated on creating conditions essential for an increase in sustainable and environmentally sound tourism activities in Petra, Wadi Rum, Jerash, and Kerak, and to realize tourism-related income generating projects at the potential sites (Aid Coordination Unit, 1997: 10).

13. www.padeco.co.jp/middleeast.html2003. Accessed February 15, 2005.

14. Meeting with Ms Monique Aggiouri. Debbbané Palace, Mutran Street, Saida, Lebanon. February 18, 2002.

15. Meeting with George Audi and Other Soap Factory staff, Audi Foundation, Saida, Lebanon. February 18, 2002.

16. http://www.rhariri.com/youthzone7.aspx. Accessed October 30, 2005.

17. Meeting with Mr Mustafa Wahbeh al Tell (the grandson). May 15, 2004.

References

Adham, Khaled (2005) Urban boundaries and new spaces of capital in Cairo. *Social Science Fourteenth Annual Symposium: The Transformation of Middle Eastern Urban Landscapes: From Modernism to Neoliberalism*, The American University of Cairo (AUC), Cairo, Egypt, May 12–15, 2005.

Aid Coordination Unit (Ministry of Planning, Jordan) (1997) Bilateral agreements signed in 1997. *PID: Partners in Development – Newsletter of the Aid Coordination Unit, Ministry of Planning* 7, 2–11.

Al-Asad, Mohammad (1997) *Old Houses of Amman: 1920–1950*. Amman: Turab.

Al-Rai' newspaper (2005) Saraya Project in Aqaba. May 19 (12659), 13. Amman, Jordan.

Al-Rai' newspaper (2005) New projects in Amman. May 21 (12661), 17. Amman, Jordan.

Al-Rai' newspaper (2005) Second priority tourism development projects implemented by the Ministry of Tourism of Jordan. October 5 (12798), 3. Amman, Jordan.

Al-Sayyad, Nezar (2001) Global norms and urban forms in the age of tourism: Manufacturing heritage, consuming tradition. In N. Al-Sayyad (ed.) *Consuming Tradition, Manufacturing Heritage: Global Norms and Urban Forms in the Age of Tourism* (pp. 1–33). New York: Routledge.

Anderson, L. (1995) Rethinking public space. *Journal of Architectural Education* 49 (1), 2–3.

Brecher, Jeremy and Costello, Tim (1998) *Global Village or Global Pillage: Economic reconstruction from the Bottom Up* (2nd edn). Cambridge, MA: South End Press.

Brenner, N. and Theodore, N. (2002) Cities and the geographies of 'actually existing neoliberalism'. *Antipode* 34 (3), 349–90.

Chang, T. *et al.* (1996) Urban heritage tourism: The global-local nexus. *Annals of Tourism Research* 23 (2), 286–99.

City of Minneapolis Planning Department (2000) *Metro 2000 Plan: Minneapolis Metro Center.* Minneapolis: Downtown Council of Minneapolis.

Crawford, M. (1995) Contesting the public realm: Struggles over public space in Los Angeles. *Journal of Architectural Education* 49 (1), 4–9.

Dahdah, Linda (2004) Bsous museum offers journey into Lebanon's silk heritage. *The Daily Star,* May 28, 2004.

Daher, Rami (1999) Gentrification and the politics of power, capital, and culture in an emerging Jordanian heritage industry. *Traditional Dwellings and Settlement Review,* X (II), 33–47.

Daher, Rami (2000) Heritage conservation in Jordan: The myth of equitable and sustainable development. In Irene Maffi and Rami Daher, *CERMOC Document # 10: Patrimony and Heritage Conservation in Jordan* (pp. 17–42). Beirut, Amman: CERMOC (Center for Studies and Researches on the Contemporary Middle East.

Daher, Rami (2002) The heritage [in] between: The discourses of 'region' and 'nation' in Bilad al Sham. *The Eighth Conference of the International Association for the Study of Traditional Environments (IASTE),* Hong Kong, China, December 12–15.

Daher, Rami (2004) Notable families of Bilad al Sham as patrons of art, heritage, and culture. *The Daily Star of the Herald Tribune,* No. 11430, July 3, 2004.

Daher, Rami (2005) Urban regeneration/heritage tourism endeavors, the case of Salt, Jordan: Local actors, international donors, and the state. *International Journal of Heritage Studies* 11 (4), 289–308.

El-Sheshtawy, Y. (2004) The Middle East city: Moving beyond the narrative of loss. In Y. El-Sheshtawy (ed.) *Planning Middle Eastern Cities: An Urban Kaleidoscope in a Globalizing World* (pp. 1–21). London: Routledge, Taylor and Francis Group.

Fanstein, S. and Gladstone, D. (1999) Evaluating urban tourism. In D. Judd and S. Fanstein (eds) *The Tourist City* (pp. 21–34). New Haven: Yale University Press.

Fainstein, S. and Judd, D. (1999a) Cities as places to play. In D. Judd and S. Fainstein (eds) *The Tourist City* (pp. 261–72). New Haven: Yale University Press.

Fainstein, S. and Judd, D. (1999b) Global forces, local strategies, and urban tourism. In D. Judd and S. Fainstein (eds) *The Tourist City* (pp. 1–17). New Haven: Yale University Press.

Gray, Matthew (2002) Development strategies and the political economy of tourism in contemporary Jordan. In George Joffe (ed.) *Jordan in Transition 1990–2000* (pp. 308–29). London: Hurst & Company.

Hall, Colin (1996) *Tourism and Politics: Policy, Power, and Place.* England: John Wiley & Sons.

Hazbun, W. (2002) Mapping the landscape of the 'new Middle East': The politics of tourism development and the peace process in Jordan. In George Joffe (ed.) *Jordan in Transition 1990–2000* (pp. 330–45). London: Hurst & Company.

Hunter, F. Robert (2003) The Thomas Cook archives for the study of tourism in North Africa and the Middle East. *Middle East Studies Association Bulletin* 26 (2), 157–64.

IMF External Relations Department (2001) How we lend. On WWW at http://www.imf.org/external/np/exr/facts/howlend.htm. Accessed on June 14.

Inam, Aseem (2002) Meaningful urban design: Teleological/catalytic/relevant. *Journal of Urban Design* 7 (1), 35–58.

Itani, Nabil (2005) The legal framework as preservation strategy: A comparative look at the CHUD approach in Lebanon. *City Debates 2005: Urban Heritage and the Politics of the Present – Perspectives from the Middle East*. Beirut: American University of Beirut (AUB).

Joffe, George (2002) Introduction: Jordan in transition. In George Joffe (ed.) *Jordan in Transition 1990–2000* (pp. xi–xxii). London: Hurst & Company.

Kabbani, O. (1997) Public space as infrastructure: The case of the postwar reconstruction of Beirut. In P. Rowe, and H. Sarkis (eds) *Projecting Beirut: Episodes in the Construction and Reconstruction of a Modern City* (pp. 240–59). Munich: Prestol.

Khalaf, S. (1998) Contested space and the forging of new cultural identities. In P. Rowe, and H. Sarkis (eds) *Projecting Beirut: Episodes in the Construction and Reconstruction of a Modern City* (pp. 140–64). Munich: Prestol.

Lynch, Michel (1999) *State Interests and Public Spheres, the International Politics of Jordan's Identity*. New York: Columbia University Press.

Maffi, Irene (2002) New museographic trends in Jordan: The strengthening of the nation. In George Joffe (ed.) *Jordan in Transition 1990–2000* (pp. 208–24). London: Hurst & Company.

Manna', Adel (1992) Continuity and change in the socio-political elite in Palestine during the late Ottoman period. In Thomas Philip (ed.) *The Syrian Land in the 18th and 19th Century: The Common and the Specific in the Historical Experience* (pp. 69–90). Stuttgart: Franz Steiner Verlag.

Mosley, Paul and Toye, John (1988) The design of structural adjustment programs. *Development Policy Review* 6 (4) (December), 395–414.

Reiker, Martina (2005) Symposium thematic introduction. *Social Science Fourteenth Annual Symposium: The Transformation of Middle Eastern Urban Landscapes: From Modernism to Neoliberalism*, The American University of Cairo (AUC), Cairo, Egypt, May 12–15, 2005.

Robinson, Mike (1999) Tourism development in de-industrializing centers of the UK: Change, culture, conflict. In M. Robinson and P. Boniface (eds) *Tourism & Cultural Conflict* (pp. 129–60). Oxford: CABI Publishing.

Robinson, Mike (2001) Tourism encounters: Inter- and intra- cultural conflicts and the world's largest industry. In Nezar Al-Sayyad (ed.) *Consuming Tradition, Manufacturing Heritage: Global Norms and Urban Forms in the Age of Tourism* (pp.34–67). New York: Routledge.

Rowe, P. (1998) The socio-economic framework for the reconstruction of Beirut. In P. Rowe and H. Sarkis (eds) *Projecting Beirut: Episodes in the Construction and Reconstruction of a Modern City* (pp. 135–9). Munich: Prestol.

Sadiq, Rula (2005) Dazzling Dubai: The 'invisible' hand of global competitiveness. *Social Science Fourteenth Annual Symposium: The Transformation of Middle Eastern Urban Landscapes: From Modernism to Neoliberalism*, The American University of Cairo (AUC), Cairo, Egypt, May 12–15, 2005.

Saliba, Robert (1997a) The Prince of Wales' Urban Design Task Force in Lebanon: The difficult reconciliation of Western concepts and local urban policies. *Urban Design International* 2 (3), 155–68.

Saliba, Robert (1997b) Emergency preservation of Beirut's Peri-center districts: A framework for debate and action. *Journee D'etudes Du* (April), 1–7.

Schriwer, Charlotte (2002) Cultural and ethnic identity in the Ottoman period architecture of Cyprus, Jordan and Lebanon. *Levant: The Journal of the Council for British Research in the Levant* 34,197–218.

Sharpley R. (2000) Tourism and sustainable development: Exploring the theoretical divide. *Journal of Sustainable Tourism* 8 (1), 1–19. University of Northumbria, UK.

Summer, Doris (2005) Neo-liberalizing the city: Transitional investment networks and the circulation of urban images in Beirut and Amman. Master's thesis in Urban Planning. Beirut: American University of Beirut (AUB).

Swarbooke, John (2000) Tourism, economic development and urban regeneration: A critical evaluation. In Mike Robinson (ed.) *Reflections on International Tourism – Developments in Urban and Rural Tourism* (pp. 269–85). Sunderland: Center for Travel and Tourism.

Swyngedouw, E., Moulaert, F. and Rodriguez, A. (2002) Neoliberal urbanization in Europe: Large-scale urban development projects and the new urban policy. *Antipode* 34 (3), 542–77.

Tiesdell, S. *et al.* (1996) *Revitalizing Historic Urban Quarters*. Oxford: Butterworth-Heinemann.

Tyler, Duncan (2000) A framework for analyzing urban tourism. In M. Robinson *et al.* (eds) *Developments in Urban and Rural Tourism* (pp. 287–99). Sunderland: Center for Travel and Tourism.

Urry, John (1990) *The Tourist Gaze: Leisure and Travel in Contemporary Societies*. London: SAGE Publications.

World Bank and CDR (2002) *Cultural Heritage and Urban Development: Summary Progress Report (December 2002)*. Washington, DC: World Bank, and Beirut: CDR.

Yahya, Maha (2005) Spectacular Beirut: War, cities and mobile geographies. *Social Science Fourteenth Annual Symposium: The Transformation of Middle Eastern Urban Landscapes: From Modernism to Neoliberalism*, The American University of Cairo (AUC), Cairo, Egypt, May 12–15, 2005.

Chapter 11

Tourism and Power Relations in Jordan: Contested Discourses and Semiotic Shifts

SALAM AL MAHADIN

Introduction

Any consideration of tourism today cannot be divorced from its epistemological concerns. The construction of economic, social, political, cultural and religious paradigms of tourism analysis reveals an inadequacy inherent in examining each of these constituents separately. The tension demonstrated by such risk is more palpably revealed upon the failure of each dimension to explore, examine and act independently as a point of reference for the success and failures of tourism on various levels.

Tourism has not always had its history rooted in the economy. Its modern form is heir to a modernist tradition of travelling to foreign lands, completely uninvited and unsolicited by locals, thus engendering a knowledge about the real and epistemological geography of the destination as Said (1979) argues. The general trend of social sciences to consider it as yet another source of national income emasculates the profundity of tourism as a cultural phenomenon, first and foremost. Harvey (1993) argues that ideology, values and power relations are inscribed in our very notion of what constitutes a 'place' and its representations. In the academic discourse of today, tourism mostly belongs to the domain of figures and numbers. Its only viability resides in the ability of nation-states to develop valid strategies for attracting tourists through various context-based strategies. Hall and Jenkins (1995: 5) reveal that tourism has been constrained by 'the lack of well-defined analytical and theoretical frameworks'.

But whilst the economic dimension of the tourism sector demands painstaking attention and incorporation into the wider framework of respective countries' economic super and supra structures, the more important aspects of tourism necessitate a critique of the cultural and discursive representations that galvanize this sector.

The former type of concern stems from the unique nature of tourism 'to generate foreign currency . . . the fact that tourism is labour intensive, and creates employment throughout the economy . . . [and] does not, on the whole, require expensive or complex technology or a highly skilled workforce' (Gray, 1997: 4)

The latter affiliation between tourism and cultural studies owes its allegiance to an exploration of the reciprocity intrinsic to the experience of travelling to be found in the medium of representation that governs the interaction and, indeed, encounter between the traveller and nationals on the one hand, and nationals and the state on the other.

This chapter will focus on the latter aspect with particular emphasis on Jordan as a case study. I shall refrain from engaging in generalizations about other countries as that would mask the importance of rendering the uniqueness of each context. Adopting a Foucauldian methodology, I shall examine the definitive attributes of image construction, discursive practices and power relations in establishing a multiplicity of epistemes that operate in both the context of the locale, Jordan, and that of the prospective traveller/tourist.

In recent years, literature on Jordan has focused on the economic and political liberalizations initiated in 1989,[1] prior to which Jordan had been largely dependent on Arab and international aid and remittances from its nationals working in Gulf states. The country's status as a rentier state had collapsed in the late 1980s as the drop in oil prices took its toll on Jordan's Gulf benefactors leading to huge cutbacks in aid and the return of many expatriates as jobs in the Gulf were increasingly lost. The concomitant economic and political changes to Jordan's discursive landscape are of the greatest importance, not to tourism per se, but to their dynamics on issues of legitimacy and regime survival of which tourism as a sector is but a symptom and representation. My aim is to demonstrate that, contrary to conventional wisdom, Jordan has never addressed the tourism sector as a source of national income, even in the late 1980s, as much as it has sought to transform it into one – especially following the economic crisis of the late 1980s – via the traditional role tourism and the semiotics thereof have always played in entrenching issues of regime survival, which is part and parcel of the legitimacy of Jordan as a state and Transjordanians[2] as a dominant minority.

Jordan, Tourism and the Question of Government

In the TV special documentary on Jordan entitled 'The Royal Tour', produced by Discovery Channel, King Abdullah embraces the role of a tourist guide to promote Jordan's historic sites. Premiered on cable channels in May 2002, the 50-minute programme introduces a rationale of space/time that prefigures a terrain of knowledge about who and what Jordan 'is'. The voice of the authority – authority of knowledge, experthood and representation on Jordan – is entrusted to the instrumental body of the establishment; metonymically, the King of Jordan. The deontology of such representation is the outcome of a historic-political horizon that infuses knowledge about Jordan with identity, legitimacy and power-relation problematizations.

The incongruity of associating tourism with the definitive nature of such problematizations disappears in the annals of governmentality: a keyword in gaining insight into the modern conditions of tourism in Jordan. Mitchell Dean (1999: 19) capitalizes on Michel Foucault's study of governmentality to argue that governmentality in the modern sense 'retains, and utilises the techniques, rationalities and institutions of both sovereignty and discipline, it departs from them and seeks to re-inscribe and recode them'. Government of a 'body of a nation' necessitates an inter-meshing regime of practices that focus on the 'subject' of government to produce a system, a discipline, a body of knowledge and by default institutions in which concomitant notions of power and authority are encoded.

Tourism is an instance of such practices of government. Its schemata, forms of social planning and policy-making define a historical moment of rationalization in propagating notions of legitimacy, identity and sovereignty. As such, the question of 'who rules?' becomes marginal to the important consideration of 'why rule as such?'. Tourism is a partial answer to the question. It forms a node in a web of power relations that delimit and define the possibilities of action and the 'forms of knowledge and identities and agencies by which governing operates' (Dean, 1999: 29). In this vein, Foucault (2000) distinguishes between three types of government. First, the state of justice that is a territory of a feudal type. Second, the administrative state where most power resides in the state and the judiciary branch regulates and disciplines the population. Third, the state of government or the modern state where economic knowledge and economic power become instrumental in policy-making.

In this instance of the modern state, the production of knowledge becomes intertwined with economic power and policy-making. Applied to tourism, it defines an interconnectedness between the industry, its concomitant policies and resources and a wide array of discourses diffused by knowledge of what constitutes and demarks sovereignty, identity and legitimacy.

A careful consideration of the history of modern Jordan traces a vision of multi-layered legitimation that could be directly linked with tourism: the legitimacy of the nation-state, the legitimacy of the monarchy and the legitimacy of a Transjordanian identity in contrast with a Palestinian-Jordanian one. These by default require 'imagining' a nation, a monarchy and a community. Such imagining and demarcation in exclusion to others demands a constellation of representative forms that by inclusion and exclusion introduce a legitimating form of knowledge regarding these three layers. Such legitimating forms are going to be the focus of this chapter in an attempt to shed light on the intricacy and importance of associating fields such as tourism with a conceptual approach that redeems power relations to the interests served by tourism.

Identity Formation: Tourism, Iconography and Policies

Tourism is associated in the minds of most with the desire to leave one's own space to embark on journey in a space occupied by an 'other'. The fascination with difference defines that moment of choice of where to go. Reasons pertain to recreation and holidaying in the first place: a focus of modern studies of tourism. Tourism's development into an industry is a 20th century novelty as the sector became 'an integral part of the machinery of modern governments and many government programmes in both developed and less developed countries' (Hall & Jenkins, 1995: 1).

This ties in with my attempt to demonstrate the indispensability of analysing tourism in Jordan today as a industry sector shaped by the interrelation between two driving forces: the role of tourism in animating representative forms of sovereignty, nationhood and identity and its importance as a source of national income. The two do not necessarily converge, which explains tourism's failure to establish itself as a viable economic force.

Richter (1989) emphasizes the importance of adapting tourism studies to incorporate the politics of tourism. As Hall (1994) reveals, such studies are still scant and tourism public policies are rarely contextualized within the wider framework of the community in which they operate on to develop better understanding of their operatives and effective history.

Jordan is a unique case of the first instance of representative variables that have shaped the tourism industry in the kingdom. As a new country, it had to continuously defend its reasons for existence (as opposed to being replaced with a homeland for the Palestinians), for being ruled by a monarchy that originally came from Hijaz in modern Saudi Arabia and finally, for being identified as a country inhabited by Jordanians as opposed to one by Palestinians who form of the majority of its inhabitants.

The three layers are deeply implicated in each other. An examination of each cannot possibly dissociate itself from the other two as they collaborated in creating 'knowledge' about Jordan, Jordanianess and Jordanian rule. Although such knowledge is ubiquitous in other fields, it is almost striking how prevalent it is in tourism, with the latter's indispensable continuums such as history, historic sites, museums,[3] festivals,[4] postcards, postage stamps,[5] promotional programmes and leaflets, and last but not least, national policies for the development of tourism. Each of these contributes to the debate of tourism and power relations.

The official discourse regarding the history of Jordan is an interesting point of departure as it presents a 'nation' that pre-dates the creation of the political entity called Jordan but nonetheless attempts to achieve historical continuity for the country in terms of time and space. The effective history[6] of Jordan, however, offers a different rendering while a comparison between the two sheds light on the dynamics of touristic sites and the underlying reason for the importance impressed upon some and the utter disregard for others.[7]

Until 1921, Jordan's history had that of a vaguely defined territory without a separate existence. Its history had always been linked with more prominent neighbouring entities such as Palestine in the West, Syria in the North and Saudi Arabia in the East and South. The Jordan region reached the height of its importance in ancient times under the rules of Greeks, Nabateans, Romans and Byzantines. Following the advent of Islam, it gained a lot of importance, not as Jordan, but as part of Southern Syria when the Umayyads proclaimed Damascus the capital of their empire. When the Abbasids defeated the Umayyads and moved their capital to Baghdad, the Southern part of Syria (what is now known as Jordan) was demoted to a provincial backwater far from the centre of the empire. During the era of the Fatimids, which witnessed the conquest of Jerusalem by the Crusades, the region of Jordan gained new importance as the Crusades sought to secure the protection of the route to Jerusalem prompting the Crusader King Baldwin to build a series of castles down the backbone of what is now modern Jordan. The Ayyubid and Ottoman rules, which came on the heels of the Fatimids, saw the region flung again into oblivion until the First World War, which saw the end of the Ottoman empire and the creation of modern states in the Middle East, one of which was Jordan. The new ruling family, the Hashemites, had struck a deal with the British to declare a general revolt against the rule of the Ottomans in return for declaring the then Sharif of Mecca, Hussein Ben Ali, King of all Arabs. The Great Arab Revolt, usually promoted by official discourse as an emancipatory historical movement, failed miserably to attain the desired effects. Sharif Hussein's sons were consequently placed at the reins of the newly initiated nation-states of Jordan, Iraq and Syria. Prince Abdullah, eldest son of Sharif Hussein, was destined to rule an area of land carved out of Southern Syria, primarily known as Transjordan and later the Hashemite Kingdom of Jordan.

The metaphor of landscape and historical boundaries articulated an official discourse that imagined a separate political entity for a country called Jordan in the midst of all these formative dynasties. Jordan, more than any other newly formed state, still suffers the ambivalence that surrounds the legitimacy of its existence up until today. In the annals of imagining itself as a country, a narrative has been tailored whereby importance was shifted from Jordan as part of Southern Syria (ancient times), as North of the historical land of Palestine (during Islamic eras) and as both part of Southern Syria and Western and Southern Arabia (during Ottoman rule) to centre on a historical narrative of a country that *has always existed* as an independent 'Jordan'. In other words, the importance attributed to the region of Jordan as part of these periods was reformulated to focus on an entity called Jordan, thus stripping Jordan of any marginalization.

Official discourse was translated into a representative reality and articulated in semiotics of sites. Whilst ancient sites have been preserved and integrated into the organizational structure of the touristic map, the era of Islam with the exception of the Umayyad's castles and the Crusaders' fortresses has been largely ignored. The Ottoman legacy of mosques and castles has been the most to suffer from such negligence. This is nowhere more evident than in school curricula and official publications and brochures on the history of Jordan.

But why do certain sites become laden with performative discursive meaning while others are fated to wither away in the abyss of official disinterest? To answer this question, two points must be explored. First, the issue of Jordan's legitimacy and its turbulent history. Second, the concomitant legitimacy of the Hashemite establishment.

Carved out of the area known as Greater Syria or Bilad Al-Sham, Transjordan was born as a political entity in 1920. But in contrast to many states born on the periphery of national movements, 'it had no reason to be a state on its own rather than a part of Syria, or of Palestine or of Saudi

Arabic or of Iraq, except that it better served Britain's interests to be so' (Wilson, 1987: 3).

Amir Abdullah, later King Abdullah I, was the first ruler of the new state. Himself an outsider, the son of the then Sharif of Mecca in Hijaz, he had to grapple with the political turbulences on both the national and international levels. The pressing issue of the moment in 1921 was linked to whether Transjordan, renamed the Hashemite Kingdom of Jordan in 1946 upon given its independence, was to be incorporated into Palestine under the British mandate and by default become part of the territory promised to the Jews. Neither Abdullah nor the British favoured such an arrangement but for different reasons. Britain 'favoured the so-called Sharifian solution by which various sons of Britain's wartime ally, Sharif Hussein of Mecca would be set up as rulers or governors of various portions of the Middle East under British Patronage' (Wilson, 1989: 3). The British position would ward off French ambitions and protect British interests in the region.

By the time of its establishment, the country was inhabited by three groups with three distinct loyalties; villagers and town dwellers oriented to the Western part of the river, Palestine, scattered villagers and tribesmen of Northern Jordan, associated with Syria and the tribesmen of Southern Jordan, affiliated with the Arabian Peninsula (LaBianca, 1997). The incohesive structure that suddenly found itself identified by the name of Transjordan in 1921 was further complicated by the form of government embodied in the person of the Hijazi emir who was declared sovereign. Emir Abdullah had two major tasks at hand crudely summarized as the urgent need to promote a *raison d'etre* for his country and one for himself in the midst of this incongruent group of inhabitants to form a nation.[8] Over the following 80 years, Jordan invented itself as that nation and won recognition both internationally and nationally but not without paying a hefty price. The monarchy also persisted in reinventing its legitimating discourses whenever those came under threat.

Himself not raised in a Bedouin context, Prince Abdullah based his legitimacy on congregating his subjects under the mantra of Bedouin loyalty.[9] The theme of religion also figured highly on his agenda with a great emphasis on his status as a supranational leader due to his being a direct descendant of the Prophet Mohammed. Maffi argues that 'through the institution of a privileged relationship between the Bedouin tribes and the dynasty, the Hashemites re-assert their task as guardians of the culture and the traditional customs and the legitimacy of their political role' (1995: 89). This partially explains the focus on the development of a Bedouin identity for the Hashemite as evidenced by the folklore museums of the early 1970s. The inextricable role afforded to Bedouins could be more viably reconstructed by the importance Emir Abdullah placed on winning over Bedouin loyalty. This was especially vital in a country that lacked a cohesive social structure. In later years, following the influx of hundreds of thousands of Palestinians in 1948 and 1967, tribalism and tribal affiliations gained momentum as both tribes and the establishment 'imagined' a common threat to their existence, namely, the great number of Palestinians that made up the majority of the population. Whilst museums in the early 1960s and 1970s were focused on Bedouin life and the Great Arab Revolt, they later began to reflect a more pronounced Jordanian identity in the late 1970s and onwards. In this sense, museums as sites of power, have not been merely created to cater for foreign visitors as they usually figure highly as a tourist attraction but also geared for local consumption. The Museum of Political Life is primarily a documentation of the life and achievements of King Abdullah I. Established upon the directives of the late King Hussein, the museum is promoted by the ministry of culture as one of the main touristic attractions. Documents, pictures, records and audio-visual media shed light on the life of King Abdullah and circumstances leading to the establishment of modern Jordan. The ministry mentions as one of the museums objectives emphasizing King Abdullah's adherence to the values and principles of the Great Arab Revolt. Other museums in Jordan have also focused mainly on folklore and archaeology with the former being promoted as 'authentic' Jordanian traditional costumes, crafts and traditions including Amman Folklore Museum, Jordan Museum of Popular Traditions and Jordan Crafts Centre. The Martyr's Monument and Military Museum is another venue for creating an official narrative of Jordanian military history and identity formation.

Museums as displays of 'public history' often evoke an innocuous sense of objectivity serving to mask definitive knowledge that has created, shaped and reshaped and often manipulated 'objects' of display to displace and replace historical narratives. It is not a coincidence then that Jordan has 'institutionalized' museums, imposing and suffusing 'objects' of display with a Jordanianess that ultimately aims at transcending their history as objects born on the periphery of pre-Jordan historical 'ambivalence'.

The 1970s have been very important in defining Jordan's orientations in the field of tourism both on domestic and international levels. The events of Black September marked a turning point when the country was flung into a civil war as Palestinian factions sought to take over and transform Jordan into a Palestinian homeland. The bloody encounter between

Palestinian guerrilla fighters and the Jordanian army once more threatened the existence of Jordan, its Transjordanian population and its monarchy. From that point onwards, the country witnessed a shift in the balance of power that has influenced many sectors including tourism. Palestinians have been excluded from government posts, the biggest job provider in the country, and were thus forced to enter the private sector of which they now control over 82% (Abu-Odeh, 1999). The state engaged in a series of policies as Transjordanians, mostly congregated in tribes and the monarchy, recognized a symbiotic relationship to survive the threat by Palestinians.[10]

To understand how this influenced tourism, one has to emphasize several spin offs of these policies. The crisis of September 1970 deflated the intrinsic national identity that encompassed Jordanian-Palestinians and Transjordanians. The subsequent disunity between the two witnessed a resurgence of a tribal and monarchical control of all aspects of the public sphere. Control of the public sector embodied by the majority of Jordanian-Palestinians, subcultures of favouritism, bureaucracy, state-controlled and Royal non-governmental organizations (NGOs) defined a culture fashioned by Transjordanian interests.[11]

In the aftermath, the image of what Jordan 'is' had to be assigned a new set of discursive practices. Such representation extends to how Jordan is promoted and perceived abroad and also on the national level. Concomitant policies have gravely affected fields such as tourism where it seemed that the importance of that field lay in achieving international recognition of Jordan as Transjordanian rather than set the sector as an income-generating industry.

In the 1970s and 1980s, at the peak of Arab aid to Jordan and remittances from expatriates working in the Gulf, the field of tourism was virtually neglected andwas not considered in any plans for sustainable development in Jordan. The political economy of the decade did not necessitate viewing tourism as a source of national income as the country basked in the economic benefits of foreign aid. Mapping tourism was thus confined to state patronage of cultural projects that promoted Jordanianess as opposed to promoting Jordan as a touristic site. Martial laws, which had been in effect up until 1989, excluded the private sector from the dynamics of decision-making and investment. The absence of a viable form of civil society also entailed the exclusion of most of the population from such a process.

It is essential to draw a distinction in the knowledge associated with tourism between the pre-1994 peace agreement with Israel and after. The former period could be argued to have been one where tourism was source of national narratives as opposed to national income. As an example of constructed fields of signification, any observer would not fail to notice how certain sites in the country that supported national identity construction had been specially chosen to represent the semiotics of places in Jordan, Petra being the most prominent example. The Nabatean city of Petra was born as symbol laden with meaning in the aftermath of the unification of the West Bank (Palestine) and the East Bank (Jordan) in 1951.[12] Postage stamps bore the first images of the association between Transjordanian identity and Petra. Stamps issued from 1951 until 1967 bore the distinctive images of Petra and the Dome of the Rock in a newly conceived contingency of identity. Transjordanian identity could be said to have been born in response to a Palestinian-Jordanian one. The importance of Petra did not lie merely in its historical and archaeological value as a touristic attraction as Jordan did not place any particular emphasis on the tourism as an industry back then. It formulated a parallel between the Hashemite and the Nabateans. The latter were Bedouins who spoke Arabic and established an ancient civilization that linked East and West. Thus, the history of Jordan not only harks back to ancient times in this narrative of continuity but also the Hashemites have borrowed elements from history to justify their rule. Maffi (1995: 93) succinctly summarizes this by arguing that archaeology has been used in Jordan 'to transform ancient history into a battlefield where the political claims of the present states clash'. Petra has thus been envisaged as a political tool rather than a major touristic site.

Another era of interest in the annals of identity construction was the Umayyad era. Similar to Petra, the castles dating back to that dynasty were not part of systematic development plans as touristic sites but were stressed in school curricula, history books and official representations of Jordan due to the nexus between their rule and that of the Hashemites. Creators of the Arabic name of Jordan, *Jund Al-Urdun*, the Umayyads who ruled between CE 661–760 defeated the Byzantines and ventured into the lands of Syria where they established Damascus as their capital. Although the Jordan region was part of Syria back then, it is featured in official discourse as political entity called Jordan rather than a small region by the name of *Jund Al-Urdun*. The Umayyads were introduced into official discourse as the mediators between the East and West – similar to the role Jordan has always aspired to play in the region. The castles that bear witness to that era are scattered all over the deserts of Jordan. Again, they have been promoted as identity creators rather than developed as touristic sites until the 1990s when the private sector in Jordan began to divert its attention to these sites as touristic attractions.

Inclusion is as important as exclusion. Nothing testifies to this fact more than the complete disregard of Ottoman sites and buildings. Once more, politics presents itself as a driving force that overcame the considerations of archaeological value. Having ruled the region for more than 400 years, the Ottomans left a legacy of many mosques and castles that slowly descended into disrepair due to official neglect. It would not be an exaggeration to claim that Jordan would rather erase from its collective memory the centuries of Ottoman rule. Modern governmentality in Jordan, in the process of nation-building, has been constructed along a narrative very antithetical to Ottoman rule. The Great Arab Revolt of 1916 in which an alliance was formed between the Hashemite of Hijaz and the British to oust the Ottomans has furnished Jordan with its heroic tale of emancipation from the oppressive Turks. The Hashemite rule was precisely determined by their willingness to depose the 'despotic' Ottomans and replace them with a true Arab leadership. It is within the dialectical annals of this narrative that Jordan has 'redeemed' its story as a nation. The semiotic stress is always on this notion of 'redemption' and 'emancipation' from the 'colonial' Ottomans, which implies that Jordan has always existed but as an entity under oppressive rule. Celebrating the Ottomans in the form of heritage conservation would be default cast doubts not only on the history of Jordan as a nation that pre-dates the creation of the political entity of the nation-state but also, most importantly, on the rule of the Hashemite and the legitimacy of their sovereignty. It is not by coincidence that more than 330 years of heritage have been left to fall into a general state of disrepair.[13] These include mostly urban buildings, mosques and centres on the Pilgrimage route to Mecca. Jordan's importance during those three centuries stemmed mainly from its geographical and strategic importance as a pilgrims' routes further emphasized by the construction of the Hijaz railway system, which linked the Saudi territory with its Levantine neighbours. Efforts undertaken in the late 1990s to establish a database of the thousands of heritage sites around Jordan still ignored Ottoman buildings.

The 1970s and 1980s also witnessed the theme of folklorization. Jordan embarked on the task of recording its 'national' narratives: 'It is the staging of Jordan as a Bedouin nation, where customs, costumes, and the daily objects of the Transjordanian tribes become the symbols of idealized universe of values' (Maffi, 1995: 88). The valorization of a specific form of folklorization aimed to periodize and delimit knowledge of what a Jordanian 'is' and 'has always been'. Modes of staging Jordan as a Bedouin nation became a ubiquitous phenomenon in the museums that sprang up during this period. These were complemented by the number of cultural festivals such as the Jerash, Zarqa and Fuehis festivals, venues for exhibiting national costumes, reviving traditional songs and dances and traditional crafts. The Palestinian constituent was always almost absent from these endeavours.

It would be to safe conclude that the array of discourses that associated knowledge about time and space in Jordan and the concomitant semiotics of sites were not geared towards tourism development due to the special political demands of the pre-1990s era and the lack of need for tourism to metamorphose into an income-generating industry. Heritage was thus either conserved or neglected to support the pressing notions of legitimacy at any given time.

Post 1980s

The sluggish economy of the late 1980s was the direct result of Jordan's dependency on foreign aid and remittances, both of which witnessed a severe decline as the decade closed in on a country grappling with a weak economy made worse by the lack of aid – especially in the aftermath of the second Gulf war when Jordan abandoned its usual allies to side with Iraq in the wake of its occupation of Kuwait. The private sector had been crippled by years of martial law and bureaucracy, not to mention economic lethargy as the need had never truly set in to develop this sector. Efforts by the International Monetary Fund (IMF) and the World Bank to introduce reforms were viewed by many Jordanians as oppressive especially when the proverbial lifting of subsidies occurred, leading in April 1989 to a standoff between the government and the Southern cities of the Kingdom.

Jordan had to face a new reality, but not an economic one, however. The regime's survival was in danger. The political and economic liberalization that followed were not, as some argued, the result of international pressure and local economic concerns[14] but a contingency necessitated by the establishment sensing the looming danger of economic hardships in an atmosphere of political oppression.

The motto 'No taxation, no representation', which had suited the establishment for more than three decades, was replaced by the pressing need to implement political reforms in order to placate the angry public. In 1989, Jordan held its first Parliamentary elections in more than 30 years.

In 1994, Jordan signed a peace agreement with Israel, touted at the time as the economic *'deus ex machina'*, which was going to bring about unimaginable economic benefits. As Hazbun (2000: 333) rightly argues, it soon emerged that tourism in Jordan, which was purportedly to reap the fruits of the agreement, quickly suffered a severe blow. The logic of 'economic rewards in the wake of peace', which 'made the option of peace more attractive and made the selling of peace easier domestically', emphasized the rationale that has underlain Jordan's notions of governmentality: economic and political reforms are contingent on regime survival and the legitimacy of the establishment. As such, the peace agreement was not the result of economic considerations but was marketed as such to ensure minimum opposition. The false hopes for the tourism sector engendered by the peace accord – hailed in 1994 as the saviour of economy, mainly through the rejuvenation of the tourism industry – were soon dashed. Between 1994- 1996, the private sector rushed to invest in tourism as evident from the phenomenal number of hotels, facilities and development projects that sprang in that period. This rush however was not supported by government policies to ensure long-term revenues.

More importantly, the control exercised by the government over the tourism industry was not matched by efforts to embark on serious international endeavours to market Jordan as a tourist destination. The boom in the tourism industry lasted only two years between 1994 and 1996 before regressing to its former state. During those two years, the sector expanded at unprecedented rates. Everyone was eager to benefit from the influx of tourists by haphazardly investing in tourism-related ventures. The result was disastrous on the environment and local populaces (mostly excluded from projects carried out in their locales), and led to the reification of local heritage sites (almost invariably marketed as five-star tourist destinations rather than sources of cultural experience). The lack of coordination between the private and public sectors in addition to the minimal role of civil society not only impacted on investors but also on local populations, sites and thousands of small businesses. The peace accord reneged on its purported promise to deliver quick, easy revenues.

Seen within this context, it would be safe to argue that in retrospect tourism was nothing but a strategy to prod the public to grin and bear the peace accord. Once the accord was ratified, the government returned to its usual business without much being done to realize the 'aims' of the peace accord.

Post 9/11

Tourism as source of national income was thus another strategy in the legitimating schemata of the Kingdom. This need has recently been affirmed when a post-9/11 world order presented Jordan with a new set of threats in the form of the spectre of 'terrorism' that has plagued Arabs and Muslims since. The violent epistemes that have arisen in the aftermath of 9/11 produced an indissoluble nexus between Arab/Muslim/Terrorist. However precarious the link seems between the three 'signs', the semiotics of their influence and dominance cannot be denied. In the absence of serious undertakings to deconstruct the universality of such a link and the power of the contexts that produced such forms of knowledge about Arabs and Muslims, especially the US, one opportune way out of the constraints of these stereotypes was to play down one's Arab and Islamic affiliations. Jordan has been one of those countries to opt for this ideological strategy. The modus operandi was once more the survival of the regime in a volatile region.

But achieving this is no mean feat. It requires marketing Jordan as Hashemite and Jordanian rather than Arab or Muslim, on both the domestic and international levels. Within the rationale of this formulation, the tourism sector becomes a vehicle rather than an end in itself. Engendering such Jordanian and Hashemite affiliations was invested in the body of the establishment. The king and queen of Jordan played both an individual and collective role in affirming Jordan's status as moderator between East and West and in distancing the country from any fanatic Islamic and Arab affiliations that would threaten the stability of the regime in view of the discursive and actual risk inherent in being seen as purely Arab or Muslim. A careful examination of a number of articles that appeared in mainstream Western newspapers about the Jordan establishment between December 1999 and October 2002, reveals the special 'knowledge' about Jordan engendered by the establishment's visits abroad, the presentation of the queen as 'very western, far from the image of extremist fundamentalists as most Arabs and Arab women are oftentimes portrayed through the biased spectacles of the media',[15] and that most apparent upon first glance was 'she does not wear the veil that many might expect to see covering the face of a Muslim woman',[16] and that

> negotiating the paradox between modernity and monarchy is the least of their problems . . . the queen has emerged in the West as a model of Muslim moderation, an implicit rebuke to those who cloak and silence women in the name of Islam . . . In the Arab world, more conservative elements frown upon her westernization, and some would like her to take a back seat rather than be as flamboyant as she is.[17]

The monarchy has been Jordan's main promoter abroad to the extent that Jordan has become associated as a locale with a king and a queen rather than a geography, history and destination. The tributary knowledge about Jordan rests its discursive foundations on what the monarchy 'is' and 'represents'.

In October 2002, the king initiated a project to promote a national endeavour under the slogan 'Jordan First'. In his letter to the prime minister of Jordan, the king affirms, through the subtle discursive strategies of the letter, the country as Hashemite and Jordanian. This has been adopted by government spokespeople throughout the period that followed. It is enough to note that upon the murder of a USAID worker in Amman in October 2002, the minister of information released a statement asserting that 'Our Jordanian and Hashemite values and beliefs go against the tide of such murders.' The imagined identities of Jordan and the Hashemite have thus been transformed into a source of values and beliefs that transcend the Arab and Islamic affiliations of the Jordanian people. The ministry of tourism and antiquities has also allocated funding for the promotion of Jordan abroad as 'Hashemite and Jordanian' divorced from its Islamic and Arab historical ties.[18] The government has also initiated a programme to revive traditional Jordanian songs and arts.[19]

The slogan 'Jordan First', which many have construed as an attempt on Jordan's part to distance itself from any potential threat against Iraq in the first few months of 2003, is in fact another tool for affirming the existence of a country called 'Jordan'. It is geared for local consumption but mainly for a international display of moderation, detachment and anti-fanaticism; themes the regime constantly attempts to revive to secure its survival. The 'Royal Tour' mentioned above underscores this by opening the programme with the contention that Jordan is situated in 'rough neighbourhood' against the backdrop of a map of the region and a list of the countries considered rough: Iraq, Syria, Palestine, Saudi Arabia and Lebanon. The semiotics of 'rough neighbourhood' evokes images of poverty, violence and crime as the viewer is left with a conception of Jordan as modern, advanced and peaceful once the commentator follows that with 'but don't let geography frighten you. Jordan is traveller-friendly.' The comparison between Jordan and other countries in the 'rough neighbourhood' ties in nicely with the image the country is trying to project; one where fanaticism and popular Arabism are depicted as anti-modern, violent and terrorist. The vivid arena of images later depicted in the documentary further emphasize this fact; the image of a mosque followed by a church then finally a belly-dancer with the voiceover 'this is a modern state with a considerable Christian population and an active night life'. However awkward the comment may sound, it recaptures the message of 'Jordan First' where religion is conveniently a personal and private issue while the public realm acquires the guise of modernity and sexual freedom, which is conventionally very antithetical to extremism and religiosity. Examples in the programme abound but it suffices to mention another comment by the presenter on why Jordan has social power that sets it apart from the rest of the Middle East, which in this instance is attributed to 'the country's leadership having always had strong ties with the West'. The scope of this chapter does not allow for a full analysis of the programme but the viewer is ultimately left with a impression of a Westernized country that seeks 'peace' and thrives on a set of values primarily Jordanian/Hashemite rather than Arab or Islamic.

The very terms that have driven the marketing of Jordan have been implicated in the annals of legitimation and survival. The impasse is thus not economic but ideological and requires that Jordan as a touristic site be reconsidered on a wider economic spectrum if the industry is ever to metamorphose into a viable source of national income. Otherwise, tourism is destined to remain a pawn in the game of political and social considerations.

Notes

1. Joffe's *Jordan in Transition* (2000) offers a comprehensive review of economic, social and political shifts in Jordan in the last decade.
2. The term Transjordanians refers to the idigenous population while Palestanian-Jorandians is used to refer to nationalized Palestanians who came to Jordan in the aftermath of the 1948 and 1967 Israeli occupation of Palestine.
3. See Maffi (1995) (2000) and (2002) for a detailed account of the role of museums in identity formation.
4. See Massad (2001) for a further discussion on the role cultural festivals in imagining a Jordanian identity.
5. See Katz (1999).
6. Effective history refers to a Foucauldian consideration of history as series of discourses with a genealogical affiliations and their role in shaping the history of locales. See Goldstein (1994).
7. Anderson (2001) explores the role of school textbooks in representing the official discourse of Jordanian identity and national formation.
8. For a detailed account of the early history of Jordan's formation see Wilson (1987). Massad (2001) offers a theoretical account of the formation of Jordanian identity through the medium of legal and military discourses.
9. See Salibi (1998).
10. See Abu-Odeh (1999) for an exploration of Palestinian/Jordanian relations in the aftermath of the 1970 standoff between Jordanian government forces and Palestinian factions operating from Jordan.
11. Power structure has narrowed the role of NGO's and introduced royal patronage. See Brand (2001), Wiktorowicz (2002) and Lynch (1999).

12. Katz (2000) and (2002) demonstrate the role Petra has played in asserting Jordanianess on an international level during the era of the unification of the West Bank and Jordan. The West Bank was mainly promoted for its holy sites, considered back then part of Jordanian heritage rather than the Palestinian one.
13. Daher (1999) and (2000) offers an interesting review of the politics of heritage conservation in Jordan.
14. See Nsour (2000) in Joffe (2000) and Kassay (2000) in the same volume.
15. Ray Hanania, Queen Rania captivates American TV audiences. *The Star* (Jordan, Middle East), 04.06.2000, p. 4.
16. Carin Gorrell, Queen Rania Al-Abdullah. *Psychology Today*, 05.01.2002, p. 36.
17. Ann Gerhart, *Washington Post* staff writer, Thoroughly modern monarch; Jordan's Queen Rania never expected a crown, but she wears it well. *The Washington Post*, 03.01.2002, p. C01.
18. Interview with a producer who spoke on condition of anonymity. She also informs me that none of the proposals presented to the ministry so far have been convincing in selecting sites that distance Jordan from its Islamic and Arab past.
19. Interview with a director working on the project. Jordan Television, 31.12.2002.

References

Abu-Odeh, A. (1999) *Jordanians, Palestinians and the Hashemite Kingdom in the Middle East Peace Process*. Washington DC: United States Institute of Peace Process.

Anderson, B. (2001) Writing the nation: Textbooks of the Hashemite Kingdom of Jordan. *Comparative Studies of South Asia, Africa, and the Middle East* 21, 5–14.

Brand, L. (2001) Development in Wadi Rum? State bureaucracy, external funders and civil society. *International Journal of Middle East Studies* 33, 571–90.

Daher, R.F. (1999) Gentrification and the politics of power, capital and culture in an emerging Jordanian heritage industry. *Traditional Dwellings and Settlements Review* 11, 33–45.

Daher, R.F. (2000) Heritage conservation in Jordan: The myth of equitable and sustainable development. *Patrimony and Heritage Conservation in Jordan* (Document Du Cermoc No. 10) (pp. 17–42).

Dean, M. (1999) *Governmentality: Power and Rule in Modern Society*. London: Sage Publications.

Foucault, M. (2000) Governmentality. *Power: The Essential Works of Foucault 1954–1984* (Vol. 3) (pp. 201–22). New York: The New Press.

Goldstein, J. (1994) *Foucault and the Writing of History*. Oxford: Blackwell.

Gray, Matthew (1997) The political economy of tourism in Syria: State, society, and economic liberalization. *Arab Studies Quarterly* 19, 57–69.

Hall, C.M. (1994) *Tourism and Politics: Policy, Power and Place*. London: Belhaven Press.

Hall, C.M. and Jenkins, J.M. (1995) *Tourism and Public Policy*. London and New York: Routledge.

Harvey, D. (1993) From space to place and back again: Reflections on the condition of postmodernity. In J. Bird, B. Curtis, T. Punam, G. Robertson and L. Tickner (eds) *Mapping the Futures: Local Cultures, Global Change*. London and New York: Routledge.

Hazbun, W. (2000) Mapping the landscape of the 'new Middle East': The politics of tourism development and the peace process in Jordan. In George Joffe (ed.) *Jordan in Transition 1990–2000* (pp. 330–45). London: Hurst & Company.

Joffe, G. (ed.) (2000) *Jordan in Transition 1990–2000*. London: Hurst & Company.

Kassay, A. (2000) The effects of external forces on Jordan's process of democratisation. In George Joffe (ed.) *Jordan in Transition 1990–2000* (pp. 45–65). London: Hurst & Company.

Katz, K. (1999) Jordanian Jerusalem: Postage stamps and identity construction. *Jerusalem Quarterly File* 5, 17–27.

Katz, K. (2000) Holy places and tourist sites: Welcome to Jordan, the Holy Land (1948–1967). *Proceedings of Al-Urdun al-Jadid Social History Conference*, Amman, Jordan.

Katz, K. (2002) Conferring authority, increasing legitimacy: Jordan and the patriarchs of Jerusalem. *Third Social History Conference*, Al-Urdun al-Jadid Research Centre, Amman, Jordan.

LaBianca, O.S. (1997) Indigenous hardiness structures and state formation in Jordan: Towards a history of Jordan's resident Arab population. In M. Sabour and K. S. Vikør (eds) *Ethnic Encounter and Culture Change* (pp. 143–57). London: C. Hurst and Co.

Lynch, Michael (1999) *State Interests and Public Spheres, the International Politics of Jordan's Identity*. New York: Columbia University Press.

Maffi, I. (1995) De l'usage del l'histoire par le pouvoir en Jordanie: Les musees et la construction de l'identite nationale a partir de 1967. *CERMOC Special Reports*, pp. 84–97.

Maffi, I. (2000) Le statut des objets dans la mise en scene museographique du passe en Jordanie: Le discours historique, la narration mythique et la tradition. *Patrimony and Heritage Conservation in Jordan* (Document Du Cermoc No. 10) (pp. 3–16).

Maffi, I. (2002) New museographic trends in Jordan: The strenghening of the nation. In George Joffe (ed.) *Jordan in Transition 1990–2000* (pp. 208–24). London: Hurst & Company.

Massad, J.A. (2001) *Colonial Effects: The Making of Jordanian Identity*. Columbia: University of Columbia Press.

Nsour, M. (2000) Governance, economic transition and Jordan's national security. In George Joffe (ed.) *Jordan in Transition 1990–2000* (pp. 23–44). London: Hurst & Company.

Richter, L.K. (1989) *The Politics of Tourism in Asia*. Honolulu: University of Hawaii Press.

Said, E.W. (1979) *Orientalism*. London and Henley: Routledge and Kegan Paul.

Salibi, K. (1998) *The Modern History of Jordan*. London: I.B. Tauris.

Wiktorowicz, Q. (2002) Embedded authoritarianism: Bureaucratic power and the limits to non-governmental organisations. In George Joffe (ed.) *Jordan in Transition 1990–2000* (pp. 111–26). London: Hurst & Company.

Wilson, M. (1987) *King Abdullah, Britain and the Making of Jordan*. Cambridge: Cambridge University Press.

Wilson, M. (1989) Transjordan: The structure of cooperation with Britain. In C. Scharf and L. Schatkowski-Schilcher (eds) *Der Nahe Osten in der Swischenkriegszeit* (pp. 52–64). Stuttgart: Franz Steiner Verlag.